The Cutting-Off Way

WAYNE E. LEE

The Cutting-Off Way

Indigenous Warfare in Eastern
North America, 1500–1800

The University of North Carolina Press *Chapel Hill*

This book was published with the assistance of the H. Eugene and Lillian Lehman Fund of the University of North Carolina Press.

Set in Arno Pro by Westchester Publishing Services
Manufactured in the United States of America

Library of Congress Cataloging-in-Publication Data
Names: Lee, Wayne E., 1965– author.
Title: The cutting-off way : Indigenous warfare in eastern North America, 1500–1800 / Wayne E. Lee.
Description: Chapel Hill : The University of North Carolina Press, [2023] | Includes bibliographical references and index.
Identifiers: LCCN 2022058207 | ISBN 9781469673776 (cloth ; alk. paper) | ISBN 9781469673783 (pbk. ; alk. paper) | ISBN 9781469673790 (ebook)
Subjects: LCSH: Indians of North America—Wars—Atlantic Coast (North America) | Surprise (Military science)—North America—History. | Guerrilla warfare—North America—History. | Strategic culture—Atlantic Coast (North America) | Atlantic Coast (North America)—Military relations—History.
Classification: LCC E81 .L39 2023 | DDC 970.004/97—dc23/eng/20221214
LC record available at https://lccn.loc.gov/2022058207

Cover illustration: F. D. Briscoe (1843–1903) drawing of forest glen used as background. Courtesy of Library of Congress Prints and Photographs Division.

Contents

Illustrations ·

Acknowledgments

This book has been built on many years of research and the edifice of debt to others' help, encouragement, documents, and discussions is larger than I have the skill to describe or enumerate. Done right, academia is truly a cooperative and cumulative profession. In recent years, this project has been a subcomponent of my larger investigation into how conquest worked, or was imagined, in different types of preindustrial societies around the world. Peter Wilson and Erica Charters encouraged me to publish a version of my theory in their edited volume *A Global History of Early Modern Violence* (2020), and I only wish I could acknowledge individually all the seminar participants who contributed to that work—they were a remarkable group and I took in information like a sponge. That conference helped me realize that my larger project needed more data first. I had to write this book before I can write that one, and when I returned to the archives of Native North America to build on things I had done before, I found welcome support, advice, and references from Mike Oberg, James Rice, Brian Rindfleisch, Christina Snyder, Joshua Piker, Claudio Saunt, Christopher Bilodeau, Garrett Wright, Evan Haefeli, and Aubrey Lauersdorf. Kathleen DuVal read through the whole manuscript and I couldn't be more grateful for her edits, suggestions, and corrections. David Preston read some key sections of the manuscript, saved me from some silly errors, and also provided some truly apropos documents at the last minute. Liz Ellis was a critical sounding board at various times, especially for chapter 3, and her discussions with me about the problems of Native sovereignty have been invaluable. For assistance with the geography in chapter 2, I'm grateful to Teiowí:sonte Thomas Deer and the Kanien'kehá:ka Onkwawén:na Raotitióhkwa Language and Cultural Center. The staff of the David Library of the American Revolution (especially Meg McSweeney), formerly in Washington Crossing, Pennsylvania, once again provided me a productive space to research and write. The library is now moved into downtown Philadelphia and I will greatly miss its former bucolic environs.

Several of the chapters here, although now substantially revised, were originally published elsewhere in different forms, and I'm grateful to those publishers for their permission to reprint here. I'm also grateful to the people who helped me at the time of their original publication, and I gladly repeat my thanks to Ian Steele, Fred Anderson, Karen Kupperman, Elizabeth Fenn, Michael Galaty, Jason Warren, Stephen Carney, Alex Roland, Bob Angevine, Steve Warren, Tom Baker, Glenn Crothers, Brad Wood, Holly Brewer, John Nelson, Jacob Selwood, David Edwards, and Paul Grant-Costa. I had many conversations with Kevin McBride about New England Native fortifications, and he supplied me with much unpublished archaeological data and his own keen insights. Charles Heath provided me with crucial archaeological material on the excavations at Neoheroka, and for this book he also provided me with a more recent site sketch. I would also be remiss if I did not acknowledge the editorial work of the editors of *Britain's Oceanic Empire* (2012), Elizabeth Mancke, John Reid, and Huw Bowen. They made what became chapter 7 in this book a much better essay. And as always, I am grateful to Peter Wood for grounding me in Native American studies many years ago. It was during those same years as graduate student that I met Rhonda, and I am forever encouraged by her support and improved by her incisive editing.

The Cutting-Off Way

CHAPTER ONE

Introduction

The Eastern Woodlands

By about 1000 C.E. maize agriculture had transformed the subsistence systems of a vast kaleidoscope of Indigenous peoples living in eastern North America—the so-called Eastern Woodlands.[1] Social and political systems adjusted in a wide variety of ways, leading in some cases to centralized chiefdoms asserting authority over an array of smaller communities who provided corn as tribute to a dominant central place. Other Nations maintained themselves on a smaller political scale, distributing authority over decision-making more broadly, although related and cooperating communities could number in the tens of thousands. Despite this political and cultural variation, the forested landscape, the animals that lived in it, and now the maize and other crops cultivated in the fields hacked into it, constituted a zone with many qualities of life in common. Woods and rivers, deer and rabbit, corn and beans, along with the absence of domesticated draft animals, were all shared basic realities. Competition for resources, a desire for security, and ultimately war were also a part of those shared realities.[2]

For the next 500 years Native Americans warred with each other using relatively homogenous technologies of combat and transportation while sustained by similar forms of subsistence (in contrast for example, to the very sharp differences between sedentary-agricultural and nomadic-pastoral forms of subsistence in contemporary Eurasia). There *was* a kaleidoscope of difference, but there were also certain basic continuities and similarities. As the peoples and Nations in this zone warred with each other, they developed more or less common means and modes of doing so, along with beliefs and expectations about the meanings and objectives of war.

Then, starting around 1500, new European-derived societies were slowly added to the kaleidoscope, faster after 1600.[3] Initially they were not powerful at all, but they were equipped with new technologies and new modes of subsistence. Indigenous systems of war were turned against the newcomers and also used alongside them. Over time Native systems of war shifted, adapting to the new variables of steel, gunpowder, disease, horses, cattle, and more. But many continuities remained, as did enmities with older enemies. Those continuities and changes are the subject of this book, viewed primarily from the perspective of the Native Americans themselves, ambitiously including all of the Eastern Woodlands because it was a truly coherent zone of shared material realities.

This book insists that we take Native Americans and their modes, systems, and beliefs about war on their own terms. Their practice of war reflected autonomous and fundamentally Indigenous systems of subsistence and forms of governance, as well as their cultural visions of appropriate conduct. Too often analyses of Native American warfare have proceeded strictly through a narrative lens that centers European expansion and then asks only "who fought who, where and when, and what happened?" Among other things, such an approach consistently puts Indigenous Nations on the back foot, responding defensively to European encroachment—even when the point of the analysis is to emphasize Indian agency and power within the broader Atlantic world. Native Americans had a long history of war, diplomacy, and geopolitical maneuvering prior to the arrival of Europeans, and that history continued to shape their wars both with each other and with Europeans in the postcontact era. This book starts from that assumption of a deeply rooted system and culture of warfare, and takes a cultural and structural approach that centers Native American interests, examining mostly intra-Indian warfare, but also encompassing their wars and alliances with European colonists and empires.[4] We must begin with the very fundamentals of Native societies: how they divided labor; how they extracted subsistence from the landscape; how they imagined territorial sovereignty; and how they moved and sustained their military forces across the continent.[5] Only with those basics in mind can we then sense the purpose and function of warfare and their strategies within it.

In the Eastern Woodlands of North America after 1500 most Native American societies practiced some combination of agriculture heavily supplemented by seasonal hunting and gathering, sometimes even including regional migration. They lived in cooperative clusters of generally politically autonomous towns, very often strung along a waterway. Those geographic and subsistence basics in turn greatly influenced how they claimed sovereignty, and in turn those claims influenced their strategic thinking. How did social, political, economic, and cultural goals—for individuals *and* communities—determine the function of and planning for war parties?

The Cutting-Off Way begins to answer these questions by laying out a paradigm for how Native Americans in the generally coherent ecological zone of the Eastern Woodlands planned and executed their attacks against other Native Nations—the cutting-off way of war.[6] Chapter 2 describes the paradigm in more detail, but a brief sketch now sets the stage. The term comes from a common English expression from the period, "to cut off," because it so accurately describes the tactical and operational goals of an Indian attack, at both small and large scales—indeed its scalability is one of its primary strengths. Lacking deep reserves of population and also lacking systems of coercive recruitment, Native American Nations were wary of heavy casualties. Their tactics demanded caution, and so they generally sought to surprise their targets. The size of the target varied with the size of the attacking force. A small war party might only seek to "cut off" individuals found getting water or wood, or out hunting. A larger party might aim at attacking a whole town, again hoping for surprise. At small or large scales, most often the attackers sought prisoners to take back to the home village. Once revealed by its attack, the invading war party generally fled before the defenders' reinforcements from nearby related towns could organize.

If a large war party arrived at an enemy town and failed to surprise it, they might offer battle—this was especially the case in warfare with other Indian Nations—but this seems primarily to have been to save face or reputation rather than an earnest effort to fight a large-scale battle in the open.

Sieges occurred, but were rare, simply because of the strategic depth of the defending town clusters that could rush reinforcements to the scene, usually in numbers far greater than the attackers. Such sieges as did happen often took the form of a blockade, with the besiegers making it impossible for the defenders to hunt, get water or firewood, and so on.

Encounter battles in the spaces between Nations were also relatively rare, but they also would usually lead to a face-saving exchange of fire and then retreat. That being said, however, Native Americans had a tactical system for the encounter battle called the half moon, in which they maneuvered as individuals, from tree to tree, trying to find and then slide around the edges of their enemy, flanking them, denying them the cover of a tree, but never surrounding them (they preferred to leave the enemy the option to retreat and thus avoid bloody last-stand fighting).

As a key modification to this tactical system in the postcontact era, Indians had learned that the most vulnerable point of a European army on the march was its logistics, and they adapted the half-moon technique to focus on the baggage train. Sometimes the "attack" at the head of the European column seems likely to have been a diversion to cover the real intention to attack the baggage.

I originally formulated this cutting-off model in response to Patrick Malone's *The Skulking Way of War*, which I believe has led many subsequent scholars astray in their understanding of the real nature of Native American warfare.[7] I believe his claimed dichotomy between a relatively low-casualty raiding system of combat in precontact times that was then altered by European total war practices into something more absolute and destructive is fundamentally misguided. Furthermore, the "skulking" term, widely repeated by nonspecialists, replicates a European adjective that was intended both to be derogatory to Indian courage and to dismiss the rational calculations behind their mode of combat.

I first began to articulate the cutting-off paradigm as part of my research into the Tuscarora and Cherokee defenses of their homelands, here discussed in chapter 5. Since then I have repeatedly found the concept useful as a kind of key that helped me decode the sometimes obscure sources that I was reading, and I have deployed it several times in other work. Chapter 2 presents it here more completely, and it is threaded throughout the book as a foundation for the more complex arguments that follow.

To this tactical and operational description we must add logistics. I have argued elsewhere that one of the most fundamental structuring forces on the nature of any society's mode of warfare is its subsistence system and the related logistical systems used to sustain war.[8] The technology of combat matters, of course, but the key logistical issue in the preindustrial world was food. It is true that in North America, as David Silverman has pointed out, access to guns could lead to cascading victories as one gun-equipped society took advantage of another's lack, but the equilibrium of equal access to guns was fairly quickly reestablished.[9] Although the introduction of guns and the need for gunpowder had major effects on strategy and diplomacy, that story is relatively well known, and will be covered here in chapter 6. To tell the story of Native American warfare more thoroughly, however, we must begin with subsistence. What we will find is that subsistence dominated logistics, and logistics ultimately shaped what Indians expected from victory.

Native Americans' "Demographic Space"

Like all other societies, Native Americans lived within a constructed "demographic space" within which they acquired food and organized their daily lives. The term, borrowed from John Landers's study of preindustrial western Europe, refers to the spatial and human-modified relationship between people and the organic energy produced from the fields and forests around them.[10] Those "spaces" differ by ecosystem and social organization, but they were all constructed by human action, and their nature defined what a society then wanted from victory.

Native Americans modified and exploited their environment in competition and sometimes in conflict with their neighbors as much as did the inhabitants of the rest of the planet. When Europeans arrived they thought they saw a "wilderness" inhabited by "savages," who went to war to resolve slights or insults, or to take revenge for earlier raids. In reality, Indians modified their landscape as farmers, hunters, and gatherers; they competed with each other for control of those resources; and their methods of warfare reflected material needs and goals as much as did their cultural constructs surrounding revenge and individual or group reputation.[11]

Native American demographic spaces in the historic Eastern Woodlands were defined by the town.[12] It was the primary sociopolitical and productive unit, and its needs determined the shape of much of the surrounding landscape. Generalizing greatly (key exceptions are noted below), beyond small close-in vegetable gardens, a town generally had several active agricultural fields, dominated by maize, but usually intermixed with beans and squash, on the edges of a nucleated cluster of homes. Depending on location and community size, those fields could be the massive expanses of maize cultivated by the Wendats in what is now Ontario—so massive that Gabriel Sagard, a Recollet friar and missionary to the Wendats in the 1620s, remembered getting lost in them more often than he did in the forest or meadows.[13] Or they could be more diminutive, like those found in the smaller towns of what is now eastern North Carolina, as pictured here for the Secotans in figure 1.1.[14]

A town's assortment of homes sheltered populations varying from hundreds to as many as a few thousand, and might or might not be enclosed within a palisade wall, depending on the recent history of regional conflict. The town's inhabitants cut fields out of the forest using slash-and-burn agriculture, and then farmed them for several years before cutting new ones. The abandoned fields would grow into meadow, attracting deer and creating a fruitful zone for "close-in" spring and summer hunting. As Douglas Hurt points out, the system was more complex than this simple portrait, as Indians often used different varieties of corn that ripened at different rates, and supplemented the classic "three sisters" of corn, beans, and squash with a wide variety of other cultivated or gathered plants.[15] Every five to twenty years the town itself would move and rebuild, in response to wood rot, distance to firewood, waste accumulation, and so on.[16] The abandoned town site would slowly become meadow in the forest, and the town, old town, fields, and old fields were all connected by a dense network of paths (see figure 1.2).

Some of those paths radiated out to nearby related towns, clustered together in a way that defined a core territory for the larger group: the Nation.

FIGURE 1.1 The Secotans' Town in what is now eastern North Carolina, drawn by John White, ca. 1585. Courtesy of the British Museum.

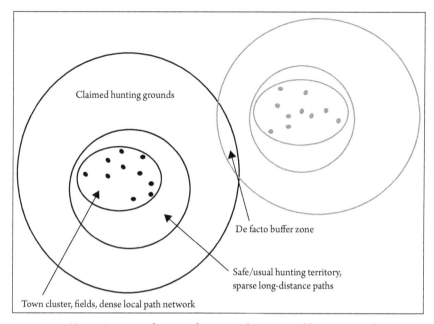

FIGURE 1.2 Native American demographic space, showing neighboring town clusters and their territorial claims. The circles are not to scale. The outer circle could be very extensive indeed in relation to the size of the cluster of towns. Drawn by the author.

The towns were usually clustered closely enough to offer mutual support when attacked, but far enough apart to allow for the process of town-and-field rotation, and the cluster of towns was almost always strung out along a waterway of some kind (see maps 1.1 and 1.2, and comparable town cluster maps in chapter 5). As just one example of land requirements, Peter Thomas calculates that a village of 400 Indians in the New England area, where aquatic protein sources reduced land requirements in many ways, would require roughly 1,000–2,300 acres of farmland to sustain itself over a fifty-year period.[17] Those calculations did not account for claims to hunting or gathering territories, and indeed the town cluster was in turn surrounded by and connected to a much larger hinterland claimed for hunting or gathering needs, typically conducted in the fall or winter, when, depending on the location and climate, either the town's male population or the entire town would head to the hunting grounds and scatter into smaller winter camps, often moving frequently over the course of the winter and early spring. As suggested in figure 1.2, claims to hunting territories could be contested, with some parts securer than others; some areas could become a true buffer zone where Nations feared to go regularly.

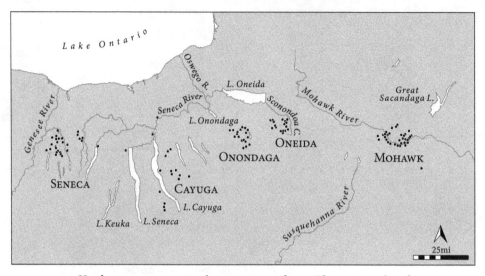

MAP 1.1 Haudenosaunee town sites, between 1500 and 1700. These sites are based on archaeological evidence; not all would have been occupied at the same time. Each cluster here represents the space within which town sites circulated, and one can clearly see the space between the clusters. Matilde Grimaldi, based on Eric E. Jones, "Population History of the Onondaga and Oneida Iroquois, A.D. 1500–1700," *American Antiquity* 75, no. 2 (2010): 387–407.

This generic portrait had nearly endless small and large variations, depending on climate, elevation, proximity to lakes and oceans, and especially in the historic period, adaptation and reaction to the arrival of Europeans. There are four variables that are especially worth mentioning. The first two are geographic and relatively well understood. First, maize production in North America was more or less impossible in the Far North, and communities there relied much more on hunting, although there is also evidence of those societies both raiding and trading for maize from their southern neighbors.[18] Second, access to coastal and riverine protein sources allowed for a somewhat more sedentary or at least a more short-range semisedentary lifestyle, with less need to distribute the population over the winter.[19] As a general rule, this is reflected in the smaller territorial range of coastal peoples when compared to inland groups' claims to very extensive hunting territories, although the vast hunting claims that become detectable in later sources also reflect the pressures of the fur and deerskin trades.

The other two key variations on the town cluster pattern reflect sociopolitical changes over time. The first was the dramatically different precontact Mississippian culture area of the Southeast and Midwest. Mississippian socie-

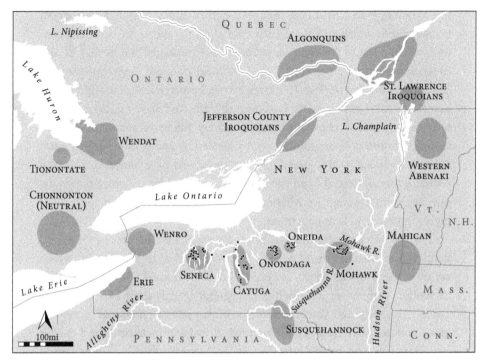

MAP 1.2 This map expands the view from map 1.1, still showing the Haudenosaunee town clusters over time, but now showing the relative positions of other Nations in the vicinity about 1534. Each shaded area indicates a region of intensive habitation, not the limit of their territorial claims; the spaces between, however, do suggest the likely jockeying for access to hunting grounds. Matilde Grimaldi, largely based on Eric E. Jones, "Population History of the Onondaga and Oneida Iroquois, A.D. 1500–1700," *American Antiquity* 75, no. 2 (2010): 387–407.

ties featured large urban complexes surrounded by smaller subordinate communities, with clear indications of a powerful centralized political authority. Cahokia, near modern St. Louis, is the most famous, with a population exceeding 10,000 by 1100 C.E., with 20,000 or 30,000 more in the immediately surrounding towns and farms.[20] But even a smaller site, like Moundville (now in Alabama), had a peak population of 3,000 in the mid-fourteenth century, and it apparently acted as the controlling political center of a large number of smaller settlements, ranging from substantial towns down to hamlets, all of which seem to have contributed some of their food production to the center.[21] Maize cultivation in the late Mississippian world seems to have been much more intensive, and people ate less meat, especially those in subordinate populations. Modern analysis of human remains shows associated nutritional deficits and disease vulnerability.[22] Much of the political centralization within the Mississippian world had collapsed before contact, and early Spanish invaders of the 1530s and 1540s encountered only some of the surviving centralized chiefdoms. The Spanish *entradas* likely hastened the further decentralization of those chiefdoms during the next hundred years, but we have few sources for that period. To a large extent, however, whether of their own accord, or hastened along by European diseases and slave raiding, that pattern of centralized chiefdoms supported by intensive maize cultivation among subordinate communities had vanished by about 1600, largely if not entirely replaced by the generic system described here, embodied in new societies that coalesced from the wreckage of the older system. At any rate, our ability to reconstruct Mississippian warfare practices and logistics is highly limited, and is not attempted here.[23]

The last key exception to this general pattern was the process of partial denucleation that occurred around Native America across the eighteenth century. Many towns began to spread out, with houses at a distance from each other, sometimes described as "straggling," usually along a river or creek. Often these were new towns, created as Indian peoples migrated to new regions and reconstituted new communities, notably including the Lenapes and Shawnees who moved into the upper Ohio watershed in the eighteenth century. These new towns with their relatively scattered houses sometimes were built alongside or even among white settlements. But this new layout also emerged among peoples who had remained within their precontact territories, including the Mohawk and the Cherokee. The shift was so profound in some places that when French military engineer Pierre Pouchot, writing in the 1750s, described a "standard" village of Indians, he did so in a way that would have been unrecognizable to his seventeenth-century forebears accustomed to densely nucleated, palisaded towns: "The huts of an Indian village are scattered along a river or a lake, sometimes over a distance of one or two leagues."[24] In part this shift was because the old nucleated villages, even if palisaded, had proven indefensible when attacked by gunpowder-equipped European expeditions, but it may also have reflected demographic shifts, a desire to settle closer to European trading posts, and even an awareness of how diseases were transmitted.[25]

This last exception to the generic description of demographic space within Native America is also a reminder that nothing was static during the period covered in this book. New technologies and modes of subsistence brought by Europeans rapidly affected this general portrait in various ways. We have already mentioned how the increasing trade interaction with Europeans put pressure on hunting territory as the demand for furs and deerskins sent Native hunters ever further afield. European animals—pigs, cattle, horses, chickens—became another subsistence option, sometimes raised locally, but also reliable targets for raiding in wartime. European trading stations and forts became economically attractive sites to form a new town—they offered proximity to trade goods, guns, gunpowder, and in wartime, to subsistence aid from the imperial powers. Although this book attempts a Native perspective throughout, their perspective was inevitably shifted or affected by the possibilities and problems presented by the colonial settlers and their imperial governments.

Sources and Organization

In addition to being attuned to the omnipresence of European-induced change, we also must be sensitive to the limits of our sources. The vast bulk of them for this period and this region derive from English, French, and some Spanish sources. Their biases and blind spots naturally obscure how Indians actually thought about war and its functions. Archaeology, linguistics, and inherited traditions among modern Native populations help enormously, but the problems of understanding intent remain. Supposition is inevitable. This book examines not only how Indians fought, but how they sustained their expeditions, managed war's violence, responded to new technologies and new enemies, and even ultimately how they imagined the political object of war—what was victory and what did they seek from it? Historians, when dealing with a fully documented historic society that composed its own records, traditionally have begun at the top, examining stated political intentions; and then, over generations of effort, they have worked their way down through various levels of analysis: Did the stated reason or reasons for the war reflect the real political calculations? How did those intentions translate into the deployment of troops and ships? How were armies and ships built, equipped, manned, and supplied? How did they fight once in contact with the enemy? What were the economic and political consequences of the conflict? What did the soldiers and sailors experience, and did they take those experiences home in some way—either as trauma or new political intention? And so on.

All of these questions could and should be applied to Native American war, but our sources impose a different sequence of analysis. We know the most about *how* Indians fought, because that was the behavior European settlers saw most often and worried about most minutely. European explorers and colonizers had very practical reasons for wanting to understand the threats they faced, and although they would occasionally belittle or diminish them, the threat was nonetheless real, and for all their bluster, they knew it. The bluster means we cannot utterly trust those sources—quite the contrary. However, it does suggest that studying a large number of accounts of Native tactics and operations can expose patterns of repeated behavior and increase the reliability of our suppositions. Our European sources' biases mean we are on the safest ground when discerning patterns in *how* Indians fought, and from there we can assess how those patterns of operations and tactics reflected other underlying realities of logistics, strategy, politics, and values. In briefer terms, the visible operational and tactical patterns within Native American warfare ultimately tell us something about their culture of war more generally.

This somewhat bottom-up program of analysis organizes this book. Chapter 2 begins with operations and tactics, generally when on the offensive (even if part of a defensive war), because those actions generated most of our sources. On that foundation we can build more reliable discussions of how Native American subsistence translated into expeditionary logistics (chapter 3); how violence was constrained by structure, rule, and ritual (chapter 4); how Natives defended themselves when attacked in their homes (chapter 5); and then how Native American societies responded to technological and demographic changes during the contact period (chapter 6). Chapter 7 digresses somewhat to a European perspective to examine how the imperial powers took advantage of Native skills originally developed for war among themselves, but in doing so we can see clearly the continuance of military power exercised by Native Nations. And, finally, chapter 8 then fills in some of the many gaps in what we think we know about Native American political intentions and expectations of wars' outcomes.

Ultimately, Indigenous operational techniques within the cutting-off way of war, with their ability to sustain large attacks or a long series of smaller ones, while preserving the lives of the attackers, and sustained by a logistical and transportation system organic to the broader region of the Eastern Woodlands, allowed war to fulfill a variety of political purposes. Natives could take prisoners as future kin, as labor, or as commodities; they could impose tribute and even establish regional hierarchical chiefdoms; they could maintain a protective reputation for ferocity; and, they could displace enemies from their homes and thereby claim new sovereign hunting territories.

Terminology and Names

Words matter. *The Cutting-Off Way* makes two very deliberate choices about words and names; one may seem anachronistic, while the other may at first seem unfamiliar. In an effort to take seriously the depth of strategic thought and the preparatory skill involved in Indian warfare, I have chosen to use a few modern technical terms in reference to military operations. It is common among military writers in the modern world to refer to different "levels" of war: tactical (how troops act in combat); operational (how forces are moved in space and time to gain an advantage at the moment of contact); and strategic (how leaders allocate resources and determine a target or targets that will lead to the submission or destruction of an enemy). There are variants and subcategories, but these are the three used here. Those terms and distinctions appear in this book because I believe they help clarify rather than confuse. Native Americans' tactical techniques—meaning how they shot bows or guns, used trees as cover, tried to surprise enemies in various ways, and so on—are often the most visible behavior in our sources and in many historical analyses. In this book I also try to recover how they imagined a campaign proceeding. How would they travel from home village to enemy countryside? How would they plan their supplies (their logistics)? How would a connected series of raids constitute a strategy for forcing their enemy to do as they wanted? I hope that the use of these terms, rather than being jarring, instead emphasizes and reveals the power and planning that Native Americans put into the problem of conducting war. As James Rice recently suggested, we need "to de-exoticize Native American warfare." Yes, it was culturally and historically specific to its context, and we must and will explore those aspects, but we also must not mark it "as fundamentally different from war in the rest of human history."[26]

In the same spirit of acknowledging the humanity and sovereignty of the many different Nations discussed in this book, I have to the extent possible tried to use Native American personal names instead of misunderstood titles (Wahunsenacawh *vice* Powahatan) and a Nation's endonym rather than the more commonly known exonym (Haudenosaunee *vice* Iroquois). It is an unfortunate fact that many of the "tribal" names most commonly used in English were originally names given to them by other Indians, often with a derogatory meaning. James Axtell once noted that most Native Americans divided the world's inhabitants into three categories of person: those who were within their immediate social group, usually named by some variation of "the true people," or just "the people"; others, often denominated by some form of epithet; and a third category of spiritual beings in constant interaction with them, and indeed living alongside them.[27] The second category is often the name that stuck in English sources, and modern historians and Indigenous people have been slowly recovering the original names in the original languages.

Some Nations have adopted their exonym and use it to this day, and in those cases I will continue to use it (e.g., Mohawk or Tuscarora). In one case, I have preferred Creek to Muscogee because modern Nations use both names. Personal names are more difficult since many Nations had a tradition of name changes at key life stages, and even a seeming European name could have been authentically used.[28] It is also difficult to standardize spellings of places and endonyms, since many Nations' names were connected to place names that shifted when that Nation moved. So referring to the Mohawks of Gandaouagué is a different thing from referring to Caughnawagas or Kahnawakes, although all were in one sense closely related.

In addition, the general trend in writing about Native Nations in North America has been to avoid the use of the word "tribe." Earlier in my career I tended to blend it with "people,"—which had the advantage of corresponding to many groups' names for themselves. In this book, however, I follow other ethnohistorians in generally using the word Nation.[29]

Finally, a note on judgment. This is a book about war, and therefore inevitably contains within it descriptions of extraordinary violence and even cruelty. I believe that virtually every human society in our long history has engaged in war of some kind, and has also therefore engaged in violence and cruelty. The forms and patterns and extremities have differed, but to say that Indians were violent is not to say they were worse than others, or more violent than others. They were equal participants in a worldwide pattern of using violence to achieve ends of various kinds. Similarly, at various times in the past, and in the text of these very chapters, I have referred to Native American war as being endemic. This was intended neither as a condemnation, nor as the basis for dismissing the quality or sophistication of their social systems. In this specific context, my intent was and is only to counter notions of an idyllic and exceptionally peaceful past. It would obviously be true to say that war among European nations was equally endemic. That, at least, no one doubts.

CHAPTER TWO

The Cutting-Off Way of War

In 1725 an English emissary from South Carolina arrived in Coweta town to demand an apology from the Creeks (Muscogees) for their recent attack on an English trader in Cherokee country, and further to demand that the Creeks make recompense by helping the English against the Yamasees.[1] The Creeks reluctantly agreed, and sent out a war party. It was quite likely that the Yamasees were already aware of their approach, as they had relocated from their usual town into a newly built fort closer to the coast. The Creeks' guide took them to the old town site, where they launched a surprise dawn volley at what turned out to be an empty fort. Their firing awakened a nearby detachment of Yamasees left behind as sentries or as an ambush party, but who had been asleep as the Creeks passed them in the night. Now, alerted by the volley, the sentry party hurried to warn the new fort. The Creeks finally found and attacked the new fort, but with "litle Success." They did, however, find a Yamasee chief, the "Huspaw King," and his family outside the fort; they captured three of them, and got "several Shott at the Huspaw king and are in hopes have killed him." At that point a party of Yamasees emerged from the fort and fought a short battle, losing one of their leaders in the process. The Creeks then blockaded the fort from a distance for three days, hoping "to take some More but to no purpose." When the Creeks finally withdrew the Yamasees pursued. Turning on their pursuers, the Creeks drove the Yamasees into a pond and were about to press them further when they were distracted by the coincidental arrival of a force of Spaniards. When the Creeks resumed their march homewards, the Yamasees pursued and attacked again, and it was in this "Batle in which they did us [the Creeks] the most Damnadge." All told, the Creeks killed eight Yamasees, and brought home those scalps, nine prisoners, and some plunder. The Creeks lost five killed and six wounded.[2]

The events of this raid are entirely typical of the "Cutting-Off Way of War," an operational pattern that could scale up or down depending on the size of the attacking force, and that very likely persisted in its essentials from well before European contact into the nineteenth century. It began with a war party attempting surprise, which in this case was foiled by fortifications and the belated alertness of a sentry force. The Creeks then attacked individuals or small groups they found outside the fort, and offered battle to the defenders near the walls. The Yamasees, perhaps to maintain their reputation, accepted battle but lost their "captain" in the ensuing fight. The Creeks then lurked in a kind of distant blockade around the fort hoping to snipe at the occasional exposed person, and after three days headed for home. The Yamasees immediately pursued, hoping to take advantage of a party spread out on the march. A series of running battles damaged the Creeks and sped them on their way home.

This pattern can be detected throughout eastern North America; it fills our European-derived sources, and it surely existed before the European arrival as well. Saying this, however, requires first wrestling with older interpretations of Native American systems of war, some that date right back to the era of first contact, and which I argue misrepresent and downplay the sophistication and lethality of Native American warfare.[3] Many previous readings of the evidence, both by some early European explorers or settlers and by some modern historians, have described Native American tactical techniques as relatively innocuous and bloodless before the arrival of the Europeans, and even long thereafter. Some scholars have argued more specifically that before contact, Native Americans greatly preferred to engage in linear pitched battles fought in a ritualistic manner, with much mutual firing and dodging of missile weapons, and not many casualties.[4] A corollary to this interpretation was that the arrival of European technology and more lethal metal arrowheads, rapidly followed by clumsy but lethal guns, led Indians to abandon the pitched battle and rely entirely on ambush. This line of thinking has occasionally been taken to extremes, with some arguing that the Europeans introduced the Indians to torture and scalping, and even to the deliberate killing of enemies in battle.[5] In one example, after describing the death of fifty Indians on one side in battle in 1669, one of the most frequently cited historians of Native American warfare calmly asserts what is in fact unknowable: "Such heavy losses in a single action were unheard of before the arrival of the white man and his weapons."[6] Colin Calloway, whose understanding of these sources is otherwise unrivaled, at one time subscribed to this view of a relatively limited and ritualistic form of warfare prior to contact as well. In his marvelous history of the Abenakis, who lived in the mountains of what is now New Hampshire and southern Quebec, Calloway asserted a postcontact escalation based on Indian "competition for furs and dominion." In support of this claim, he cites the abandonment of Iroquoian settlements on the St. Lawrence near Quebec City (then Stadacona) between the arrival of Jacques Cartier in 1535 and the French return under Samuel Champlain in 1603.[7] The problem with this interpretation is not that the settlements were abandoned (they were), or that the inhabitants were pushed out by war (that seems likely), but that we should assume that such a displacement due to war had never happened prior to European contact. This assumption is all the odder given that Cartier himself reported that two years *prior* to his arrival, the Toudaman Indians had surprised some 200 sleeping Iroquoians (men, women, and children) inside a temporary palisade. They set fire to the palisade and then killed everyone who rushed out, leaving only five survivors.[8]

In the same vein, Patrick Malone, whose book *The Skulking Way of War* created a paradigmatic phrase for this view of Native American warfare, argued more specifically that war in early seventeenth-century New England could vary in scale, but that combat itself was "on a small scale," mostly ambushes and raids, with some sieges and occasional battles, and "in all these forms of warfare, relatively few participants were ever killed."[9] Malone's use of "skulking" has been widely cited by generalists as the best way of describing Native American fighting techniques.[10] The term was indeed in common use among Europeans as a way to describe Indian martial capabilities that they themselves could only dimly perceive. It was not complimentary. It somehow managed to imply both a lack of seriousness (in that it supposedly resulted in few deaths) and a lack of honor and openness. Indians "skulked": meaning that they sneaked, they lurked, they attacked without warning and without rules. For us to retain it as a common descriptor for their way of war is thus *at least* semantically problematic in its denigrating quality.

More importantly, however, the paradigm of the skulking way of war is fundamentally flawed in other ways. First, its emphasis on tactics distracts from the extent to which Native American forces moved and fought to fulfill strategic intentions, and not just to satisfy bloodlust, or even a desire for revenge.[11] They warred; they did not just feud. Second, even at the tactical level, the paradigm overemphasizes the shift to ambush as a response to firearms. Ambush had long been a crucial component of Native American warfare as a style of combat well suited to smaller-scale societies, and thoroughly documented in other comparable societies around the world. Firearms were not required to make ambush a critical component of their tactical repertoire, although guns likely *did* lead to open battles becoming less common.

Finally, the skulking paradigm likely underplays the level of lethality in precontact warfare in North America. There is archaeological evidence for the long continuity of a style of war that could be highly destructive and lethal. Three examples are the large-scale massacre at Crow Creek in South Dakota in the fourteenth century; a cemetery site in Illinois from the same era indicating a persistent series of violent attacks; and a recent reexamination of 119 precontact burials in southern New England showing that a remarkable

15 percent of them had died from violent trauma, 20 percent of whom were women or children.[12] Furthermore, the documentary and archaeological evidence for the Mississippian societies of the Midwest and Southeast strongly suggests a pattern of elaborate and deadly warfare.[13] In a later era, admittedly postcontact, the Narragansetts' advice to the English in 1637 was clear and stark: "The assault would be in the night when they [the Pequots] are commonly more secure and at home, by which advantage the English, being armed, may enter the houses and do what execution they please." The Narragansetts did request, however, that women and children be spared—likely so they could be taken prisoner.[14]

To account for this evidence of willingness to kill and for the growing archaeological evidence of extensive and lethal precontact warfare, recent anthropological work has developed a more complex and convincing description of Native American warfare that sees highly lethal and highly ritualized warfare coexisting, with one superseding the other depending on the circumstance.[15] Part of the argument of this book is that the basic operational pattern of Native American warfare in eastern North America made those transitions naturally simple. In other words, Calloway could be absolutely correct about the devastation of the St. Lawrence settlements, but wrong in suggesting that it represented some revolutionary change in style or intention for warfare. Anthropologist Kevin McBride, in reassessing the traditional argument for the low lethality of precontact Native warfare, sees not so much a change in *method* as a change in "scope and purpose" generated neither by European technology nor new notions of total warfare, but rather by changing "political, social, and economic objectives."[16] This book is not ultimately about precontact warfare and its level of violence, but it does argue that the operational pattern described here, the "cutting-off way of war," is fully compatible with both high levels of violence in war and with seemingly ritualized low-casualty battles. It encompasses both small ambushes by small war parties and the devastating destruction of towns.

Like skulking, the "cutting-off" phrase was English, and it could simply mean killing, or it could be used to imply the wholesale destruction or elimination of towns, forts, or forces in the field.[17] The phrase was frequently applied to war with and by the Indians, and it sometimes appears as the English translation for what Indian emissaries supposedly said. British Lieutenant Edward Jenkins, for example, reported in June 1763 that when the local Indians had asked to talk to him, they seized him (as a part of what is sometimes called Pontiac's War), and informed him that "Detroit, Miamis and all these posts were cutt Off, and that it was a folly to make any resistance therefore desired me to make the few Soldiers I had in the Fort Surrender, otherwise they would put us all to death in Case one man was killed."[18] In another example, the Cherokees explained to George Chicken in 1715 that "it was not plunder they wanted from them [the Creeks] but to go to war with them and cut them of[f]."[19] It is impossible for us at this remove to discern the idiomatic subtleties that either of these emissaries may have intended, but the phrase is suggestive, and ultimately it is also descriptive. Indian war parties on offensive expeditions, whether to exact revenge, gain prestige, acquire prisoners, assert sovereignty, or perhaps administer a political lesson, sought to "cut off" enemy villages or individuals through surprise and ambush—an event that could be highly lethal, especially on a per capita basis. Furthermore, repeated success at or around a village could render it uninhabitable, functionally cutting it off from its cluster of related villages.

Referring back to the discussion of "levels" of war in chapter 1, it is important to emphasize that the cutting-off way of war is a description of warfare at the strategic and operational levels—not the tactical. It is about selecting targets, moving forces toward the enemy sometimes great distances (often along separate paths), and then bringing to bear superior numbers—hopefully by surprise—against the enemy at predesignated points. Whether what followed was an ambush, a battle, an assault on the walls, or a siege was a matter of tactics in response to being in contact with enemy forces.

What exactly did a cutting-off attack look like, and how did it respond to shifts in circumstance, enemy action, and so on? Whatever strategic motive might be in play, and we will explore those motivations in later chapters, the operational goal of an Indian offensive force, or war party, remained generally similar—and that was to "cut off" a selected segment of the enemy's population, whether large or small, and to do so with impunity.[20] Native American societies were politically and demographically wary of heavy casualties. The larger communities (as discussed in chapter 1) might be tens of thousands in population, but they were segmented into clans and towns, each with their own structures of relatively consensual authority. Coercive recruitment did not exist, nor could leaders retain their position after sustaining heavy losses.[21] This fear of disaster demanded relying on surprise in the attack and a basic cultural willingness to retreat rather than fighting to hold ground. In some ways, the mobilization of the war party would determine the nature of the target. A politically important or emotionally charged situation could inspire a large war party which in turn could hope to cut off a whole enemy town. Smaller raiding parties targeted and cut off individuals or small groups, usually in the open. In either case, surprise was central. The usefulness of this approach lies in its flexibility. It can be used in warfare from a raid to conquest and empire building. The operational key was surprise and then avoiding effective pursuit by a larger force.

It is in light of this system that we should understand John Norton's description of a Haudenosaunee campaign. Norton was born in Scotland of a Cherokee father and a Scottish mother, and he later became a British soldier, a fur trader, and a key associate of the Mohawk Joseph Brant late in the eighteenth century, even being adopted by the Mohawks. Writing early in the nineteenth century, he described how the Haudenosaunee previously had raided the Cherokees and Catawbas:

> The Warriors sought fame to the South of the Ohio, in desultory excursions against the Cherokee and Catawbas. . . . [They] left home in parties from two hundred to ten. . . . [and traveled until they] came upon the Head Waters of Holston, along the Banks of which the Cherokee Hunters were frequently scattered;— these they often surprised, killing and taking them prisoners. At other times, they proceeded to the Villages, but only in small parties to prevent discovery,— the Main Body generally remaining [behind at various camps now in] the State of Kentucky. . . . When the party detached, had gained Scalps or Prisoners, they fled to where their comrades awaited their return, to support them in case they might be surprised by superior force. . . . Many of these Parties were overtaken [during their march home],—others triumphantly returned with Scalps & Prisoners.[22]

In this account large parties moved over long distances, probably combining land and water travel, and then split up into smaller groups for actual raids on towns or enemy-hunting parties. Norton also adds a key logistical detail—to which we will return in the next chapter—noting how the main war party established a camp as a rendezvous for the return trip home.

Norton's account neatly matches up with another from a hundred years earlier, this one a Jesuit account of a Haudenosaunee expedition in 1662. The missionary described how a hundred men of the Mohawks and Oneidas set out to ambush the Ottawas when they would be using a portage around some rapids on a river. They traveled "depending on their muskets for provisions, and using the Woods . . . as courtyard, kitchen, and lodging place." As they approached the enemy's country "they began to prowl along the shores of the Lake of the Hurons, seeking their prey." Unfortunately for this war party, they were discovered and surprised by yet another Nation and forced to flee after suffering heavy casualties.[23]

There are countless similar accounts that reveal aspects of this system, although few of them are as comprehensive as Norton's. For the most part European witnesses saw only parts of the system at a time: the initial attack, the sense of being besieged by small wandering parties, or the need to pursue a fleeing war party.[24] A few Europeans, usually those long resident among a Nation as trader or missionary, sometimes provide a more comprehensive view. Jerome Courtance, for example, living among the Chickasaws in the 1750s, kept a detailed journal that described their fighting with the Choctaws over several months in late 1756 and into the spring of 1757. There is a sense of constant raids and counterraids, with enemy war parties surprising small numbers of men and women outside their village and killing them, as well as occasional larger confrontations. One incident beginning on April 19 can stand in for the others. Courtance reported that an "Army of Chactaws [sic]" had been discovered within thirty miles of the Chickasaw towns. The Chickasaws apparently prepared to defend themselves in a way that made it obvious to the Choctaws that their attempt at surprise had failed, and so they adapted: "The said Army finding themselves discovered declined attacking the Chickasaw Nation in a Body, but formed themselves into small Parties and spread round the Nation. One Gang of them fell on a Chickasaw hunting Camp consisting of ten Fellows and killed three of them and carried off one alive together with all their Horses and Skins and every Thing they had at Camp."[25]

War parties like this Choctaw one may never have intended to attack "in a body" as Courtance assumed. As Norton's account suggested, a main body might travel together to some point within striking distance and then separate into smaller parties better suited to achieving surprise. In a separate account, Norton described in more detail what this might look like. A small war party encountering the tracks of a hunting party would follow them and charge them: "Killing till they meet with no farther resistance, they then make prisoners of the remnant, and return home. One rencounter is all that is sought for in an expedition." If they meet none on the way, "they proceed to the villages or Settlements of the enemy, and there either make an attack on some little hamlet, or lay an Ambuscade into which they endeavour to draw some of the enemy into the snare prepared for them."[26]

This pattern of subdividing and waiting was particularly appropriate if the enemy was fortified, and thus more dangerous to try to attack by surprise. In that case it was common to focus on smaller groups of vulnerable individuals moving in the vicinity of the towns, often over a period of days, in a kind of distant siege. The British commander of the garrison at Fort Loudoun, built at Cherokee request in the midst of the Overhill Cherokee towns, was able to observe Cherokee methods more closely than most. He reported in July 1757 that the Cherokees had gone on a raid against a French camp, and found that it was already fortified, so they spent "several Days watching, but no Success, till one Morning he [the Cherokee war leader] sent five of his Men pretty early near the Fort, and lay in Ambush, when this young Man [a French officer] came out and they shott him."[27]

Shooting to kill from a distance, however, was not always a sufficient reward. As virtually all of our authorities, past and present, agree, one key motivation for individuals on a war party was to take prisoners. Prisoners could serve a range of purposes, but the necessity to take some was clear, and doing so clearly required hand-to-hand combat.[28] Once a war party was revealed, especially if in the midst of a cluster of enemy towns, as Norton's descriptions suggested, the war party would typically flee before the defenders could gather reinforcements from nearby towns.

One of the great weaknesses of colonial settlements was their frequent inability to pursue. European frontier communities would build blockhouses or small forts as places to gather when surprised, but they were usually unable to gather quickly enough for effective pursuit, and were also afraid of being ambushed in the process. During Grey Lock's War in the 1720s in northern New England, the Missiquois' entire strategy was predicated on this reality: they could stage repeated "raids" on New English settlements, even as the white settlers resorted to working in their fields in ever-larger groups, and the Missiquois could flee without fear of effective pursuit. Governor William Dummer warned about this problem, since "the Indians alwaies make a Sudden onset & then retire forthwith so that if your forces remain as they now are [in reserve well to the south of the frontier] before they can be got together & march to the places attackt the enemy will probably be got out of reach & so it will be too late to follow them."[29] In another example in another part of the continent, this time in the late 1780s, a group of Americans pursuing a war party after its attack began to worry about what happened if they succeeded too well in keeping up with their "fleeing" enemy: realizing they had been spotted, they stopped to hold a council to decide what to do, and, "Knowing their mode of warfare, and believing that they had discovered us; we were aware that if they thought they could not stand us, they would scatter in the woods and we could not find them, but if they thought they could stand us, they would waylay us in some convenient place, take the first fire and we might be defeated as there was but fifteen of us. We therefore concluded to pursue them no further."[30]

In contrast, effective pursuit by Native American defenders meant that the attackers had to balance the need to retreat quickly while also securing their line of march. Norton's descriptions are again helpful: "After having made an assault, and killed and taken some of the enemy, if his men are all young and active, none of them wounded and the prisoners able to keep up with them, will return by the most direct path home," while placing guards in the rear to warn of pursuit and perhaps to stage ambushes of any pursuers.[31] Norton interviewed an older Cherokee man who spoke of the back-and-forth raiding between the Cherokees and the "Northern Tribes" [generally the Haudenosaunee, among others], noting that not only did the Cherokee suffer losses, "but very frequently the aggressors suffered in their turn, ... in being overtaken by the enraged and injured pursuers." Norton's witness further related how he had gone on a raid against the Piankashaws on the Wabash River, and had succeeded in killing several and "brought off their scalps," but the pursuit force nearly ran him to the ground; ultimately he barely escaped.[32] Another of Norton's interviewees described how the pursuit was managed. First they had to figure out what Nation had attacked them, and therefore what direction they would be fleeing. They then "take a straight course, with all expedition to some pass in a mountain by which they [the enemy] must go, or crossing place on some great River, and there lie in ambush for them until they arrive." Lacking such a place, they would use an alternate path to get to the frontiers of the enemy country and then determine if the enemy war party had already gone by, and if not, "they seek the war path, which communicates with the two nations; and should they there perceive no signs of their having yet passed, an ambuscade is fixed."[33]

In all of the examples thus far, no real distinction has been made based on the size of the raiding party, simply because the cutting-off pattern works in very similar ways at large and small scales. And repeated persistent small-scale attacks can have major strategic outcomes. It is also true that even the scale of an attack does not always lend itself to an easy interpretation of motive. As David Silverman points out regarding Haudenosaunee attacks on their traditional enemies in the 1630s through the 1650s: the "usual pattern" saw the Haudenosaunee march from their homelands in upper New York to the St. Lawrence and Ottawa Rivers to attack fur-bearing convoys of canoes. In bands of ten to fifty, they would stake out a section of the river, driving the canoes to shore with gunfire, and then descend on the paddlers, killing some and capturing others. In this case the technique was not focused on the enemy homeland, but it effectively found small groups of enemies away from support, and cut them off from home or destination, and such a successful raid netted honor, prisoners, and furs. Which one was the main motive? Furthermore, persistent raids on those rivers cut off their traditional enemies from trading with the French and thus weakened them. The fact the attacks were conducted on a small scale does not mean that they were not part of a larger strategic calculus.

On the other hand, it is quite possible that smaller-scale raids, like the one on the Piankashaws described to John Norton by an older Cherokee, mostly fulfilled individualistic goals of satisfying blood debt or enhancing personal status. In that case, it had been simply he and a friend who had travelled together all the way from eastern Tennessee to the Wabash River in Indiana. But the line between personal vendetta and ongoing war between Nations is hard to draw. The parties of ten to fifty that Silverman suggests were the normal pattern of Haudenosaunee raids on fur convoys, for example, could have been opportunistic small-scale raids within a larger cultural framework of persistent enmity between "traditional enemies"—in which young men took the opportunity for blood revenge or social stature enhancement by attacking those with whom their Nation was already in a persistent feud or even war.

Some options within the cutting-off way of war, however, were only possible at a larger scale. When political considerations dictated, such as the need to administer a serious political message, or perhaps even to remove an enemy as a potential threat or competitor, then a large-scale operation could ensue, and hundreds of men would gather for an offensive. The operational goal would remain cutting off a segment of the enemy, detaching it from the larger whole, although in this case the target would likely be a whole town within the cluster of towns described in chapter 1.[34] As usual, such an attack depended on surprise (especially if the target was fortified) because low casualties among the attackers and the killing and capture of people remained the goal, just now on a larger scale. If the enemy shut themselves up in a stockade, and no relief from other towns was forthcoming, then the attackers could either settle in for a siege and assault, or fall back on raiding the surrounding territory hoping to cut off straying individuals or isolated farmsteads.[35] It was rare for the attackers to remain in a body around an enemy town for more than a few days, however. Most "besiegers" would usually leave before enemy reinforcements from other tribal villages could arrive. We even have the spectacle of a Choctaw leader in 1730 who was helping the French besiege the Natchez, after two full months of siege, approach the Natchez walls to convince them to surrender, saying, as evidence of their earnestness, "Do you remember or have your ever heard it said that Indians have remained in such great numbers for two months before forts?"[36] Apparently the very idea was incredible. In an older analysis of Native warfare, anthropologist Wendell Hadlock turned this on its head, arguing that defenders could not rely on tribal reinforcements because the raids would not last long enough. He mistook the cause for the effect: the attackers were very aware of the timing and likelihood of reinforcements and calculated how long to continue a siege or a raid in order to avoid them.[37] In the case of the French siege of the Natchez, there were no other Natchez towns to send relief.

A Mahican-led attack on a Mohawk town in 1669 provides an illuminating example of a war party miscalculating this exact probability, although only barely. The details of this particular encounter show nearly every step of a cutting-off attack on a large scale, as well as the defenders' responses, and so merits narrating here in some detail. Throughout the 1660s the Mohawks were in constant conflict both against assorted Algonquian Nations in New England and against the French.[38] In 1666 the French launched a major invasion of Mohawk country. The Mohawks moved their population into hiding, and abandoned their towns to the French torch, but suffered almost no casualties. When the French force returned to Canada, the Mohawks simply rebuilt their towns in new locations north of the Mohawk River—although the loss of crops and goods was substantial.[39] The precise dating of this destruction and relocation is one reason we can be relatively certain about the number and location of Mohawk towns at the time of the Mahican attack in 1669, since those sites have been identified archaeologically.[40] Map 2.1 represents a specific Mohawk version of the demographic space described generically in chapter 1: three or possibly four towns, fortified, each closely associated with water, and separated from each other by six to fifteen miles, centered within their larger territorial claim (the towns destroyed in 1666 were in essentially similar places, just south of the Mohawk River). At this time there were probably some 2,000 Mohawks spread across those four towns.

In August of 1669, perhaps stirred by the recent killing of six Mahicans along the St. Lawrence, wrongly attributed to the Mohawks, but also part of a longer ongoing conflict, the Mahicans pulled together a coalition of allied Indians from the greater New England area (often collectively referred to as Algonquians, referring to their related languages) to launch a major attack on the most easterly Mohawk town of Gandaouagué. This attack, siege, retreat, and battle have been occasionally discussed or mentioned by modern historians, but none of them seem to have fully understood the role of neighboring towns in creating and dispatching a relief force, which became the pursuit force.[41] Their retellings have not been "wrong," but the cutting-off model helps us see the nature of the attack and response more clearly. Lastly, although there are only two original accounts of this particular event, we are unusually blessed in that one comes from a French source who had some

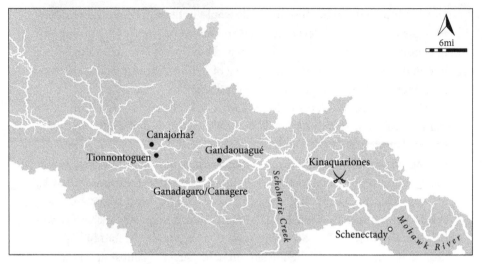

MAP 2.1 The Mohawk towns in 1669. The location of Canajorha is somewhat speculative, but likely. Schenectady is shown at its present-day location for reference. Matilde Grimaldi, based on data in Dean R. Snow, *Mohawk Valley Archaeology: The Sites* (University Park, Pa.: Matson Museum of Anthropology, 1995), 411–13, and with thanks to Teiowí:sonte Thomas Deer for further clarification and a variant of this map from the Kanien'kehá:ka Onkwawén:na Raotitióhkwa Language and Cultural Center. Hydrography is publicly available; Kinaquariones location from Percy M. Van Epps, "The Battle of 1669 at Kinaquariones," *New York History* 13, no. 4 (1932): 420–30.

insight into events from the Mohawk point of view, and the other from an English source, who spoke to the attacking Algonquians after their return and provides their perspective.[42]

The Mahicans, supported by allies from among the Massachusetts, some "Praying Indians," and possibly some Narragansetts, all resentful of years of Mohawk raids, totaled either 300 or 600–700. This number apparently included twenty-four women, and their likely role in logistics is a subject to which we will return in chapter 3. Once assembled, they marched west overland to the Hudson River and then up the Mohawk River, camping a night's march away from Gandaouagué. The route spanned something over 200 miles, and our English source for the march (Daniel Gookin) clearly did not understand Indian logistics, which he disparaged as slow, relying on food acquired "as they travel, by hunting, fishing, and gathering roots; and if, in their march, they are to pass any Indian towns or plantations; which they will go out of their way to visit and find quarters in, rather than pass them; at such places they will stay several days, until they devour all they can get; boasting, vapouring, and prating of their valour."[43]

We will explore these supply options further in chapter 3, but for now it suffices to say that Gookin's disparagement ignores the operational freedom provided by not having to carry food or baggage. And, despite his concern for their "prating," the Mahican/allied force in this case arrived completely by surprise outside the palisade walls of Gandaouagué at dawn on August 18. Gookin was clearly not aware of all the details of the initial assault, and merely notes that the Mahican force settled in to besiege the fort for several days. The French priest Jean Pierron, however, then resident about twelve miles away at the Mohawk capital of Tionnontoguen, tells us more. The Mahicans had achieved surprise, but the palisade walls served their primary purpose of preventing a surprise from becoming a massacre. No doubt finding the gate closed, and unwilling to risk the casualties of an assault, the Mahican force unleashed a volley from outside the walls (in fact, I suspect that these surprise volleys "at" palisade walls may have actually been done by poking muskets through the gaps between poles and shooting into the longhouses; musket balls would penetrate the longhouse walls, unlike arrows). The volley killed four and wounded two more. The men in the sleeping village "at once took gun and hatchet in hand; and, while they defended the palisade, the women began, some to make bullets, and others to arm themselves with knives and defensive weapons."[44]

The precise timing and sequence of what happened next are not completely clear. But the critical and oft-overlooked part is that the noise of the volley alerted the residents of the "neighboring village"—presumably Ganadagaro—who quickly sent messengers to Tionnontoguen. This is an eventuality that the Mahicans clearly would have anticipated, and so the question from their point of view was, how much damage could they do before they were beset by Mohawk reinforcements? Jean Pierron makes it seem as if those reinforcements had mustered and set out by 8:00 A.M. (supposedly including Pierron himself). This is not at all improbable. In August, predawn light for the Mahican attack would have been available by 5:30 A.M., giving Mohawk messengers more than enough time to get to Tionnontoguen and for the word to spread through the longhouses and men to gather their equipment. Meanwhile, Pierron says a two-hour battle in the open in front of the palisade had been taking place. All this is contradicted by Gookin, who claims the siege lasted for a couple of days before reinforcements arrived. Gookin, who was not there, may have combined the final night march, the day's fight, the night's retreat, and the next day's battle into a single multiday siege, but it is highly likely that he was wrong about the duration of the siege itself.[45] Reinforcements were close by and apparently moved quickly. The

Mohawks of Tionnontoguen and possibly Canajorha rushed to the scene, where they found the Mahicans had already sensibly retreated, having suffered apparently only one dead. This is *precisely* what we should expect, notwithstanding some historians' claims that the Mahicans had "not much military sense," or had "run out of ammunition."[46] They had calculated exactly how much time they had to push the fight at Gandaouagué, and then they had fled.

What followed, however, was simply one side outthinking the other. The Mahican and allied forces were retreating the same way they had come, expecting pursuit, but figuring they had a head start. The Mohawk reinforcements, however, "finding the enemy no longer there [at Gandaouagué], promptly had cornmeal prepared, that they might pursue him in his retreat. The provisions being ready, they immediately embarked in Canoes on our river, which is very swift; and, as they followed the current of the stream, they made very good progress." Thus using the river, the pursuing Mohawks overtook their attackers in the night, silently ascertained the location of their camp, and then prepared to ambush them on the trail the next morning at a place called Kinaquariones (see map 2.1). As was usual, the Mahicans moved out that morning in single file, and in the rough ground only the leading twelve or so were initially caught up in the Mohawk ambush. They took some casualties, but then fled back to the sheltered (and possibly entrenched) camp, which the Mohawks continued to attack through the day right up to nightfall. The Mohawks attacked, however, with great care, taking turns firing from behind the shelter of a carried tree. Even so, casualties on both sides were considered fearful: perhaps forty Mohawks and fifty of the allied force. Under the cover of darkness, the Mahicans continued their retreat, and escaped home.[47]

Reading these details through the lens of the cutting-off model suggests the usefulness of the model. Four different modern retellings of the attack significantly underplay the role of the reinforcements from Tionnontoguen. Understanding their operational significance not only helps clarify the contradictions in the sources about the length of the incident, but also helps us see how disease and population loss could render highly vulnerable those Indian Nations reduced to a single town. The cluster of towns that was the usual pattern of a Native Nation's demographic space not only aided their subsistence by spreading out the population across a wider belt of land; it also gave them strategic depth when attacked.

The events at Gandaouagué included a battle outside the walls, and although we do not have a firsthand description (neither Pierron nor Gookin was there), we can turn to other sources to explore what "battle" looked like in the cutting-off way of war, and ultimately we can assess its function. If an attacker found the defenders to be safe behind their walls, as the Mohawks appeared to have been at Gandaouagué, the attacker could assault the walls, blockade the fort, or go home.[48] Assaults were relatively rare, because they lacked the tools to breach the walls, although we know fire was sometimes used.[49] More often, if the attackers knew they had some time before reinforcements would arrive (because of distance, or in the case of colonial forts, because of the general slowness of militiamen), they would create a form of blockade, usually from a substantial distance, that made it impossible for the defenders to hunt, or get water, firewood, and so on, as the Haudenosaunee did to the soldiers defending Fort Frontenac in 1687. Those French soldiers lacked ready reinforcements and most of them were dead of scurvy by spring.[50]

On some occasions, however, the defender might choose to come out from the walls and offer battle in the open—often in the immediately surrounding agricultural fields. Such battles were documented on several occasions by early European explorers. Samuel Champlain participated in one against the Haudenosaunee in 1609.[51] The Powhatans enacted a mock battle for the benefit of the early Virginia colonists.[52] And in the mid-sixteenth century, Jacques Le Moyne de Morgues provided both a drawing and a description of the Timucuas of Florida lined up for battle in a deep, massed formation.[53] Even later witnesses in New England continued to describe Indians as occasionally lining up for battle. Roger Williams described their "pitcht field" battles as seldom killing twenty men, since "they fight with leaping and dancing, that seldome an Arrow hits, and when a man is wounded, unlesse he that shot followes upon the wounded they soon retire and save the wounded."[54] These open battles, as Williams indicated, proceeded without much result. Very few casualties, and possibly even the first letting of blood, sufficed to end the battle, and each side would return home.[55] In this sense, battle could be ritualized and only marginally lethal, but this says nothing about the lethality of war more broadly.

Rather than view open battle as the main object of a military expedition, it is probably more accurate to consider these encounters as moments in which the attacking expedition already had failed, having lost the benefit of surprise.[56] Battle was thus a last resort, perhaps only a kind of face-saving measure, or maybe a test of strength. On some occasions, in the right circumstances, it could have decisive results. An example was the battle of "Sachem's Field," fought between the Narragansetts and the Mohegans in Connecticut in the summer of 1643. Miantonomi led a force of some 900–1,000 Narragansetts into Mohegan territory (both sides apparently still primarily armed with bows and hatchets), almost certainly hoping to surprise Uncas, the Mohegan sachem. After learning of their approach from his scouts, Uncas sent for help from his tributary villages. Gathering together about 600 warriors, he refused to be shut up in his fortified town of Shantok, which at sixty meters square probably could not have usefully accommodated 600 men anyway. He instead moved to meet Miantonomi on an open field, where the two sides approached to within bowshot. A parley was proposed, and Uncas offered to settle their dispute in a single duel. Miantonomi, with the greater numbers, declined, and Uncas gave the signal to begin the attack immediately. Miantonomi was wearing a European mail shirt and, slowed by its weight, was seized by Uncas. Some Narragansetts, perhaps thirty, were killed. The vast majority fled unhurt.[57]

Notice the key role of failed surprise and the defending Mohegans' appeal to their nearby allied or tributary villages. In this case, failed surprise and timely reinforcements allowed the defenders to offer open battle. In other circumstances, however, successful surprise might carry the walls and lead to truly large-scale success and lethality. The most notable recorded example of such a large-scale successful surprise occurred during the Haudenosaunee invasion of the Wendat lands in 1648 and 1649—perhaps the most famous and most interpretively debated of all the intra-Indian wars. It has also been called one of the most decisive. The scholarly debate centers around the motivation for the Haudenosaunee Confederacy's attack.[58] Some scholars have argued for essentially material causes: the Haudenosaunee sought to dominate the fur trade with the Europeans and therefore they attacked and drove out their most serious competitor. Others have at least partially accepted this explanation, but only in the context of European influence, arguing that such materialist-motivated warfare did not exist prior to contact. The most recent interpretations of the war suggest that there was no (or very little) material motivation, and that in fact the Wendat and Haudenosaunee were engaged in traditional warfare based on an old enmity and a desire to gain captives for adoption.

This Haudenosaunee-Wendat war also merits a moment's pause to consider the geopolitical consequences of cutting off entire towns. The story begins with the French settlement in the St. Lawrence region in the early seventeenth century. They eventually came into contact with the powerful Wendat Confederacy on the far northeastern extremity of Lake Huron. For the Wendat this new relationship meant the arrival of missionaries and new material goods, purchasable through the sale of beaver and other furs, and the Wendats quickly became significant trading partners with the French. The restrictive French trading system, however, limited the trade in firearms. Meanwhile, in 1614 the Dutch established a trading post at Fort Orange (now Albany) on the Hudson River, where they cultivated a similar trading relationship with the Haudenosaunee Confederacy, ancient enemies of the Wendat. The Dutch proved more willing to trade guns and powder and eventually the Haudenosaunee, for whatever reason, determined to take advantage of their edge.[59]

In 1648 the Haudenosaunee began a series of major offensives into the Wendats' home territories. They had been attacking outlying Wendat villages for a number of years, and David Silverman argues that the Haudenosaunee used their superior access to firearms to achieve almost complete freedom of movement within the Wendats' home territory prior to 1648.[60] But, beginning that year, and especially in the attack of 1649, the conflict became a much more concerted affair.[61] The Haudenosaunee cut off and destroyed two frontier towns in the summer of 1648. Then in the summer of 1649 a thousand Haudenosaunee warriors "well furnished with weapons,—and mostly with firearms . . . arrived by night" without warning outside the Wendat town of St. Ignace (Taenhatentaron).[62] After a winter-long approach march of hundreds of miles, the Haudenosaunee warriors crept up to the weakest point in the town's palisade wall (a fifteen-foot-high stockade and ditch), breached it, and entered the town before the Wendats became aware of their presence. All but three men among the 400 Wendats in the village were captured or killed.

Those three warned the next village, St. Louis, some three miles away, and many of its inhabitants immediately fled, leaving only about eighty defenders. The Haudenosaunee force shortly arrived and assaulted the palisade around St. Louis. After two or three attempts they cut their way through the stockade, overwhelmed the defenders, and burned the town to the ground, while preserving the palisade wall for their own uses. That night other towns of the Wendat Confederacy, alerted, rushed to the French Jesuit post at Ste. Marie, and the next morning lay in wait to ambush the approaching Haudenosaunee and defend the French fort. The second day of the attack proceeded in a seesaw fashion as each side in turn gained an advantage, but fundamentally the Haudenosaunee had lost the advantage of surprise. They made an attempt on Ste. Marie, took heavy casualties, and chose to return home. Facing a long march, and presumably worried about the arrival of more Wendat reinforcements, they burned the remainder of St. Ignace, killed many but not all of their captives, and headed south. In typical fashion, the Wendats of yet another town dispatched a pursuit force, but it failed to catch up. Although the Haudenosaunee had suffered more casualties than they had hoped for, they had successfully destroyed two towns (in addition to the two of the previous summer), and had killed perhaps as many as 700 Wendats.

There is much in this narrative that is "typical"—corresponding precisely to the cutting-off model—but it also stands out for its scale and the level of destructiveness.[63] Attacking a fortified village was fairly standard, but in this case a successful breach combined with the size of the raiding force meant that once they were inside the walls they killed and captured the inhabitants to a startling degree. Emboldened, and unusually, the Haudenosaunee immediately attacked a second village. It was only after that second success that the normal rallying of reinforcements from other nearby Wendat villages occurred. Then, as usual, the Haudenosaunee headed for home and the defenders pursued, but in this case the damage to the Wendats had been devastating. In combination with the previous year's major attacks and further raiding, this attack decisively forced the Wendats to disperse. They no longer felt safe in their home territories; the separate clans headed in separate directions, putting themselves under the protection of other groups.

In addition to the battles fought outside the walls of a town, there could be encounters on the move, when two groups either deliberately or accidentally encountered each other in the open, and not via ambush. Encounter battles such as these do not seem to have been the norm, since neither side was prepared to surprise the other. Both sides might engage briefly, exchange fire, and then retreat. But there was a tactical system for the encounter battle called the "half-moon," in which warriors moved individually, using trees as cover, while trying to slide around the flanks of their enemy (thus denying them the cover of a single tree).[64] John Norton describes the firing and moving in great detail, a technique he elsewhere identified as advancing like "black birds":

> In marching to the attack, they advance by files, leaving such intervals between each, as may enable them to outflank him. As soon as they come in contact, they all run up, and form; not so exact perhaps as regular troops, but sufficiently to support each other. If the Action commences with firing, they cover themselves by trees and ravines. In plains where these advantages are not to be had they lie on their faces. Parties advance with their guns loaded, which they discharge on the enemy, these are immediately succeeded by others, until they come in close contact, when use the spear and tomohawk.[65]

The half-moon formation was widespread, and would become most famous as used against European columns, and it was apparently so common as to merit a single word in the Narragansett language: *Onúttug*, meaning "An Halfe Moone in war."[66] John Smith encountered it in the early days of James-town and later white settlers on the frontier were so familiar with it that they did not even bother to explain it.[67] Some militiamen in Virginia in 1758 simply noted that the Indians (either Shawnees or Cherokees) tried to attack them during a negotiation, and it turned into a running fight, and "the Indians tryed to get them into a half Moon three Times which at last they effected, [two Indians fell]. . . . At last the Enemies' half Moon being broken, both Parties fled from each other."[68]

KNOWING THE BASICS of Native American operational methods, and having these examples for reference later, allows us to now open up broader issues of logistics, motivations, levels of violence, and ultimately the purpose and function of war. Some hints are already there. The pattern of going and returning tells us something about logistical requirements, and it also suggests what a defender had to be prepared for. Furthermore, it suggests something about political intention—it was not expeditionary warfare designed to take and hold territory—but it could by constant repetition make a space at first indefensible and then ultimately unlivable. Constant successful small-scale raids over a campaign season suppressed the defenders' awareness of what was going on. Small groups became afraid to go out, and without those warning encounters, a major surprise became more likely. A group that found itself unable to retaliate effectively would eventually have to decamp to some other location or submit. One way to describe this process might be "conquest by harassment"—a concept we will return to in chapter 8.[69] Indians were fully willing to engage in complete destruction, and arguably were so willing even prior to European contact, limited only by the relative balance of defense versus offense in precontact years. But truly dramatic victories demanded successful surprise, and that was rare. Our early European witnesses thus passed down an impression of innocuous battles, missing the deeper demographic impact of repeated small-scale raids. The varying availability of European technology—both steel axes (for attacking palisade walls) and guns—upset the balance of offense versus defense, introducing new possibilities for successfully storming and destroying a whole village, but the desire for extensive lethality had always been present.[70] As European technology spread evenly across the continent, however, the balance among Indian Nations was restored, even as demographic loss due to disease and social disruption increased the fear of debilitating casualties.[71] War retained its many functions, however. Nations defended themselves or sought expanded access to goods and even territory, while individuals satisfied their need for social recognition, prestige, and revenge. These were not mutually exclusive goals, and we will see their interaction in the remaining chapters.

CHAPTER THREE

The Indians Went Hunting

Native American Expeditionary Logistics

During the summer of 1755, as part of General Edward Braddock's campaign to attack the new French fort at the forks of the Ohio, his troops and colonial support forces hacked a series of roads into the forest. The roads would allow the movement of supply wagons and artillery, but they also represented yet another British intrusion into Lenape (Delaware) territory. The Lenapes had already been displaced from their ancestral lands further east by fraudulent treaties earlier in the century, and when the Lenape leader Shingas (along with other Native leaders) asked General Braddock "what he intended to do with the Land" if he defeated the French, Braddock replied that "the English Should Inhabit & Inherit" it. Shingas pressed Braddock, asking if those Indians who were friends to the English would not be allowed to "live and Trade Among the English and have Hunting Ground sufficient To Support themselves"? To which Braddock doubled down, saying, "No Savage shou^d Inherit the Land."[1]

Unsurprisingly, many Lenapes swiftly joined the French cause, and small parties of Lenape warriors spread out along the track of both Braddock's road and Burd's road to disrupt the roadbuilding and the movement of provisions. One such war party, joined by a Kanesetake, captured James Smith near Bedford, Pennsylvania.[2] Having secured Smith and killed his companion, they immediately left the site of the ambush and did not stop for fifteen miles. They lit no fire that night. The next morning "they divided the last of their provision which they had brought from Fort DuQuesne," giving Smith an equal share, amounting to "two or three ounces of mouldy biscuit." That was all the food the party had for the remaining fifty miles of their journey to Loyalhanna, apart from "a young Ground-Hog, about as large as a Rabbit, roasted, and also equally divided." They then reunited with several other war parties converging on this rendezvous, where some men had already been present, hunting and gathering food. They all had venison that night, and the next day the reunited force arrived at Fort Duquesne. Smith remained a captive for some time, and in June 1757 he joined a large encampment of "Wiandat [Wendat], Odawas, and Ojibwas" near the French fort further west at Detroit, a gathering place from which warriors supplied themselves and then headed off to raid the English frontier settlements in Virginia and Pennsylvania. They left Smith behind, having consigned him to a female role. Smith soon realized that in the absence of all the warriors that "we were very scarce of provision; and tho we did not commonly steal from one another; yet we stole ... any thing that we could eat from the French, under the notion that it was just for us to do so; because they [the French] supported their soldiers; and our [women], old men and children were suffering on the acccount of the war, as our hunters were all gone."[3]

Carefully picking through Smith's account we find much that is representative of Native American subsistence systems and campaign logistics, and it also hints at other issues that only become clear when compared to other sources. At the war party level, Smith's captors seamlessly integrated their logistical needs into their operations and tactics. Still carrying some French-supplied biscuit when they attacked Smith's group, after their successful attack they were prepared to go astonishing distances without food. They also hunted on the move for smaller game, while still holding on to the remnants of the French biscuit. On an operational level (referring to the coordinated movements of separate elements), the group that captured him was one of several that had dispersed to both raid and hunt separately, and then meet at predesignated rendezvous points (or cache points). Smith specifically noted that a hunting party had remained continuously at the rendezvous preparing for their return. In Smith's longer narrative of his time as a captive, lasting several years, we also see the strategic pressure created when the men were not available to hunt for the community, creating subsistence vulnerability and a heavy reliance on European allies to supply provisions. Only with this outside help could the men continue to raid on a year-round basis.

The Lenapes' methods of provisioning on the move showcase how Native American campaign logistics provided them with enormous geographic and operational flexibility, but also limited their ability to engage in months-long campaigns. Smith's account also shows the extent to which they had hybridized their logistical systems through their alliances with Europeans—Smith's captors began their raid with French biscuit and later sustained their families through the offices of a French fort. Their overall flexibility is further indicated in the title of this chapter, a quote taken from the journal of a British army engineer, Captain John Montresor. His entry for August 16, 1764, noted simply that when his army of some 2,000 white soldiers and at least 300 Indians encamped at La Riviere de Villejoint, "The Indians went hunting. Provisions issued to the Troops."[4] This brief journal entry encapsulates much of the difference between European and Native American expeditionary logistics—one was flexible and seemingly limitless, but only for a single campaign year, or even just a season. The other was inflexible, road- or river-bound, was pushed forward from the rear, but could be sustained year over year on the basis of agricultural production elsewhere.[5] The French in North America in many ways overcame this limitation, but primarily because their expeditions were almost always conducted jointly with Natives and relied on Native logistical systems.

This contrast may state the seemingly obvious, but not only were there key variations in how Native Americans managed logistics in ways beyond simply hunting, but the question has crucial implications for the nature of Native American offensive warfare and associated political aspirations. Too often historians—even those interested in warfare—have ignored the logistical systems that underpinned Native American warfare, or they have simply assumed a kind of effortless ability to "live off the land."[6] Ultimately, understanding the specifics of Native American campaign logistics will contribute to assessing the political function of war in Native polities.

Chapter 1 laid out the basic arrangements of homes, fields, and towns in a hypothetical Native Nation's "demographic space." Indians did not live in the "wilderness"—they lived in an environment that they had shaped over many generations. This may seem a ridiculously simple point, but the ubiquity of that word in the mouths of our European witnesses continues to mislead or obscure key realities about the human-modified and human-managed landscape of eastern North America. Scholars have achieved a certain clarity with respect to the nature of towns, fields, and even town clusters through site-based archaeological work and the greater reliability of European witnesses when they were describing town buildings and associated public activities like farming and eating. But the nature of the spaces *between* town clusters remains less clear. It also, however, was not wilderness. It was a world filled with transportation networks and contested or semicontested territorial claims associated with hunting and gathering grounds, both of which represented key components of Native American expeditionary logistics.

Long-distance movement occurred overland and by water. The latter required appropriate technologies and a knowledge of portage routes from one drainage system to another or around fall lines. Those portages were also linked into the beaten paths that stretched across North America. Some of the overland paths have become famous, such as the "Warriors' Path" roughly paralleling the Blue Ridge Mountains in Virginia and North Carolina, connecting the southern piedmont from the South Carolina/Georgia border ultimately via several northern branches to the Haudenosaunee (Iroquois) towns in upstate New York. The path served as the regular route for war parties of Catawbas or Cherokees heading north, or Haudenosaunee heading south, in the long-standing conflicts between those Nations. White settlers later appropriated and widened long segments of the path to create the "Great Wagon Road" connecting Lancaster, Pennsylvania, to western Virginia and the Carolina backcountry. Beyond this well-known example, local historians in North Carolina, Virginia, Pennsylvania, and Ohio have reconstructed the complex and far-reaching Native-built paths connecting the many different peoples of the region, both to each other and to distant hunting grounds.[7] Militarily speaking, these paths channeled movement into relatively predictable paths. Any large group moving long distances could be counted on to choose among a limited number of options (whether land, water, or a combination). Overall, this constructed environment of fields, roads, hunting grounds, portages, and so on shaped Native tactics as well as their strategic thinking as they sought advantages from war beyond simple revenge or reputation.[8]

Before turning to the specifics of logistics on the move, we must elaborate somewhat on the material from chapter 1 about Native American subsistence. Their traveling diet derived from their diet at home and its caloric realities, and so requires a deeper look. Dietary variations among different groups during the historic period are generally well understood, but maize corn had been the staple of Native American farming in the Eastern Woodlands since at least 1100 C.E., generally mixed with beans and squash.[9] In some areas, among the Wendats, for example, maize thoroughly dominated the annual caloric intake, whereas hunting played a relatively larger role among their near neighbors in the Haudenosaunee Confederacy.[10] Among the Algonquians of coastal Virginia, estimates vary, with one scholar suggesting that only 25 percent of the annual diet was from agriculture, and the rest from hunting, fishing, and gathering (likely reflecting the value of aquatic protein sources), while another argues that maize provided more calories than any other single food.[11] And, although Susan Sleeper-Smith rightly emphasizes the enormous farming capacity of historic-era Indians in the Ohio River valley, even there hunting was seasonally and economically essential, as it was for *every* society in the region, sometimes on a large scale. The Virginia Algonquians, for example, despite ready access to maritime proteins for much of the year, included deer drives in the deep part of the winter, usually some distance upriver from their towns, and using groups as large as 300 men to drive deer. This was supplemented by a postharvest (August to October) dispersal into small groups to live by small-scale hunting, fishing, shellfishing, and gathering.[12] The Lenapes also used large groups for deer drives.[13] Deer hunting's caloric significance was supplemented by its economic value in the deerskin trade with Europeans, but archaeological evidence makes clear that deer had been the primary hunting prey in the Mississippian era as well.[14] Depending on local climate, access to shoreline, and so on, the seasonal system included a period of relying on stored food in the late winter into the spring planting season (the labor for which was mostly or entirely done by women), supplemented by fish runs and gathering. The summer and fall usually saw "close-in" hunting near the town areas. After the harvest, hunting parties, composed either mostly of men or of the whole village, would head out for long-range hunting, intended to gather and cure large quantities of meat for the winter.[15]

This kind of seasonal movement and shifting of food sources provided the skill set and the capacity to travel long distances without carrying much food. Instead, Native peoples developed systems of plant caretaking and hunting that enabled them to feed themselves while they were on the move. We see some of its forms both in campaign narratives and in captivity narratives that relate the kinds of traveling food used during the seasonal process of hunting or dispersal.

To simplify somewhat, traveling food took five forms—defined here partly by what they were, but also by how they were prepared—supplemented by one behavior. The first and most well known was ground parched corn, carried in a small bag, and it could be eaten dry or mixed with water into a paste. The Haudenosaunee who captured David Ogden in the early 1780s marched an entire day without a halt, "except for a few minutes, when the Indians took from the packs a little parched corn, which had been pounded fine in their mortars, before they left Niagara; this they mixed in water in some wooden dishes, which each Indian carried with him, then drank it down, pounded corn and all, leaving the chewing process to be carried on by the stomach." The second category was very closely related, but the requirement for a fire led Ogden to carefully distinguish this cold use of corn flour from "samp," elsewhere called "sagamite," which required boiling of the same parched corn (sometimes ground or pounded, sometimes not).[16] The third category of traveling food was dried meat, taken at some earlier hunt and prepared for easy transport, typically venison, but sometimes bear. The Seneca chief Chainbreaker recalled Senecas using dried venison specifically to increase their speed while evading pursuit after taking prisoners; it allowed them to avoid making fires.[17]

The next two categories were less reliable, but provided greater freedom of movement since they did not require carrying food at all. The first was "expedient" food: a whole class of edibles that European witnesses derisively called "trash." This could include a wide assortment of wild vegetable matter, but also the meat of smaller animals more readily hunted while on the move. The Wampanoags who captured Mary Rowlandson in 1676 were suffering from both English and Mohawk attacks, and as they moved from place to place that year they turned to expedient foods, variations of which can be found in nearly every captivity narrative. In Rowlandson's case she observed that the Wampanoags would

> starve and dy with hunger: and all their Corn that could be found was de-
> stroyed, and they driven from that little they had in store, into the Woods
> in the midst of Winter. [But, they] would eat that, that a Hog or a Dog
> would hardly touch. . . . The chief and commonest food was Ground-
> nuts: They eat also Nuts and Acorns, Harty-choaks, Lilly roots, Ground-
> beans, and several other weeds and roots, that I know not. They would
> pick up old bones, and cut them to pieces at the joynts, . . . and then boil
> them, and drink up the Liquor, and then beat the great ends of them in a
> Morter, and so eat them. They would eat Horses guts, and ears, and all
> sorts of wild Birds which they could catch: also Bear, Vennison, Beaver,
> Tortois, Frogs, Squirrels, Dogs, Skunks, Rattle-snakes; yea the very Bark
> of Trees; besides all sorts of creatures, and provision which they plun-
> dered from the English.[18]

It is true that the Wampanoags were under extreme pressure, but Rowland-son's account rings true to other relations of war parties moving quickly and relying on expedient local foods to keep moving.

In the last category, war parties on the move could stop for more intensive hunting, preparing the food for further travel, caching it, or even breaking up into groups (as we saw in James Smith's narrative), designating some men to hunt, while others continued on, anticipating a later rendezvous. More exam-ples of this kind of hunting on the move will be discussed later, but for now it is important to point out the time that it required. Mary Jemison noted that the group she was traveling with from Ohio to New York, although already carrying horseloads of provisions, chose to stop for two days to hunt.[19] Jemi-son's group was not a war party, but it reminds us that deer were not just wait-ing around to be hunted, especially if a large war party was moving through the woods. Hunting larger game required time, as did preparing the meat, a task usually done by women, and one that they seem to have sometimes done even for war parties on the move.[20] In addition to these five categories of food, there was one additional "behavior" that emerges in the sources—a behavior also found in other warring societies around the world who otherwise lacked ready access to food while on the move—and that was to gorge when food was available, and then correspondingly go without for surprisingly long periods.[21]

Having established these basic food sources, let us consider the caloric possibilities. As a general rule, a person needs around 2,000 calories per day to stay moderately healthy; U.S. Food and Drug Administration (FDA) guidelines for an active adult male recommend about 3,000 calories per day, while modern military field rations, assuming strenuous activity, aim considerably higher at 3,750.[22] British Army rations in the mid-eighteenth century had a core daily allowance of one pound of bread and one pound of meat, supplemented on a rotating basis by butter, peas, rice, or oats. This produced a daily total of roughly 2,500 calories (varying on whether meat was fresh or dry, and so on, and the total calories would be increased by beer when available).[23] How much would it take to meet these approximate standards using the most common Native American traveling foodstuffs? Unmodified dried corn is roughly 1,800 calories per pound (as kernels or in flour form).[24] One 200-pound deer, boned and gutted, produces 100 pounds of meat, at 680 calories per pound (in reality, much of the "discards" could or would also be cooked into a stew, drawing out the value per warrior). If we imagine an idealized equivalent to a British soldier's ration: one pound of corn plus one pound of fresh deer meat would provide about 2,480 calories. Bear's meat is considerably fatter, at almost double the calories per pound.[25]

In short, measured strictly in terms of calories and pounds, Indian rations and European military rations did not differ that much (corn is somewhat more caloric than European bread, but beef and pork are more caloric than venison). The difference lies in the way they were procured, stored, carried, and eaten. A British soldier's beef and biscuit would be transported along with him in barrels, in wagons, on packhorses, or as live cattle driven along with the army. This might be less true when a British army maneuvered within populated Europe, but wagon trains and packhorses were the rule on the frontiers of North America. In contrast—as the rest of this chapter shows—Indians carried relatively small amounts of prepared food overland; they could combine that food with meat taken while on the move (even at the cost of some delay, but often by designating hunting groups to provision the whole); they took advantage of a wide array of naturally available foods in the landscape; and they combined fasting and gorging as a matter of course.

This basic understanding of caloric possibilities must be laid alongside the model of Native American operations laid out in chapter 2. The raids, sieges, or battles of the cutting-off way of war were all conducted at the end of a march. What was a Native American "march" like? How did they move to their enemies, and how did they sustain those movements? Long-distance movements by water were logistically simpler, as canoes could carry supplies and were usually faster than travel on foot, but water routes were also more predictable and detectable by an enemy. Long overland marches were also common, and even when a war party moved mostly by water, there were usually a minimum number of days of overland travel at one or both ends of the route. Consider the long war between the Catawbas and the Haudenosaunee over the course of the eighteenth century. Although the war parties in that case were often relatively small, they were conducted almost entirely overland, over a distance of some 600 miles or more, meaning at least thirty days' travel each way at a generous estimate of twenty miles a day. And there are other examples. In 1663 a Seneca force of some 800 men marched 300 miles to attack a Susquehannock fort in southern Pennsylvania.[26] In 1759, 200 Chickasaws set out to intercept a party of Savannahs, and traveled for twenty-six days before almost blundering into them.[27] This willingness to travel long distances was already an organic part of Native American societies. David Silverman has shown how Indians traveled enormous distances to acquire arms and powder from distant traders. He reports that William Johnson warned General Jeffery Amherst at the outset of Pontiac's War that the Indians were likely to seek out French traders far away in the Illinois country, with Johnson remarking that "I well know that distance is little regarded by Indians."[28]

The approach march could also be shaped to provide a logistical network once in enemy country, including caches, or, as with James Smith's account, a rendezvous point where hunters remained at work. The war party that captured Jean Lowry during the French and Indian War, for example, four days after her capture met up with "two other Indians, that had been left to Hunt, got some fresh Venison, and struck up Fire and prepared Victuals." To that point she had only been given food (bread) once.[29] Chapter 2 quoted John Norton describing how the Mohawks attacking the Cherokee homeland established a hunting camp as a rendezvous, to which the war parties returned.[30] Elsewhere Norton filled in some of the details of how this looked, varying according to the scale of the expedition. On the lower end, with only "small parties of from ten to fifty warriors," the men would kill game and provide an "abundance of provisions." Just before their arrival "in the neighbourhood of the enemy's settlements, they cure a sufficient quantity with smoke, for their sustenance while they have to remain there, as also on their retreat"—allowing them to avoid fires or even stopping. On larger expeditions by a whole

"Nation," runners would be sent to "surrounding tribes and villages" whose women would "immediately begin to prepare parched corn flour and bread for provisions to the warriors." As the men marched toward the rendezvous, "The warriors spread out on each side of the path, to hunt the animals of Chace [i.e., normal prey], for provisions, assembling at noon, when those which they have killed are divided among the party."[31] The details Norton provides here are very rare, and even rarer is his separation of logistical systems by scale. Even this description, however, lacks some specifics, and needs both more explanation and a deeper exploration. Having established the basics of Native subsistence, combined with a sense of the operational system of the cutting-off way of war, and now guided at least initially by Norton's suggestions, we can go deeper into exactly how expeditionary logistics functioned, beginning with routes and means of transportation and carriage.

Expeditionary Logistics: Routes

Very many routes relied heavily on water travel, and carrying provisions afloat presented few problems. Strategically, the real issue presented by water travel was that it channeled war parties into fairly predictable paths, especially at key portages either joining the heads of two rivers, or passing around major fall lines. European maps from the period emphasized the course of rivers and regularly provided portage details (see figure 3.1). A portage could vary from a matter of feet to many miles, but in combination with the appropriate boat-building technology they could connect water routes for hundreds of miles, especially in the Great Lakes region and down the Ohio and Tennessee River drainages into the Mississippi.[32]

For using these networks Native Americans possessed essentially two boat-building traditions, both of which could carry substantial loads. Some Nations, generally the more northern ones, built canoes from tree bark, typically elm or birch. Pierre Pouchot reported that elm canoes were more fragile and were limited to three to nine people and their equipment. He particularly noted that elm canoes were more commonly used for war parties, possibly reflecting the apparent ease of building them and then likely discarding them to travel overland (although it is also worth noting that elm trees also grew much further south; birchbark canoes brought into Illinois country were called "north canoes").[33] Birch canoes were more sophisticated than the elm version, and could mount three, six, twelve, or even twenty-four benches, carrying up to 3,000 pounds, but were light enough for only four men to carry

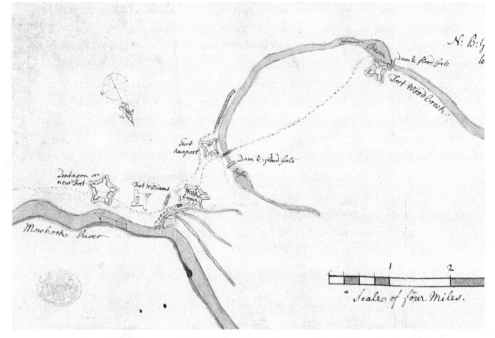

FIGURE 3.1 A detail from a 1758 map of the "Great Carrying Place" showing the path, river, and portage connections between the Mohawk River and Lake Oneida. Detail of map, ca. 1758. "The Course of the Wood Creek from the Mowhock River at the Onoida or Great Carrying Place to The Onoida Lake. Representing the Forts built on the Carrying Place by order of General Shirley: and Afterwards destroyed by Major Generl Webb." British Library and Granger Historical Picture Archive.

across a portage.[34] Bark canoes could be made relatively quickly from local materials. William Preston in 1756 reported how the Cherokee allies accompanying his expedition rapidly put together canoes to float downriver after their party emerged from an exhausting march through the mountains.[35]

Dugout canoes, or pirogues, on the other hand, were essentially an entire tree, painstakingly hollowed out, but capable of carrying even larger numbers of people. Thomas Hariot reported from the Roanoke colony in the 1580s that the locals there made dugouts capable of carrying "well xx [twenty] men at once, besides much baggage: the timber being great, tal, streight, soft, light, & yet tough."[36] Peter Wood's survey of the archaeological and literary evidence for pirogues in the lower Mississippi drainage as well as elsewhere in the Americas finds vessels regularly in the twenty-five-to-forty-foot range, sometimes carrying forty to fifty men. One account from Hernando de Soto's expedition described a dugout with twenty-five oarsmen (paddlers) to a side with an additional twenty-five or thirty warriors in the middle.[37] In 2017 such a dugout was found preserved in the mud in the Red River in Louisiana, measuring thirty-four feet.[38]

In contrast to these Native technologies, European riverboats were harder to drag around a portage and were poorly suited to traveling upriver. William Johnson, the long-standing British agent among the Mohawk—they adopted him into the Nation in the 1740s—advised Colonel Henry Bouquet on the use of boats for his expedition into the Ohio country in 1764. He pointed out that the Indians would travel freely up and down the Muskingum and Scioto Rivers in any season, but he doubted that European boats could make it back upriver.[39] One reason the French were more effective at long-distance logistics in North America is precisely because they had become more familiar and adept with Native boat-building technologies, and deployed them on a large scale.[40]

The nature and capacity of Native American canoes and dugouts are generally well known, and need not detain us long, but there are two related points to make with respect to logistics. The first is that there seems to have been a cultural practice of leaving boats on riversides, where travelers could find and use them (European distinctions between "stealing" and "legitimately borrowed" do not seem to fit properly). At times the permission was explicit, and seems to have been readily given. The Baron de Lahontan, on the upper Missouri in 1688–89, seeing some fifty pirogues lined up at the bank of a village, asked the local chief for four, "which he granted very frankly, allowing me to pick and choose." In Peter Wood's estimation, this sort of accommodation was the norm, with boats "lent and swapped . . . freely," although he suggests that in this region French demands for boats may ultimately have made them unwelcome participants in that system of sharing.[41]

A narrative from the Seneca chief Chainbreaker suggests other ways that canoes might simply be lying on the riverbank, and it also opens a window into the problems of combining land and water travel over long distances. In 1775 Chainbreaker and a party of other Senecas were asked to meet with an American commissioner. They traveled overland initially for several days to the mouth of French Creek. There they stopped "in order to build bark canoes to go down the river as far as Pittsburgh." They took several days to build the canoes, and they hunted as they did so: "Sometimes we took five or six deer every day while we stayed at this place." The implication here is clear: The initial overland stage to French Creek was done carrying light loads. As they prepared to travel by water, they laid in supplies (they also traded venison for bread with a local resident at French Creek). They then paddled downriver to the meeting (in January!). With the meeting completed they went to a camp at the mouth of the Monongahela, where they "threw away some canoes," and kept three to carry their provisions upriver, partly walking, and partly pushing the canoes.[42] James Smith, during his long captivity with the Kahnawakes, regularly buried birchbark canoes for later use, and equally regularly made elm bark canoes as expedient substitutes for better ones.[43]

Those canoes Chainbreaker "threw away" may have helped another traveler on another day, but his story also illustrates the second issue to be considered with respect to understanding the limits of long-distance travel by boat. As soon as any overland leg (other than a portage) intervened, supplies had to be left behind. When a group of Mohawks captured Isaac Jogues in 1642, the journey back to their village took ten days by canoe and then four more on foot. Jogues recalled that he had foolishly disdained the food "which our canoes had supplied abundantly," and was reduced to starving during the last four days of travel. Jogues no doubt failed to understand the pattern of gorging and then starving! This despite him describing the amount of "baggage" that his captors were carrying: when they stopped once on the second day of walking to put a kettle on a fire "as if to prepare food," it was instead "merely to enable us to drink as much as each chose of the water thus slightly warmed"—presumably filling stomachs (although it may have been lightly floured with cornmeal—so-called corn water).[44]

In addition to the frequent combination of land and water travel, some campaigns were conducted mostly or entirely overland, sometimes for hundreds of miles. Supporting this overland movement were dense networks of paths that surrounded and connected towns within a cluster, and the somewhat sparser networks that stretched out over great distances, connecting important crossroads towns, portages, mountain passes, and hunting grounds.[45] Already mentioned was the Warriors' Path along the edge of the Appalachian Mountains, but there were many more, not least the path through the Cumberland Gap that followed the buffalo migration route to the salt licks in northern Kentucky near the Ohio River—now more popularly known as the buffalo trace. Crucially, these paths were normally simply that: single-file tracks through the woods, suitable for humans and packhorses, but not wagons. The paths shown in figure 3.2 represent the results of older research into these networks, and notably exclude many paths now known in Virginia and eastern North Carolina (at least), but they give a sense of the extent of the network. Similar maps exist for Ohio and Pennsylvania. Knowing these regional connecting paths was crucial for Europeans interested in trade or military movement, and they were commonly shown on contemporary maps, as in figure 3.3.[46]

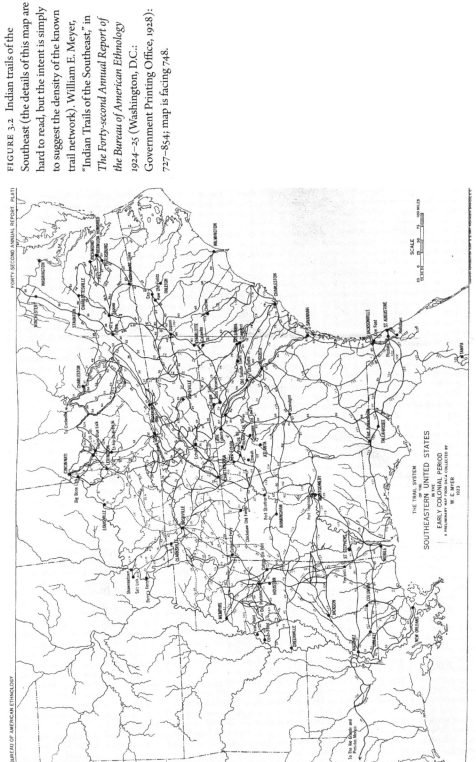

FIGURE 3.2 Indian trails of the Southeast (the details of this map are hard to read, but the intent is simply to suggest the density of the known trail network). William E. Meyer, "Indian Trails of the Southeast," in *The Forty-second Annual Report of the Bureau of American Ethnology 1924–25* (Washington, D.C.: Government Printing Office, 1928): 727–854; map is facing 748.

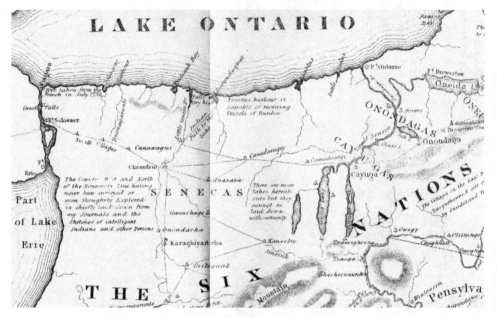

FIGURE 3.3 A 1771 map of the upper northwest portion of the Haudenosaunee Nations, showing the regional paths between Confederacy towns and other key locations in upper New York and along the lakes. An extract from a map prepared by Guy Johnson for Governor William Tryon, 1771, reprinted in Jonathan Pearson, *A History of the Schenectady Patent in the Dutch and English Times* (Albany, N.Y.: 1883), foldout map preceding 433.

Expeditionary Logistics: Carrying Food

Once on the path, to what extent did Native American war parties carry provisions? Many of our sources seem to claim that when Indians left their homes on foot to go to war, they did not carry much. The Algonquians of southeastern New England, described by Roger Williams in the 1630s, used parched corn as a traveling food, eaten hot or cold mixed with water. Williams further specified how he had "travelled with near 200 of them at once, near 100 miles through the woods, every man carrying a little basket of this [parched corn] at his back and sometimes in a hollow leather girdle about his middle, sufficient for a man three or four daies."[47] Given the calorie calculations, it seems likely that the *most* each man carried was three to four pounds of parched corn for their three- to four-day walk—a pretty light load! One of the best French observers we have, Jesuit missionary Joseph-François Lafitau, noted that when the Indians departed for war they would "march ceremoniously" out of the village, wearing all their decorations and carrying nothing but their weapons. But when they had gone just a short way down the path their women would be waiting for them with their provisions. The men then stripped off excess decoration "and gear[ed] themselves as travellers, giving back to their wives or relatives all that they do not absolutely need, burdening themselves as little as possible," carrying only "their arms, some utensils needed for camping, and provisions of flour."[48] An account of the Natchez on the march in 1730 also conveys this logistical lightness, adds in the security measures associated with the cutting-off style of war, and stresses the need to abandon the campaign if discovered (or, as here, reduce it to a smaller-scale attack):

> The war-Chief appoints the day of departure, that each one may prepare provisions necessary for the campaign. . . . When on the war-path, they march in single file: four or five men who are the best walkers lead the way, and keep in advance of the army a quarter of a league, to observe everything, and give immediate notice. They encamp every evening an hour before sunset, and lie down about a large fire, each one with his arms near him. Before they encamp, they take the precaution to send out twenty warriors to the distance of half a league around the camp, for the purpose of avoiding all surprise. . . . as soon as they have supped, they extinguish all the fires. . . . When the war-party is considerable, as it enters the enemy's country, they march in five or six columns. They have many spies, who go out on scouting expeditions. If they perceive that their march is known, they ordinarily adopt the resolution of retracing their steps, leaving a small troop of from ten to twenty men who detach themselves, and endeavor to surprise some Hunters at a distance from the Villages.[49]

Despite descriptions like these of seemingly unburdened warriors marching out of their village, it is clear from other accounts that for nearly all journeys at least some food was carried—sometimes quite a lot. The usual mechanism was some form of pack, supported by a tumpline or *"hoppas"* (carried from the forehead by women or around the shoulders by men, see figure 3.4). Quite a number of captives or semiethnographic accounts described this kind of pack, but it is not always clear whether it was used by war parties who may have traveled more lightly, as in the Natchez example mentioned earlier, or only by hunting parties. Pierre Pouchot noted that "when they travel overland, each person carries his own little parcel on his shoulders suspended from his forehead by a belt. Their belongings are all in a blanket folded at each end and tied up with the straps of the belt in a very artistic way. This closes off the two ends like a pouch."[50] Charles Johnston, taken captive along the Ohio River in 1790 by a multinational war party, described a *hoppas* as a fourteen-to-fifteen-foot strap,

FIGURE 3.4 A Creek Indian going hunting, clearly showing the *hoppas* around his shoulders. Drawn by Philip Georg Friedrich von Reck, ca. 1730. NKS 565 4°, Von Reck's drawings, Royal Danish Library.

by which the pack is secured to the back. It is about two and half inches wide in the middle, and gradually narrows towards each end to the wideth of one inch, or three fourths of an inch. A length of near two feet, in the middle, or broadest part, is very closely woven, and neatly ornamented with beads and porcupine's quills, stained of various colours, and tastefully wrought into fanciful forms. The hoppas is so tied to the pack, that this ornamented portion passes over the breast and upper part of the arms, and is all that can be seen in front. It is curiously plaited by the hand, and is made from the bark of a wild plant closely resembling hemp, and quite as strong.[51]

His captors tasked Johnston to carry a bag of bear oil, but he could only manage it for a mile or so, after which he gave up and threw it to the ground. His captors calmly picked it up and carried it themselves.

Other captives also reported large loads being carried, although not always with Johnston's eye to detail. Captive Mary Rowlandson remembered being "favored" in her load, carrying only her knitting work "and two quarts of parched meal." Her Wampanoag captors were then in the midst of a rapid march to escape an English army, and she was once denied permission to eat any of that flour, and she also remembered them stopping to glean fields, gathering groundnuts and other expedient food, all while on the move.[52] Other captives mention packs, but omit details. Zadock Steele in 1780 described the Caughnawagas who captured him as they returned from their raid on Royalton. There were some 300 in the war party plus captives from Royalton, and Steele observed that "many of the prisoners" were carrying their captors' packs, "enormous in size, and extremely heavy, as they were filled with the plunder of pillaged houses." Steele complained of unsavory food on the march, but admitted to getting an equal "share of their best."[53] When Shawnees captured Mary Jemison in the spring of 1755 she remembered them plundering the house, primarily for bread, meal, and meat, and "having taken as much provision as they could carry, they set out," traveling till dark without stopping or eating. In fact, there was no food or fire during the first night of her captivity; instead they all ate while they walked the next morning, eating the "provision that they had brought from my father's house."[54]

Such packs, whatever their precise configuration, could apparently carry enough bread or meal sufficient for the entire distance for shorter trips and smaller parties—or at least one way with an assured resupply from an ally at their destination. In the fall of 1779, for example, the Six Nations general council agreed with a British request to go to war against the Americans, and the Senecas determined to rendezvous at Fort Niagara to meet with British officers there, a journey of some sixty miles overland. One participant remembered that every man was to take his knapsack "with Indian Bread calculated to last on the away journey toward" the fort.[55] This provisioning assumed that their British allies at the fort would supply them thereafter.

In discussing packs, we must note that by the middle of the eighteenth century, many Indian Nations had access to horses for carrying loads. Eastern Woodland Nations' access to horses varied enormously over time. Virginia DeJohn Anderson noted that colonial authorities in seventeenth-century Massachusetts tried to ban selling horses to Indians, as did the Plymouth Colony. In 1665 an exception was made for Metacom (a.k.a. King Philip), the Wampanoag chief, in deference to his status, but the associated bureaucratic fuss only serves to highlight the English fear that the Indians would acquire horses on larger scale.[56] During King Philip's War, which broke out soon after this legal wrangling over a horse for Metacom, a witness to a gathering of al-lied Indians east of Albany claimed he saw some 300 horses there. On the other hand, an anecdote from the 1701 Grand Peace negotiations suggests that early in the eighteenth century horses were still rare among the Nations of the *pays d'en haut* (the wider Great Lakes region).[57] By the French and In-dian War Pierre Pouchot's memoir contradictorily claims both that the "Indi-ans travel on foot or by canoe" and that "in summer journeys on foot are always short," and simultaneously that "the Iroquois & those who live along the Ohio have horses which they have stolen from the English. . . . They have considerable numbers of them, but they do not raise them themselves."[58] Studies of the Creeks suggest they acquired horses from the Spanish as early as the beginning of the eighteenth century, and found them especially useful in transporting deerskins for that trade.[59] Tyler Boulware has shown how Native Americans in the Southeast were heavily dependent on horses by the mid-eighteenth century for economic exchange and more.[60]

It is not at all clear, however, how often horses carried loads in war parties. Jason Warren's study of King Philip's War concludes that Indians did use horses occasionally for transport, but not as a means of travel for a war party.[61] Indeed Warren suggests that over longer distances Indian men on foot were faster and more sustainable than men on horseback. James Carson agrees, asserting that the Choctaws did not find horses useful in war through the eighteenth century, although raiding *for* horses picked up late in that century. Accounts of raids often mention horses being taken as plunder, but just as often the raiders arrived on foot, and horses did not seem to be a part of the logistical calculation. A Lenape raid in 1755 against Penn's Creek took captives and horses, and allocated two of each to an Indian named Galasko, but the clear implication is that the raiders arrived on foot, and they allowed the cap-tive girls to ride during their retreat.[62] Mary Jemison, taken captive by the Shawnees in 1755 and then adopted by the Seneca, recalled one problem with relying on horses: when a party she was traveling with caught some aban-doned horses and loaded them up with food, they found themselves unable to move later when the horses strayed for over a week (their loads then being on the ground).[63] James Smith, during his extended life among the Kahn-awakes and Wendats in the 1750s, repeatedly bemoaned the lack of horses on assorted hunting expeditions, leaving himself and others in the party to carry everything on their backs. And at one point, the Wendats he was with went on a raid for horses specifically to solve this problem.[64] Later in his account, however, Smith also relates that a major war party set out in June 1756, appar-ently taking quite a lot of food with them. Smith was left behind with the old men, women, and children, and the war party was gone so long that the village began to run short of food, lacking their young men to hunt. Smith and an older man went hunting for deer, and soon thereafter encountered the returning warriors who brought with them prisoners and captured horses, laden with meat, intended to refresh the women and children left at home.[65]

Interestingly, Smith also points out the role of Indian women as porters on these hunting expeditions, raising another possibility for the carrying of food.[66] Many narratives mention women bearing burdens on hunting expeditions, and this gender-based division of labor was clear. Pierre Pouchot described how a husband would return from hunting and light his pipe, and then, "after a little while, he says to his wife: 'I have killed such and such an animal more or less at such and such a place in the forest' . . . the woman sets out, brings the animal back on her shoulders & skins it." On the other hand, there is less evidence for women as burden bearers on war parties, and Pouchot was explicit about this as well, suggesting that "wives accompany their husbands everywhere together with her family, *except to war*."[67] An account of the Oneidas from probably around 1660 suggests that women prepared the provisions after war was decided on and then marched with the men, carrying that food for the first full day's march. There the whole group would stop to hunt, and the women would then carry much of that food back to the village, presumably as part of providing for the town while the men were gone, in this case usually for four to six months.[68]

There are some examples, however, of women continuing with the war party. The Mahican assault on Gandaouagué, narrated in chapter 2, apparently included twenty-four women as part of the march column of some 500 men, probably for food preparation purposes. A truly striking example comes from the Battle of Lake George in the fall of 1755, which was a fight of the French versus the English; but Indian allies, some related to each other, accompanied both armies. In that battle the Mohawk leader Theyanoguin, originally on horseback, was unhorsed (or abandoned his horse), and in one account, as he was heading for cover, he "fell in with the French Indians baggage guard [apparently the contingent from Kahnawake] of young Lads and Women who having no fire arms stab'd him in the back with a spear or bayonet, some pretend today it was committed by a squaw, the Lads being too young to attempt it and by the manner of his being scalped it is probable a woman did it" as the scalp was very small.[69]

But the real issue here seems to be porterage as a gendered construction, and if "women" were not always available for that labor, then those *deemed* women might be pressed into service carrying burdens, notably prisoners, slaves, or sometimes the youngest men. As Lafitau noted, "When there are no women" the youngest of the war party "lights the fire and has the duty of making the pot boil and of doing all the rest of the household chores."[70] This "feminized" status of the youngest could also be applied to prisoners or captives. This is a complex area, as the status of captives within Native American societies varied over time, by Nation, and even within the same Nation at the same time. At one extreme, some captives (usually adult men) were killed as part of a communal ritual of grieving and exultation. At the other extreme, many were adopted as replacement kin and considered fully a part of those Nations.[71] Between these extreme outcomes, there was certainly a precontact Mississippian tradition of enslaving captives, and we know that various Mississippian chiefs provided Hernando de Soto's expedition with enslaved porters in the hundreds.[72] That tradition of porterage service persisted in some places in the colonial Southeast—whether enslaved or not is less clear. Spanish administrators in Florida in the mid-seventeenth century repeatedly asked for warriors from the Timucuas, Potanos, and Yustagas to help defend St. Augustine. On one occasion, they had requested that each arriving warrior carry his own corn to the fort. The chiefs' (*holatas*) response was interesting: they were offended at the idea of themselves or other elites within the Nation acting as porters; this was a job for captives or those lower on the social ladder. They ultimately agreed to provide soldiers, but specifically said that their elites would not carry corn.[73]

That particular social construction of captive porters may have been a holdover from the Mississippian era specific to the larger chiefdoms, but there is also substantial evidence from elsewhere during the colonial era for the occasional claim of a captive as "slave," or at least evidence for a captive being assigned some sort of lesser status, and they later reported that they were used as menials.[74] Such reports from white captives are difficult to assess, as they were not accustomed to Indian lifeways, and they may have simply confused different with degrading. Some European observers, with a bias about gender roles and status, assumed that some captives were relegated to a menial labor role because they were working alongside the Indian women. French soldier Charles Bonin in the mid-eighteenth century, who at least recognized the possibility of differential fates for captives, claimed that "prisoners taken are either adopted, enslaved, or condemned to death. Slaves do most of the menial work, such as cutting firewood, cultivating the fields, harvesting, pounding Indian corn or maize to make sagamite, cooking, mending the hunters' shoes, carrying their game, and, in general, anything that women do."[75] But, as an example of how complicated this could all be, the French

Jesuit priest Jean Filleau described an incident among the Mohawks in 1641, when they captured thirty young Algonquian women, tortured them, but spared them for marriage into their own Nation. The next spring, however, they were put to work as porters for Haudenosaunee war parties, something that the ethnohistorian Bruce Trigger claims was not done by free Haudenosaunee women (although the story just related about the battle at Lake George would seem to contradict that). As it happened, those women sought their first opportunity to escape, and did so.[76] In one analysis of Iroqouian slavery, the authors claim that slavery existed within and alongside the adoption process, and in that mode it may have created the space for assigning purely menial porterage duties to male and female captives.[77]

That the process of "adoption" could also be a process of creating a subordinate laborer is supported by Brett Rushforth's work in Siouan and Algonguian linguistics. Rushforth's analysis puts enslavement for local labor (not for sale to Europeans) at the center of war in the *pays d'en haut*, concluding that "slaves stood at the heart of both Natives' regional war culture and the diplomacy that kept warfare from overtaking the region." In the region's cultural formulation, the slaves were "dogs" rather than "women"—although male captives too assumed feminized roles: being supervised by women, and carrying loads on hunting expeditions as women did. The captives taken for this purpose were clearly not adoptees, as they were mutilated in some way to mark their permanent subordinate status.[78]

Expeditionary Logistics: Finding Food on the Move

In general it would appear that overland war parties carried only limited amounts of food to sustain their journey. Very many war parties would have combined land and water travel, and movement by water allowed for bringing along provisions sufficient for at least a few days of carriage overland. For short trips, that might be sufficient, but longer overland travel seems instead to have relied on travelers obtaining food in other ways. Before breaking down each of the possible categories of supply, let us consider the assorted components of the logistical complex that sustained movement in several examples from in and around the white settlements in the Virginia Appalachians from the 1750s through the 1790s. There we will see a whole variety of methods in play, although we only see them from the perspective of the white settlers and soldiers the Indians were attacking. For clarity's sake, each type of supply method mentioned in this short narrative will be in **boldface**.

From the 1750s and through the late 1770s white settlers began coalescing in scattered settlements among the mountains west of the Shenandoah River in places like Warm Springs, Virginia, and what is now Greenbrier County, West Virginia. The latter area conveniently connected via the Greenbrier River to the New River, then to the Kanawha and on down to the Ohio. During the French and Indian War, Indian Nations from further west, generally supporting the French, targeted these intrusive settlements. Many were Shawnees, based in towns on the Ohio River near its confluence with the Big Sandy. In 1756 the Virginia government authorized an expedition to attack the Shawnee towns, and even secured substantial assistance from the Cherokees. The so-called Sandy Creek Expedition headed northwest from Fort Frederick on the New River in February, and immediately struggled to sustain itself in the face of cold weather and high water. Early in the expedition, when their Cherokee allies arrived, joining the column of men and packhorses, the now-combined force of some 340 men **stopped to hunt**, which initially brought in fresh meat "in abundance." But only two days later, when the expedition again stopped to hunt, game was elusive, both that day and the next (many of the Cherokees had been sent ahead to scout and were thus not available to hunt). Hunting improved over the next few days, but meanwhile the **packhorses** started to break down, no doubt in part because they were forced to cross and recross the same creek sixty-six times over just fifteen miles. The situation continued to worsen and within a few days, and after more failed attempts at hunting, the white companies began to desert. When the Virginian commander consulted with the Cherokee chief Outacity (Ostenaco), the latter expressed surprise and said that "the white men could not **suffer hunger** like Indians, who would not complain of hunger." The Cherokees suggested that once they got to the forks of the river (the Tug Fork, near modern Panther, West Virginia) they should "**make bark canoes** to carry themselves down the river, which was immediately put into practice." Even so, the men ultimately refused to slaughter the pack animals, and the expedition returned home.[79]

Those same settlements around Greenbrier and Warm Springs were also stopping points on branches of the Warriors' Path from the Haudenosaunee to points south. The Haudenosaunee seemed to treat them as **convenient neutral towns** en route, where they could rest and resupply war parties. In 1763, for example, a British army captain at Warm Springs reported that some seventy-eight Haudenosaunee had recently passed through, claiming to have been on their way to attack the Cherokees. They had initially camped in Greenbrier and had then "distributed themselves ... among the [white] Inhabitants, by Six & Seven to a House, for the Convenient Collection of Refreshments." They stayed there for five to six weeks, and then moved further south, closer to Cherokee country, where they camped again for two weeks—presumably to stock up and **cache** supplies.[80]

Then, during the American Revolution, this part of the Virginia frontier saw occasional campaigns by both settlers and Indians. One Indian raid (possibly Wendats) in May–June 1778 was remarkable for white awareness of Indian logistics. The attack began with probably 100 to 200 Indians attacking Fort Randolph at the junction of the Kanawha and Ohio Rivers. The attack failed, but the Indians, who had presumably **arrived at the fort by water**, drove off the garrison's cattle and horses and used them to sustain their raid as they pushed deeper into the mountains, heading for the settlements at Greenbrier and elsewhere. The white commander at the fort assumed, probably wrongly, that the Indians had simply killed all the cattle. Several days later (moving overland) the Indians attacked a small blockhouse (Donnally's Fort) in the midst of the Greenbrier settlements. The soldiers at Fort Randolph had gotten a message through to warn the settlers, in part because the messengers "overtook the enemy, & found them **dispersed in groups hunting**." Virginian reinforcements arrived during the attack on the blockhouse and drove off the Indians, but they noted how the Indians had come "well equipped with **pack horses and driveing [sic] cattle**."[81]

The forks of the Kanawha and the Ohio saw renewed conflict as the new American states tried to control and claim the Ohio country after the War of Independence. In 1790 Charles Johnston traveled by river from Greenbrier Courthouse down the Kanawha to the Ohio, where he was captured by a war party of multiple Nations, most of them from what is now western Ohio. This group seems to have combined a seasonal hunting trip (it was late March) with a plan to raid passing river craft. They had gathered on the banks of the Ohio, **prepared a large base camp**, and after several successful attacks—including the one that captured Johnston—they split up to return to their home nations (the group was composed of Shawnees, Lenapes, Wendats, and Cherokees). Immediately after his capture, Johnston was marched to the base camp where he found a fifty-foot-long campfire with the Indians seated all around it, with rifles behind them on a forked stick within easy reach. He is vague about numbers, but the campfire size suggests as many as one hundred men, and he specifically mentions at least six mostly older women, two captive white children, and a black man, formerly enslaved, also with the group. The Indians divided the prisoners among the Nations, and the plunder in

general was distributed by the chiefs "in a manner that seemed perfectly satis-
factory to all," to include flour, sugar, and chocolate. In his new, possibly feminized role, Johnston was put to work making bread. When his Shawnee
captors took him from the camp on the river, they **stopped at a cache** about
five miles away, where they had stashed horses recently stolen from Kentucky
and "a quantity of dried bear's meat, venison, peltry, and some of their
people." They also **slaughtered a recently acquired cow**, and **packed all the
food on the horses**, but, as they travelled "through a trackless wilderness"
his captors **relied entirely on the abundant game** along their route, as "their
plan was to carry home the dried meat for the summer use of their families."
His captors also demonstrated the value of **gorging** as a traveling strategy,
when they killed a bear and "we remained on the ground where he was taken,
until all his meat was consumed." His captors repeated this for the duration:
any time a bear "was killed, . . . they swallowed a plentiful repast of it; or if any
other food was procured, which afforded them an abundant meal; immediately after satisfying their appetites, they laide themselves down to sleep."
And when they woke up, they would eat all the remainder. In sum, while
carrying loads of preserved meat to their home villages, during this whole
march of about four weeks across the whole diagonal breadth of modern
Ohio, "**we subsisted on bear's meat, venison, turkeys, and racoons**, with
which we were abundantly supplied, as the ground over which we passed afforded every species of game in profusion, diminishing, however, as we approached their villages. But we were destitute of bread and salt, necessaries of
life to a white man, while they are considered mere superfluities by the Indian
warrior or hunter, when he is occupied in war or the chase."[82]

Although spanning three decades, these campaigns through the mountains of Virginia and into the forests of Ohio shared several things in common: they were conducted overland for long distances (even if combined
with river travel); they combined multiple modes of supply; and they responded effectively to the changing conditions created by the intrusion of
European settlers and animals. At this stage, trying to dissect a precise process of change over time beyond the brief previous discussion of the introduction of packhorses is outside our scope. And addressing the interaction of
European and Native logistics on combined expeditions must also await
another venue. But we can turn now to each of the on-the-move logistical
methods highlighted in the preceding paragraphs: neutral/friendly villages
en route, caches, gorging, and hunting and foraging on the move.

When the Haudenosaunee war party stopped in the Greenbrier settlements in 1763 and found food, shelter, and entertainment with the local set-

tlers, they seem to have simply been folding the white community into an older Native system of using neutral settlements along key war paths to provide refreshment and hospitality.[83] Hospitality for travelers is well documented as a central component of many Native American societies, as is European abuse of that system, whether it was the English garrison at Roanoke in 1585 or the colonists at Jamestown from 1607 through 1614 (and beyond). That pattern repeated throughout the early colonial period and all around the Eastern Woodlands. In the early years of the Spanish outpost at St. Augustine in Florida, for example, one local Indian Nation provided boatloads of corn to keep the colony alive.[84] French voyageurs in the Mississippi River basin typically relied on a combination of hospitality and trade to provision themselves on their long travels up and down the rivers.[85]

Whether or not this general system of hospitality could have been used by large war parties on a regular basis, however, depends on whether Native towns could reliably have sufficient surplus food, and the evidence for that is not entirely clear. Among other issues, it would have depended on both the season of the year and the nature of that year's weather. Neither factor was something that Europeans (our usual witnesses) really understood. That large surpluses did sometimes exist is clear. Susan Sleeper-Smith has documented the vast productivity of Indian agriculture, suggesting that the Wendats retained a two- to-four-year surplus of corn stored in underground pits.[86] Major Morrill Marston in 1820 described how the Sac and Mesquaki raised 7,000–8,000 bushels of corn each year ("besides beans, pummpkins, mellons &c") and sold 1,000 of those bushels for trade, and stored all but five bushels per family in "holes in the ground for their use in spring & summer."[87] One study of southern New England Indian farms in the interior (i.e., noncoastal) estimated a family could produce perhaps 280–340 pounds of maize per person per year, which would equate to 68 percent of the annual daily intake, and since they would not eat all that corn every day, there was likely some surplus available for trade, hospitality, and so on.[88] Samuel Champlain in the St. Lawrence region saw Natives storing maize corn for winter in woven "bags" buried in deep trenches and covered in sand.[89] Archaeologist Stephen Potter, reviewing the archaeological and historical records for the Potomac and Chesapeake regions (as well as regional comparanda from the Late Woodland period), claims that pit storage outside the tidewater was substantial and common, but in the coastal plain of the Potomac it was rare or very limited, and there is no evidence for stored corn. But he also admits that Henry Spelman and other early Virginia colonists described instead whole storage houses filled with baskets built above ground. The Powhatan paramount chiefdom seems to have demanded and received substantial amounts of corn as tribute from subordinate towns, and it was then stored in granaries in the chiefdom's capital. Furthermore, Wahunsenacawh supposedly paid a 500-bushel ransom for Pocahontas, despite this being (we now know) a period of extreme drought, and there were many examples in John Smith's travels of him successfully trading European goods for hundreds of bushels of maize, although he also encountered dearth.[90] Potter suspects that the so-called "treasury" buildings identified by John Smith, William Strachey, and Spelman may have served as subsistence storage, possibly of tribute. Potter goes on to argue, however, that this form of aboveground storage may reflect the stratification in Wahunsenacawh's chiefdom, in which the deliberately visible granaries under the paramount chief's control were a symbol of his power—implying that such a high level of surplus should not be considered the norm during the historic period.[91] Similarly, the vast surplus encountered by Hernando de Soto in his wanderings through the still-centralized chiefdoms of the Southeast from 1538 to 1541 must be considered an exception. They were able, however, to supply his rather large (and wholly unprovisioned) force repeatedly and in large amounts, while de Soto regularly eyed their fields to estimate how much of an army they could supply.[92] In a later era in the colonial Southeast, aboveground corncribs were certainly the norm for storage, and although William Bartram and other travelers in Georgia, Florida, and Alabama frequently mentioned them as a feature of Indian farms, they did not provide much data on available surplus.[93]

Even lacking certainty about surplus and storage, we do have concrete examples of towns serving as logistical way stations for war parties. Perhaps the most well known was Shamokin, at the forks of the Susquehanna River. Something of a refugee town, it was home to about 200 Indians from various Nations, created more or less by Haudenosaunee policy between the 1720s and 1740s. It served as a way station on the Warriors' Path, and there are several accounts of war parties stopping there as they headed south to raid the Catawbas in the Carolinas.[94] And although the Moravian-converted Indians at Newcomerstown may be a slightly different example, they were able to resupply Colonel Daniel Brodhead's force of 300 men after his raid on the "revolted Delaware Towns" nearby.[95] An Apalachee expedition in the late seventeenth century received river crossing assistance from an ally along their route, after which the whole expedition stopped for two days to gather supplies for the remaining march.[96] It is difficult to track how common such neutral/friendly logistical support was, but Daniel Gookin, in his critique of the Mahican expedition discussed in chapter 2, disparaged the Indians as normally relying on Indian towns along the route for supplies and to rest. If neutral provisioning was as common as Gookin thought it was, it suggests a new program of research into the functions and purposes of Native American diplomacy.

In terms of march planning, however, such neutral support was unlikely to be available either close to one's own towns on the last stretch home, or within easy striking distance of the enemy's towns. For both of those purposes—sustaining the first and last legs of the return march—there is substantial evidence for Native war parties caching food. As just discussed, storing food underground within towns was a matter of course (at least outside the tidewater). When one party of Senecas traveled across Ohio and New York they happened upon a recently abandoned Lenape village, and the Senecas immediately found where the Lenapes had "buried their provision in the earth, in order to preserve it from their enemies, or to have a supply for themselves if they should have a chance to return." Apparently it was "completely dry and as good as when they left it."[97] And of course, in one of the most famous stories from early English colonization, the newly arrived "Pilgrims" on their first day ashore in the New World discovered about ten bushels of buried corn as they explored, a discovery that helped tide them over through the winter of their landing.[98]

These skills of storing food safely underground were readily transferred to war parties. The Seneca chief Chainbreaker described how both corn and venison could be stored underground in preserved form, and he also specifically recalled how one could see caches of food stored all along the river.[99] Elizabeth Hanson, captured in 1724 in New Hampshire, traveled for twenty-six straight days heading north. She noted that her captors, prior to the raid, had concealed nearby some old beaver-skin mantles, which they recovered at the beginning of the return march and used as food. She also recalled expedient small-game hunting and foraging, including the bark of trees, "but had no corn for a long while," including "three days together, without any sustenance but cold water."[100] The Kahnawakes captured Zadock Steele in October 1780 as they returned from a raid on Royalton. We encountered Steele previously complaining about the "enormous" packs loaded with plunder he and the other prisoners were put to carrying. Just a "few days" into the return trip, his captors came to a mountaintop where they, "on their way to Royalton, had secreted a number of bags of fine flour, which they brought with them from Canada, and now regained." The whole return march lasted seven days, suggesting that the cache had been carried from Canada no more than two or three days, and then buried to sustain their return.[101] An account from later and further west, written by Thomas Forsyth, an agent for the Kickapoo, Sac, and Mesquaki Nations in 1827, declared that "in going to war, the Indians always travel slowly and stop to hunt occasionally, where the[y] deposit their jerked meat for their return." He clarified that "before making an attack they send forward some of their smartest young men as spies, the attack is generally made a little before day light, the great object is to surprise, if defeated every one makes the best of his way home, stopping and taking some of the meat jerked and buried on the way out."[102]

This last quote from Thomas Forsyth can begin the discussion of the key role of hunting on the move. All of the examples thus far highlight the many different methods that Native Americans used to sustain war parties over long distances. But other than perhaps simply using canoes to carry a large amount of supplies over long distances, hunting on the move has long been understood as the primary basis of Indian strategic mobility. As should be clear from this chapter, however, not only was it supplemented enormously by the methods cited here, it was also more complicated than it might appear. As almost any hunter will tell you, game does not appear at the snap of a finger, much less game in the quantities needed by a large war party. Even so, European observers long emphasized Indians' ability to conduct warfare almost magically logistics-free. Indians are described as enduring hunger, traveling lightly, and most importantly, as hunting when they needed food. William Smith, writing in 1765 about the best way to fight Indians on the frontier, noted that Indians on "their expeditions live chiefly by hunting, or on wild fruits and roots with which the woods supply them almost everywhere."[103] As a young militia officer, George Washington complained about settlers' unsecured cattle sustaining Indian raids in Virginia, but also was aware that they "depend on their dexterity in hunting."[104] This apparent ability to subsist through hunting on the move was almost an article of faith, and was real enough. There are very many instances of Indian war parties subsisting through hunting, and they sometimes provided fantastic amounts of food in a short time, not least the hunting party that brought in one hundred deer in a single day to feed the delegates to the Canandaigua treaty negotiations in November 1794.[105]

Nevertheless, several issues emerge in the sources that make this option more complicated than it seems (and a good deal less magical). First, as several examples here have already noted, hunters must split up to cover ground, whether the small groups sent out from a war party or the seasonal hunting parties from a single village. Hunting for subsistence for any kind of large group encounters several challenges, from the need to access a large hunting territory to distributing the meat as rations to problems of preservation.

Historian Colin Calloway identified the political implications of the territorial requirements of Indian subsistence. As the new United States began intruding into the Ohio country in the 1780s and '90s, Indian efforts to confederate and resist were hamstrung by the problems of bringing so many Indians together in the same place to fight. In Calloway's reckoning, doing so "placed enormous pressure on the food resources of the area, and warriors frequently dispersed to go hunting. The Indian army needed British supplies to help keep it together."[106] In fact, the American general Arthur St. Clair assumed that these problems would prevent the Indians from being able to resist him, but the further he advanced, the easier it became for Indians to rely on corn carried over the decreasing distance from their home villages.[107] Even so, the Indians had to manage the delicate balance of concentrating forces at the right moment and location while also dispersing to hunt, and it deprived the Ohio Indian confederacy of a substantial fraction of their numbers prior to the battle in 1791 where they defeated St. Clair's army. One source suggests that as many as 300 of 2,100 Indian warriors were out hunting at the time of the battle (and 600 more arrived late).[108] John Norton reported a similar story and a similar operational problem for the warriors who gathered to oppose General Anthony Wayne's advance into the same region in 1794. At the beginning of summer the warriors of many Nations began to rendezvous in their hundreds, but "not having sufficient store of provisions to await the approach of General Wayne and his Army they proceeded to meet him, in two divisions, and by separate routes, the better to secure the provisions, by hunting." One group had some 1,000 men of various Nations, and the other was just over 300 men.

> The Confederate warriors advanced by moderate days journeys, searching the woods as they went, for game. When a number hunt together they sometimes extend the line for several miles, leaving a space from a hundred to two hundred paces between each man, the two flanks generally projecting a little in advance. They start and partly envelope all the game contained in the extent they pass over, and overwhelm them with bullets. This method of hunting is called wa-eneaghrontye, and is only practiced by War parties, and villages when the inhabitants hunt in a body, to procure meat for a feast.[109]

As for preservation, unless meat is butchered immediately, especially in any sort of weather above about forty degrees Fahrenheit, it quickly will begin spoiling from its internal heat.[110] Smaller game is safer, as the carcass cools more quickly. But all meat, if not eaten very soon after being taken, will spoil unless dried or salted, and either operation takes time. As indicated earlier in the quote from Pierre Pouchot, in peacetime hunting trips the men often expected their wives to retrieve a carcass and do the skinning and butchering.[111] And several of the captivity narratives surveyed here mentioned stopping to prepare recently acquired meat for travel. Indeed this is why Charles Johnston's captors hunted along their route and ate fresh meat—including "gorging"—while keeping already preserved meat packed up on their horses.[112]

Finally, if small parties of hunters were providing for a larger war party on the move, those hunters would have to be organized and directed, both in how to find the main body again, and in the distribution of meat. There were well-established mechanisms for this, including the already mentioned system of setting up a hunting camp as a rendezvous point for distributed war parties on raids. A war party hunting for itself divided up the game and the associated labor of cooking. Thomas Forsyth observed that "the Indian who carries the Kettle is the cook for the party and when encamped the warriours must bring him wood and water[,] furnish meat &c the cook divides the vituals, and has the priviledge of keeping the best morsel for himself."[113] On a larger scale, as observed by an American army officer, the Shawnees on a winter march in January 1786 conducted their movement with "great regularity; that the whole appeared to be formed in certain squads, equal in number, and when any of their young men or hunters would kill meat, it was brought, laid down by the chiefs, one of whom cut it into as many shares as there were squads or fires (for every squad had their own fire) and sent it off by men, who appeared to serve as fatigue men for the day; so there was no one lived better than another, but all fared alike." James Adair observed a similar procedure among southeastern Indian war parties, in which every war captain chose a noted warrior to "attend on him and the company." That attendant was responsible for giving out the rations, and although every warrior carried "on his back all his travelling conveniences, wrapt in a deer skin," they would only eat when given food by the "waiter." And to return to another example from the Indians of the Ohio confederation, according to William Wells, who fought alongside Little Turtle (Michikinikwa), the chief "divided his men into bands or messes, to each mess twenty men. It was the business of four of this number alternately to hunt for provisions. At 12 o'clock each day it was the duty of the hunters to return to the army with what they had killed. By this regulation, his warriors were well supplied with provisions, during the seven day's [sic] in which they were advancing from this place to the field of battle."[114] This system of dividing a force up into squads, and constantly sending out small parties of hunters, was likely a solution to the meat preservation issue. This solved the time-delay problem of accumulating and preserving a large stock of meat and the army could continue to move.

Perhaps the best evidence for the efficacy of Indian hunting on the move, however, comes from a whole other set of sources. Most of the hunting discussion thus far has tried to focus on those sources that provide even a tiny glimpse into Indian practices when acting on their own, according to their own style of war. But when we expand the source base to include how European military forces relied on Indian logistical aid, the examples multiply rapidly.[115] In expedition after expedition, white forces moving beyond the line of white farming settlements regularly found themselves relying heavily on allied Indians hunting for them, even when the number of such hunters remained very small. The Sandy Creek Expedition discussed previously repeatedly failed to find game, except when their Cherokee compatriots were with them.[116] Peter Schuyler's 1691 expedition to Canada, ultimately a failure, became almost entirely dependent on the hunting skills of his Indian allies after some canoes carrying European-style provisions overturned.[117]

European military planners were occasionally explicit about this need for Indian hunting assistance. Captain Stoddart wrote to William Johnson in May 1753 reporting on French movements down to the Ohio River, and noting that some "500 Indians of the Coghnawagees, Scenondidies, Onogonguas, Oroondoks & Chenundies [Kahnawakes, Okas, Abenakis, Adirondaks, and Tionontati] would not engage to go to war with the English & on Ohio but are employed at so much P[e]r Month to Hunt for ye army."[118] On a smaller scale, and much later, American general Josiah Harmar in 1787 wrote from Kaskaskia and mentioned that his party of thirty-three men had marched 160 miles over seven days, supplied by two Miami Indians "who hunted and supplied the party with meat (buffalo and deer), both on the march and upon our return."[119] This use of Indian hunters could even extend to stationary garrisons. An intelligence report on French forces at Venango in 1759 noted that the one-hundred-man garrison there was provided meat by several Indians hunting around the fort. In the same region twenty years later, Colonel Daniel Brodhead in 1780 declared that he would be unable to supply the American forces at Fort Pitt any more meat, and he recommended that the commander there employ "two or three faithful Indians to hunt near the fort."[120]

Finally, we should consider how all of these logistical methods often demanded that large parties of warriors on the move should travel somewhat separately, in "packets." Doing so made it easier for each group to feed itself, whether through hunting on the march or relying on local communities for hospitality. Normally our sources do not allow us to see a large war party in its many component parts while on the move, but there have been hints in this chapter with respect to multiple parties operating from a single base or hunting camp set up within enemy territory. European forts could fulfill a similar function. Those forts, expected to supply their allies once an Indian force arrived, functioned as both rendezvous and cache, and were thus easily folded into Indian logistical systems. Groups approaching the fort could travel separately for easier sustainment, and then coalesce around it as they entered or neared enemy territory. Unusually, we can see exactly this sort of process at work when the Cherokees sent a large expedition to support the British move against Fort Duquesne in 1758. The Earl of Loudoun, the British commander in chief in North America, wrote to the president of the Virginia council, asking both for interpreters to meet with the Cherokees, and for logistical support for a hoped-for Cherokee march to join the British army in Winchester, after which point the army would provide for them. William Byrd, acting for Virginia in coordinating the delivery of gifts to the Cherokees, wrote to Loudoun in March, mostly about the difficulties of transporting the gifts, but also noting that "many parties of the Indians are gone, & others going out, some one way, some another." A muster of the separate Cherokee companies taken in Winchester in late April 1758 shows how they arrived: a total of 595 Cherokees arrived in twenty-three separate groups, varying in size from eight to seventy-five, originating from sixteen different towns, and arriving between November 16, 1757, and April 21, 1758, with the vast majority arriving in late March and early April.[121] In those smaller groups, marching through what they presumed was friendly country, they could far more easily sustain themselves until they arrived at Winchester.

Conclusion

This chapter opened with a narrative of Lenape logistics, as narrated to us by their captive James Smith. During his years living with different groups of Indians, Smith experienced a full range of Native American seasonal subsistence and campaign provisioning, foreshadowing for us many of the techniques that have now been described in somewhat more detail. Perhaps it makes sense to close with another, similar account, this one from Frenchman Pierre Pouchot. Pouchot was a regular soldier in the French army who fought in North America, and in his memoir he described how the French allied Indians went to war (he was being deliberately generic, not indicating the specific Nation involved). After the necessary rituals, the men would march out of the town, preceded by a young warrior carrying the medicine mat. Then, "A number of girls follow the party carrying the gear of the young warriors. They sometimes accompany them for three or four days, after which they return to the village. They travel always by canoe, because the rivers are the only highways of the country." The camp chores were done by the younger men (after the women had departed). Each day

> they set up camp early in order to hunt, since they bring with them no other provisions than their ammunition. Nonetheless, they sometimes have a small bag of *sagamité,* which is mashed corn, grilled & cooked in a copper pot with fat & maple sugar. They save this type of flour for the time when they are near their enemies, or for when they are short of food. Simply by mixing it with water, they can make a meal which is healthy, nourishing & pleasant to the taste. Two handfuls of this food a day are sufficient to sustain life if they fear that food may be in short supply. When they are in enemy territory, they do not fire their guns. If they do not have a bow and arrow, they live on fish, a few roots and their *sagamité.* But as soon as they are on the point of attacking, or when they are retreating, or after an operation, they will go three or four days without food

When they were close to the enemy they would "hide their canoes, together with all their packs & ornaments." After the attack, having agreed on rendezvous points, they would head home, and "they hardly ever indulge in pillaging. If they have time, they kill animals to eat."[122]

In Pouchot's account, and in the accumulated evidence here, we can see how closely tied Native American campaign logistics were to the very nature of their societies and their normal patterns of subsistence. Indeed, in some ways the campaign was simply a more intense extension of the seasonal winter hunting trip. It relied on the same communications and portage infrastructure: canoes, long-distance paths, pack-porterage (although women's role as porters seems reduced on a war party), and eventually packhorses, combined with the fruits of hunting. Strategically these systems in combination provided very long reach, but when the raiding force arrived at its target, it was by then at the end of a tenuous logistical tether. Operationally, once in or near enemy territory, behaviors shifted to suit wartime conditions: stop building fires; stop using guns; cache food for use during a sudden retreat; set up hunting camps as both rendezvous point and food cache, and so on. Tactically, they would go into battle carrying almost nothing but their weapons, and then flee precipitously after either a successful or an unsuccessful raid, perhaps traveling several days with virtually no food, until arriving at cache or rendezvous.

All in all, these logistical systems lacked the capacity to sustain wars that would take and hold territory. But that does not mean that Native Americans did not *want* territory, either to move to, or to hunt upon. What it did mean was that a strategy to force an enemy to cede territorial claims generally required repeated smaller attacks, the kind easily sustainable by this logistical system, even year after year, *although not year-round*. Occasionally, a few successful large-scale assaults could accomplish the same thing, but in neither case did the successful attackers then claim the land by occupying it. To do so would have denuded their home village of male hunting labor for the winter season. To enable a year-round "garrison" of Indians would have required them to disperse locally to hunt within the newly captured territory, rendering them vulnerable. Or it would have required bringing women from the home village to tend the fields around the new "garrison" and essentially to re-create the entire community system in a new location. Interestingly, we see exactly that sort of community reconstruction when a Nation was displaced by war and forced into a new territory, not as conqueror, but in retreat.

During wars when Native Americans were allied with European powers, one finds the French or the English committing to provide food for families left behind, and on that basis expecting the warriors to sustain their attacks repeatedly throughout the winter, and perhaps even in successive winters.[123] But that was only possible through European logistical support and after overcoming the cultural inertia that resisted such expectations. The men wanted to conduct raids and win glory, prisoners, and perhaps plunder and then return home to their communities.

The French friar Gabriel Sagard saw all this clearly enough among the Wendats in the first third of the seventeenth century, although he missed some of the political intention behind their campaigning. He interpreted their tactics as focused on "surprises and treachery," but those Wendat attacks were conducted *throughout* Haudenosaunee territory, every year, in the spring and for the whole summer. Scattered across Haudenosaunee country, 500–600 warriors would have rendered the entire region dangerous, cutting off small parties or individuals. He also noted how those warriors "carry with them their ordinary food, each one on his back, a bag full of corn meal," which they combined with water, not needing a fire. He thought that they would subsist on that for the duration of a six-to-eight-week campaign, after which "they come back to refresh themselves in their own land and the war is for a time at an end, or they go back again with another supply of food."[124] Finally in 1648 and 1649 the Haudenosaunee launched two full-on offensives against the main Wendat towns, surprising some, and assaulting and taking others. But even this massive tactical and operational success resulted primarily in the Wendats departing and moving west. In the earlier decades, the Wendats had had no capacity to take and hold Haudenosaunee territory through persistent raiding. And now, even after the shocking Haudenosaunee success in destroying Wendat towns (possibly enabled by the possession of steel axes), the Haudenosaunee similarly lacked such a capacity.[125] What the Haudenosaunee did get was a new freedom of access to this vacated territory, many prisoners to adopt and thereby restore their population, and the strategic flexibility to attack further west and south and push other enemies into various forms of tributary status.

On the other hand, the role of war in a competition for resources blended, sometimes indistinguishably, with its more cultural functions associated with individual status, communal grieving, and reputation management. War was not just a political process in a naked competition for power among peoples. It was also a cultural construct, spurred, mediated, and restrained by beliefs that are explored in the next chapter.

CHAPTER FOUR

Peace Chiefs and Blood Revenge

Patterns of Restraint in Native American
Warfare, 1500–1800

War in any society is conditioned by cultural forms and needs as much as it is by calculated strategy or the nature of logistics.[1] War served key functions in Native American societies, beyond and in addition to its political or material aspects. Young men could gain status and authority through demonstrated courage and aptitude in war.[2] Groups could gain or protect territory at the expense of others, incorporate prisoners into their population as kin or as labor, and even impose tribute on other peoples. Above all, the killing of a member of one group mandated revenge on the perpetrator's people. Blood demanded blood. The rewards and requirements of war were so thoroughly entwined in Indian societies that irrespective of the arrival of the Europeans, a nearly endemic state of war existed throughout much of the Eastern Seaboard and beyond. Equally thoroughly entwined within Indian societies, however, were structural and cultural limitations on the scale and devastation of warfare.

Modern work on European and Indian conflict almost assumes that the experience of contact escalated the intensity and violence of Native American warfare. The only disagreement has been on the exact mechanisms of that escalation. Older explanations have emphasized economic pressures: the availability of valuable European goods led Indians to war for more wide-ranging and absolute goals, including conquest and/or economic domination. With more demanding goals came more frightful violence. Others have suggested that Indian warfare escalated from a kind of technological, material, and, especially, demographic shock. The disease and social disruption brought by Europeans demanded the restoration of balance; the only available cultural solution was war and the incorporation of prisoners. According to this argument, a different kind of balance had also been upset by the arrival of European technology: the military balance of offense versus defense had slipped in the face of iron and gunpowder. War had become more lethal through European technology, eroding war's utility in restoring demographic health through the adoption of prisoners. Most recently, some historians have argued that warfare escalated in intensity and violence because of a clash of New and Old World military cultures. Each side violated the other's expectations or norms of war, and was thus led to discard their own usual limitations.[3] Unfortunately, an essential foundation has been missing from this debate: What exactly were the restraints on war in Native American societies? Only after answering this question can we hope to understand how European contact may have broken them down. Could, in fact, either combatant's structures of restraint hold up in the face of an enemy with an entirely different system?

The subject of the level of violence in precontact Native American warfare is contentious, so let me be clear. Native American restraints on warfare were no more perfect than European restraints. Indians had not balanced war into harmony with their other cultural values and thus scaled down warfare into some kind of ritualized, nonlethal nonentity. Given the opportunity and the right motive Indians were prepared to wage intensely lethal violence on another people. Much of the time, however, structural restraints built in to Native American social organization, combined with their own values about war and interpretations of its meaning, restrained its scale and intensity. Contact with Europeans dramatically affected the nature of their social organization as well as their beliefs about the meaning of war. Not all of those changes happened at once. Nor can any one moment or incident be identified as that when restraints were cast off. Native Americans continued to try to regulate war, and they tried to preserve the traditional nature of their social organization, all while trying to adjust to the opportunities presented and damage caused by the presence of Europeans.

Unfortunately, the nature of the sources severely limits our ability to comprehend the probable changes in Native American ways of war at the very outset of contact. The first caveat is that sixteenth-century sources are sparse and interpretively debated, while the earliest seventeenth-century descriptions of Indian war are more voluminous, but may reflect societies and behaviors that had already markedly changed.[4] The second caveat is about the nature of the generalizations used here. As discussed in chapter 1, there was of course no such thing as "Native American society." There was variation and difference from Maine to Florida, or even from one valley to the next. But in addition to the shared ecological zone of the Eastern Woodlands, it is also the case that societies regularly in conflict usually experience some form of convergence in techniques and values of war, partly from military necessity and partly from mutual self-interest.[5] This study is necessarily synthetic, and faces the task of trying to explain traditional restraints on warfare within a context of constant flux aggravated by European contact. Furthermore, the analysis here is primarily structural and cultural, rather than about how specific political configurations or diplomatic decisions may have restrained or unleashed war. Nevertheless, focusing on the periods of contact and of competitive imperial colonialism (roughly 1500–1800) lends a certain coherence.[6] In short, the basic generalizations in this chapter about eastern Native North American restraints on war are safe, although by no means universal. Two specific examples of Native Americans at war, chosen to complement those from earlier chapters, can serve as foundations for the more diverse and generalized evidence that will follow.

The Powhatans and the 1622 "Massacre"

English settlers arrived in the Chesapeake area of Virginia in 1607, and within a few weeks had built themselves a town and a fort at Jamestown. Almost immediately they became embroiled in conflict with the local paramount chief Wahunsenacawh, often referred to as Powhatan, largely because of the colonists' persistent inability to feed themselves. Apparently, Wahunsenacawh had only relatively recently become *the* Powhatan, having led the Nation of the same name to dominate an array of peoples within a wide arc around the Chesapeake Bay. His "empire" was unusual for its size and the extent of his personal control, although it had some parallels with the earlier paramount chiefdoms of the Mississippian cultures to the south and west. Some scholars have even suggested that Wahunsenacawh was motivated to this level of conquest as a defensive measure against an expectation of further European arrivals. The inhabitants of the region, and perhaps even Wahunsenacawh himself, had had some unpleasant experiences with earlier abortive English and Spanish settlement.[7]

At any rate Wahunsenacawh quickly perceived the English both as interlopers within his sphere of influence and as potentially useful allies. He therefore sought to bring the tiny, struggling Jamestown community within his orbit. From his point of view that process involved creating both familial and political ties, the first through marriage and adoption, the second through rituals of submission by the English. The English were unclear about the meaning of these activities, and frankly thought that they were leading Wahunsenacawh through rituals of submission to the English. In a classic scene of partially understood meanings, the English brought a crown to Wahunsenacawh in 1608 with which they hoped to mark him as a vassal of James I. Wahunsenacawh repeatedly ignored their signals for him to kneel and accept the crown. Finally one of the English pressed hard on his shoulders, Wahunsenacawh "a little stooped," and Christopher Newport put the crown on his head.[8]

Partly through this lack of understanding, partly through the settlers' single-minded pursuit of quick riches, and partly because each side sought to dominate the relationship, the two peoples remained in periodic conflict until the diplomatic marriage of John Rolfe and Pocahontas in 1614. Anthropologist Frederic Gleach has interpreted these early years of conflict as a repeated effort by Wahunsenacawh to use war to bring the colonists' behavior into line with his perception of their subordinate status. He had no desire to exterminate, only to control.[9] Wahunsenacawh's daughter Pocahontas fell into English hands in 1613 as a hostage, leading to peace negotiations. Within a year Pocahontas and Rolfe were married and peace achieved. Peace through marriage was a diplomatic technique understood in both societies, and that connection maintained an uneasy peace until 1622.

The breakdown has been handed down to history as the "Massacre" of 1622, but the Powhatan attack in that year needs to be considered within their vision of war. Several things had happened since 1614. Pocahontas had died in 1617 while visiting England. The numbers and extent of the English settlement had expanded dramatically from what Wahunsenacawh might have guessed in 1614, and Wahunsenacawh himself had "resigned" in 1617 (he died in 1618). His powers passed to his brother Opitchapam (later Itoyatin), but there is some suggestion that Opitchapam was "decrepit and lame," and that real rule shifted to the other brother, Opechancanough.[10] There is some disagreement on what precise powers Wahunsenacawh had had. Gleach argues that part of Wahunsenacawh's success at centralizing and expanding his chiefdom came from his holding civic, religious, and foreign relations powers in his own hands—in other words, he was simultaneously peace chief, war chief, and shaman.[11] It was far more common in Native societies of this period, however, for those powers to be divided, and there is good evidence that Opechancanough had been acting as war chief, directing the Powhatans in war and also managing other "external" relations—a role he continued under Opitchapam—while Wahunsenacawh had managed the civic and internal affairs of the chiefdom (and perhaps its religious affairs, although that is more obscure). Regardless, Wahunsenacawh's resignation and death seem to have concentrated power in Opechancanough's hands, and he had developed an abiding fear of growing English power and presence.[12] After trying and failing to persuade the English to help him in one of his own wars to the west, Opechancanough changed his name, often a signal of coming war, and prepared to administer what he thought would be a decisive "lesson" in the proper subordination of the English to his control. They would strike at the English, punish them for their transgressions, and await the restabilizing of the relationship in the proper roles. Gleach calls this kind of political status quo–seeking attack a "coup"—implying the French term for a strike or a blow—to emphasize its limited political objectives.[13]

The attack came on March 22, 1622. The Powhatans went about their business normally at the beginning of the day. By this time many of them had regular personal or economic contacts within the English settlements, and at the prescribed moment, all around the English colony, the Indians, already intermingled with the populace, picked up various agricultural tools (having come in unarmed) or appeared from the surrounding woods and set upon the English. They killed all those who came within reach that day, probably more than 350 people, completely wiping out some settlements. Tellingly, however, there was no follow-up. Having administered their lesson, the Powhatans went home. They surely expected retaliation, even as they would from another Native society, but they would not be caught unawares, and probably expected to be able to prevent any kind of equivalent damage to themselves. They prepared for the cutting-off war of raid and counterraid, but presumed that their initial successful attack would give them the advantage in the long run.

Furthermore, the Powhatans' attacks were almost exclusively confined to the outlying English settlements, and this may provide the "text" of the lesson—that the English should remain within their proper area.[14] Political objectives provided one kind of restraint, but so too did cultural practice. The overall damage to the settlements was limited by warnings of the impending attack given by Indians living among the English, particularly the warnings provided to Jamestown by a Christianized Pamunkey Indian named Chanco (or Chauco) and another unnamed Indian living with the English.[15] As we will see, the exchange of residents between communities often served to limit the possibility of surprise and its consequent high level of fatalities.

Despite these limits to the attack, the English did not respond to the lesson in the expected manner. They prepared to fight a war according to their own model of continuous campaigning: not raiding, but taking, destroying, and hopefully exterminating—largely in the hope of establishing their control over more land. In this the colonists succeeded to a horrifying degree, usually failing to catch very many Indians, but deliberately and thoroughly destroying their towns and crops. Indian efforts to negotiate a peace were repeatedly rebuffed until the war crept to a close in 1632.

The Creek-Cherokee War, 1715–1753

As a second example, we can examine how a long-standing enmity between large Native groups resulted in an episodic war, continued with starts and stops over many years, in this case in the mountains of the Southeast between 1715 and 1753. The outbreak of this particular war is both relatively well documented and illustrative of the role of codes of war and diplomacy, as well as of the more usual alternative to take and hold conquest: endemic raid and counterraid. Although the Creeks of Georgia and Alabama and the Cherokees at the junction of Tennessee and North and South Carolina had had a long history of occasional violent conflict, this particular conflict (and our knowledge of its origins) resulted from the diplomatic efforts of the English.[16] In 1715 the Yamasees of piedmont South Carolina had turned against their former English allies, and in the process had persuaded a host of other peoples to join them, including the powerful Creek confederacy. The hard-pressed South Carolinians also sought Indian allies, winning the Tuscaroras to their side, but they particularly aspired to gain the Cherokees' assistance.[17] To help convince them, Colonel Maurice Moore marched a small expedition into the Cherokee towns to force serious diplomatic negotiations. Although hospitably received, the English quickly found themselves confined to a relatively passive role as witnesses to internal Cherokee debate and factionalism over how to respond to the English request.

The Cherokees, like most other Native societies, were not a unified political body. Each town grouping, or even each town, had its own say in whether it would be willing to help the English. The "Lower" towns were initially reluctant to help against the Creeks (too close and therefore too threatening), or the Yamasees (too closely related), but they would help against some of the other small piedmont Nations. Meanwhile, representatives from the Cherokee "Overhill" towns were pushing for war with the Creeks, and in fact some had already been to Charlestown to promise their support to the South Carolinians.

While the English emissaries were touring the towns trying to rally support, the Cherokees requested that the Creeks send an embassy for talks. A Creek delegation duly arrived in the Lower Towns, but while in the town of Tugaloo an anti-Creek faction within the Cherokees unexpectedly killed them. Word of the incident spread like wildfire. The Cherokees realized that this violation of the sacred status of a diplomatic embassy, not to mention the deaths of several prominent persons, would bring swift Creek retaliation, and they prepared to meet it. Their short-term defensive strategy is as revealing about Indian warfare as is the fact that this dramatic violation of the codes of diplomacy led to nearly forty years of endemic warfare.

Expecting an attack from a large nearby Creek encampment, the Cherokees immediately put themselves and the visiting English in a defensive posture, clustering close to the village the night of the killing, and the next day marching about three miles south of town "to waylay the pathe."[18] They waited in ambush all that day for the approach of any Creeks, took some prisoners, and then, fearing their intentions discovered, they abandoned their position and returned to the village for the night. The following day, realizing that the killing of the embassy was still undiscovered, the Cherokees, with their English allies, advanced still further south, hoping to catch the main Creek force by surprise. They continued advancing in stages, each time getting closer to the Creek encampment, but by the time they arrived, the Creeks had abandoned it. Failing in their attempt at surprise, the whole Cherokee-English force returned to Tugaloo.

The Creeks eventually did find out about the murders, sought blood revenge, and the war began in earnest. Over the next ten years the Cherokees appear to have fortified a number of their more vulnerable towns, but in nearly forty years of on-and-off warfare they could not always be alert, and several of those towns were surprised and destroyed.[19]

Ultimately, many of the southernmost Cherokee towns were abandoned entirely, their inhabitants joining with villages in the interior of their homeland. As the war dragged on, the South Carolinians pressed for peace out of a desire to trade with both sides. Finally, after a Cherokee victory at the battle of Taliwa and a highly successful series of Creek raids in 1752, both sides agreed to allow the British to mediate a peace.[20] It is important to note that the Creeks did not proceed to occupy the abandoned Cherokee territory—although they would later make explicit territorial claims based on victory.[21]

In combination with the longer case studies from the earlier chapters, these two examples highlight several issues central to a discussion of the restraints, and the lack thereof, in Native American warfare. Of particular importance are the role of blood revenge, the political divisions within Nations, the importance of resident visitors from other peoples, the reliance on the raid with possibly dramatic results if surprise was achieved, the willingness to besiege towns, the importance of prisoners and prestige, and finally the tendency to engage in endemic, although not *continuous*, warfare.

Restraints

War, no matter how well regulated, is by its nature destructive. Consequently, the first issue facing any culture in its efforts to restrain war is to set limits on its frequency and duration. The phrase "to set limits" implies conscious choice, and in moments of actual diplomacy there could certainly be deliberate recognition of the problem of "too much war." In general, however, what concerns us here is how Native American social organization and cultural visions of war drew boundaries around its frequency and duration. Once war is under way, the remaining problem is to find ways to regulate its destructiveness, primarily to one's own side but, for various reasons, also more generally. The remainder of this chapter uses the preceding examples of war and additional evidence to examine these two questions. The organization is roughly step by step within the framework of an imaginary war. We will begin with the causes of war, and discuss how Native Americans provided some alternatives to war. We will then turn to ritual preparation, warrior mobilization, and the style of war itself.

There were three basic functions of war in Indian society. The broadest, and slipperiest to interpret, was the use of war to solve political or economic problems, whether to gain resources or to administer political "lessons" in proper relationships between groups (as suggested here for the Powhatans in 1622). Although the existence of political war is generally acknowledged, it is less clear to what extremes Native Americans would press war in a political cause. For example, could such political adjustments through warfare include outright conquest?

The other two functions for war, both broadly "cultural," are seemingly more clearly understood. A great deal of Native American conflict was filtered through the demand for blood revenge coupled with the expectation of achieving personal status through war. The mandate that relatives take blood revenge for the killing of one of their own was arguably the single greatest factor in patterning violent relationships both within a people and between Nations. The need to take revenge could outweigh a variety of other considerations, At the outset of the Creek-Cherokee conflict just described, for example, when George Chicken tried to convince the Cherokees not to attack the Creeks because they would have had time to remove their effects and their dependents, the Cherokees replied: "It was not plunder they wanted from them but to go to war with them and cut them of[f]."[22] Furthermore, young men in virtually all Native American societies looked to success in war to assert adulthood and to increase their status within the group. Warriors returned home bearing enemy scalps or prisoners as their individual possessions, and although sometimes such prizes were redistributed upon arrival in the village for the benefit of all, for that moment, possessing trophies redounded solely to their own credit as men.[23]

These three motives or functions for war did not exist in isolation from each other. Even if war arose from material or political causes, it was frequently enacted through the blood feud. To put it another way, the recruitment of individuals for a succession of raids that might have political or material consequences still relied on blood feud requirements and the lure of status to motivate young warriors.[24] Of course the problem with these latter two motives for war is their potential endlessness. There are always new young men in need of proving themselves, and each act of revenge typically begets a fresh desire for revenge from the other side. In fact, however, although extraordinarily awkward to contain, the seemingly endless loop of the blood feud had both structure and restraint.

The basic principle of blood debt was simple. The killing of any person, accidental or otherwise, placed an obligation on the dead person's kin to exact revenge on the people of the killer. This belief had two crucially open-ended facets. The timing and intent of the original killing were irrelevant. An accidental killing, a deliberate murder (as a European would define that term), or death in battle all equally mandated vengeance. The other open-ended component was the lack of specificity in who should be on the receiving end of the revenge. Any member of the killer's people would do—in the case of an intragroup killing, the killer's "people" meant himself and his relatives. If the killer were from outside one's own Nation, then any member of his Nation would suffice.

Naturally two different systems developed to cope with this mandate: one for intra-Nation killing and one for inter-Nation killing. If the blood debt was within a Nation, the general expectation was that the relatives of the killer either would withdraw their support from that individual, acknowledging that revenge against him was justified, or would offer to pay a blood gift to the family of the dead person.[25] The situation became more complicated when the killer came from outside the group. First, the possibility of a blood gift sufficing to calm relatives was reduced dramatically, although not completely. Diplomatic overtures could avoid the outbreak of war, but success depended on the willingness of the clan council and the dead person's relatives to accept it.[26] Second, there could be no expectation that the killer's relatives would stand aside, and in fact, the individual identity of the killer ceased to matter. Furthermore, in blood revenge situations between Nations, there was no expectation that the other side would simply accept the second, revenge killing as evening the debt. The suggestion could be made that one killing had balanced another, but convincing the other side to accept it proved difficult. The Cherokees of the town of Keowee, for example, threatened the Catawbas that a failure to accept a recent killing as squaring the balance would lead to escalation:

As the Catawbas were coming home . . . finding one of our Women there, they kill'd her in Revenge, . . . that was the Reason why We in Return kill'd one of their Women in this Place. This is only the Talk of this Town, and if the Catawbas continue to take Revenge, we will not only go against them Ourselves, but draw the whole People of our Nation against them: but if they are satisfied we are also, for as they began first, and laid our People in heaps, we have kill'd two of them, and laid them on our own; and now we are satisfied, if they will be so; but if they are not, we will soon go against them, as we think nothing of them, and as it was intirely their own Fault.[27]

Furthermore, the whole concept of "balancing blood" implies a mathematical precision within the system that did not exist. Much early scholarly work on blood debt focused on its transactional quality, with investigators trying to unlock how participants weighed one death versus another, or a death versus a compensatory payment or gift. Recently, historians of emotion have tried to complicate our understanding of the role of grief in this process. Matthew Kruer, for example, suggests that "labels such as 'grief' or 'fear' are not legible in any straightforward way." Instead we should understand that when Susquehannocks, for example, spoke "about murdered kin, women and children in danger, and the primal feelings evoked by these circumstances, they tapped into a reservoir of enormous political power. When the cruelty and malice of others ruptured the bonds of intimacy, it demanded a reckoning."[28] In this landscape of primal emotion, "balancing" blood was a tricky business at best, and the problem was made worse by the very nature of a war party. A war party mobilized to avenge a blood debt, even a small one, was unlikely to be able to contain their damage to one person—even if they wanted to.

This is where the blood debt system overlapped with the use of war for personal status to produce endemic states of conflict. A war party ostensibly mobilized for revenge but composed of individuals hoping for status, especially young men, had no desire to limit their attacks to one person. Once in contact with an enemy group, individual desire for success in war quickly led to the taking of as many scalps and/or prisoners as could reasonably be accomplished—because in those prizes lay status.

There follows an obvious response. Any deaths inflicted by the first war party created a need in the targeted group for their own retaliatory strike. This cycle was the weak link within Native American restraints on war. The cultural mandate for revenge proved extremely difficult to overcome. Historian John

Reid summarized the problem: "A [Cherokee] warrior who had recently lost a brother in a Creek raid might tell a Creek peace delegation that he would bury the bloody hatchet after he had taken one Creek scalp. If he succeeded, it would be for the brother of his Creek victim to decide if the war would continue. Peace negotiations therefore were largely promises to forgive and forget."[29] In some cases the original source of enmity between two groups might be lost in the depths of time, but endemic raiding back and forth continued nonetheless, as each new killing reinvigorated the blood debt.

There were, however, certain restraints within the need for revenge. The scale of the avenging party, and thus its destructive potential, was limited by the mobilization process. Decisions for war were reached by consensus, and Native American leaders lacked the capacity to coerce participation.[30] As indicated in the Cherokee-Catawba conflict quoted above, it was unusual to mobilize warriors from outside the family or from members of other towns. Unless the dead person was a prominent figure, it was unlikely that his or her death would stimulate a multitown mobilization. An influential leader with a significant following could possibly expand the pool of recruits, but he could do so only as long as his reputation held out.

While a lack of coercive political structures limited the scale of war, another fundamental limitation was the Native ideology of revenge. The revenge motive did not carry with it the motivation to pursue the wholesale destruction of the enemy people—a few scalps and prisoners would suffice. This "tit-for-tat" understanding of war was unfocused in its targeting since any victim would do, but it was limited in its scale. This limited notion of revenge differed dramatically from the European ideology of revenge in war. The Europeans also had notions of retaliation, but they were much more thoroughly lethal. The European ideology of revenge presumed that an original violation of norms, however "small," authorized a no-holds-barred retaliation.[31] It was just this kind of ideology that the Virginia colonists unveiled in their response to the 1622 attack. Materially they may have been seeking land, but ideologically they justified their efforts at wholesale destruction by citing the "treacherousness" of the Indians. Edward Waterhouse summed up the Virginians' explanations, writing, "Our hands, which before were tied with gentelnesse and faire usage, are now set at liberty by the treacherous violence of the Savages, not untying the Knot, but cutting it: So that we ... may now by right of Warre, and law of Nations, invade the Country, and destroy them who sought to destroy us."[32] In this light the blood revenge system seems much less destructive.

When we turn from the blood feud as a cause of war to the question of political and economic causes, we enter one of the most contentious issues in the study of Native American warfare. There are well-rehearsed arguments that Indian societies did not pursue conquest or economic/territorial gain in their waging of war, or that if they did so, it was only because of European-induced changes—particularly the introduction of new trade items. There is strong evidence to the contrary, however, particularly in the chiefdoms of the late prehistoric Mississippian Southeast who clearly demanded tribute from submitted peoples.[33] Wahunsenacawh's rise to becoming a paramount chief also fits that general description, as his relationship with subordinate towns also involved enforced submission and tribute.[34]

Even without certainty regarding their ultimate motives, however, Native Nations do appear to have distinguished between "grand" and "little" war.[35] On occasion, sufficient motivation existed—whatever it might be—for large parties of warriors, perhaps 600 to 1,000, to attack their enemies "in the name of the tribe," rather than as part of a limited blood feud, apparently in the hope of inflicting damage well beyond the norms of the "little war," the tit-for-tat war, practiced in the blood feud.[36] Expeditions such as these were intended at least to force a reformation in relationships between groups, even if not intended to conquer territory or impose tribute. They attested to the power and vitality of the attackers, and sought to arm-twist their enemy into modifying their behavior in some way. In that sense they *were* political wars, but with limited goals. As Neal Salisbury described the motivations of the Narragansetts of New England: "To the Narragansett warfare was a contest in which one sought to intimidate and scatter one's enemies through a combination of physical and supernatural weapons. The result might be a favorable shift in the balance of power but certainly not the elimination of any existing communal entities."[37] This interpretation focusing on shifting the balance of power has been applied to many of the larger attacks on the European settlements: the Powhatan attack on the English in 1622, and the Tuscarora attack on North Carolina colonists in 1712, are examples. It is fair, however, to ask whether "scattering" one's enemies is simply a relationship adjustment. The Haudenosaunee attack on the Wendats in 1648–49 described in chapter 2 was clearly war on a large scale, and it resulted in the complete displacement of the Wendats, with all the suffering associated with the forced movement of an entire population and the reestablishment of subsistence systems. It was not merely resetting relationships.

It is also difficult to draw a line between little and grand war, in part because Native American societies did not necessarily recognize that duality. The little war of the blood feud could escalate, through repeated frustration, into large-scale attacks that might lack the political or economic intent of grand war.[38] Conversely, a Nation could launch a long series of small-scale little war–style raids, but with a larger political purpose in mind: attempting in effect to achieve "conquest by harassment," in which repeated attacks rendered a zone uninhabitable.[39] The Narragansetts, for example, advised the English in 1637 to attack the Pequots over the "space of three weeks or a month, [and] that there should be a falling off and a retreat, as if you were departed, and a falling on again within three or four days."[40] It was even possible to resolve disputes through single combat between champions: truly a "little war" but with larger political import.[41]

Nor did Native Americans draw a stark line between war and peace (perhaps in part due to the endemic nature of blood revenge needs). Peace did not exist as a formally declared state so much as it was achieved through the mollification of hostile feelings.[42] Since within their cultural system it was nearly impossible to completely erase hostile feelings within every individual, the possibility of attack always existed. Declarations of war did occur, such as sending the red stick, or flying the red flag of war, but there also existed a level of conflict between peace and outright war during which significant levels of violence could be in play, perhaps intended to carry a political message, or perhaps intended to let off young men's steam without a full commitment to war.[43] Essentially, there was another point on the spectrum between the poles of peace and war, which for lack of a better phrase, I call the "not quite war" level of conflict—in early Jamestown John Smith called it "sometime peace and warre twice in a day."[44] The "not quite war" is politically motivated as an effort to affect relations between groups, but employs only the small-scale methods of "little war." It may perhaps even be deliberately disavowable *as* little war (a personal grudge only) if peace is determined to be a better alternative. Furthermore, the "not quite war" functioned very well within the imperial context, helped along by the autonomy of individual towns within the Nation, easing the process by which Indian headmen could "capitalize on [their] decentralized, kin-based politics to cultivate connections with rival colonies and so avoid dependence on a single European power."[45]

As an example of such behavior, consider historian Tom Hatley's analysis of a Creek attack on the English trader John Sharp's home near the Cherokee town of Nayowee in 1724. The Creeks approached his house, fired several volleys, wounded Sharp in the leg, and then plundered his house. All of this was done within sight of the Cherokee town whose residents declined to interfere. Hatley interprets Sharp's survival as proof that the Creeks were merely making a point, "a symbolic statement about the strength of Creek men to the onlooking Cherokee villagers."[46] They could equally as well have been making a point to the English and the traders, but at any rate Sharp was neither killed nor captured, nor were the Creeks then "at war" with the English.

The Cherokees engaged in a similar round of "not quite war" with the English in 1758. Nominally allied with the British during the French and Indian War, some of their warriors returning home from Pennsylvania were attacked and killed by Virginia militia in a dispute over stolen horses. As a matter of course, the relatives and townsmen of the dead men sought blood revenge, and were aided by anti-British factions within the Cherokees who hoped to join with the French. Small groups of warriors began to raid the white frontier in Virginia and North Carolina, and in fact continued to raid the frontier throughout the summer and fall of 1759. Strikingly, at the same time all remained peaceful around the British forts in the Cherokee towns. Trade and relations there continued, if with greater worry and tension. There was no sense of the two peoples being "at war," even while some Cherokees were undeniably wreaking havoc elsewhere. When diplomatically confronted, the Cherokee leadership downplayed the violence, describing it as young men out of control. The conflict thus was both simple blood debt and a political contest at the same time, all while the Cherokees tried to avoid a broadening of the conflict.[47]

Once "at war," whether at the "grand," "little," or even the "not quite war" level, a number of factors built into Native American society tended to limit the extent of the conflict's lethality and overall destructiveness—for both the attacker and the defender. These structures were not absolute, and they may or may not have originated as deliberate efforts to restrain war, but there is little doubt that they served that function in practice.

To begin with, Native American war demanded a certain level of ritual preparedness and sacred purity. Meeting those needs had an impact not only on the frequency and relentlessness of war, but also on individual behavior within war, notably with regard to rape. Although much of Native American warfare was at least nominally motivated by the desire for revenge, ostensibly one of the more "bloody-minded" and unlimited approaches to war, it still occurred within a cultural framework that carried certain spiritual expectations. Those expectations reined in the potentially unrestrained attitudes arising from revenge-based warfare. Prior to the departure of any war party the community, the leadership, and the warriors partook in a series of ritual activities designed to insure the success of their endeavor. Southeastern Indians retired to the war chief's winter house, remaining there for three days and nights, fasting and drinking potions, intended both to purify them and protect them from danger.[48] John Gyles, captured by the Abenaki in 1689, described a feast in preparation for war that served both ritual purposes and identification of those willing to volunteer.[49] Mary Rowlandson, captive among the Wampanoags, witnessed a ritual dance prior to the departure of a war party that seemed in its details to embody the classic prehunt dance in which the warriors enacted the events of a successful raid.[50] The preparatory rituals of the Miamis lasted for a full five days and nights and attendance was mandatory.[51]

Common to many of these prewar rituals was the expectation that proper access to spiritual power would provide protection in war.[52] Such a belief attested to the Native American outlook that the spiritual and material worlds were in fact coterminous. Spiritual power was immanent in the world and only required ritual skill to tap it.[53] Such a powerful belief in the importance of ritual to the successful outcome of war meant that an offensive could easily be derailed by bad omens, whether natural or deliberately manufactured. The sensitivity of a small-scale society to casualties enhanced this probability. If the spirits seemed unwilling to support an attack, the people could not afford to ignore them and risk defeat. Attakullakulla (Little Carpenter), a Cherokee leader in 1758, explained that their expedition to aid the British war effort could not leave because the "Conjurers" had produced omens of a "Distemper" that would afflict them after the first two months of the expedition.[54] A raid by the Indian Nation living on the Gaspé Peninsula in 1661 saw half of its participants depart when one of their number "just now recalled" the command of a dying relative (and therefore spiritually significant) not to participate in the raid.[55]

Sacred restrictions included a prohibition on sexual intercourse, which extended to prohibit the rape of enemy women. Although as we will see, women were targets in other ways—for capture, adoption, and possible marriage—there appears to have been no equivalent in Native American societies to the European soldiers' propensity to indulge in rape as a perquisite of war.[56] This is in fact an arena in which we can identify a Native American expectation of war that almost certainly came into conflict with those of the Europeans. There is not much direct evidence on the subject, but there was one definite example of English soldiers raping Cherokee women that contributed to starting a war, and other examples that led to local retaliation.[57]

Finally, acknowledging the fundamental spiritual harm caused by the taking of life, some societies expected returning warriors to undergo a period of purification prior to their full reentry into society. Anthropologist Charles Hudson described the general process for the southeastern Indians as a process much like that before setting out: three days of fasting under the guidance of the war chief, accompanied each night by the women singing songs outside the war chief's home.[58] The Shawnees practiced a similar postraid purification through isolation and fasting.[59] This need for purification after a raid created a basic limitation on the frequency of war, since it at least nominally prevented those warriors from simply resupplying and returning to the attack.

Where the needs of the spirit world provided a kind of halting, awkward, and unpredictable restriction on warfare, the more immediate and loudly voiced expectations of the people on their leadership created a different and more abiding set of limitations. The coercive power of Native American leaders was extremely limited, and it was thus difficult to raise large armies or to maintain one's leadership position after a defeat.[60] Authority within a people usually derived from the consensus of the elders channeled through a peace and a war chief (internal and external chiefs might be better terms). We will return to the exact nature of their relationship later, but for the moment it is sufficient to observe that this division of power and authority restrained the usually more aggressive tendencies of the war chief.

Furthermore, the group's religious figure or shaman wielded a separate authority through his more extensive contact with the spirit world.[61] In military terms this divided structure of leadership dependent on the consensus of the group imposed two significant limitations. The first was the inability to coerce warriors to go to war—the mobilization problem. We have seen how grieving relatives could persuade others, usually young men in search of status, to join them in a blood feud. To raise troops for more "political" warfare required an almost identical, and therefore equally fragile process. As hinted in the preceding discussion of ritual preparation, warrior mobilization and purification were an intertwined process. James Adair, a trader and traveler in the eighteenth-century Southeast, described the process of mobilization:

> In the first commencement of a war, a party of the injured tribe turns out first, to revenge the innocent crying blood of their own bone and flesh, as they term it. When the leader begins to beat up for volunteers, he goes three times round his dark winter-house, contrary to the course of the sun, sounding the war whoop, singing the war song, and beating the drum. Then he speaks to the listening crowd with very rapid language, short pauses, and an awful commanding voice. . . . Persuad[ing] his kindred warriors and others, who are not afraid of the enemies bullets and arrows, to come and join him with manly cheerful hearts. . . . By his

eloquence, but chiefly by their own greedy thirst of revenge, and intense love of martial glory . . . a number soon join him in his winter house [and commence the three-day fast].[62]

The emphasis here is on volunteers, motivated by desire for revenge and status, and presumably supported in their hopes by the reputation of the war leader. A similar process of ritual volunteering occurred among the northern Iroquoian and Algonquian peoples as well.[63] One should immediately note that these recruitment processes by their very nature were confined to one town at a time. Efforts to raise warrior volunteers from other towns required extensive negotiations, travel, and even gift-giving to convince other towns to join in.[64] Despite a generalized martial enthusiasm among the young men, such mobilization techniques among an already demographically limited society further restrained the size of war parties on most occasions. In turn, a smaller war party could inflict only limited damage.

Furthermore, the fragile authority of the war chief tended to limit the risks he could take while on campaign. High levels of casualties were ill afforded, and generally defined a war party as unsuccessful. The Haudenosaunee believed that "a victory bought with blood is no victory."[65] The blame in such a case fell squarely on the war leader, usually on an assumption of his lack of ritual purity. Adair noted that "they reckon the leader's impurity to be the chief occasion of bad success; and if he lose several of his warriors by the enemy . . . he is degraded by taking from him his drum, war-whistle, and martial titles, and debasing him to his boy's name."[66] The Illini apparently systematized the process: two failures simply ended a war leader's career.[67] Serious disasters put the war leader's very life in jeopardy. After the English destruction of the Pequot village of Mystic in 1637, the Pequots very nearly killed their leader Sassacus.[68] Such punishments, combined with the minimal standards for success of any single raid (a few scalps or prisoners would do), encouraged the war leader to avoid risk, thus limiting the likely destructive potential of any given raid.

In practice, to "avoid risk" meant relying on the cutting-off way of war, with its emphasis on surprise, flight before enemy defenses could rally, and battlefield tactics that emphasized cover over firepower. As discussed in chapters 2 and 3, the operational patterns of the cutting-off way were driven heavily by logistical considerations, but equally important was the desire to avoid casualties among the attackers. There was no inherent reluctance to killing large numbers of the enemy, although as we will see, the hope for prisoners did mean an initial preference for capturing over killing.[69] A casualty-averse war party's best option was always surprise. If this was successfully achieved, either by ambushing a smaller party, or by attacking a sleeping village, the relative casualty ratio for the defender could be quite high. But surprise was not easy. An alert enemy, or one informed by "resident aliens" as discussed below, would be prepared, leaving the attacking war party with the options discussed in chapter 2: they could return home, offer open battle, or lay siege to a palisaded town.

Alert defenders behind walls posed a problem. A direct assault on the walls was relatively rare, particularly during the precontact era, because of the technological balance between offense and defense and the strong likelihood of high casualties. Fire was one option to speed the assault, and was certainly resorted to on occasion, even prior to the arrival of Europeans.[70] In general, however, attackers seemed to prefer the blockade, supplemented by sniping at the walls from the cover of the woods, and trying to cut off any individuals straying outside the fort, avoiding casualties while offering the possibility of taking isolated prisoners or scalps and gaining the associated air of victory and prestige. As discussed in chapter 2, the attackers could instead offer open battle, but doing so had a ritualistic quality. The defenders would have to agree to it and come out from behind the walls; with both sides prepared, casualties were likely to be light, and the whole affair may simply have been an exercise in saving face.

The technological and tactical balance of the offense and the defense both in siege warfare and in open battle meant that warfare prior to the arrival of Europeans would usually be a relatively mild affair. Successful surprise, however, overcame that limitation, and could immediately produce huge per capita casualty ratios.[71] The European arrival did not introduce the concept of lethality in warfare; what it did was introduce new technologies that upset the parity of offense and defense, making the open battle more lethal and a successful siege and assault more likely. In the face of the inability to either dodge bullets or heal bullet wounds, the ritual battle, probably never the true centerpiece of Native American warfare, rapidly disappeared.[72] It still happened, of course, that large war parties could encounter each other while far from their villages with neither side having the benefit of surprise. In such a case, battle might follow, but not the linear open battle described by the early sources. Instead individual warriors "took to the trees," firing from cover and endeavoring to outflank their enemy with the "half-moon" formation, negating the enemy's use of a single tree as cover.[73]

We have returned to these tactical issues and contact-era adaptations in this chapter because they relate to the larger problem of whether Native

Americans practiced "total war." It is a common argument that Native American warriors prior to European contact did not seek the indiscriminate destruction of the old, the women, and the children, nor did they usually burn villages or crops in the European tradition of laying waste the countryside. Francis Jennings and Patrick Malone have even argued that Indians were taken aback by the European destruction of villages and crops.[74] In one instance some Pequots literally queried the English about their style of war, asking "if we did use to kill women and children?" It is possible that the English reply that they "should see thereafter" may have been a bit of a shock.[75] Later in the conflict, the Narragansetts, although allied with the English against the Pequots, sent a message through Roger Williams expressing their desire that the killing of women and children be avoided.[76] And, most famously, when the English and the Narragansetts utterly destroyed the Pequot village at Mystic, killing hundreds of all ages and sexes, the Narragansetts "came to us, and rejoiced at our victories, . . . but cried Mach it, mach it; that is, is is naught, it is naught, because it is too furious, and slays too many men."[77]

Contrary to the idea that this oft-quoted passage supposedly expressed a Native American horror at an all-too-thorough European way of war, there is substantial evidence that Indians were well prepared to carry out fairly indiscriminate destruction. Fire by definition was indiscriminate, and we find early Wendat and Haudenosaunee fortifications specifically designed with fire prevention in mind, while Jacques le Moyne provided a very early engraving of Indians firing an enemy village.[78] There is no denying the occasional killing of women and children during the historic era, although as we will see, many of them could be adopted instead of killed. As early as 1540 the Spanish reported both sexes and children being scalped in the Southeast, and the same Pequots who queried whether the English killed women and children, upon hearing the Englishmen's vague answer, immediately replied that they would go to Connecticut to "kill men, women, and children, and we will take away the horses, cows, and hogs."[79] The subject remains contentious, however. The basic counterargument is that this level of violence arose only in reaction to European methods of war. There is much to be said for that argument, but it may be that more is explained by understanding such killings within the context of a style of war that so highly valued prisoners.

One way to interpret the Narragansetts' "Mach it, mach it" complaint about their English ally's destruction of the Pequots at Mystic is that such destructiveness denied them the opportunity to take prisoners for prestige or adoption. It is in the Native American attitude toward prisoners that one paradoxically finds both the most and least restraint in the overall violence of their warfare.

Prisoners served three and sometimes four overlapping purposes. Bringing prisoners back to the home village certified the overall success of the mission, and warriors gained individual glory by pointing to particular prisoners as "theirs." Scalps were also a mark of success and prestige, but were considered a poor second best to a live prisoner. The preference for prisoners over scalps arose from prisoners' other three functions. A prisoner, particularly an adult male, could become the target for their captors' rage and grief at their other losses. Elaborate and extended rituals of torture unto death existed in many of the Eastern Woodland societies. Scholars continue to struggle to understand their exact meaning, but it is clear that at the center of the process was a tremendous outpouring of violent grief, an outpouring in which the whole town—men, women, and children—participated. Native prisoners were well aware of what awaited them, and sought to remain impassive in the face of excruciatingly inventive torture. Not crying out certified their personal bravery, and some captor tribes sought to partake of that bravery through a ritual cannibalism in which they imbibed the courage and spirit of their prisoner.[80]

The third function of the prisoner was that of the adoptee. Adoption of prisoners may have been less universal than torture, but some incorporation into the captor group, either as kin or as a kind of servant, remained extremely common. Most familiar are the processes associated with the Nations of the Haudenosaunee Confederacy, in which the taking of prisoners in war was designed both to assuage grief and to restock their own population. In this "mourning war" complex Haudenosaunee families adopted prisoners to replace dead kinspeople, while torturing those not selected in a venting of their grief. Daniel Richter, Jose Brandão, and Jon Parmenter have rooted most if not all of the Haudenosaunee wars, particularly of the seventeenth century, in the temporarily successful but ultimately vain pursuit of sufficient prisoners to replace their losses in war and from disease.[81] Prisoner adoption was by no means exclusive to the Haudenosaunee; the process is simply most clearly understood for them. Among other trends it is well known that the demographic disaster of disease and war over the centuries of contact forced many peoples to reconfigure themselves through assimilation of other peoples; included in that process was prisoner adoption or incorporation.[82]

In addition, as briefly discussed in the preceding chapter with respect to porterage, recent scholarship is making increasingly clear that for some Nations, a captive could become something much closer to a slave than a replacement relative, even as terms associated with fictive kinship might continue to be used. Brett Rushforth's linguistic analysis of the Anishinaabe speakers and Miami-Illinois speakers of the *pays d'en haut*, for example, finds a strong sense of captives being degraded as "dogs," being marked by mutilation to indicate their lower status, and even to have been considered individually owned.[83] It is important to note that this discussion is entirely about those captives *retained* by the captors, essentially remaining within a fundamentally Native American paradigm of war and their notions of social formation—whether as adoptees or forced labor. It is not about how European settlers persuaded Indians to raid other Indians and then sell the prisoners into a European slave labor market (see chapter 6).

This overdetermined desire for prisoners limited the destructiveness of Indian war.[84] In battle it was difficult to seize a prisoner at all, and if one succeeded, one was unlikely to return to the fray to take another, leaving the first prisoner either unguarded or subject to competitive confiscation by one of his fellow warriors.[85] While some of the prisoners would be tortured to death, others would survive as adoptees (or ransomees), limiting the total lethality of the conflict. Furthermore, the most likely adoptees were women and children, and so the goal of prisoner adoption, if not a generalized revulsion against total war, tended to limit the killing of the defenseless. Finally, and most speculatively, the extremity of torture practiced on individual prisoners may have played a role in limiting the need for further warfare. Since much warfare was originally motivated by a desire for revenge, a desire that Kruer has reminded us was intensely emotional, the lengthy and elaborate rituals of torture practiced on a few individuals standing in for someone "responsible" for the original death may have forestalled or obviated the need for killing greater numbers of the enemy group.[86] Ironically, torture may have helped end feuds.

The logic of taking prisoners and its apparent limitations on overall violence had a flip side, however, and that became the side usually emphasized by Europeans. The targeting of women and children as preferential prisoners for adoption violated European norms of war that nominally exempted women and children from the theater of conflict at all. Furthermore, the torture of prisoners, particularly the communal public torture of prisoners, also violated European norms.[87] In John Lawson's otherwise sympathetic description of southern Native American life in 1709, he called it the one thing "they are seemingly guilty of an error in."[88] Finally, the long and difficult return marches after a successful raid, often under pursuit, meant that the captors ruthlessly weeded out the unfit or incapable: in their minds this was a mercy killing to be preferred to slow starvation.[89] This logic, however, could also lead to mass killing. When a successful surprise of an enemy village resulted in hundreds of prisoners, as after the Haudenosaunee capture of St. Ignace in 1649, logistically there was almost no way to guard that many prisoners for the long trip home. Fearing pursuit, and not wanting to release their enemies, the Haudenosaunee on that occasion summarily killed many of their prisoners.[90]

Native Americans explicitly expressed this thought process when arguing with their European allies against the European practice of exchanging or paroling prisoners. In their world view, to return prisoners to the enemy made no sense. They would lose the chance to both grieve and exult, and their enemies would live to fight them again. The Creeks and Cherokees, assisting in an English attack on St. Augustine, witnessed such a prisoner exchange and accused the English of conducting a sham fight.[91] More famously, the French-allied Indians complained about the negotiated surrender of Fort William Henry in 1757, refused to abide by the terms of the surrender, and attacked the retreating British troops. Even in this incident, however, one can also see the other restraining effects of war for prisoners. The successful acquisition of prisoners and plunder usually meant the end of an expedition, so that once the Indian allies of the French in 1757 had in fact acquired some prisoners and plunder they promptly abandoned the French offensive.[92]

The end of an offensive, however, did not mean the end of hostilities, and the resumption of peaceful relations required complex diplomacy. The full range of diplomatic activity and techniques lies beyond the scope of this chapter, but there are some structures and practices designed to facilitate the process of peacemaking that are worth elaborating here. First, Native Americans typically extended protections over enemy embassies to facilitate the beginning of negotiations. We have already seen how the Cherokees' violation of this code in 1715 brought lasting enmity with the Creeks.[93] This fundamental need to allow for the safe passage of negotiators was almost the sine qua non of limiting warfare among Europeans, and its role was perhaps even more important in an environment of endemic, revenge-based warfare.

The attack on the Creek embassy notwithstanding, the more normal protections for diplomatic parties can be seen in the peace negotiations between the Haudenosaunee and the French and their allies in 1644 and 1645. The French-allied Indians released a Haudenosaunee prisoner to return to his people to carry a message about the possibility of peace. Alternatively, a third party could be invoked to serve as an intermediary for this initial and most dangerous establishment of contact.[94] In this case, the Haudenosaunee sent back three negotiators and also released a French prisoner as their own gesture of good faith. The three negotiators were then hosted as eminent guests and treated with more than kindness.[95] Similarly suggestive of the process through which Native peoples sought to end war was the Pequots' approach to Lion Gardiner's fort on the Connecticut River in 1637, "calling to us to speak with them." Gardiner and a translator went out to negotiate, and the Pequots asked if they had "fought enough." Although no peace was forthcoming at this attempt, both sides obeyed the dictates of the negotiating truce.[96]

Of course the approach of one side asking for peace did not mean that the other had to accept it, but the divide between civil and military authority within a people helped the process of choosing peace. Civil chiefs, especially in those Nations where the civil chief's authority passed through hereditary succession, did not have their personal prestige or power vested in successful war.[97] Where the war chiefs, supported by eager young men, might prefer to continue to pursue opportunities for victory, or to overcome recent reverses, those pressures did not apply to the civil chiefs in the same way. The Creeks went so far as to force their White, or peace, chiefs to take an oath that they must always be devoted to the white path of peace and that they must never shed human blood.[98] Furthermore, the ruling council tended to be made up of older men, respected for their wisdom, and already possessed of war honors.[99] Unfortunately, over the course of the colonial era, the power of the war chiefs tended to rise. European traders and diplomats almost invariably conducted negotiations with war chiefs, or younger members of the council who served as spokesmen for the real power behind the curtain.[100] As conductors of those negotiations, they both received the diplomatic gifts presented by the Europeans, and were assumed to be the real authority of the group. European bestowal of titles like "emperor" or "king" did not make it so, but over time this process weakened the influence of the civil and/or religious authority.[101] One can speculate that this decline made it more difficult to move from a state of war to one of peace as dealing with Europeans grew increasingly important.[102]

In a similar way, Europeans affected the role of women within Native societies and their ability to restrain warfare. The political power of women varied widely among Native Americans, but some of the most prominent Nations, including the Haudenosaunee, the Shawnees, and the Cherokees, vested substantial political power in women. In many instances it was the women's desire to take vengeance, to grieve, or to replace their lost kin that could start a war, but in other instances they could prove a driving force to end one.[103] In some ways women could shift more easily from war to peace, since they, like peace chiefs, did not derive their social status or authority from success in war. Europeans' failure to understand women's roles, and their preference for dealing with war chiefs in general, helped to undermine the potentially (although not universally) ameliorative role of women.[104] As did European technology, so did European diplomacy upset certain balances within Native societies that had helped to contain the capacity for endemic warfare. Claudio Saunt's comment about the Creeks is more generally applicable: "Though Europeans observed only inconstancy and disorder, Creeks saw a healthy tension between female and male, old and young, and peace and war."[105]

If making peace was difficult, and required a minimal level of trust, keeping the peace was perhaps even harder. Ultimately, creating "peace" was about building some kind of alternative relationship between Nations, substituting forms of fictive kinship, fostering trade, and even exchanging people.[106] Getting to that point, however, was not easy. The first stage might include a formal declaration of peace between groups, but initially that likely simply meant, as John Reid has suggested, less looking over one's shoulder.[107] The elders recognized they could not fully control the desires of their young men to seek glory—and perhaps continued revenge—and thus in their creation of a peace they also had to seek ways to make such adventuring both less likely, and less likely to be successful.

One component of the solution was a varying combination of hostages, resident aliens—the latter often created by marriage between peoples—and even resident diplomats, or *fanimingos*. Even to use the word "hostage" is to imply a forced residence among an enemy people that does not always fit. Wahunsenacawh, for example, deliberately took in and developed personal attachments to several young Virginia colonists.[108] To the English they were captives or runaways who naturally needed to be restored to their own people. To Wahunsenacawh, as for most if not all Eastern Native American Nations, the exchange of people was supposed to both create a more lasting relationship and serve as a carrier of information between the two peoples. Taking in others established kinship through marriage or adoption, and kinship served as both a preventative to war and a path toward peace—although even kinship was no guarantee.[109] In this case Wahunsenacawh regretted the flight of the English boy Thomas Savage, saying that he was "my child, by the donative of Captain Newport, in lieu of one of my subjects Namontacke, who I purposely sent to King James his land, to see him and his country, and to return me the true report thereof."[110] Englishmen living with the Powhatans served both as hostages at risk in the event of an English attack, and as sources of information warning Wahunsenacawh of such an attack (and thus lessening the likelihood of a highly fatal surprise).[111] The Europeans and the Powhatans were closer to the same understanding of the diplomatic role of marriage, but differed on the details. Both sides clearly saw Pocahontas's marriage to John Rolfe as a marriage of peace, and the English even sought another of Wahunsenacawh's daughters for that purpose. Wahunsenacawh refused in frustration, pointing out that he only had so many daughters, and that he dealt with many Nations.[112]

Marriage, adoption/incorporation, and hostage-taking were not the only ways that visitors were introduced into the villages. It was common practice for members from many Nations to live in, or lengthily visit, another people for trading or political reasons. At the simplest level, the presence of visiting Creeks in a Cherokee town, for example, made it less likely that the Creeks would try to attack another Cherokee town for fear of the fate of the visiting Creeks.[113] More systemically, resident aliens or long-term visitors maintained interests in both camps. They frequently served as conduits of information between the groups, both formally and informally.[114] Themselves fearing the total destruction of either group in which they now had a vested interest, they warned of impending attacks, preventing the horrifying casualty rates of a successful surprise, if not derailing an attack completely.[115] Resident aliens could also step into the role of peace negotiator. Lacking the taint of blood revenge, they were a safe choice to send to the enemy to open negotiations. Chanco (or Chauco), who warned Jamestown in 1622, apparently also later served as an emissary from the Powhatans proposing peace, bringing with him a released prisoner.[116] James Quannapaquait and Job Kattananit, both Christian Nipmucs, expected to fulfill this role from their position as resident aliens among the English during King Philip's War. They offered to go to King Philip to "suggest somthing [sic] in order to the enemies submission to the English & making peace if they found the enimy in a temper fit for it."[117] This "resident alien" system is in fact the system into which the Europeans at first fit relatively naturally. Traders and later forts and garrisons set up within a Nation's territory were desirable both for their role as conduits for material goods, and for their certification of good feelings between the two peoples.[118]

This "resident alien" role found a more formal expression among some southeastern peoples in the institution of the *fanimingo*. As historian Robbie Ethridge describes it among the Chickasaws, a part of the population was obligated to contemplate paths to peace at all times. Its members formed the "peace moiety" of the Nation. Among their duties was to formally adopt someone from a Nation with whom they sought a new relationship. The adoptee would represent Chickasaw interests to that other Nation, and it, in turn, would adopt a Chickasaw to represent their interests among the Chickasaws.[119]

Escalation

The structures of keeping the peace naturally merged with those which helped to prevent or limit the frequency of war. Thus we have come full circle.[120] But it is important to note that restraint was not necessarily the dominant characteristic of Native American war. Peace chiefs (male or female) might play a role in limiting the resort to war, or help bring a war to a halt, but the more persistent and durable drive was blood revenge reinforced by the desire for personal status. That was the true circle of Indian war, where one act led to retaliation, and that retaliation demanded yet another response, and so on. Breaking the cycle of vengeance proved extremely difficult in a society ill suited to top-down coercion. Nevertheless, if war was endemic, it was also usually conducted on a small scale, and usually without the more destructive goal of outright elimination of an enemy people. Calling war among Native Americans "endemic" is not a denigrating comparative judgment. In the early modern world, war was pretty much endemic everywhere; it certainly was in Europe. There were differences in scale and intent, however. Where European warfare of the era was persistent, thorough, and when believed necessary, all-consuming, Native American warfare was usually episodic and personal, with easily satisfied goals, although it might be no less fatal on a per capita basis than its European counterpart.

One question repeatedly raised in this chapter and indeed in this book is whether the Indians began to shed their own restraints in response to the Europeans' way of war. Scholars have argued that a "collision of military cultures" occurred in which each people acted in ways that violated the other's expectations of war, leading to an overall escalation in violence. We have seen probable examples such as the Indian attitude toward rape, and the European response to the capture of women and the communal torture of prisoners. Such violations of norms naturally led to angry retaliation, and war spiraled out of control.[121] A more structural explanation suggests that the introduction of European diseases, technology, and materialist systems of exchange wrenched Native American warfare out of its comfortable, restrained path into something more terrifying and destructive.[122] Daniel Richter, for example, suggests that high levels of fatality from disease overwhelmed the capacity of the mourning-war complex to produce the "calm minds" necessary for peace. More and more captives were needed to replace people lost to disease, dramatically escalating the frequency of war.[123] There is much in both of these arguments, but the real story is probably even more complex.

Escalation in contact-era warfare was not just the result of simple anger at the violation of codes and expectations, nor can it be entirely attributed to the Native experience of dramatic demographic and economic change. There were also fundamental disconnects between the systems of restraint imbedded in each side's culture of war. Conventions designed to limit the destruction of war fell flat without the participation or at least the understanding of the enemy. For example, Europeans understood hostages and diplomatic marriages, but they did not understand the cautionary or peacekeeping function of resident aliens.[124] In one dramatic instance, when an English emissary to Wahunsenacawh demanded the return of William Parker, who had been living with the Powhatans for some time, Wahunsenacawh complained that "you have one of my daughters [Pocahontas] with you, and I am therewith well content, but you can no sooner see or know of any English mans being with me, but you must have him away, or else break peace and friendship."[125] The English furthermore never learned to trust or truly value the presence of Christianized Indians living among themselves as sources of information and warnings of attacks, famously ignoring John Sassamon's warning of King Philip's impending plans for war.[126] In an exception perhaps proving the rule, the Plymouth settlers allowed Squanto and Hobomock to live among them, where they seem to have served much as resident aliens. In at least one instance Hobomock and his wife played an active role in maintaining peace between the Pilgrims and Massasoit, the Wampanoag sachem and grandfather of King Philip.[127]

Fundamentally the English rapidly learned to use allied Indians as aids in war, but only rarely as aids to peace. The English refused to live with Natives, instead separating them into their own towns or reservations. The "Praying Indians" of Massachusetts, for example, already segregated into their own towns, were rounded up and confined on an island in Boston Harbor during King Philip's War.[128] In numerous Euro-Indian conflicts, militias repeatedly massacred peaceful, converted Indian groups, apparently unable or unwilling to distinguish between friendly and enemy peoples.[129]

Other failures to synchronize systems of restraint have been noted in this chapter. European systems of prisoner exchange and parole clashed with Native American ideas of the ways in which prisoners could be used. There is no question of "better" or "worse" here. The European system preserved prisoners' lives, but within the context of a much more lethal style of war. The Native system killed fewer outright, but then regarded prisoners as a prize of war—some to incorporate congenially into the captor's society and others to be tortured and killed, but on a very limited scale.[130] Ian Steele has pointed out that by the mid-eighteenth century British imperial negotiators had begun insisting on the return of all prisoners as a condition of peace.[131] Such a demand usually proved impossible for Indian leaders to enforce and therefore only prolonged conflicts. When the demand was met, it broke up nascent resident alien linkages between the two societies that might have helped defuse future wars. In another example of incongruence, European revenge could be unlimited in scale and target, but the desire for revenge was not triggered by simple death in open battle. Those killings were recognized as legitimate. Not so for Native Americans, for whom any death warranted blood revenge. In contrast, Indians could put aside revenge needs once the proper rituals of peace had been concluded; Euro-American colonists frequently proved incapable of doing the same.[132] On the more diplomatic front, European centralized governments expected similar coercive capabilities from Native Americans. Their repeated efforts to foster such centralization ended up strengthening war leaders, undermining one of the most fundamental of Native American structures of restraint: the peace chief.

As a general rule, the success of systems of restraint depends upon a minimal level of congruence between both sides' understanding of those systems.[133] Over time in North America, Europeans and Indians learned about each other, and moved to a certain level of understanding. Diplomacy became possible; intermarriage took place; wars ended. But in a deeper sense neither side ever fully came to terms with the other culture's overall vision of war, and thus they never succeeded in meshing their systems of restraint. Failing that, war became more extreme and more destructive.

CHAPTER FIVE

Fortify, Fight, or Flee

Tuscarora and Cherokee Defensive Warfare
and Military Culture Adaptation

In 1713, the second year of the "Tuscarora War" found the Tuscaroras facing the continued threat of joint English-Indian attacks on their villages along the Neuse River and Contentnea Creek in eastern North Carolina.[1] Over the course of the war the Tuscaroras had progressively refined their traditional defensive palisades, culminating in the complex fortification near the town of Neo-heroka. Now besieged in that fort, and threatened with ever-closer trenches, siegeworks, cannon, and even an underground mine, the Tuscaroras resisted desperately. They burrowed out underground bunkers, dug countertrenches, made arrowheads of broken glass, and inflicted significant casualties on the attacking force by keeping up a constant fire from both muskets and bows. The final furious assault by the English and their Indian allies took three days. They stormed the fort, set it afire, and killed or enslaved its nearly 1,000 inhabitants.

In contrast, in 1760 and 1761 two separate expeditions of British regulars marched into the Cherokee towns to retaliate for attacks on backcountry homes and forts. Both expeditions encountered occasional resistance while struggling to supply themselves and care for their wounded, but inflicted only limited direct damage on the Cherokees, mostly by burning empty towns. The regulars then departed, and in November 1761 a peace settlement ended the war. The Cherokees, diminished but not destroyed, rebuilt their towns, having suffered perhaps sixty to eighty men, women, and children killed by the British.[2]

This brief sketch highlights the ways Native American military culture shifted and adapted to the challenge of European military techniques across both place and time. Although the preceding chapters of this book have generalized about the strategy, logistics, and even the cultural aspects associated with the cutting-off way of war, that basic system was also constantly shifting in response to changing conditions. Indians rapidly learned about European capabilities and adapted their strategic conceptions and tactical techniques to the best of their abilities. This chapter unlocks part of that process of adaptation in two ways. First, it focuses on two specific, related case studies. The case study approach allows us to examine military decisions in detail, rather than relying on evidence from around the continent. Furthermore, these two particular cases allow us to compare a relatively early Anglo-Indian conflict with one from later in the eighteenth century, both within the Southeast and further linked by the Cherokees' role as English allies in the attack on Neo-heroka.[3] Second, this discussion narrows the evidentiary complexity of decoding the Indians' motives and ideologies of war by focusing on that most fundamental of military problems—home defense, the survival of the village. The Tuscaroras and the Cherokees each faced a direct European threat to their towns almost fifty years apart. Their changing strategies reflected the process of cultural adaptation to military necessity. The Tuscaroras, as we will see, had refined their fortification techniques in response to the European threat, but, to their cost in 1713, had not yet learned the full efficacy of European siegecraft. The Cherokees had also traditionally relied on defensive fortifications to protect their homes, but over the course of the century, as the English threat moved closer, they adapted, changed their techniques, and although ultimately in a doomed effort, prolonged their resistance.

Admittedly, the problem of identifying and explaining change is a difficult one. Our understanding of precontact Indian warfare is naturally limited, and even the earliest English or French sources for Indian warfare provide details of warfare among communities that may already have been affected significantly by the spreading ripple of sporadic European contact in the sixteenth and early seventeenth centuries.[4] Historians must recognize that different Nations faced different strategic problems, depending both on improvements in European technology and on their relative proximity to a Nation's home territory.[5] David Silverman's analytical framework has helped in showing how a "gun frontier" moved around the continent, temporarily creating a technological gradient among Indian Nations, as one gained access to guns before another, and used that advantage to its benefit.[6] Even with his work, however, it remains difficult to accurately assess the earliest Native American adaptations to the European military challenge. This chapter emphasizes that process of adaptation and change, showing that it was both continuous and flexible, albeit not always successful. Beyond merely learning how to cope with and then use firearms in the seventeenth century, Native Americans of the eighteenth century continued to adjust tactical styles in response to changes in military conditions. The Tuscaroras, who lived just inland from the coast, and by 1710 had experienced only limited military conflicts with the thinly spread European settlers of eastern North Carolina, provide us with a model of a "partially informed" group's reaction.[7] For the better-informed

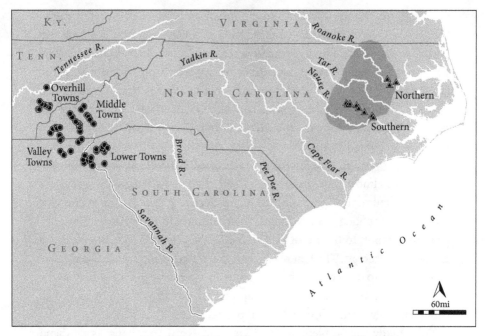

MAP 5.1 General locations of Cherokee and Tuscarora towns in the eighteenth century. Matilde Grimaldi.

mid-eighteenth-century Cherokees there is even more substantial evidence, and it is possible to fairly accurately trace a number of changes in their methods of warfare, at least in regards to the specific problem of home defense (see map 5.1).

Making sense of defensive strategies first requires understanding the threat. For Native Americans accustomed to wars with other Native Nations, that threat was the cutting-off war at varying levels of intensity. Their "vision" of how to defend themselves was rooted in that particular threat, as described in chapter 2. The initial impact on that system was not the Europeans themselves, but the availability of their technology in the form of metal axes and guns. Those implements shifted the potential of a cutting-off attack, and defenses adjusted accordingly. Over time, as Indians came into conflict with the Europeans themselves, and began to understand the strengths and weaknesses of their expeditionary forces, defensive strategies would adjust once again, although the threat of attacks by other Native American societies remained real for many decades as well. As we saw in chapter 2, when facing the threat of cutting-off-style warfare, the best defense was above all to prevent surprise, secondly to protect the noncombatant population by fortification

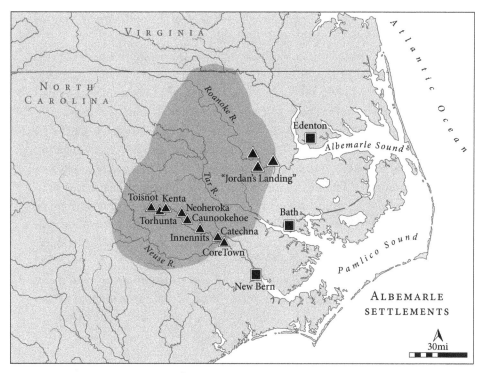

MAP 5.2 The Tuscarora towns (the "northern" towns along the Roanoke River are underrepresented due to a lack of archaeological work and fewer narrative sources. The southern town sites are known with some precision). Matilde Grimaldi.

or concealment, and finally, to pursue retreating raiders. It was from this baseline conception of defense against Indian enemies that first the Tuscaroras and later the Cherokees progressively adapted to the European military challenge.[8]

The Tuscarora People and Palisades

The Tuscaroras were an Iroquoian-speaking people living in the coastal plain of upper North Carolina and Virginia (see map 5.2).[9] The Tuscaroras appear to have migrated into the region as early as 600 C.E., and during the ensuing centuries they seem to have become the most powerful and populous group in the region, with the exception of the more politically centralized Powhatan chiefdom to the north.[10] Most Tuscarora towns sat astride the fall line, where the rivers make their final drop into the coastal flatlands. Such a location presumably aided their active role in long-distance trade. European settlement (beyond the abortive Roanoke colony) did not occur in their immediate vicinity until the 1650s, when a sprinkling of English settlers began arriving in the Albemarle Sound region overland from Virginia.

The Tuscaroras lived on agriculture, hunting, and fishing, residing primarily in permanent village sites, but dispersing annually to nearby hunting camps in the late fall for the relatively brief winter.[11] In the early historic period there appear to have been approximately twenty Tuscarora villages, each of which was largely autonomous.[12] Seven or eight of those villages clustered around the Roanoke and Tar Rivers, comprising the northern component of the group, while the remaining villages were situated primarily along the Neuse River and Contentnea Creek to the south. By the beginning of the eighteenth century, European diplomatic preference for a single chief had pressured the northern and southern villages into a mild political consolidation, each headed, or at least represented, by a dominant personality (Tom Blount and "King" Hancock respectively). Village autonomy remained strong, however.[13] Although the total population is difficult to determine, by 1700 there may have been about 5,000 people, down from 6,000–8,000 in the 1670s.[14] Of particular relevance to the question of village defense was the settlement pattern within and around the permanent villages, whether scattered or nucleated. The available historical sources describe only the settlement patterns of the southern villages, but recent archaeological evidence supports the idea that two different kinds of settlement styles existed, corresponding to the northern/southern division of the villages (although the evidence remains tentative). Prior to contact and in fact up through the outbreak of the Tuscarora War in 1711, the Tuscaroras' southern villages were composed of loosely clustered homes and farms spaced outwards from an identifiable center, but in no sense nucleated or palisaded. When Colonel John Barnwell marched through the region in 1712 he described the houses as much scattered: "no where 5 houses together, and then 1/4 a mile such another and so on for several miles."[15] Baron Christoph von Graffenried, captured by the Tuscarora just prior to the outbreak of fighting, gave a similar impression of dispersal in his account, noting specifically that King Hancock's house was some two miles from the village proper.[16] Archaeological evidence supports the literary evidence. A survey of the Contentnea Creek region (the southern village area) identified five obvious clusters of settlement, but in each case the cluster was composed of scattered hamlets or farmsteads.[17]

This lack of fortification and nucleation among the precontact southern villages contrasts with the clear evidence for palisaded villages in the northern Tuscarora towns, and with the extensive precontact palisading among other Native peoples in the region. Although there has been no archaeological survey of the northern villages, and their refusal to join the southern villages in the war against the English has limited the surviving descriptions of their villages at that time, there is strong evidence that at least some of the northern villages were palisaded. Excavations at the Jordan's Landing site, a northern Tuscarora village located on the Roanoke River, and apparently occupied year-round during the prehistoric era, have revealed evidence of a village palisade.[18] Furthermore, when Graffenried, still a prisoner, was transferred from the southern village of Catechna to the northern village of Tasky in a diplomatic concession to the Virginia governor, he described his new surroundings as "fortified with palisades."[19]

Archaeologist John Byrd has suggested one possible explanation for the differential existence of fortifications in the two regions. He points out that the northern villages were in frequent and violent contact not only with the coastal Algonquians of North Carolina, but more especially with the Powhatan chiefdom to the north. In contrast, south of the southern villages lay the relatively sparsely populated Sandhills region of North Carolina.[20] Furthermore, the main trading path from the Powhatan chiefdom heading west and south ran through the Tuscaroras' northern villages.[21] In short, it seems clear that the Tuscaroras were familiar with some form of fortifying their villages, but did so in response to the nature of the regional threat—preferring not to fortify when unthreatened.[22]

Not only did the Tuscaroras employ two settlement types, but there were also a variety of precontact precedents for fortification techniques. One of the most familiar images of a Native American village is John White's 1585 painting of the palisaded village of Pomeioc from coastal North Carolina (see figure 5.1). White's painting, combined with Jacques le Moyne's from Florida[23] and the narrative and archaeological evidence of the palisades of Iroquoian peoples to the north,[24] provides a fairly uniform portrait of circular or oval palisades of wooden posts, sometimes surrounded by a ditch, using an offset overlap to create a narrow gate—sometimes called a baffle gate.[25] More complex versions of these palisades had multiple, concentric lines of posts, with branches or bark interwoven through the posts to close the gaps seen in White's and le Moyne's portraits, and then watchposts and ramparts added at the tops of the walls to allow for observation and for firing from the walls.[26]

Furthermore, there is archaeological evidence in southeastern North America for an even more sophisticated style of fortification—one associated with the pre-Columbian Mississippian cultures of the region. In this more

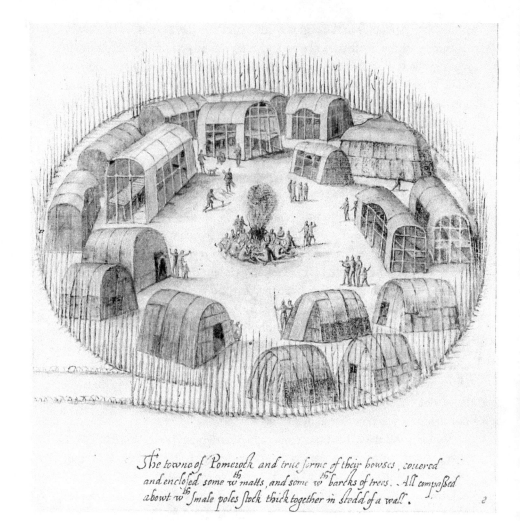

FIGURE 5.1 The palisaded village of Pomeioc from coastal North Carolina, by John White, ca. 1585. Courtesy of the British Museum

complex version, generally surrounding the much larger towns of the Mississippian chiefdoms, the palisade lines featured periodic square projections that allowed bowshots down the length of the wall (see figure 5.2).[27] For simplicity's sake we can call these projections "simple bastions"; they were *not* the angled bastions of contemporary European artillery fortresses, but they represented a significant improvement over a circular palisade that lacked them. A palisade system on Potomac Creek in Virginia, dating to around 1300 and believed to be ancestral to the Patawomecks of the historic period, seems to have been something of a hybrid. Its wall was essentially an oval, several

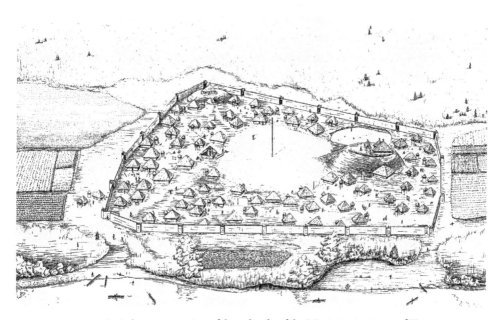

FIGURE 5.2 Artist's reconstruction of the palisade of the Mississippian town of Toqua. Drawing by Thomas R. Whyte, courtesy of the Frank H. McClung Museum, the University of Tennessee, Knoxville.

lines of posts thick, and also included five circular projecting bastions to help protect the walls.[28] Within the decades immediately preceding 1712 in eastern North Carolina, however, the standard palisades seem to have lacked even these simple bastions. This distinction is significant (as we will see), because at least by the time the Tuscaroras were fortifying themselves against the threatened English attack in 1712, they too were using palisades with bastions, some more complex than the simple ones associated with Mississippian sites. The question thus arises whether the Tuscarora bastions were an innovation derived from knowledge of European-style fortifications, or whether they had already learned the technique from the Mississippian peoples to the south with whom they had traded, even though most of the more centralized Mississippian states had collapsed by the seventeenth century at the latest.[29]

All of this background sets the stage for the Tuscaroras' reactions to the problem of European attack in the early eighteenth century. In sum, the Tuscaroras were prepared, if necessary, to rely on fortifications as a part of the defense of their home villages and territories. Virtually the whole eastern part of the continent had in fact seen a vast increase in the use of palisades over the preceding several centuries.[30] Those defensive fortifications traditionally had consisted at least of a circular palisade and ditch. Ramparts and/or watchtowers were known throughout the East Coast, but are not portrayed on the simpler palisades of the coastal Southeast. Finally, although the evidence is unclear, there is a possibility that the Tuscaroras were already aware of the advantages conveyed by squared walls supplemented with projecting bastions.

The Tuscarora War

Within the broader effort to understand Native American reactions to the European military problem, the Tuscarora War represents an "early" response in the relative chronological scale of military experience with the English. Although this was an eighteenth-century war, the Tuscaroras had had only limited conflict with Europeans up to this point. South Carolina's wars had been directed largely west and south, while the Virginians had fought mainly with the Powhatans and Susquehannocks to their west and north. The small numbers of English arriving in the Albemarle region in the late seventeenth century did not constitute much of a threat, and in fact Thomas Parramore has argued that the Tuscaroras completely and deliberately hemmed those settlers in.[31] The Tuscaroras had of course long been in contact with the Europeans, and had adjusted their trade networks to accommodate the new arrivals.[32] Militarily, however, it is likely that their vision of European techniques and eventual potential was still unclear. Although hostile relations had developed with the English in Albemarle and Virginia by 1701, and continued to escalate until the outbreak of the war in 1711, there had not been much outright warfare.[33] The Tuscarora War itself would then last for several years, with the most active period lasting over a year and a half, catapulting the Tuscaroras from uncertainty about European military techniques to a thorough familiarity over a relatively long conflict. Within that lengthy war the Tuscaroras coped, adapted, and changed.

The reasons for the outbreak of the war are complex and controversial.[34] Traditional explanations focus on the Tuscaroras' and other local Algonquian groups' resentment at white encroachment on their land, taking of Indians as slaves, and dishonest dealings by white traders. Frustration had even led the Tuscaroras to ask for permission to settle in Pennsylvania, which request depended on the North Carolina government certifying their past good behavior. When North Carolina refused, Pennsylvania's permission was withdrawn.[35] In an alternate interpretation, Parramore has emphasized the power of the Tuscaroras rather than their weakness. He argues that the Tuscaroras saw their hard-won regional ascendancy, and their continued efforts to extend their dominance over the coastal tribes, threatened by the arrival of the Swiss and Palatine German settlers at New Bern in 1710 (see map 5.2). They thus lashed out to reassert their control.[36]

Both explanations for the start of the war, however, find their catalyst in the founding of New Bern, and either explanation suffices to explain the nature of the Tuscaroras' original attack. First of all, New Bern threatened the southern Tuscarora towns, not the northern, and it would quickly become clear that the northern towns preferred neutrality. As for the Tuscaroras' and their Algonquian allies' military goals, in either case, they sought a reformation in their relationship with the Europeans.[37] They desired a reassertion of their dominance, or a change in English/German settler behavior, or, more probably, some of both. To achieve those aims they waged war, but with limited goals. As we saw in chapter 4, Frederic Gleach has called this kind of war a "coup," using a term implying a single blow or a strike, by which he means that they used military force to make a point, and then expected a renegotiation of their relative positions. They attacked according to their understanding of war as a punitive tool, designed to assert their ascendancy and persuade the Europeans to remain confined to a bounded territory. It was not a war of extermination or conquest, but a warning.[38] Furthermore, they did not anticipate that the various European groups within North Carolina would act jointly in response. The Tuscaroras initially attacked the English settlers around Bath and New Bern, but deliberately avoided the Swiss and Germans, although that exception did not persist.[39]

These political calculations, combined with the traditional cutting-off operational technique, dictated the style and scope of their initial attack. They opened hostilities without warning on September 22, 1711, attacking isolated farms and houses, killing and capturing those they could find, while bypassing larger groups or settlements, and then retreating with their prisoners. As the North Carolinians proved powerless to respond, the Tuscaroras attacked again, even besieging the small fortifications or garrison houses hastily thrown up by the settlers.[40] The Tuscaroras expected retaliation in return, but they expected it to be of the same type and intent—the transitory quest for isolated victims as part of a political wrestling for ascendancy. That was, of course, not the colonial response. The colonists did not see the policy; they saw only atrocity, and they reacted accordingly.

Outraged at the supposed treachery of the attack and horrified at the reports of torture and mutilation, North Carolina's government sought to wreak destructive vengeance.[41] In the short term, however, its initial response was panic and impotence. No force could be gathered within North Carolina, and settlers holed up with each other in fear of further attacks. North Carolina turned for help to the neighboring colonies, and eventually South Carolina would send two different joint white-Indian expeditions (mostly Indians) to attack the Tuscarora towns.[42] Without retelling the whole course of the war, what we can do is look more closely at Tuscarora defensive strategies and how they changed over the next year and a half.[43]

North Carolina's inability to retaliate meant that the Tuscaroras had few opportunities to demonstrate defensive techniques in the early months of the war. Two incidents or points, however, stand out. The southern villages, as discussed earlier, were not fortified at the outbreak of fighting. Therefore, when a report arrived in Catechna that a force of sixty English and Palatines were on their way to attack the village, the Tuscaroras immediately evacuated the women, the elderly, and the children to a "fine corn field . . . in the midst of a swamp, that is, in a wild place, a portion of forest in the morass, and water on one side and the other it is next to the river."[44] Thus forewarned, young men arrived from the other villages the next day, and set out to ambush the approaching white column. They successfully surprised the Europeans and sent them fleeing to their settlements. The Indians pursued for two days, but without doing much damage. This is the classic pattern of Indian warfare with Indians, and it conformed to the Tuscaroras' expectations. Their initial attacks were responded to by a raid (by the sixty Europeans). They abandoned their unfortified village in favor of the swamps, while the men prepared to do as much damage to the invaders as possible, but without engaging them decisively (only one European was killed). The colonists' raiding force, failing surprise, and confronted by the combined population of several villages, retreated and was pursued by the defending force, which itself had been built up from several related towns. From the Tuscaroras' point of view this was the cutting-off style of war—back-and-forth raiding, seeking surprise and the consequent cutting off of a group of victims, all while avoiding the same.

Expecting that such a war of raid and counterraid was about to commence, the Tuscaroras turned to the familiar option of fortification. The best defense was to detect an approaching enemy with sufficient warning, attack them while on the march, and call for reinforcements from nearby villages. Failing that, a simple palisade, or "refuge" fortification, protected an unaware village. A refuge-style fortification could not hold out against a determined siege or assault, but could provide immediate shelter and sufficient time for a relief force from other villages to arrive, particularly given the regional clustering of Tuscarora villages.[45] The Tuscaroras thus set about building fortifications, generally one per town. Some of these were more sophisticated than others, perhaps in the expectation that the simpler ones would serve against smaller raids, but a larger threat would require a more concentrated defense. The Tuscaroras were still in the process of completing them when South Carolina's first white-Indian expedition arrived under the command of Colonel John Barnwell.[46]

Barnwell and his army of thirty white men and five hundred Yamasees and other Indians encountered the first generation of Tuscarora forts in the winter of 1712.[47] As he first approached the towns, Barnwell noted in his journal the proliferation of small unfinished forts. He saw nine in one area, "none of them a month old," in which the men "sleep all night & the women & children mostly in the woods."[48] He found the towns themselves hastily abandoned, with much plunder left behind. He successfully assaulted one fort near Narhantes (Torhunta), although he and his Yamasee allies were surprised upon breaking through the wall to find two "blockhouses" more stoutly built than the palisade itself. The Tuscaroras defended desperately, "the very women shooting Arrows," killing seven and wounding thirty-two of the allied troops.[49] The next day a Tuscarora force from nearby Kenta harassed Barnwell's column, but the majority of the Tuscarora war effort seems to have been directed at continuing to raid the settlements to the east. Barnwell then progressed from town to town, occasionally fending off an ambush or surprise attack, finding abandoned towns and more unfinished forts (all of which he proceeded to burn).[50] Finally, he learned that the Tuscaroras were concentrating their men at Hancock's Fort: the fort adjoining, although not surrounding, Catechna—King Hancock's Town.

In short, it appears that Barnwell achieved strategic, but not tactical, surprise. The Tuscaroras were surprised at his arrival in the region, and thus decided against defending most of their unfinished forts, and in fact left a lot of plunder behind for Barnwell's army. But they had sufficient warning of his coming to evacuate their population and begin to concentrate their men in the completed fort at Hancock's Town (all while continuing to raid the settlements). There was an important strategic choice here. The Tuscaroras were defending in a manner that committed them to fight from a static fortification, but *not* in order to protect their population or even the towns themselves. Hancock's Fort was not built around Hancock's Town (Catechna), nor was the population inside the fort. Prisoners informed Barnwell that the old, women, and children had fled to Virginia in small groups.[51] It may be that the Tuscaroras had realized that Barnwell's techniques represented something beyond cutting-off warfare. His persistence in moving from village to village, besieging, assaulting, and burning, may have stimulated them to try something different: hide the population, while the men stayed to fight from within a fort.

After some delay, Barnwell marched to Hancock's Town, found it deserted, and then scouted the approaches to Hancock's Fort. It was built along the riverbank, "having a large Earthen Trench thrown up against the puncheons [palisade poles] with 2 teer of port holes; the lower teer they could stop at pleasure with plugs, & large limbs of trees lay confusedly about it to make the approach intricate. . . . The Earthen work was so high that it signified nothing to burn the puncheons, & it had 4 round Bastions or Flankers."[52]

This is clearly more than a simple circular palisade with an overlapped entrance in the manner of the John White painting (figure 5.1). The deep ditch and palisade are archaeologically attested elsewhere in the Tuscarora homeland and thus do not represent a change in practice.[53] The real apparent difference here is the presence of projecting towers or bastions to provide covering fire along the length of the wall. Barnwell, himself surprised at the complexity of the fort, claimed that a runaway black slave named Harry had taught them the technique.[54] It is equally probable, however, that the Tuscaroras already knew of the simple bastions found in late Mississippian fortifications, or had seen the European so-called *trace italienne* angular bastions on the fortifications present in Virginia and South Carolina. European forts used such bastions as artillery platforms, but they also effectively protected the line of the wall between the bastions more effectively than round bastions projecting from rounded walls.[55] Whatever the source of the idea, it would seem that the Tuscaroras had already enhanced their simpler traditional style of fortification in response to their understanding of the European threat.

Hancock's Fort was sophisticated enough that Barnwell's siege proceeded only with difficulty and only through the careful use of European siegecraft. Barnwell ordered his troops to fashion 200 "Fashines" (i.e., fascines: large bundles of sticks). Behind these his troops first approached the ditch; they then threw the bundles into the ditch to fill it, and followed up with an assault on the wall. Despite his preparations, and his hopes that the defenders were as yet unprepared, the fire from the fort was intense enough to repel the assaulters. Barnwell responded by building a counterfort thirty yards from Hancock's fort, taking advantage of a bend in the river to command the Tuscaroras' access to the river and thus their water supply. Barnwell noted that it was only at this point that the Tuscaroras began to fear being trapped in the fort, and they tried to evacuate by canoe. The fire from Barnwell's counterfort forestalled their escape, so the Tuscaroras turned to the expedient of using their English captives as water bearers and continued to hold out. Barnwell pressed the siege, and finally the Tuscaroras tortured and even killed one captive to force Barnwell to negotiate. He agreed to lift the siege on the promise of the captives' release, and he marched away on March 8, having spent five days approaching, assaulting, and then besieging the fort.[56]

Barnwell and his army retired to the coast and awaited the expected return of the hostages.[57] The truce shortly collapsed, and Barnwell prepared to mount a return expedition against Hancock's Fort. He at first hoped to surprise them by appearing suddenly with a small force audibly if not actually "enlarged" by numbers of drums and trumpets. Instead, the Tuscaroras again left Barnwell scratching his head. Creeping up to the fort, he was disconcerted to discover that the Tuscaroras had expanded their fortifications to enclose "the ground of my former attack," effectively preventing him from retrying his counterfort tactic. Barnwell pulled back, built himself a fort nearby to use as a base of operations, brought in reinforcements and supplies, and introduced a new variable—artillery. He procured, perhaps on the advice of Graffenried, "2 three pounders, 2 patteraros, 7 Granardo shells, [and] 22 Great Shott."[58] Although Barnwell lamented the relative lack of powder, and he reported that they had to improvise a mortar to throw the grenades, Graffenried claimed that the "savages . . . had never heard nor seen such things before," and thus that the artillery would be decisive in finally ending the siege.[59]

At this early stage, however, the siege was far from over. Having prepared his ground, Barnwell closed in on Hancock's Fort, commencing siege operations on April 7. Barnwell's force, now consisting of 153 whites and 128 Indians, spent the next ten days digging approach trenches until close enough to assault the ditch and palisade. The Tuscaroras not only resisted the approaching ditches, but also strenuously fought off the final assault. Barnwell's own words best convey the tenacity of their defense:

> [The] Subtell Enemy finding the disadvantage they were under in sallying open to attack our works took ye same method as we did and digged under ground to meet our approaches, wch obliged us to make sevn traverses and false approaches to deceive them. At last we got to the ditch and ye enemy had a hollow way under their pallisades that as fast as we filled ye ditch they would carry away the Fashines, & tho' we fired ye pallisades yet we could not maintain it. . . . We gained ye ditch & sevn times fired ye pallisades wch ye enemy like desperate villians defended at an amazing rate. This siege for variety of action, salleys, attempts to be relieved from without, can't I believe be parallelled agst Indians. Such bold attacks as they made at our trenches flinted the edge of those Raw soldiers.

His approach trenches now actually at the palisade wall, and apparently on the verge of success, Barnwell offered terms to the Tuscaroras, which they accepted.[60] The terms included the release of the white captives, and the demolition of the "flanks [bastions] next the attack," and later the whole fort, with the agreement not to build any more. The terms of the truce also allowed for Barnwell to enter the fort, satisfying European notions of victory by holding the ground (and indeed a ceremonial entry to mark the occasion). Barnwell was "amazed" at the fort's complexity, for "I never saw such subtill contrivances for Defence."[61]

From the Tuscarora point of view the whole affair was nothing less than two successful defenses, and in fact, Lieutenant Governor Spotswood in Virginia similarly interpreted it as a defeat for Barnwell.[62] For the Tuscaroras the truce terms were not so important as their apparent ability to resist a European incursion, protect their population—most of which continued to hide in the swamps during the siege—and extract terms.[63] On the one hand, the successes of Barnwell's expedition (he did after all burn several towns) would have encouraged the Tuscaroras to more strenuous efforts. On the other hand, the great difficulties Barnwell had at Hancock's Fort might have convinced them that they were on the right track. As Lieutenant Governor Spotswood put it: "'Tis encouraging to the Heathen, who are not such fools as not to perceive their [the Carolinas'] weak efforts in carrying on the war, as well as their easiness in making peace."[64] The Tuscaroras had begun the defensive part of their war relying on small, simple refuge forts, supplemented by tactics of harassment and ambush. Although there is some contradictory evidence, it also appears that the Tuscaroras used the refuge forts to protect their civilian population from surprise.[65] Meanwhile they built larger forts, like Hancock's Fort, to function as what John Keegan calls a "stronghold"— a true fighting platform.[66] The stronghold fort indicates a defensive strategy designed to make the Europeans fight them in their fort, extracting casualties and straining the invaders' logistics (this being Barnwell's greatest weakness). In short, their still-evolving understanding of European military capabilities led them to rely on improving their fortifications rather than abandoning them. That decision would prove fatal in the next year's campaign.

From Barnwell's point of view the war was over, and he quickly departed for South Carolina, although not without taking advantage of the opportunity to enslave some Indians, and thus help sow the seeds of the rapid dissolution of the peace.[67] Fighting quickly broke out again, the Tuscaroras "fortified themselves still more securely," and again North Carolina had to call for help.[68] Again South Carolina clapped together an expedition, this time composed of 33 white men and 850–900 Indians (Yamasees, Cherokees, and others) under the command of Colonel James Moore.[69]

The initial response of the Tuscaroras to the arrival of Moore's expedition is not known, but they were surely aware of its presence. A heavy snow and North Carolina's failure to coordinate logistical support held up Moore's troops in the Albemarle region for as much as three months after his arrival in North Carolina.[70] Moore, reinforced by at least one company of North Carolinians, eventually began his march and headed directly for the Tuscarora town of Neoheroka, and their new fort built nearby. Fortunately for historians, Moore, or a member of his expedition, prepared a detailed diagram of the fort and the ensuing siege, and the site has recently been excavated, confirming many of the details in the diagram.[71]

The details of the fort's design reveal the halting nature of the process of adapting European techniques into Native military culture (see figures 5.3 and 5.4).[72] The fort is clearly equipped with projecting angular bastions to increase the effectiveness of defensive fire, and at least some of the bastions were roofed to make a kind of blockhouse. The Tuscaroras also had learned from their experience at Hancock's Fort and had dug a concealed and at least partially entrenched route to the riverside for fetching water. Furthermore, perhaps in anticipation of the artillery and mortar fire briefly used against them at Hancock's Fort, they innovated entirely by constructing underground bunkers (Moore called them "caves") as a last refuge, and as a place of security for the noncombatant population—this time brought *into* the fort.[73] But their mastery of the *trace italienne* was not complete. Although Moore drew the walls of Neoheroka as straight lines (as a European would have expected), modern excavation has revealed that in fact the palisade line tended to bow outwards, reducing the effectiveness of the bastions in covering the line of the wall.[74] Even so, this was a stronghold fort, and the Tuscaroras would make taking it costly, but at an unanticipated cost to themselves.

Moore arrived outside the Neoheroka fort sometime in early to mid-March. He scouted the vicinity, and spent an indeterminate amount of time digging the zigzagging approach trenches, culminating with an elevated blockhouse (at A on figure 5.3), a battery (at B), and even a subterranean mine under the line of the wall (at C). Those works were complete by March 20. The Tuscaroras meanwhile had not remained idle. Aware of the implications of the approaching trenches, they had dug a countertrench out from their wall (at M), designed to fire down the line of the approach trench.

The attackers set off the explosives under the wall (at C) on the twentieth, thus signaling the assault. The "damnified" (corrupted) powder in the mine had little effect, and the attacking English and allied Indians suffered significant casualties in their assault on the wall. This was particularly true of the

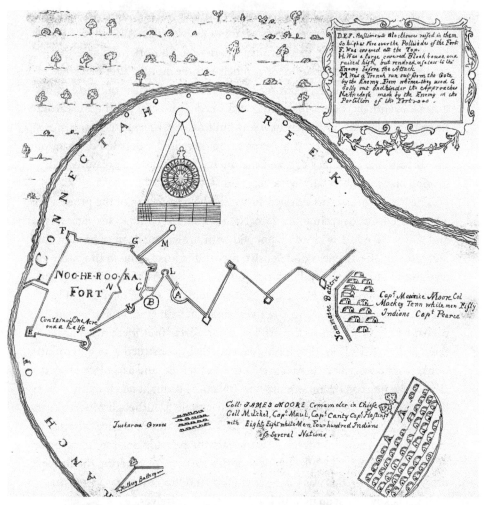

FIGURE 5.3 Detail of Moore's map of the siege of Neoheroka. The Cherokee "battery" is just off the upper left corner. From a tracing printed in the *South Carolina Historical and Genealogical Magazine* 10 (1909).

attack that mistakenly went in between bastions E and D, got caught in the crossfire, and was badly mauled. The English and allied Indians were able to gain the wall between bastions G and K, and the Tuscaroras responded by digging a trench line within the fort to seal off that part of the wall (N), and by firing from bastion F at the attackers near bastion G. The attacking forces then started fires at various points along the wall, including (by morning) firing the blockhouse within bastion F. Now moving into the second day of the assault, the Tuscaroras continued to resist as the attackers fought their way

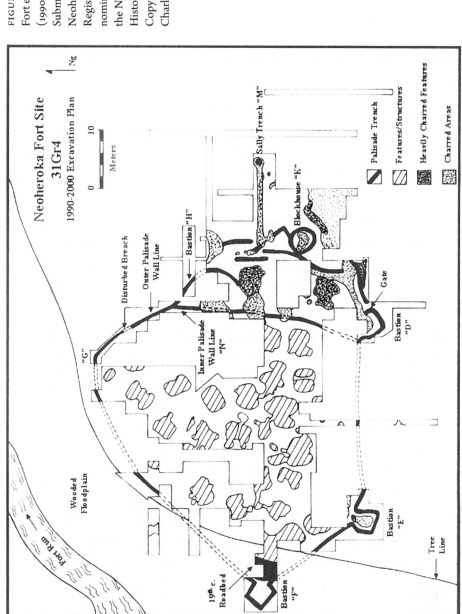

FIGURE 5.4 Neoheroka Fort excavation plan map (1990–2000 field data). Submitted as part of the Neoheroka National Register of Historic Places nomination, archived with the North Carolina State Historic Places Office. Copy provided by Charles L. Heath.

Neoheroka Fort Site
31Gr4
1990-2000 Excavation Plan

Ng

0   10
Meters

Palisade Trench
Features/Structures
Heavily Charred Features
Charred Areas

Wooded Floodplain

Fort Run

19th c. Roadbed

Bastion "F"

Bastion "E"

Tree Line

"G"

Disturbed Breach

Outer Palisade Wall Line

Bastion "H"

Inner Palisade Wall Line "N"

Sally Trench "M"

Blockhouse "K"

Gate

Bastion "D"

from house to house and through the interior trench line (at N). Many re-treated into the underground bunkers, while others retreated to the covered way to the river, enhanced the fortifications there, and held out until the third day of the assault (March 23) when all resistance finally ceased, many perishing in the flames. Graffenried, although not present, described the final defense: "The savages showed themselves unspeakably brave, so much so that when our soldiers had become master of the fort and wanted to take out the women and children who were under the ground, where they were hidden along with their provisions, the wounded savages who were groaning on the ground still continued to fight."[75] This remarkable and desperate effort cost the colonists twenty-two white men killed, thirty-six whites wounded, thirty-five Indian allies killed, and fifty-eight Indians wounded.[76]

The cost to the Tuscaroras, however, was much higher. Their hopes for their fortification program had brought together far too many people in one place: 392 prisoners were taken, 192 scalps taken from the fort, 200 more Tuscaroras killed and burned in the fort (and therefore presumably not double counted as scalped), plus an additional 166 killed or taken during scouts or sorties from the fort. The prisoners were sold into slavery.[77]

This was an enormous casualty count for any Native society, and it devastated the southern Tuscaroras. They immediately abandoned another fort, and began to retreat north and west, presumably hoping to link up with the Five Nations of the Haudenosaunee, who had promised aid, and who in fact may have sent a party to convince the still-neutral northern Tuscaroras to join them in raising the siege.[78] Sporadic fighting dragged on for several years as the Tuscaroras' local allies continued to resist from ever deeper in the swamps of eastern North Carolina. Many of the Tuscaroras eventually moved north to become the sixth Nation of the Haudenosaunee Confederacy. The others, particularly those of the neutral northern towns, remained, while Tom Blount patched up another treaty with North Carolina, this one affirming him as the ruler of the Tuscaroras.[79]

The lesson of the siege of Neoheroka seems clear. European-style siege-craft (even if substantially carried out by Indians as in this case), with sufficient logistical support, and particularly when supported by artillery, would always overcome a Native fortification that itself lacked artillery. The now well-established European methods of approach trenches, mines, bombardment, entrenched artillery batteries, and the use of fire in the final assault, were not defensible with the material and techniques available to Native Americans.[80] If the attacking force ran out of food or supplies, that might blunt their attack, but the Indians quickly realized that there were better ways to take advantage of the European necessity for supply trains. Those ways depended not on static fortifications, or even stronghold-style fighting platforms, but on mobility and rugged terrain. At Neoheroka, one group of intelligent observers absorbing this lesson were the Cherokees. They formed a significant minority of the Indian allies under Moore's command, as shown by the "Charikee battery" on Moore's diagram. They would remember the lesson.

The Cherokees' Defensive Strategies

It is of course impossible to document specific Cherokee decisions about defensive strategy in relation to their memories of the Tuscarora War (or any other specific war), but it is certainly clear that they very much remembered the war itself over the next forty or more years. The Cherokees repeatedly reminded the South Carolinians of their assistance during the Tuscarora War, and Tittigunsta, a headman of the Overhill Town of Tanassee in 1751, specifically said that he had been present when they had, in his translated words, "cut off" the Tuscaroras.[81] It is also possible to document the changes in Cherokee uses of fortification and defensive techniques both in the wake of that war and in response to changing conditions around them.

The Appalachian Mountains and their sheer distance from the coast gave the Cherokees more time to adjust to the presence of Europeans and to become familiar with European military capabilities. That familiarity extended so far as to include the adoption and adaptation of many European techniques and items of equipment, most obviously firearms, but also many of the symbolic and customary practices normally associated with European forces, such as the firing of salutes and the use of flags of truce.[82] But the Cherokees continued to war with Native adversaries, and had to accommodate that threat as well. In short, over the course of the eighteenth century the Cherokees' remoteness from European settlement, combined with their continued wars with Indian enemies, forced them to progressively adapt their defensive strategies depending on the nature of the threat. The Cherokees' wars with the Creeks to the south and with the "Northward" Indians (a common catchall phrase usually but not exclusively referring to the Haudenosaunee) meant that palisades continued to be viable, even necessary, defensive structures until the British built forts at the Cherokees' request in the midst of their villages. It was only then that the Native palisades disappeared. Shortly thereafter, when faced with a European enemy, the Cherokees adopted a completely different defensive strategy.

By the beginning of the eighteenth century the Cherokees, also an Iroquoian-speaking people, comprised a loose confederation of towns totaling perhaps 12,000–15,000 people, in three or four equally loose groupings, residing in the mountains of what are now North and South Carolina, Tennessee, and Georgia (see map 5.2).[83] The four main groups, divided not only by geography but by three mutually intelligible dialects of the Cherokee language, were the Lower Towns (closest to South Carolina, Elati dialect), the Middle Towns (Kituhwa dialect), and the Valley and Overhill Towns (Otali dialect). The town groupings were politically decentralized; each town retained considerable autonomy, and even within the towns decisions depended on consensus. Individual decisions to go to war remained personal, and chiefs lacked coercive power. Alexander Longe described the mobilization process in 1725: "When the war king has a mind to go to war with any strange nation, he sends for all his warriors. When assembled, he [says] . . . All of you that are willing to go with me to war and gain honor for yourselves and revenge the death of your countrymen that has been killed by such a nation, you must give me your names and number."[84] What unity there was sprang from a kinship system based on seven matrilineal clans represented throughout the towns.[85] As trade relations with the British widened in the early eighteenth century, the British sought to impose some diplomatic centralization through the creation of an "emperor." That effort failed from the British point of view, but over the long term their pressure did lead to the elevation of the war chiefs over the priestly class.[86]

Cherokee life and subsistence revolved around their towns. Houses were nucleated around a large "Townhouse" and a plaza for public and ceremonial activities. By the late eighteenth century, however, that pattern of settlement had become more dispersed, and with more European-style houses. This denucleation presumably paralleled the decline in the use of palisades described in more detail below, as dispersed houses could not be contained within a palisade.[87] The Cherokees followed an even more sedentary subsistence pattern than the Tuscaroras, depending primarily on the produce of their nearby fields and hunting. Unlike the Tuscaroras, however, when the men departed for the hunt, the women, children, and elderly remained in the village, exacerbating the need for village defense during those times of absence. Hunting absences only increased with the rising European demand for deerskins and the increased Cherokee involvement in European trade. The sacred role of the townhouse and the periodic absence of many of the men put a priority on some kind of village defense strategy. A common option, extending back into prehistory, was to palisade the village itself.

Understanding the Cherokees' knowledge of fortification, however, demands a consideration of their relationship to precontact Mississippian societies, and unfortunately the nature of that relationship is not entirely clear.[88] To make a complex archaeological argument short, it would seem that the eighteenth-century Cherokees lived in a region with two different prehistoric traditions of fortification, and that they had participated in one if not both of those traditions prior to contact. Archaeologists generally agree that the historic Cherokee homeland fell within the periphery of the urban, centralized Mississippian societies of the precontact Southeast. In the 200 years or so preceding European arrival, a culture known as Early Qualla to archaeologists, presumably Iroquoian speaking, resided in the mountainous heartland of the later Cherokee territory (the upper reaches of the Tuckaseegee, Little Tennessee, Chatooga, and Little Hiwassee Rivers). The Early Qualla culture replicated many of the characteristics of the contemporary surrounding, more urban, Mississippian cultures. When those larger Mississippian chiefdoms began to collapse in the late sixteenth century, the Qualla/Cherokees emerged from the mountains, incorporated other ethnicities, and occupied new territory—in particular the Overhill Towns region, but also presumably some of the Lower Towns. Within that larger region now occupied by the historic Cherokee, archaeologists have uncovered two basic patterns of precontact fortification—the Mississippian and the Pisgah—both geographically peripheral to the original Early Qualla region, but both presumably known to those people who would emerge as the Cherokees.

Mississippian fortifications have already been discussed, and a relatively sophisticated version is shown in figure 5.2. Supporting the archaeological evidence are the narratives of the leaders of the sixteenth-century Spanish *entradas*, who encountered and described a number of these forts.[89] Again, while the Cherokees were probably not the architects, builders, or sixteenth-century occupiers of those fortifications, the forts' existence on the Little Tennessee River, some in locations later claimed by the Overhill Cherokees, meant that their ancestors had almost certainly experienced or witnessed them.[90] Pisgah and Qualla sites, such as Warren Wilson, Garden Creek, and Coweeta Creek, have revealed both fortified and unfortified villages. The fortified versions were simple round or oval log palisades, sometimes two lines of logs set close together, one behind the other. The "gates" were the same overlapping walls (baffle gates) as seen in the John White painting. The Garden Creek site provides evidence that even some of these simpler palisades may have included simple bastions.[91]

By the seventeenth century the Cherokees were certainly occupying their historic-era locations, although the sites of individual towns would continue to shift. The earliest English visitors to those towns, and those of their near neighbors, confirm the picture of a common, if not universal, reliance on palisades as part of their system of village defense. Their descriptions also add details of wall platforms (battlements) unavailable to archaeologists. In 1674 Henry Woodward visited the Westo Indians on the Savannah River, downriver from the Cherokee Lower Towns, and found their town "duble Pallisadoed" on three sides, and singly along the riverbank. The Westos claimed to need this protection for their regular wars with the Cherokees.[92] A year earlier, Abraham Wood had described substantial fortifications at the Cherokee Overhill Town of Chota on the Little Tennessee, which he said had cliffs on the riverside and on "the other three sides trees of two foot over, pitched on end, twelve foot high, and on ye topps scafolds placed with parrapits to defend the walls and offend theire enemies which men stand on to fight."[93]

After Wood's early visit to the Cherokee villages in 1673, European descriptions and knowledge of Cherokee home territories precipitously declined for the next four decades. Not so the Cherokees' knowledge of the Europeans. They quickly entered into a trading relationship with the English, possibly supplementing earlier relations with the Spanish in Florida. Although trade with the English initially appears to have been indirect, with the English focusing their attention on the Creeks, the Cherokees did have early contact with European military techniques and fortifications.[94] They accompanied an English expedition against the Guales in 1680, and may have participated in, or been aware of, the later expeditions against the Apalachees in 1704 or even the regular siege (including artillery and mortars) against Spanish St. Augustine itself in 1702.[95] We have already seen how they sent a large force to aid against the Tuscaroras in 1713.

Our knowledge of the Cherokees' defensive techniques and use of fortifications expands dramatically with the outbreak of the Yamasee War in the spring of 1715.[96] The South Carolinians found themselves at war with a host of Indian groups, and they shortly came to believe that they would be doomed if the Cherokees also threw their weight in the war against them. Diplomatic exchanges aimed at securing Cherokee neutrality if not outright aid finally evolved into Maurice Moore leading an expedition of some 300 men (including "100 Negroes and Indians") to Tugaloo in the Lower Towns in a bid to impress and persuade.[97] One of the subordinate officers, Captain George Chicken, kept a journal of the expedition, and it provides some critical detail on Cherokee preparedness and defensive thinking.[98] During the course of

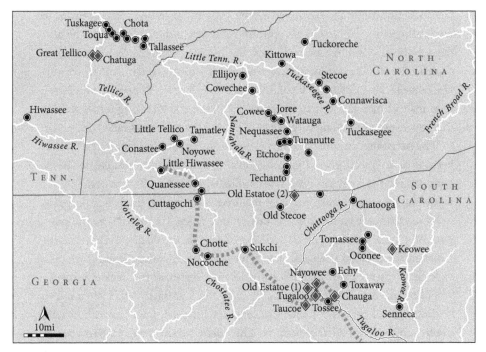

MAP 5.3 Cherokee towns in 1725. Diamond markers indicate fortifications. Other towns might or might not have been fortified. Tomassee was not. The dotted line shows the route taken by George Chicken ten years earlier; all those towns he visited were not fortified at that time. Matilde Grimaldi.

extended negotiations, Chicken, in company with other expedition leaders, toured a number of the southernmost towns of the Lower Towns and Valley Towns (see map 5.3).[99] At no time does he mention fortifications at any of those towns. While this may seem rather loose negative evidence, in comparison to his detailed accounting of Cherokee fortifications in 1725 (discussed below), it would have been a remarkable omission—particularly given what happened next.

Moore hoped to convince the Cherokees to aid the English against all their current enemies, but especially the Creeks (who had joined the Yamasees in their war against South Carolina). Factions within the Cherokees wavered over which other Indian Nations they would be willing to war against, and an anti-Creek faction seized the moment to irretrievably start a war. As described in chapter 4, a Creek delegation traveling under a flag of truce was attacked and killed in Tugaloo. The Cherokees, realizing that Creek vengeance would be forthcoming, tried to preempt it. Presumably in part because they lacked fortifications, they gathered a large force and marched south of town "to waylay the pathe."[100] No Creeks appeared that day, and the Cherokees the next day advanced closer to a known Creek encampment, only to discover it abandoned. The whole incident fits the mold of a group engaged in cutting-off warfare while lacking defensive fortifications. The village being open to attack, the men instead marched out to intercept the presumed attacking force, seeking their own surprise. Failing surprise, the "defensive attack" was called off.

The surviving accounts from 1715 leave some uncertainty about the Cherokee use of fortifications at that time, but the scenario becomes clearer when compared to the events of 1725. The conflict with the Creeks that began in 1715 would be long and bitter, much of it unrecorded by the English. It appears, however, that at least some of the Lower and Valley Towns foresaw the prospect of a long war, and invested in fortifying their villages. When George Chicken returned to the Cherokee towns in 1725, this time leading his own expedition, he recorded a significantly different response to Creek offensives.

Following the end of the Yamasee War, the Carolinians had returned to trading with all parties: Creeks, Cherokees, Chickasaws, and any others who could supply them with deerskins. The colonists saw inter-Indian wars as inconvenient interruptions to the trade, and the Carolina Indian agents and commissioners repeatedly sought to both keep the peace and exclude the French. The Cherokee-Creek War continued intermittently nevertheless, and flared up hotly again in 1725, just after George Chicken arrived as Indian trade commissioner on a mission specifically designed to keep the peace.[101]

Looming violence with the Creeks led Chicken to tour a number of the Lower, Valley, and Overhill Towns, view their defenses, and encourage the Cherokees in their efforts to repair their fortifications. He found "enforted" villages, with "Muskett proof" houses at Great Tellico and Chatuga, while Old Estatoe was "well ffortifyed all round with Punchins and also ditched on the Outside of the sd Punchins (wch Ditch) is Stuck full of light wood Spikes so that if the Enemy should ever happen to fall therein, they must without doubt recieve a great deal of Damage by those Spikes. I also observe that there are Sevl New fflankers made to the ffortificacons of the Town and that the Town house is also Enforted." He also reported fortifications in "Togelo parts," Keowee, and Chauga (see map 5.3).[102] His descriptions indicate a significant effort at fortification, unreported in 1715, but also much less sophisticated than what the Tuscaroras had attempted at Neoheroka. There are "new flankers" at Estatoe, but those could represent either continuity with Mississippian simple bastions, or the adoption of more angular European-style bastions, and Estatoe seems to have been exceptional. The other towns apparently retained simple palisades with some interior townhouses being reinforced against gunfire. These are forts designed to defend against the cutting-off attacks of the Creeks, and the Cherokees were quite explicit about how they were meant to be used.

The Cherokees understood the Creek threat and resisted Chicken's efforts to impose a strategy on them. He repeatedly advised them to combine the strength of their villages and march out to meet the Creeks before "they come Nigh your Towns."[103] The Cherokees equally repeatedly insisted that they would defend their towns, and keep scouts out to prevent surprise. At one point they were quite explicit about their methodology: "[The Cherokees intend] to lett them come to their Towns, but not undiscovered, for they design to keep out lookouts every way and be ready to give them a Smash in their Towns First and then to gather all their Strength and follow them when they are upon their retreat with their Wounded men."[104] This was the defender's ideal, but of course the cutting-off technique was designed exactly to avoid getting "smashed." When an offensive party arrived outside an unsurprised village, they were content to wait, snipe, and retreat if a superior force arrived. A Creek headman described this exact process in 1725, claiming to have gone "to Warr agst the Cherokeys and Lay 15 days about there [sic] towns, waiteing ane opertunity to gett a Scalp, but to no Purpose for they ware in Forts as though they Expected our Comeing."[105] Thus offense and defense balanced, with the defenders secure as long as they were not surprised.

Of course, not every town could be alert all the time, and the Creek-Cherokee War dragged on for almost three more decades. It is not possible to reconstruct the war on a blow-by-blow basis, but the Cherokees seem to have abandoned a number of the southern towns most exposed to Creek raids—some slowly over the course of the whole period, others in a burst near the end of the war. Among other incidents, we know that the Creeks attacked and destroyed Nagouchee in the Lower Towns early in the war, and then in 1750 and 1752 the Creeks forced the abandonment of Echy, Estatoe, Keowee, Tugaloo, Oconne, and Tomassee. The refugees moved to the Middle or Overhill settlements, or built new towns further north.[106] The crosses on map 5.4 show the apparent successful cutting off of Lower, Valley, and some more southerly Middle Towns. A smallpox epidemic in 1738 may have contributed to the abandonment of some of these towns, but the pattern of abandonment seen in map 5.4 seems to correlate with the military threat of the Creeks to the south, and to a lesser extent, the attacks by Shawnees and Iroquois from the north.[107]

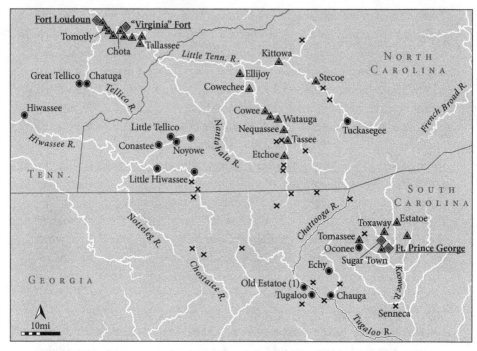

MAP 5.4 Cherokee towns in the 1760s. Diamond markers again indicate fortifications (both English and Cherokee). Crosses are sites of abandoned villages. Triangles indicate towns that were likely not fortified as of 1760. Matilde Grimaldi.

The continued existence and, in fact, the dominance of the cutting-off threat of other Native groups meant that Native palisades retained their viability even this late into the eighteenth century. There is evidence that some of the Cherokee communities displaced by the Creek War built palisades around their new settlements.[108] Furthermore, at least some of the more exposed towns that were not totally abandoned continued to be fortified (or were refortified) as late as 1752.[109] Other Indian societies in the region, particularly those further west, and therefore more remote from well-equipped European forces, also continued to rely on palisades. In 1757 a Chickasaw war party responded to the approach of a French and Choctaw force by returning to their towns, where they set "all Hands" to "fortifying ourselves in the best Manner we can, as it is a general Opinion amongst the Indians they are coming here." They built "three large Forts" and then deployed scouts. With the Chickasaws forewarned, the Choctaws' cutting-off attempt had failed, and they responded in the manner typical of cutting-off warfare: "About two hundred Men [Choctaws] came here, but did not think proper to engage us being discovered[,] returned Home after killing several of our Horses and carrying of[f] ten Head."[110] In another incident from the same period and the same region, the Shawnees defended themselves from the Chickasaws in improvised field fortifications. Further north, a multi-Nation Indian force laying siege to Detroit in 1763 built a substantial field fortification to interrupt waterborne supply to the British garrison.[111]

For the Cherokees, however, the end of the Creek War signaled a shift in their understanding of the threat. They now found themselves in an increasingly complex situation, still having to worry about other Indian enemies, but also facing the growing likelihood of having to contend with a strong European military force, particularly as hostilities erupted between France and England.[112]

The complexities of Cherokee factionalism and diplomacy in the face of the imperial contest are beyond the scope of this chapter, but it is clear that one aspect of their dealing with the situation was to persuade the British to build a fort or forts within their territory. Doing so would satisfy a number of Cherokee cultural forms and political needs. As early as 1746, and possibly a good deal earlier, the Cherokees had begun requesting that the South Carolinians build forts among their villages, and these requests picked up in frequency and intensity in the early 1750s.[113] Tom Hatley has correctly pointed out that having an English fort within their towns was one way of satisfying the Native diplomatic technique of having members of other peoples living within the community.[114] Such persons, described in chapter 4 as "resident aliens," coming from a variety of other communities, functioned as diplomatic entry points, go-betweens, and early warning mechanisms; with investments in their home community and now in the community in which they lived, they were expected to seek to prevent violence that would harm either one.[115]

The forts surely assumed this function in the eyes of the Cherokees, but Hatley then downplays how long and how insistently the Cherokees had been demanding forts, as well as the *military* reasoning behind those demands. To be sure, the Cherokees foresaw the forts' economic function in helping guarantee the continuance and regulation of the deerskin trade, and thus the availability of European goods, but they also clearly saw them as places for their own people "to fly to" and as visible guarantors of an alliance with the English.[116] The long Cherokee desire for English forts notwithstanding, willingness and funding to build such forts remained insufficient until 1753, when the South Carolinians finally financed the building of Fort Prince George in the Lower Towns.[117] For the Lower Town Cherokees this fort cemented the end of the Creek War. When reiterating their hopes for a fort in 1752 they had made sure the English would inform the Creeks and the Chickasaws of the fort's location, thereby assuring the Cherokees of safety from their attacks.[118]

With Fort Prince George in place, the Overhills Cherokees immediately stepped up lobbying for a fort of their own. Again, intra-Nation factionalism and the desire to dominate trade played a role, but the Cherokees sent clear signals that a British fort would also serve them as a refuge. The Cherokees' desires intersected with a burst of French and English competitive empire building via fort construction that itself exploded into war in 1754. This latest imperial war reinforced the British desire to hold onto the Cherokees as active allies and as a buffer against the French. As a result, and to the Cherokees' delight, both South Carolina and Virginia agreed to build a fort in the Overhills' towns. Virginia built a small square log fort at Chota in early 1756, but then failed to garrison it.[119] South Carolina, somewhat tardily, built Fort Loudoun near Toskegee and Tomatley later that year, and also established a permanent garrison and brought in cannon (see map 5.4).[120] The independent trade policies of the two colonies had frequently allowed the Cherokees to play them off against each other, and so it was only natural within the Cherokee diplomatic system to want representatives from both to reside in their area.[121]

Again, however, beyond simply diplomacy and trade, the Cherokees also saw the forts as places of refuge.[122] They specified this need in their early requests, desiring "that they may have some Place to fly to," and as Ft. Loudoun began to become a reality, a controversy arose over the siting of the fort that made plain the Cherokee vision of its military function.[123] The Cherokees saw the fort as a place of refuge for their "Wives and Children in case of danger," particularly when the men were gone to war or hunting.[124] So when the engineer, John William Gerard de Brahm, proposed a location some distance from the towns and upon a high knoll, the Indians were quick to point out the disadvantages, particularly the distance from the village. In the end, a compromise site was chosen—one much more accessible to the Cherokees.[125] Furthermore, the Indians were particularly pleased at the arrival of artillery, exclaiming that "the very name of our [the garrison's] great Guns will be a Teror [sic] to the French . . . and particularly to their Indians for they never could expect that we would have brought a Train of Artelery from such a Distance."[126]

Fort Prince George, Fort Loudoun, and even the Virginia fort (briefly), thus served as local and regional protection for the Cherokees.[127] Locally they provided refuge in the case of surprise for the towns nearest them. Re-

gionally they functioned as a visible marker of the British promise of protection from the Creeks (for the Lower Towns) and from the French-allied
Indians to the west and north (for the Overhill Towns). The forts were thus
both a diplomatic shield and a tripwire. An attack on the Overhill Towns would
almost certainly draw in the British garrison, and therefore the British
would have to continue to commit resources to defend themselves as well as
the Cherokees. And best of all, from the Cherokees' point of view, British garrisons did not march away to hunt during the winter. This style of refuge and
protection was year-round.[128] The forts certainly had an economic role, but
they also had this military one.

Further evidence of the Cherokees' vision of the British forts' military
utility is the fading of virtually all evidence for Cherokee-built town fortification from this point forward. In all of the many documents produced during the Cherokee War of 1759–61, including Henry Timberlake's detailed
descriptions and sketch of the Overhill Towns in 1762, there is evidence only
for a stockaded townhouse at Sugar Town (Conasatche) (see map 5.4).[129]
The repeated mention by different sources of Sugar Town's stockade in fact
highlights the lack of mention of similar structures at other sites.[130] To be sure,
this is negative evidence, but the three expeditions of 1759, 1760, and 1761
(discussed below) produced a wealth of sources, and the latter two actually
progressed through quite a number of Lower and Middle Towns, while Timberlake's sketch includes virtually all of the Overhill Towns and none of them
mention fortifications other than those at Sugar Town.[131]

The key here is to give the Cherokees credit for understanding the threat.
European troops quartered among them provided protection from other
enemies, but if those garrisons became hostile, Native palisades would not
suffice. Against Indian enemies in other situations, their own style of palisade
was still useful. Further west, where the European threat was still minimal,
Shawnees and Chickasaws continued to use palisades.[132] Against a large
European force, however, a new defensive strategy would be necessary.

That new notion of strategic defense became apparent during the Cherokee War of 1759–61.[133] Relations between the Cherokees and their British
allies deteriorated seriously in the summer of 1758 when some Virginia militiamen attacked and killed Cherokee warriors returning home after they had
aided in a British expedition against the French. The affected towns immediately sought blood revenge, and anti-British Cherokee factions rehashed
other, older grievances in a bid to join with the French and the Creeks in
a regional alliance.[134] The ensuing months saw increased violence on the

frontier, largely in Virginia, with the seemingly anomalous continuation of day-to-day relations between the Cherokees and the British garrisons and traders in their towns (described in chapter 4 as an episode of "not quite war"). Individual Cherokees thus sought revenge, while individual settlers continued to aggravate the situation through their own illegal activities or violence, all without "war" breaking out.[135]

The situation escalated dangerously in the fall of 1759 when Governor William Lyttelton of South Carolina, having decided to march into the Cherokee country to head off a complete break with the Cherokees, imprisoned a large delegation of Cherokee headmen who had come to Charlestown to reassure the British of their desire for peace. Lyttelton then kept them under guard all the way to Fort Prince George. During the ensuing negotiations he demanded twenty-four Cherokees be delivered for execution, and he imprisoned twenty-one Cherokee leaders in the fort as hostages against the eventual meeting of his requirements.

When smallpox began to run wild in the expedition's camp near the fort, Lyttelton hastily concluded a treaty (centered on the demand for the twenty-four guilty men), and the army hurriedly marched back to Charlestown. Lyttelton's demands were beyond the power of any Cherokee leader to meet, and the Cherokees were much incensed at the imprisonment of so many of their chief men. With Lyttelton's army gone, the Cherokees killed the local traders and began a kind of loose "siege" of Fort Prince George, as those who left the protection of the fort might find their lives in danger. This period of intensified "not quite war" ended when the Cherokees lured the garrison commander of Fort Prince George out of the fort, and then ambushed and killed him.[136] Exasperated, the soldiers in the fort killed the hostages, and the war rapidly escalated. Raiding party after raiding party descended on the Carolinas' frontiers, cutting off isolated settlements and farms. Furthermore, Fort Loudoun, on the far side of the mountains, was also cut off. There an extended siege began, as the Cherokees correctly estimated that they could "cut it off" without fear of a relief column.[137]

The killing of the hostages had touched many towns, Lower, Middle, and Overhill, and there were a host of relatives now driven to take revenge. Furthermore, the raids could be seen as an effort to reassert Cherokee potency and force the South Carolinians to reform their behavior and curb their land hunger. The rash of attacks became serious enough to attract imperial attention, and General Jeffery Amherst, the commander in chief in North America, dispatched a force of regulars to Charlestown in 1760, commanded by Colonel Archibald Montgomery, to mount a punitive expedition.

It was in response to this expedition (and to a second one in 1761) that the Cherokees opted for a different defensive strategy. The techniques were not new, merely an old alternative revived in the face of European capabilities and altered to attack European weaknesses. This alternative is the one often described as the "normal" Indian way of war, and it was simply to avoid the approaching force, abandon the village altogether for some more topographically difficult refuge, and then harass the enemy—cutting off stragglers and, in the case of European enemies, targeting supply lines. The Cherokees had not entirely changed the *role* of war within their society, as the outbreak of the Cherokee War demonstrated. What they had done was change their way of dealing with large-scale European military intrusions.

The story of Montgomery's 1760, and later James Grant's 1761, expeditions can be told in great detail—the sources are voluminous. Fortunately most of that detail is unnecessary for the argument presented here; a short description can make the point.[138] Montgomery's mixed force of regulars and provincials (militia and rangers) arrived in the Lower Towns after a relatively rapid final march, hoping to effect surprise. They found the towns abandoned and burned them. Montgomery continued his march toward the Middle Towns, and in a narrow place alongside a river near the town of Etchoe, the Cherokees attacked his strung-out column. Montgomery interpreted this as an attempt to prevent his forward progress, but a more likely scenario is that the attack on the head of his column was intended to hold his attention while they "endeavored to cut off our packhorses and cattle."[139] The Cherokees surely sought to cause casualties, and did so surprisingly well, killing seventeen regulars, and wounding sixty-seven (with a few more killed and wounded among the rangers).[140] It is probably wise, however, to assume that the Cherokees recognized Montgomery's greatest weakness: logistics.[141] And sure enough, Montgomery, after pressing through to Etchoe and evaluating his situation, determined that carrying his wounded men further into the mountains was as untenable as leaving them there.[142] He thereupon turned his entire force around, marched back to Fort Prince George (harassed by the Cherokees all the way), and thence to Charlestown, where he declared victory. Meanwhile, Fort Loudoun remained besieged.[143]

The events of the ensuing months said more about who had "won" than Montgomery's declarations. Some Cherokees were openly snide about the effectiveness of Montgomery's campaign, deriding the British military technique of "standing close together as in heaps," while admitting, with tongue firmly planted in cheek, that they sure could stand and take it.[144] Furthermore, they stepped up their siege of Fort Loudoun, eventually forcing its surrender, and their talks with South Carolina now took on the aura of bargaining from a position of strength.[145] In short, the Cherokees were quite certain who had gotten the better of Montgomery's expedition. The destruction of the garrison at Fort Loudoun in August 1760, the rising threat to Fort Prince George, and continued depredations on the frontier finally drew the imperial eye back to South Carolina and Amherst dispatched a new expedition, this time commanded by James Grant (who had been second in command on the 1760 expedition).[146]

Grant launched his expedition in the spring of 1761, quickly rolled through the Lower Towns, burning the remnants of those towns and their crops, and proceeded along the same path toward the Middle Towns. At almost exactly the same location as the previous year, the Cherokees again struck the British column. The battle lasted some hours, but as before, it consisted mostly of long-distance sniping by the Indians, and British attempts to flush them out. Again the Cherokees launched a concerted attack on the rear guard with the cattle and the flour, and again their attempt was defeated, but in his journal Grant admitted the loss of some packhorses killed and some flour loads lost or abandoned when the packhorse men panicked.[147] Grant's force suffered eleven killed and fifty-three wounded, but this time Grant was prepared for the eventuality of casualties.[148] He left the wounded with a strong force in Etchoe, and took the remainder of his troops on a march of destruction around the Middle Towns.[149] They found all of the towns abandoned and proceeded to burn fifteen of them over the next several weeks, while the Cherokees remained virtually invisible to Grant's force. Despite the lack of resistance, Grant's troops reached the end of their rope, and he made no attempt to cross to the Valley or Overhill Towns. Presuming that he had wreaked sufficient devastation, he returned to Fort Prince George. The Cherokees came forward to negotiate for peace, and a treaty was signed in the early fall.[150]

Grant's and Montgomery's expeditions were examples of the by-then standard European technique of dealing with apparently uncatchable Indians: the burning of towns and the destruction of crops, or the "feed fight."[151] In this they followed to the letter their instructions from General Amherst to "punish" the Cherokees.[152] There was little doubt that the technique had an impact, particularly in this case. Three straight years of British expeditions had created significant hardship and wastage in the Cherokee towns (the 1759 expedition did not burn towns, but left smallpox in its wake). Some South Carolinian critics complained that the Cherokees had barely suffered,[153] but others duly noted the amount of materiel destroyed, and the willingness of the Cherokees to sue for peace and then keep it.[154] Grant himself believed their desire for peace sincere, and in fact laid much of the blame for the war on the South Carolinians.[155] The Cherokees clearly suffered a great deal. Disease, disruption of subsistence, and the lack of shelter for the weaker members of the community all took their toll. This was particularly true in this case where at least some of the towns (especially the Lower Towns) had seen three straight years of disruption. If the need for steady logistics was the Europeans' greatest weakness, the inability to sustain continuous warfare was the Indians'.[156]

In *relative* terms, however, the Cherokees had escaped major damage. In one participant's words: "They kept aloof, & saved their Scalps by flight to such places as insured their safety." As a result they lost very few men to combat, maybe fifty in the first battle of Etchoe, perhaps thirty-five in the second battle (at most), with a few caught and killed during Grant's subsequent march (usually the elderly or women).[157] Many more died of disease and starvation,[158] but compared to the disastrous defense of Neoheroka, or almost any other occasion when prepared Europeans attacked a fortified Indian force (most famously the Pequots at Mystic), the Cherokees had chosen the right, if not the only, course of action.[159] Furthermore, there is strong evidence that the Cherokees quickly recovered from the disaster. The Overhill and Valley towns were untouched by the war, and when the Lower Towns people came back down from the mountains in the fall of 1761, they brought with them "their effects, their corn, & the seed which they intend to plant next spring."[160] The Cherokees proceeded to rebuild their towns and replant their corn, and they continued to constitute a significant military presence through the American Revolution.[161]

The usual historical summary of Native American use of palisades emphasizes their swift abandonment in the face of European firepower and total war techniques (including fire). For example, according to Colin Calloway's summary for the Abenakis, "The lessons of Pequot [1637] and Narragansett [1675] experiences were not lost on the western Abenakis. A palisaded village could become a deathtrap when surrounded by English muskets and put to the torch." Native Americans instead turned to a "strategy of withdrawal" in which "merely by keeping out of the way, the Indians allowed the enemy to defeat himself."[162] While this chapter might at first glance seem to be retelling the same story, the details reveal a more complex and flexible Native response to the difficult problem of European military systems. Part of the necessity for flexibility arose from the continued mixture of threats: European and other Indian enemies coexisted, sometimes in the same army. Virtually every European force to fight a Native American force included other Native

Americans—not least ironically the Tuscaroras who accompanied the North Carolina militia in Virginia's stalled expedition against the Overhill Cherokees in 1761.[163] Indian defensive strategies therefore had to encompass not only European forces, but Indian allies as well, not to mention the continuing threat of purely intertribal war. To complicate the problem even further, European capabilities continued to change. The nearly helpless and ill-equipped forces of early eighteenth-century eastern North Carolina were hardly comparable to the regular expeditions of a mid-eighteenth-century imperial power. In the face of this complexity, both the Tuscaroras and the Cherokees struggled through a learning process, and then progressively adopted courses they believed best suited to their defense.[164]

The first option, for the Tuscaroras, as well as for the Narragansetts and the Susquehannocks earlier in the seventeenth century, was to improve their forts, not abandon them.[165] For the Tuscaroras this proved to be a miscalculation, and they suffered a terrible defeat. Depending on the nature of the threat, however, palisades retained their viability and were still in use in the Eastern Woodlands well into the eighteenth century. Further west, one anthropologist has even calculated that the number of palisaded villages along the Missouri River actually increased as European contact escalated the intensity of inter-Indian conflict.[166] In an alternative strategy suited to the imperial conflict and the continued threat of other Indians, some Native Americans requested European forts be built in their midst. These forts could function defensively in a manner like their own palisades, but offered the additional security of serving as a diplomatic shield.[167]

Faced by a determined European incursion, however, the best strategy proved to be avoidance, but even this was more than a mere "strategy of withdrawal." Eighteenth-century European expeditions and forts were often at the end of a very tenuous chain of supply, and attacking that fragile chain was an efficient way to send those armies packing without having actually to destroy them. Both battles of Etchoe saw the Cherokees make determined attacks on the British baggage train. This too is evidence of a shift in Native American tactics. Ambushes and the half-moon formation—the latter designed to quickly allow a force to slip around both flanks of a force contacted in the front, making it difficult for the surrounded men to find cover and increasing crossfire—were originally employed as a way to inflict casualties on a surprised enemy while reducing one's own.[168] At the two battles of Etchoe, and at other examples discussed in chapter 6, those tactics shifted to focus on the baggage train near the rear of a European march column.[169] Montgomery and Grant dismissed these attacks on the rear in their official dispatches, preferring to emphasize the actions of their line troops rather than their baggage guards, but Grant noted the loss of packhorses and flour, and even the desperate disposal of flour to prevent capture.[170]

Unfortunately for the Cherokees, their attack was only partially successful. It did not stop Grant's subsequent march of destruction, but it does appear to have curtailed it. Saying that "we could not well run things nearer," Grant acknowledged that he was down to fifteen bags of flour by his return to Fort Prince George. Grant also crossed out a section in his official journal admitting that "it would have been impossible for us to proceed further. Our Provisions were almost Expended, & our Men worn out, . . . they have nothing left to subsist."[171] One of his officers later claimed that 1,500 of the troops were barefoot by the end of the march, many were sick, provisions were low, and the provincial regiments lacked most of the basic necessities, "the Greatest part of which they had lost."[172]

Bruce Trigger has written that "if, in the long run, native people failed to devise strategies that could halt European aggression, it was not because they were unable to understand European behavior from a rational point of view."[173] This was surely true of the Cherokees. With more time than the Tuscaroras to adapt, the Cherokees went through each of the strategies outlined here. In each case they chose the best of a series of bad options, and lived to fight another day. The "Indian way of war," although rooted in certain cultural practices and expectations, nevertheless retained an extraordinary flexibility.[174]

CHAPTER SIX

The Military Revolution of Native North America
Firearms, Forts, and Polities

Violent conflict almost inevitably accompanies interactions between imperial or colonizing powers and Indigenous peoples.[1] Conflict in turn generates
cultural exchange, as each side learns about the other's warfare practices and
adapts to or adopts them. In the storybook version of their arrival in North
America, the Europeans learned how to use canoes and snowshoes and (more
slowly) how to fight in the vast forested landscape by skirmishing, individually aiming, and hiding behind trees. Meanwhile, the Indians learned how to
use firearms and to avoid direct battles with European conventional forces.
Thus far, the story is an old and familiar one, and not entirely wrong. But it is
possible to ask deeper questions about this process and to refine the story by
adding detail. The previous chapter examined the problem of home defense
as one particular aspect of this cultural adaptation using two very specific
cases. But we can also examine the issue from a broader lens, using a model of
military change and its consequences developed for Europe in exactly this
period. European historians have suggested that in the early modern era the
technology and techniques of war underwent a profound transformation
and this transformation in turn affected European social and political organization. Although it was primarily a *military* revolution, its consequences were
far broader.

This chapter takes a similar analytical approach, examining the consequences, if any, of introducing new technologies and techniques to Native
American warfare and whether their introduction changed their way of war and
thereby changed their social and political organization. Did Native Americans
experience a military revolution, with its accompanying social and political
implications, based on technology introduced from Europe?

The European Military Revolution

For comparative purposes, it is best to begin with the European military revolution, or at least one version of it. The literature on the subject is extensive, primarily devoted to whether it had chronological limits, whether it was truly
revolutionary, and whether it actually gave the Europeans significant advantages

in the post-1500 global struggle.[2] Of the several different models, the one most relevant here is that developed by Geoffrey Parker in his landmark *The Military Revolution: Military Innovation and the Rise of the West, 1500–1800*. He suggests that the invention of castle-busting artillery in the late fifteenth century led rapidly to the creation in the sixteenth century of a new style of bastioned artillery fortress, known then and now as the *trace italienne* (or Italian style). Almost simultaneously, hand-held firearms became important on the battlefield, which, when combined with the new emphasis on siege warfare, put a premium on larger and larger armies composed primarily of drilled, volley-firing infantrymen. The horrific expense associated with the *trace italienne*, with artillery parks, and with larger armies then dominated the budgets and policies of the emergent European states, which were frequently locked in combat with each other. Brian Downing pushed this argument even further, indicating that the states most often drawn into the kind of "arms race" inspired by the military revolution were those that tended toward absolutism, whereas those less threatened, primarily England/Britain, were left with political room to maneuver that allowed for a more cooperative relationship among the commons, aristocracy, and king.[3] Parker's argument goes on to emphasize that naval developments may have constituted the real military revolution in terms of European global power, but that approach is less useful here.

A key aspect of this "revolution" was the use of firearms on the battlefield and the consequences of their use. The first firearms were highly inaccurate and took an exceedingly long time to reload. As a result, to be useful on the battlefield, they had to be used in large masses, producing volleys of shot capable of hitting large blocks of enemy infantry or cavalry. Europeans turned to ancient Roman models of discipline, as they understood them, to produce new systems of synchronized collective movement designed to make these formations more efficient. This, too, had social consequences, since the advantage of firearms was that they opened up a much wider pool of the male population to recruitment. No special skills were required to be a musketeer, only institutionalized training.[4] In the period considered here, the radical possibilities of this widening of social mobilization were contained by placing the old aristocratic elite in charge as officers, who used their disciplinary tools for social and operational control over their men. In the long run, however, firearms made it possible for all men to serve usefully in the state's armed forces, which then led to a new kind of politics and even a new kind of state. All these arguments necessarily oversimplify the historical processes, but they at least prompt the questions that we might ask about the Native American experience.

One further technical detail arising from developments in Europe needs to be addressed as well. Most of the military firearms of the early colonial period, from roughly 1550 to 1690, were *matchlock muskets*, a composite term. Although *musket* could have a very specific contemporary meaning referring to a specific model of firearm, here and more generally it is used as a catchall term for any firearm with an unrifled barrel, loaded from the muzzle. The lack of rifling and the *windage*, or the difference in diameter between the bullets and the barrel, meant that these firearms were likely to hit a human-sized target at no more than one hundred yards; the preferred range was fifty yards. *Matchlock* refers to the ignition mechanism, in which pulling the trigger dipped a prelit length of cord, or *match*, into the pan, which then ignited the charge at the base of the barrel. The obvious problem was preparing and lighting the match before needing to fire. *Flintlocks* (familiar to modern Americans from pioneer movies) and a precursor version of them called *snaphaunces* became available early in the seventeenth century. Although flintlocks were just as inaccurate as matchlocks, they did not require a prelit match. They were not widely adopted for military purposes in Europe until the turn of the eighteenth century, but the colonists abandoned matchlocks much sooner. Planners for the Massachusetts Bay Colony in 1629 suggested that eighty snaphaunces and twenty matchlocks be provided for every one hundred men, while Maryland in 1641 required men who wanted title to land to come equipped with "one musket or bastard musket with a snaphance lock," ten pounds of gunpowder, and forty pounds of bullets, pistol, and goose shot (some required of each). Despite this kind of encouragement for the newer technology, however, matchlocks had a long life, even in the colonies.[5] As we shall see, flintlocks proved much more congenial to Indian warriors than did matchlocks.

By discussing the European military revolution as background to the changes in Native North America, I am not pretending that these were directly comparable experiences. We already know, for example, that Native American Nations did not become transatlantic powers as a result of changes in military practice and naval technology. Nor am I arguing that Parker's model for Europe is correct. But the broader theoretical question remains: What were the social, political, and cultural implications of the new military technologies—firearms and fortresses—and techniques?

A Native American Military Revolution?

To discuss a revolution requires beginning with whatever came before. As chapter 2 outlined, for much of eastern North America, at least from the early sixteenth century, warfare followed an operational pattern that we have called the cutting-off way of war. As best as can be told from the archaeological evidence, the large, centralized Mississippian chiefdoms had a somewhat different pattern of warfare, the vestiges of which are faintly discernable in the accounts of the first Spanish explorers in the Southeast in the 1530s and 1540s. Thereafter, however, especially by the time English and French colonies were appearing on the coast, the majority of the Native Americans living east of the Mississippi had settled into some variation of the cutting-off way. As a strategy it was highly flexible. It allowed for large war parties that attacked whole towns or even multiple towns over several days, or, on a smaller scale, war parties repeatedly harassing enemy hunting or habitation zones. Operationally, it was carried out by war parties moving long distances across uninhabited, albeit claimed, spaces, relying on surprise, sudden attacks, the occasional open battle, and rapid retreat. Tactically, attackers who had achieved surprise might launch volleys of arrows and then rush into a disoriented opponent, clubbing them down, hoping to thus acquire prisoners. One further advantage of surprise was that prepared attackers in the precontact era would often be wearing wooden armor of various types, reducing their vulnerability as they rushed upon their surprised and therefore unarmored enemy. Fortified towns presented a tougher challenge, something discussed in more detail in chapter 5, primarily because wooden palisades, if the defenders were alert, were easily defensible against bows and clubs. They could be and were attacked by using fire, and a town could also be isolated and subjected to harassment from a distance, but that left the "besiegers" vulnerable to the arrival of reinforcements from nearby friendly villages.[6]

In the absence of surprise, therefore, whether in the open forest or a defended town, Indian systems of offense and defense were roughly balanced prior to European arrival. Single-event demographic disaster was probably rare, but was neither unheard of nor ideologically problematic (this was discussed in greater detail in chapter 4). A seventeenth-century dictionary of the Narragansett language conveys a good impression of the most important issues in Native American warfare at the outset of European contact: "They lie in the way [in ambush]," "They fortifie," "An house fired," "An Halfe Moone in war," "They fly from us / Let us pursue," and, probably most important of all, "Keep Watch."[7]

The cutting-off way of war persisted and adapted after the arrival of Europeans, in part because that arrival was not a single dramatic event that brought a single new form of military threat. Yes, European technologies, techniques, and attitudes toward war presented Native Americans with a series of challenges.

But those challenges changed significantly over time as the numbers of Europeans, their goals, and their military capabilities all shifted. To use the English as an example, the very first arrivals were mostly soldiers interested in rapid profits, who were quickly succeeded by settlers interested primarily in accumulating land and only secondarily interested in trade with the Indians. These settlers fought as a militia, with widely varying skills and persistence. Then in the mid-eighteenth century, professional military forces from Britain arrived, with more cannon and expeditionary capability, although they tended to strike and leave. Meanwhile, all Native American peoples continued to war with other Indians and thus had to take account of those groups' techniques and goals as well. Although European technologies did indeed produce some profound changes, especially at the outset of contact, cultural continuity and Native American sociopolitical structures limited their extent. Following the example of Parker's analysis of the European military revolution, I focus next on two major changes in military technique and then ask whether those innovations explain any postcontact changes in Native American polities. The first is firearms, and the second is fortifications.

Firearms

The attractions of the gun versus the bow still elicit a surprising amount of disagreement. Elaborate and convincing arguments have been made that the musket, especially the matchlocks and the snaphaunces of the early seventeenth century, held few advantages over the Native bow. All experts admit that the advent of the flintlock made the gun more attractive, primarily because it was lighter and handier than the matchlock and did not require the bright, smelly, position-revealing match. Nevertheless, Brian Given contends that even the flintlock had more faults than virtues compared with the bow.[8]

The problem with this argument is the evident and persistent eagerness of Native peoples to acquire guns and the services of gunsmiths, and their equally strenuous efforts to secure and maintain their access to gunpowder.[9] Given proposes that guns were attractive for their psychological effect against those enemies not yet supplied with them, but this does not account for the continuing long-term quest for guns, when their psychological impact had long since become meaningless. In contrast, David Silverman analyzed region after region within North America, and in each of them he finds one Native Nation gaining early access to guns and more or less immediately adopting them and thereby gaining an advantage over a less well-connected Native Nation. Usually, however, that initially disadvantaged Nation relatively quickly found a comparable source for guns and reestablished an equilibrium of sorts.[10] This simplifies his argument, and elides the fact that some Nations were in fact destroyed in this process, but the larger point for our purposes is that guns were avidly sought after, and we must ask why that would be.

As Given and others have pointed out, the Native self bow and the seventeenth-century musket had comparable effective ranges (50 yards optimum, 100–150 yards at the outside). The bow, however, could be fired much more quickly, did not require extensive material infrastructure (such as that required for making gunpowder), was generally more accurate in the hands of a skilled user, was silent, could be reloaded while kneeling, and could even occasionally penetrate metal armor (mail, not plate, especially when equipped with iron or brass arrowheads). Against an enemy accustomed to its noise, flash, and smoke, the argument goes, the musket held few advantages. Admittedly, early snaphaunces and the later flintlocks avoided the problem of the match, but they were prone to misfire more often than matchlocks due to the flint's failure to spark when dirty or dulled.

Europeans, especially Englishmen with their own tradition of using longbows, had played out many of the same arguments with one another about the relative efficacy of the bow versus the early musket. It seems clear that in Europe the gun initially replaced the bow for demographic and economic reasons, and Europeans then profited in the long term by the room for improvement inherent in firearms technology.[11] Whereas the bow required a lifetime's training to use effectively, the musket could be learned quickly. This relative simplicity of use allowed for a significant expansion in the pool of men suitable for military service, and this expansion is a key component of the argument for a European military revolution. Native societies, however, had little to gain by expanding the category of potential warriors, since virtually all men of a particular age were warriors anyway. Given all these disadvantages, why did Native Americans pursue guns so avidly?

Some of the answers are obvious, some less so. For Indians, because the bow or the musket had to serve in both war and the hunt, something in the technology had to satisfy the needs of both pursuits. Although the burning match of the matchlock was ill suited to hunting deer, a carefully prepared charge in a flintlock could be highly effective (a musket typically misfires because of dampness or after repeated firing). A musket ball was less likely than an arrow to be deflected by vegetation, and it also had a greater kinetic impact on the target. A deer struck by an arrow receives a very deep wound (arrows from modern bows can pass completely through a deer), which, although eventually lethal, might require the hunter to pursue the bleeding deer for some distance. In contrast, a musket ball penetrates flesh, shatters bone, and creates a larger wound cavity.[12] It "smacks," where an arrow "slices." According to Given's calculations, a military musket ball at 50 yards hits a target with 706 foot-pounds of kinetic energy. An arrow from a typical modern bow hits at 50 yards with 50–80 foot-pounds of energy. The arrow's energy is more than enough to penetrate flesh and tissue and produce a killing wound, but it is much less likely to drop an animal in its tracks.[13]

The musket has similar advantages against humans. Much of a human target is limbs, especially when walls or trees are used to cover the trunk of the body. An arrow wound to the leg or arm is rarely lethal, although it can be debilitating. But a musket ball strike to the arm or leg may shatter the bone and is more likely to carry debris into the wound, leading to infection, sepsis, and death. In 1612 William Strachey described Powhatan fears of such a "compound wound . . . where . . . any rupture is, or bone broke, such as our smale shott make amongst them, they know not easely how to cure, and therefore languish in the misery of the payne thereof."[14] In the immediate term, a man with a shattered leg or arm, flung to the ground by the force of a musket shot, also makes a better target for being taken prisoner or scalped. Unable to flee, he becomes vulnerable and may hold up his fellows trying to carry him away from the field. The musket's kinetic energy also made it a more reliable penetrator of wooden armor. Although there is early anecdotal evidence for Indian bows penetrating European armor, the more systematic evidence for the disappearance of wicker-and-wood armor (and shields) from the Native American repertoire is convincing proof of the difference in the penetrating power of musket shot and arrow against a semirigid surface.[15] More obviously, bullets cannot be dodged, whereas arrows in flight over any distance (especially on an arcing trajectory) can be seen and dodged. Modern film footage of the Dani people's arrow-and-javelin battles in New Guinea shows this process clearly, and numerous European witnesses commented on the Indians' ability to dodge arrows.[16]

Finally, the musket could be loaded with multiple small shot, or even, famously, "buck and ball"—a load of small shot combined with a normal musket ball.[17] This, too, could serve both hunting and warfare practices better than a bow. *Very* high levels of skill are required to take small game with a bow. An improvised "shotgun" load, however, greatly improves the odds, as it also does against humans at short range. The shotgun-style loading of a musket is described from the very beginning of the colonial experience and became famous during the American Revolution. Its ubiquity among the colonists surely informed the Indians' use of it as well. Connecticut militiamen in the Pequot War of 1637, for example, were ordered to carry twenty bullets and four pounds of shot.[18] Excavations at the Monhantic Fort, a Pequot fortified village occupied from the mid- to late 1670s, have found small shot (4–5 mm) almost exclusively, with only one full-sized bullet so far recovered.[19]

All in all, there were considerable advantages to preferring a musket over the bow.[20] With that established, we must ask what effect muskets might have had on strategy, operations, and tactics. At the very highest level, as will be discussed later, there were some key effects, because the need for a supply of gunpowder and gunsmiths changed specific national strategies as they affected relations with Europeans. At a purely military level, however, the musket's effects were distinctly limited. The cutting-off way of war had always emphasized surprise as the best means of destroying unaware villages or isolated parties while also increasing the odds of successfully taking prisoners. Guns did not change that operational preference, because they did not change the sociopolitical structure of a Native Nation, nor did they change the underlying expeditionary logistical systems in which food was more of a restraining issue than gunpowder or lead for bullets. Surprise and efficient movement through the wilderness continued to dominate operations and strategy.

Tactically, guns did not much change the use of a shower of missile fire, followed by the close-in fight with ax and club, designed to disable individuals for capture or scalping. What guns did do, however, was to make an open battle—intended primarily to display power and numbers and to sustain prestige—excessively lethal. To fight in large massed numbers, in the open, and against guns now meant that missiles could not be dodged, armor was no longer effective, and wounds were more likely to turn fatal from infection or shattered bones. Indian battles had never been fought to hold ground, and for a small-scale, relatively egalitarian society, the incentives to avoid fatal casualties were great.

"Battles" still were fought, but they tended to follow a pattern different from the massed open confrontation of the pregunpowder era, and they took place in three main contexts. In one pattern, a fortified Native village could be persuaded that the raiding party lurking in the woods outside the fort was too small to be a real threat, and the inhabitants might sally forth to attack and drive them away. As with the steppe warriors of Eurasia, however, this often proved to be a feint; the raiders might have hidden larger forces out of sight, and the sallying villagers found themselves outnumbered and cut off from their fort. This exact scenario happened to the Sokoki town of Squakheag on the Connecticut River in southern New Hampshire in December 1663.

A Haudenosaunee war party, primarily Mohawks, appeared outside the fort, and fifty Sokokis emerged from the fort to challenge them, pursued them into the woods, and ran headlong into a much larger waiting Haudenosaunee force. Eighteen Sokokis fought their way out of the trap and retreated into their fort, whereupon the raid became a siege (about which more later).[21] Nothing suggests that similar scenarios did not play out in the pregunpowder age, but without guns, an open confrontation in front of the walls of the fort (possibly in the cleared space around it) likely would have preceded the feint and chase (much like the 1643 battle on Sachem's Field discussed in chapter 2). For defenders who had walls to hide behind, such an open confrontation no longer made sense with guns in the mix because the risks were now greater.

Another type of "battle" was the classic ambush: attacking a war party, or any other group, from behind cover when they were entirely unaware, and especially when the target was small enough to be hit simultaneously all along its length. Such attacks almost certainly had always been a part of Native American warfare and were probably the sort of attack that produced the most casualties over the long term. Surprising a whole village could generate a single high-casualty event, but such major surprises were probably rare. Smaller parties on the move were easier to catch. In this sense, the "skulking way of war" phrase continues to make sense, but especially when skulking is used in its alternate meaning of "waiting in hiding" rather than "sneaking." A war party traveled to the vicinity of an enemy and waited for an opportunity to strike.

Finally, there was the large-scale meeting engagement between two large armed and prepared groups. Exemplary in this category were incidents when large European military expeditions, too large and spread out to be ambushed all at once, suddenly found the head of their column under attack. Then, as the battle progressed, Indian warriors moved from tree to tree, sliding along the flanks of the column and forming a horseshoe of fire, something that they called the half-moon formation.[22]

This technique appeared in earlier chapters, but it is particularly relevant here because of how Indians used it to attack the logistical weak point of European expeditionary columns: their baggage train. Most infamously, this was the type of attack that General Edward Braddock's army encountered in 1755 at Monongahela. In that case French regular forces blocked the path and stopped the British vanguard, but even as they did so, the allied Indians "disperse[d] to the Right and Left, forming a half Moon." As they slid along the length of the British column they quickly came to the army's baggage train, leading many of the packhorsemen to panic and flee (see map 6.1).[23] In this

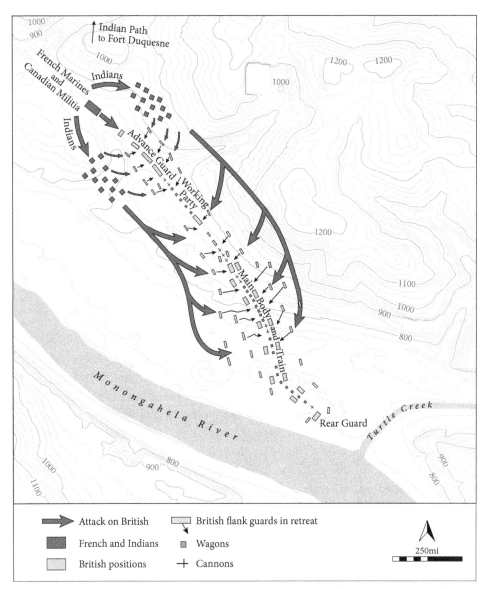

MAP 6.1 The Battle of Monongahela, clearly showing how the half-moon formation could surround a European column. Wayne E. Lee, Anthony E. Carlson, David L. Preston, and David Silbey, *The Other Face of Battle: America's Forgotten Wars and the Experience of Combat* (New York: Oxford University Press, 2021), 19. Used with permission.

sense the tactical adaptation was not so much about the technology (muskets vs. bows), but about the nature of the enemy: European armies operating in the wilderness depended on carried provisions. In Europe, they could rely on strings of depots and magazines in preplanned locations, and when they moved beyond the resupply distance of a magazine, they could turn to the countryside for supplies. In northwestern Europe, or in the settled coastal areas of North America, the countryside was densely inhabited, farmed, and beribboned with local (if poor) roads, all of which facilitated the daily collection of food and forage.[24] But in the North American forest, both Braddock in 1755 and John Forbes in 1758 had to cut their own roads to accommodate their cannon and baggage. Similar efforts slowed other such expeditions. Even forces without cannon or wagons, and thus capable of movement along narrower Native paths, used a pack train of horses to carry flour and other gear. Accordingly, when Indians attacked, they often deliberately focused not on killing large numbers of soldiers but instead on destroying their provisions, hoping thereby to turn the whole expedition around. One Lenape warrior named Lamullock was quite clear about this vulnerability: he referred to the British armies as "a Parcel of old Women," unable to "travel without loaded Horses and Waggons full of Provisions and a great deal of Baggage." Furthermore, Lamullock suggested that "we Indians are all one as Wolves[;] we can lay in Ambuscade and take you English all one as in a Trap.[25]

That the baggage was the focus of a half-moon attack, or even other forms of attacks, was not always obvious to European participants or witnesses, who often focused their accounts on the actions of regular soldiers stationed at the front or fighting along the flank. Baggage guards were often militia or provincial troops, and their activities (and attacks on them) received less attention in official accounts by regular officers. But when we look carefully at a number of such encounters the pattern is clear. Monongahela in 1755 is one example, but there are others.[26] Chapter 5 detailed how the Cherokees quite successfully executed a half-moon attack on the British baggage at Etchoe in both 1760 and 1761. The allied Indians who besieged Fort Pitt at the outset of Pontiac's War in 1763 drew the same conclusion, and when they attacked Colonel Henry Bouquet's relief column, their clear objective was his baggage train.[27] After American independence, expeditionary forces into Ohio faced this kind of attack several times, including at Harmar's Defeat in 1790 and St. Clair's Defeat in 1791. When yet another American army ventured into the Ohio country in 1794 under General Anthony Wayne, it too faced an Indian confederacy that opened their defensive efforts by attacking a pack train carrying flour to one of Wayne's supply depots. Later, at the Battle of Fallen Timbers, the Indians attempted a one-sided half-moon envelopment (much like at Etchoe, a river protected the other flank). Wayne's reliance on careful marches with daily fortified camps (explicitly following guidelines from his reading of Julius Caesar) helped secure his supplies and enabled his eventual victory.[28]

In addition to these attacks on the pack trains of expeditionary forces, it is also fairly clear that Native strategies against European outposts often focused on isolating them from resupply.[29] Attackers targeted supply convoys as they passed through known portage points—as they did at the portages between Niagara and Detroit during Pontiac's War. There, in 1763, Indians, probably mostly Senecas, attacked the "Carry[in]g Place" and "Entirely Cutt off" two companies of the 80th Regiment of Foot, but they also destroyed or carried off "the oxen[,] horses[, and] Waggons." Close reading of the various letters reporting this incident makes it clear that the real initial target was the wagon train passing through the portage with a small escort. The British infantry companies that were destroyed had been sent to help.[30]

It bears repeating, after so many words describing a specific tactical adaptation in attacking European expeditionary forces, that this was not a revolution in technique driven by technology. Instead it reflected Native awareness of European weaknesses, and could equally have been attempted with bow-armed warriors.

Gunpowder itself may have had more significant effects. Although it may not have changed tactics very drastically, the dependence on gunpowder supplies undermined an already shaky Indian ability to sustain long, repeated campaigns. A society that sends out most of its men to war loses their productive labor (typically as hunters, whether for trade or subsistence). As we saw in chapter 3, a war party on the move was operationally much more mobile and logistically self-supporting than a European force, but strategically they did not have the reserves of provisions that could be shipped in from other locations to sustain campaigns over long periods. Worse, if their primary European provider of gunpowder had become their enemy, they had to find alternative sources or risk running out—as seems to have happened to some groups in the Indian alliance in the Yamasee War in 1715 and to the Cherokees in 1761, and which was a key part of preparation for those Indians anticipating and preparing for war against the British in 1762 and 1763.[31]

The other major vulnerability for Indians created by the shift to gunpowder was in the field of artillery. There are very few examples of Native Americans successfully using artillery. The Susquehannocks' fort in 1663 and again in 1675 had cannon, but those were probably fired by European gunners the first time.[32] The Cherokees who successfully blockaded the British in 1761 in

Fort Loudoun, South Carolina (now Tennessee), confiscated the fort's cannon and hoped to force the British gunners to help them attack Fort Prince George, but the gunners escaped.[33] In 1685 a village of French Catholic Iroquoians at Sault built a pentagonal, bastioned palisade, with one 8-pounder cannon mounted.[34] In 1730, the Natchez, besieged by the French in their two forts, and under fire from a French artillery battery, returned fire with three of their own cannon, taken from the French Fort Rosalie earlier in the war, but the Africans operating the cannon were untrained, and their fire ineffective.[35] Wall-mounted swivel guns seem to have been successfully adopted, but they are not often mentioned, and using them was not much of a technical leap from a musket.[36] But these instances were clearly exceptions.

More common was the Europeans' ability to bring cannon to bear on Indian forts, which usually quickly ended the confrontation (although the Susquehannocks in 1675 held out for seven weeks). On the European side, a *trace italienne* fortress equipped with cannon was generally invulnerable to assault by Indians, although extended sieges and trickery did lead to the capture of several such European forts, and smaller stockades were also vulnerable.[37] The combination of fort and cannon, especially backed by European transatlantic capabilities, provided a kind of ultimate guarantee of security and persistence in North America. But to discuss cannon here only points up the even more interesting and variable role that fortifications played.

Fortifications

It is generally agreed that the arrival of Europeans and their goods made conflict more frequent in North America. As discussed earlier, there is more debate over whether their arrival meant an increase in the lethality of warfare, but the arrival of new players bearing desirable trade goods from an unexpected direction into an already competitive system almost inevitably generated new conflicts while also imbricating the newcomers into preexisting conflicts.[38] The proliferation of fortifications has long been understood as an archaeological marker for the intensification of conflict, and a major period of proliferation had begun across much of the eastern part of the continent beginning around 1100 C.E.[39] The arrival of Europeans apparently created another burst of fortification and in new regions. Furthermore, Native Americans responded to European military capabilities by changing the design of their forts and then finally abandoning them. How did this increase in fortification, as well as a shift in their design, change the nature of Native American political structures? Or did it?

Southern New England provides an informative case. The archaeological evidence strongly suggests that at least Connecticut, Long Island, and Rhode Island were devoid of Native fortifications before extensive contact with the English and the Dutch began in the seventeenth century.[40] Despite the absence of evidence for a tradition of palisading, archaeologists suggest that the "traditional" form of fort in the region, as was true for much of the Northeast and parts of the Southeast, was the circular palisade with a baffle gate, most famously represented in the woodcut of the Pequot fort at Mystic, destroyed by the English in 1637. Other Indian forts built in New England around this time and in the ensuing three or four decades took on a more European look: they were increasingly squared, combined a ditch and palisade, and were furnished with corner bastions projecting out from the wall that allowed the defenders to fire down the length of the wall.[41] They were not true European artillery fortresses, whose bastions could direct defensive artillery fire in crossing patterns at besiegers some distance out from the walls. These bastions were simpler, merely intended to give the defenders the ability to fire at enemies attacking through the ditch and trying to set fire to, or cut down, the base of the palisade. This need was almost certainly a result of European steel axes, which greatly improved the potential for success of this kind of attack. Furthermore, archaeologists have suggested that many of the forts in the Long Island Sound area were built to protect the production and accumulation of wampum, the carved shell beads that acquired tremendous importance in the mid-seventeenth century as a form of currency in the European-Native fur trade.

The need in New England for forts (not all of which were built *around* villages but instead were built *near* villages as refuges) may or may not have been driven by the wampum trade, but it seems clear that their design resulted from the arrival of European technology. Indians may not have been copying European fortification techniques when they adopted bastions or "flankers," which had long existed on prehistoric Mississippian forts in the Midwest and Southeast, but the suddenness and thoroughness of the change in fortifications indicate a response to a perceived threat.[42] In these early contacts with Europeans, when a besieger was as likely to be an Indian as it was to be a poorly equipped European militia, it seems unlikely that the threat was cannon.

In this first phase of Indian fortress adaptation, as Craig Keener shows, the new threat was simply the iron ax. Keener analyzes shifts in Haudenosaunee fortifications and assault techniques and finds a process of evolution occurring in the seventeenth century similar to that discussed for New England, with the difference that Haudenosaunee and Wendat precontact forts were already elaborate and common. Indeed, in the century before the arrival of Europeans, they had become progressively sturdier, using heavier poles in multiple concentric lines (as many as four), with even the earliest ethnographic sources describing watchtowers and wall platforms furnished with firefighting material.[43] Nevertheless, a sturdy circular wall without projecting bastions was vulnerable to an enemy who gained the wall and were equipped with iron axes and mantlets to protect themselves from overhead fire. Keener outlines a series of successful Haudenosaunee assaults in the 1640s, whose success he attributes primarily to their having iron axes.[44] In response, and under French tutelage, the Wendats in the 1640s began to "make their forts square and arrange their stakes in straight lines; and that, by means of four little towers at the four corners, four Frenchmen might easily with their arquebuses or muskets defend a whole village."[45] Squared, bastioned forts then proliferated in the last decades of the century, and as a result the Haudenosaunee shifted their siege tactics and had fewer spectacular successes.[46]

The success of this kind of adaptation is revealed in the events at the same Sokoki fort at Squakheag discussed previously. This fort was new, built in the early 1660s when the Sokokis, actually several communities under pressure, were coalescing into one for mutual protection. The fort sat on a high, necked hill; it had a substantial palisade, flanking bastions, a "high standard" over the entrance, and covered access to a spring for water. After the initial disastrous battle outside the walls (described earlier), the Sokokis retreated inside while the Haudenosaunee repeatedly assaulted the fort and even managed to set fire to one wall by throwing in a bag of gunpowder. Nevertheless, the attack failed, and the Haudenosaunee later admitted to suffering at least one hundred dead.[47] A Jesuit source for the siege noted that shortly thereafter, the Senecas (the westernmost Nation of the Haudenosaunee) asked for French help in surrounding "their Villages with flanked palisades."[48]

Bastioned forts' successes against Native American enemies and ill-equipped settler militias, however, proved a false security. The Narragansetts famously relied on their new bastioned fort in the Great Swamp during King Philip's War, but it proved to be a death trap in the face of persistent attack by a large English militia army. And chapter 5 of this book described how the Tuscaroras progressed from an initially successful adaptation of bastioned forts to catastrophic failure. When they successfully defended one improved fort against a joint White-Indian expedition, they committed more of their population to the protection of an even more sophisticated fort at Neoheroka the next year. That decision, however, proved to be a disaster, as European siegecraft, aided by hundreds of Indian allies, eventually overwhelmed the defenders, and the attackers killed or enslaved hundreds of Tuscaroras.

The French wars against the Mesquaki Nation (Fox) near Detroit and in Wisconsin provide similar examples of Native attempts to improve their fortifications in tandem with the associated gamble of bringing much of their population inside the walls. In 1712 the Mesquakis under the leadership of Pemoussa established a palisaded village within just fifty paces of the small French Fort Pontchartrain (Detroit), intending to threaten and isolate the French, whom they suspected of having encouraged a recent Odawa attack on their allies the Mascoutens. What followed was complex, and depended on the comings and goings of Indian groups allied to both sides, but ultimately the tiny French garrison, massively reinforced by Odawas, Potawatomis (Neshnabé), Wendats, and others, turned the tables and besieged the Mesquakis in their fort. The siege lasted some weeks, and included various devices to fire over the walls into the Mesquaki fort while the Mesquakis dug internal entrenchments to provide cover, several attempts at negotiation, desperate efforts by the besieged to secure water, and ultimately, a failed attempt to flee the fort under the cover of a thunderstorm. The French repeatedly broke promises of mercy, and their Indian allies had suffered severe losses and were thus motivated to take extensive revenge. Many Mesquakis and Mascoutens were killed during their flight.

After the disaster at Detroit, the remaining Mesquakis, still led by Pemoussa, concentrated at a town in Wisconsin overlooking Big Lake Butte des Morts, and massively reinforced the fortifications there, using steel axes to cut down thick oak trees as palisade posts, digging entrenchments inside the fort for additional cover, and using that dirt to reinforce the walls. In 1716 a large French and allied Indian army brought two small cannon and a mortar in reinforced canoes, but still failed to breach the walls. Instead the French commander began digging approach trenches and prepared to mine the walls. Pemoussa offered terms and the campaign ended with both sides declaring victory, but the inevitability of European siege techniques seems clear.[49]

Despite this record of failure, palisades were not abandoned all at once around the continent. Many Native peoples continued to battle other Indians, and palisades remained functional against Indian enemies who lacked not only artillery but also the desire to engage in a protracted digging campaign designed to approach the walls. As we saw in chapter 5, the Cherokees expanded their own fortification system against the Creeks during their war from 1715 to 1752. When facing a competent European expedition, however, most Indians quickly learned to abandon their fortifications, as the Cherokees

did in 1760 and 1761, and as the Haudenosaunee did when the American revo-
lutionaries invaded in 1779.[50]

And that is the point. Native Americans' technological and social infrastructure proved incapable of taking advantage of all of the components of
the European military revolution. They transformed their form of warfare
in the field, and they initially transformed their fortifications with fair success.
But without the ability to mount artillery on those forts or to provision them
for the long term, forts could not provide the kind of frontier or homeland
security that they did for the Europeans.[51] The forts instead became traps,
soon regarded as useless. Without a reliable base of fortifications, Native
Americans' strategic defensive options depended on their greater operational
mobility in a vast forested continent. But that mobility came at the sacrifice
of their cornfields and homes, left behind for European expeditionary forces
to burn.

Polity Adaptation?

The story of how Native American social and political organization shifted
and adapted to the many facets of the contact experience is varied, complicated, and often obscure. It was a long-term process perhaps best studied at
the level of each individual Nation. The factors influencing the process were
many, but the purpose of this chapter is to ask how changes in the techniques
and technology of warfare shifted the structures of Native American polities
generally.

To start with, the adoption of the gun meant a form of dependence, at least
in the long run. Brian Given argues that no such dependence emerged in the
mid-seventeenth century and perhaps for long after that. More recently, Daniel Silverman suggests not so much an Indian "dependence," but rather a form
of *mutual* dependence, in which Native Americans *needed* firearms, but Europeans needed Indians as well.[52] More narrowly focused, but widely cited as
also showing a lack of dependence, Patrick Malone highlights evidence from
seventeenth-century southern New England for Native Americans repairing
guns and even having their own forges with which to do so. Indeed, New
England Indians' long and close exposure to Europeans may have equipped
them better than some other Nations to master certain smithing techniques.
In addition to the forges that Malone discusses, excavations at Monhantic
have revealed a forge site probably used by Indian smiths (although white
militia operated cooperatively nearby with the Pequots, so the case cannot be
certain). The blacksmithing tools recovered from the site and some small

handmade gunstock screws suggest that the smith there was capable of relatively sophisticated work.[53]

It is nevertheless a striking and persistent truth in the records of Indian diplomacy across the eastern part of the continent that Native Americans sought out guns and gunsmiths. Broken gunstocks were easy enough for a woodworking society to repair, and matchlocks are extremely simple mechanical devices, as are the various tools used to clean muskets or make bullets. Flintlocks and barrels, however, were relatively complex metal objects and required a sophisticated knowledge base and tooling infrastructure to make repairs.[54] Ian Steele proposed that 20 percent of the inventory of actively used muskets had to be replaced or required significant repair every year. They simply broke.[55]

What was mostly true of guns and gun repair was unavoidably true of gunpowder. Even in Europe, its production was centralized in a relatively few locations, and the skills required were precise indeed, developed over a century and more of experimentation.[56] Even drying damp powder could be difficult and dangerous. Naturally enough, the records are replete with Indian requests for gunpowder (and at better prices).[57]

This dependency on Europeans for guns, gun repair, and especially for powder, had two related impacts on Native American polities. First, it emphasized maintaining diplomatic ties with Europeans in situations in which the response might otherwise have been hostility or even just simple disregard. It particularly emphasized interimperial diplomacy, so that if relations with the English, for example, deteriorated, the French could be turned to as an alternative source of powder. Long-range trade and diplomacy had always been important to Native American political and economic patterns and are amply attested in the archaeological record from the precontact era, but most long-distance trade goods had been used for prestige or ritual purposes. Although gunpowder did have ritual functions, it had become a necessity.

Second, as a side effect of this emphasis on diplomacy, many Native American polities experienced a shift in the relative power of war chiefs over peace chiefs and, in many societies, over the council of women. This is a complex subject, and could vary widely between Nations, but the basic outlines are well known.[58] Very many Native American Nations divided political authority among men designated as war leaders, and the men and women who ran the domestic affairs of the clan, town, or Nation. Both civil and military powers were usually further separated from religious authority. Ultimate political authority depended on group consensus but was usually channeled through a semihereditary civil chief.[59] When European traders and soldiers entered the scene, as outsiders they were initially invited to deal with the war chiefs—those men tasked with external affairs and with raising warriors (often the point of a European visit). They then became the initial recipients of European diplomatic gifts, and as redistributors of those goods, they gained power and influence. In ambitious ignorance, Europeans tried to formalize this process by designating individuals as "kings" or "emperors," titles that meant little in the short run, but as those men became the redistributive authority for European goods, they did in fact acquire greater power, which unbalanced normal intragroup political relations. This process would no doubt have occurred in the absence of guns, axes, and gunpowder, since many European trade goods held appeal, but war and hunting were deeply significant.[60] Even given the remarkable successes that different Indian groups had in manipulating their European suppliers, or playing them off against one another, the Native American military revolution played a role in reshaping the political structures within Native American polities.

The Native American military revolution also shifted settlement patterns. The failure of even improved fortress systems eventually led some Native peoples either to ask that European forts and garrisons be placed in their midst or to relocate (especially in times of crisis) nearer to European forts. Chapter 5 narrated how the Cherokees requested Fort Prince George to be built in their Lower Towns, and Fort Loudoun in the Overhill Towns, and even convinced the Virginia government to build another fort in the Overhill Towns, although ultimately Virginia did not garrison it. For the Cherokees, having a British fort and garrison in their midst served a variety of purposes: they guaranteed a continuance of trade; they provided a refuge for the Cherokee people if attacked; and they certified the British alliance with the Cherokees to other Indians who might refrain from attacking them for fear of dragging the British into the fight.

Similarly, during the French and Indian War, Haudenosaunee leaders conditioned their military assistance to the British on the building of forts near their towns as refuges for their women and children.[61] Then, during the American Revolution, the British Fort Niagara became a magnet for refugee or threatened Indian populations. In part, this was because British subsidies were doled out from that location, and also because of the kind of "ultimate security" that a British fort and garrison were thought to provide.[62]

There are other examples as well, as different Nations sought to find the right combination of their own fort-building traditions, European aid in building forts, European forts being built nearby, or some hybrid of all of those, depending on the political environment. After 1648–49, many Wendats coalesced around a new Jesuit stone fort on Christian Island, where the Jesuits directed the building of a new bastioned palisade for them.[63] Similarly dire circumstances persuaded the Saponis to move into the shadow of Virginia's Fort Christanna on the Meherrin River in 1714, hoping for regular access to the fort's smith as well as the protection of its cannon.[64] Native peoples similarly aggregated around the Spanish fort at St. Augustine and the French at Fort Toulouse in modern Alabama. Again, this partly reflected a desire for access to goods, but it also stemmed from the need for security in the face of failed Indian defensive systems. The Catawbas, coalescing as a new Nation from the survivors of several others, and settling on the border of the two Carolina colonies, built their own forts during the first half of the century following "concepts derived from both aboriginal and colonial models." The two Carolina governments vied to build a fort among them, but the Catawbas long resisted. Smallpox and war in the 1759–61 period eventually produced an agreement for the South Carolina government to build a fort in 1761, but it was left ungarrisoned.[65]

Furthermore, with their own forts abandoned and under increasing pressure from Europeans' landownership patterns, Indian towns frequently became less nucleated, with individual farmsteads instead "straggling" across wide spaces in the same manner as backcountry European settlers (see figure 6.1). In one well-documented example, in the years between the building of Fort Loudoun in 1756 and the American Revolution, and accelerating thereafter, Cherokee towns increasingly denucleated.[66] In another case, Mary Jemison, adopted by and living with the Senecas during the American Revolution, experienced the devastating impact of Sullivan's Expedition in 1779, which seems to have precipitated much of the population moving into outlying residences, now avoiding the nucleated town.[67] This denucleation was not a universal process, as not all Native communities were nucleated in the first place. The process by which Indian corporate territory became individualized Indian-owned parcels is not well understood and occurred in very different ways depending on local geography and local power relationships. Nevertheless it seems to have partially resulted from changes in the structure of military security. Villages inside palisades had become death traps, and nucleated towns and collective fields had become targets.[68]

But European military techniques represented more than dependence and disaster. For some Indian Nations at some times, Europeans and access to their weapons represented opportunity. David Silverman has shown how those Nations with early access to the Europeans—and thus early participation in the Native American military revolution—gained a military advantage that

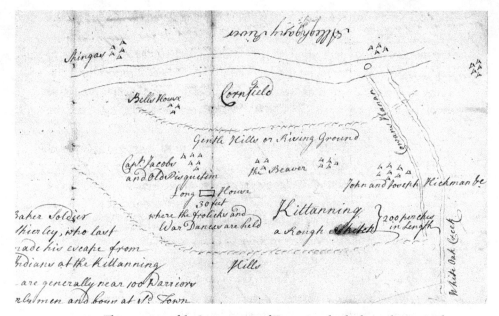

FIGURE 6.1 This 1755 map of the Lenape town of Kittanning clearly shows the scattered components of the town, with some parts of the population even residing across the river. Armstrong, John, "Plan of Expedition to Kittanning," Miscellaneous Manuscripts Collection, Mss.Ms.Coll.200, American Philosophical Society, Philadelphia, Pa. Courtesy of the American Philosophical Society.

they parlayed into greater power and influence over their neighbors.[69] For the Haudenosaunee, early access to guns (and axes) from Dutch suppliers gave them a decisive advantage over their traditional Wendat enemies, whose French trading partners long refused to supply them with guns. In contrast to earlier decades of apparent relative balance, Haudenosaunee campaigns from 1648 to 1652 forced a massive Wendat displacement, essentially forcing them out of their homeland.[70] Similarly, the New Brunswick Mi'kmaqs' readier access to French tools and weapons also seems to have enhanced the effectiveness and lethality of their raids on their agricultural neighbors to the south.[71] The Indians of the coastal Southeast experienced what seems to have been a succession of positions of power enabled by the gun trade, as one Nation and then another raided for Indian slaves to sell to the South Carolinians in the late seventeenth century, using traded guns to enhance their success as slave takers.[72]

In this respect, it is difficult to separate the effects of the changes in military techniques and technology from the broader effects created by trade and/or actual military alliance with Europeans. Were the Mohegans able to parlay their alliance with Connecticut into a greater share of regional power because they had more guns? More trade? Better diplomatic choices? The wide-ranging successes of the Haudenosaunee in the late seventeenth century are an even more marked example of the complexity of causes. Military superiority based on guns (and axes) and on a new ability to attack other Indian forts probably was a factor, but it seems unlikely to have been the primary cause of either their going to war or their success.[73] Intriguingly, Dixie Ray Haggard argues that the Westos' successes in seventeenth-century Georgia were enabled by their enemies' perception of *spiritual* power. The Westos' possession of some European technologies was more important as evidence of their great spiritual power than any actual material effect they had.[74]

Similarly, the presence of Europeans affected Native war practices in other crucial ways that were fundamentally less about technology and more about capitalism, labor, or European military inadequacy on the continent. The just-mentioned rise of Indians raiding other Indians for slaves arose from the early English colonies' quest for labor to expand agricultural production of cash crops (notably tobacco, rice, and indigo). For much of the late seventeenth century white planters sought Indians as laborers, but lacked the military capacity to force Native Americans into servitude. They instead turned to neighboring Indian Nations to act as slave raiders—trading them European goods for that purpose. The practice became widespread across the South, rapidly penetrating deep into the continent and disrupting the usual cultural systems for the treatment of prisoners. The discussion in chapter 4 of the roles of prisoners as adoptees, near kin, or even as subordinate labor was from within the Native American conception of war, and obeyed those limitations—even when the wars might have spun off from European-derived causes. In contrast, the devastating campaigns waged among successive Native Nations primarily driven by the demand for slaves in South Carolina were, in David Silverman's apt summary, "fundamentally a trade of humans for munitions in which marauding Indian slavers grew ever more formidable by selling captives for arms, while previous victims became raiders themselves in order to obtain guns for protection and predation."[75] In this case European demands did change the nature of Indian warfare, but not because of any European superiority or military technology.

The settlers' reliance on Indians to do the work of enslaving also extended to a separate dependence on Indian allies in a variety of other ways, some of which also fundamentally changed Natives' practice of war and warfare. When colonial governments introduced scalp bounties as a way of encouraging allied Indians (especially in the Northeast) to raid otherwise seemingly uncatchable enemies, for example, it changed the role of scalps as a symbol of success and spiritual power. It also likely changed how captives were treated.[76]

Ultimately, in another shift related to the role of capital in generating changes in the fate of captives, white prisoners came to be seen as a source of ransom. Native Americans quickly became aware of the lengths to which European families would go to retrieve prisoners, and the imperial wars between France and England formalized the process of redemption through ransom. James Axtell has argued that the whole prisoner-taking complex of Indian warfare shifted in response to this economic possibility.[77] Prisoners could still bring honor, but now they brought material reward as well—but only if returned. Adoption or incorporation never disappeared, but was substantially replaced by ransom (until the departure of the French) through the opposite imperial power's good offices.

Strictly speaking these changes in the function or role of prisoners were not a change to the nature of the polity itself, but they *were* a significant subversion or alteration of how Native Nations conceived of prisoners in cultural terms—where previously they had been incorporated into the Nation in some way, as adoptees or even as some form of forced labor, now, as prisoners for sale or as ransomees, they were seen and treated very differently. In this sense European arrival made a very significant mark on the nature and function of the polity, not through military technology or technique, but through capitalism.

In this same vein of multiple and complex causes, the process by which Native peoples broke apart, coalesced, confederated, or otherwise reshaped their polities in the late seventeenth century and into the eighteenth century can hardly be attributed completely to shifts in military technique, although it was closely tied to the experience of European colonization more generally. European intrusion caused a number of different demographic shocks, of which disease is only the most well known. Historians have long known about the occasional massive outbreaks of plagues like smallpox or measles, events that may have rapidly devastated single communities, but we now know that such occasions were relatively rare. Demographic analysis is beginning to show that equally if not more significant was population decline from the "slow violence" of settler colonialism: domesticated animals and shabby legal claims that nibbled away at standard subsistence practices and territories; trading interactions that persistently reintroduced diseases in endemic ways; traders who deliberately used alcohol as a primary trade good in ways that undermined families and social structures; and, in particular, the synergism between disease and the English-encouraged slave-raiding wars all around the southeast.

Under the persistent hammering of all these shocks there developed what Robbie Ethridge calls a "Shatter Zone."[78] In the Shatter Zone (which in many ways extended beyond the Southeast that Ethridge discusses), peoples broke apart, fled their traditional homes, and then recoalesced in new combined communities, reforming and even renaming themselves. Sometimes these new peoples proved to be stronger than their individual parent groups, and so they persisted and survived. In particular, the eighteenth-century confederations created by the Creeks, Cherokees, Shawnees, and Haudenosaunee were able to incorporate a host of other peoples and then use their position between competing imperial powers to assert their status as major military and diplomatic players.[79]

They did so while using the new technologies and new/old techniques of warfare, but the changes in those techniques were not themselves responsible for their coming together or for their status as regional powers in the eighteenth century. In Europe the introduction of chemical energy as a key facet of military power had produced a long-term change in the disciplinary structure of armies and a widening of social mobilization while initially retaining the old social hierarchy with nobility at the top. The resultant massive increase in the pool of labor that could be mobilized, however, eventually changed the political and social organization of the modern state. In smaller-scale Native American societies, in which virtually every male was already a warrior, the introduction of chemical energy did not change the mobilization of manpower. It was true, as David Silverman points out, that access to guns could lead to cascading victories as one gun-equipped society took advantage of another's lack of guns, but his work also shows that an equilibrium of equal access to guns was fairly quickly reestablished. And the guns themselves did not alter forms of mobilization, although the need to acquire them may have privileged war chiefs in the long run. What sociopolitical changes did take place as a result of new military technologies and techniques paled beside the slow violence of the enormous European demographic expansion and the Native American demographic decline from war, social shock, and disease. War and settler colonialism were very much part of the story, but specific military technologies were not driving the change.

CHAPTER SEVEN

Subjects, Clients, Allies, or Mercenaries?

The British Use of Irish and Native American
Military Power, 1500–1800

This chapter takes a different, mostly non-Indigenous perspective, but even as it does so, it highlights the military power exercised by Native American Nations and also compares and contrasts imperial exploitation of their power with the parallel case of Ireland.[1] English colonists and later British administrators pushing outwards into the Atlantic basin never had sufficient people or money relative to the scope of their ambitions, and European military systems provided only limited solutions. Improvements in European military technology and technique brought tactical superiority in most open-field confrontations, but battlefield superiority was not guaranteed, nor did they convey rapid strategic conquest capability over land. At sea western European superiority was more marked at both tactical and strategic levels, although Matthew Bahar has recently told the surprising story of how the Wabanaki of northern New England and the Canadian Maritimes persevered in building their own sailing navy and then contesting the control of local waters through the end of the Seven Years' War.[2] In the long run European gunpowder weapons and drilled infantry were designed to deal with peer enemies and had certain weaknesses against enemies who fought differently, especially those in large undeveloped geographic spaces. These weaknesses led colonizers and administrators to rely heavily on Indigenous power, through diplomacy, coercion, elite cooption, or some other means—a process that depended ultimately on the creation and maintenance of relationships, typically framed through Native cultural systems, including not least, trade. From necessity the English invented or altered traditional ways of mobilizing Indigenous populations to serve English military needs, and they did so in both Ireland and North America, with revealing similarities and differences.

From an imperial perspective Indigenous peoples could be employed militarily in three basic ways: as labor to be folded into a uniform military system, possibly through reclassification as a full imperial "subject"; as suppliers of specialty skills that added capability to the imperial military system (as mercenary or allied contingents—with a substantial blurring of the line between the two); or as clients who fought without direct assistance from imperial forces. "Client," as used here, implies an autonomous agent (state or "tribe") acting to benefit English interests without implying dependency. A Native Nation, for example, that warred against a third party that was also an English enemy was acting as a "client"—if only from an English perspective.[3]

Irishmen and Indians acted within each of these three categories, but with different results, emphases, and on different historical trajectories. Irish clients became too dangerous too close to home (the Spanish or French could exploit them as independent powers), and the English forced them down or out. Indians were long crucial as clients, albeit highly autonomous and often unpredictable. As specialists, the value of Irishmen declined in the late sixteenth century as the English army switched to pike-and-shot formations. As specialists, Indians proved indispensable in the continent-sized operations in North America, even in small numbers. The British continued to rely on Indian specialists through the War of 1812; Americans used them throughout the nineteenth century. But their specialty skills did not prove "exportable" outside North America. As labor in a uniform military system the Irish became progressively more acceptable, but along a bumpy road of anti-Catholicism and rebellion, and might never have been fully incorporated if not for a long fiction of recruiting "only" Protestants in Ireland. As labor Indians mostly refused to adjust to the British military system.

There was no simple linear progression in the way colonial or imperial agents imagined the Irish and Native Americans filling these needs. Nor were there exact parallels between the two contexts (and North America had *many* contexts, especially prior to 1720). Employing the Irish and Indians varied according to circumstances and administrative personalities, not to mention cultural prejudices. Furthermore, there were many variables that determined use, style of use, or nonuse of indigenous military resources.

Nonetheless, we can identify five rough parallels in the English/British experience on both sides of the Atlantic. First, English administrators sought to coopt Indigenous leaders through the granting of heritable titles, hoping thereby to centralize and simplify the process of diplomacy and mobilization. Second, Irish and Indian auxiliaries were believed to provide special military skills appropriate to a landscape lacking the infrastructure of European-style settlement. Third, personal relationships proved more successful in mobilizing Gaelic and Indian allies than bureaucratic arrangements. Fourth, English administrators depended on a lack of Indigenous unity—divide (or keep divided) and conquer was a crucial strategy. Finally, English/British authority was initially wielded through local, but nonnative, agents, whether Anglo-Irish earls (e.g., Kildare and Ormond) or provincial governments (e.g.,

Virginia and Maryland), who frequently competed with each as much as they combated Indigenes. In both arenas, a metropolitan presence and authority gradually expanded at the expense of both local authority and Indigenous autonomy. In North America, that process bred resentment among the local authorities (the colonists) and they eventually rebelled in a war that proved disastrous for Native Americans. In Ireland, Gaelic interests eventually partly merged with those of local authorities, mostly because of their shared Catholicism, but their joint rebellions failed.

Ireland

Between 1500 and 1800 the problems English administrators faced in Ireland changed dramatically. In the sixteenth century, bringing few resources to a region filled with warring locals, they were told to combine profitability with the assertion of sovereignty. Increasing hostility to English rule from both Gaels and Anglo-Irish, and the possibility of Ireland becoming a beachhead from which continental powers might attack England, complicated governance. To address these issues, English authorities inevitably involved Indigenous military resources, but also had to adjust to then-ongoing shifts in the nature and composition of European armies.

In sixteenth-century Ireland, the king's will was articulated first through a king's "deputy," himself a great lord with a personal retinue of soldiers, to which he could add additional troops at royal expense—either subject troops raised in England or Wales or mercenaries hired in Ireland. Together they comprised the King's retinue or English garrison. During the early Tudor period, the deputy was an Anglo-Irish lord, whose personal retinue derived from his holdings in Ireland, which he then supplemented with forces from allied Gaelic chiefs. In the first part of the century, the deputy was usually the Earl of Kildare, and his rental book from 1518 recorded his military arrangements with twenty-four Gaelic chiefs situated in a "wide arc around the Pale, plus a few quite remote chieftaincies."[4] Later deputies sent from England usually raised their retinues before embarking for Ireland and after mid-century relied more and more on royally financed troops. Anglo-Irish lords were expected to assist the deputy through their own "hostings" of soldiers from their lands. Locally available mercenaries supplemented the personal retinues of the deputy and Anglo-Irish lords, and were paid for by, or quartered directly on, the local peasantry.[5] English military efforts also typically drew on allies among the Gaelic lords, who had personal retinues of permanently maintained mercenaries supplemented by a "rising out" by subchiefs. Those allies were often tied to service by formal indentures.[6] In 1540 Lord Deputy Leonard Grey listed current indentures with Gaelic chiefs: for example, Cahir OmUlloy was obliged for six horsemen and forty kerne for one day and one night if given three days warning; Tybbot Burgh obliged for 120 galloglass for six weeks; and Fergananym Okarrell obliged to send twelve horsemen and twenty-four kerne to great hostings at his own charge, and eighty galloglass for three months.[7]

"Kerne" and "galloglass," both types of Irish troops, appeared in virtually every sixteenth-century tabulation of English forces in Ireland, either as mercenaries and/or as allies. A "kerne" (Irish *ceithearnach,* trooper) was both a soldier with a particular armament and a class of mercenary. Land-poor Irish freeholders could not afford armor and heavy weaponry, and so a kerne was "a kinde of footeman, sleightly armed with a sworde, a targett of woode, or a bow and sheafe of arrows with barbed heades, or else 3 dartes, which they cast with a wonderfull facillity." By 1600 they had also "growne good and ready shott" with firearms.[8] Some made such contract military service a profession. Wealthier lords retained such kerne as standing forces and quartered them among the peasantry.[9] The galloglass (Irish *galloglach* or foreign soldier), represented a truly professional class of mercenaries, originally from Scotland; by the sixteenth century they were permanently resident as hereditary clans or septs who hired themselves out to landed lords. By the final war of the century, however, they were much less visible and important.[10]

For English administrators, these troop types had three significant advantages. Endemic warfare (or at least cattle raiding) among Gaelic chiefs meant that a military profession as a kerne or galloglass was viable, even hereditary, in Ireland; and such mercenaries were often more reliable than one's own tenants or clients.[11] It was simpler to keep a body of kerne or galloglass (or both) always ready to hand. Additionally, although heavier English cavalry and longbowmen were superior in open-field battles, fighting frequently occurred in wooded, mountainous, and marshy terrain, where light Irish horse and highly mobile kerne held their own. Irish conditions and troops thus exemplified the value of Indigenous troops in an "imperial" context: they were readily available (in Ireland because of the proliferation of mercenaries; in North America because all men were warriors) and they provided abilities suited to the local environment.

Making the Irish Loyal Subjects

An enduring English objective for Ireland, from the Normans to the Hanoverians, was to have the island peopled with loyal subjects. Strategies to achieve it varied from incorporation to forced acculturation, intermingled with advocates for expropriation or expulsion. Neither incorporation nor forced acculturation prevailed as the sole approach, nor did they succeed in controlling Gaelic society or in making the Irish loyal subjects. The third and most extreme strategy was expropriation. All three found expression during the reigns of the Tudors and the Stuarts.

Central to Henry VIII's vision for tightening his lordship over Ireland was to transform "the 'sundry sorts' of people who made up the Irish population . . . [into] one class only, the king's subjects."[12] A process of elite co-option through granting English titles to existing Gaelic chiefs (called "Surrender and Regrant") proved initially successful, even allowing Henry to raise Irish recruits for wars in Scotland and France.[13] But Henry never really committed the resources to entrench the program, and the Irish refused to abandon their own systems of land tenure and succession.

In the mid-sixteenth century, as royal servitors of the Tudors began pushing hard for legal uniformity throughout Ireland, they increasingly defined Irish resistance as barbarity. This shift tilted English policy toward expropriation, beginning with the removal of local Gaelic elites and eventually even of the local Gaels. A clear division thus emerged between a royal vision of inclusion favoring legal subjecthood for Irishmen and the personal interests of the so-called New English who increasingly favored expropriation or even elimination.[14]

Elizabeth and the Conquest of Ireland

Elizabeth (r. 1558–1603) at first continued Henry's combination of sometimes violent arm-twisting with co-option. Inclusion, however, was now combined with new and forceful attempts at expropriation. There was a vicious cycle here, in which the "plantation" of English landowners and some settlers on land forfeited by rebels led to more rebellions (by both Gaels and the Anglo-Irish), and thus to more plantations. Repeated rebellions and tightening English administration finally culminated in the Nine Years' War (1594–1603) against Hugh O'Neill, the Earl of Tyrone.[15]

Throughout the century, the small English garrison in Ireland left royal administrators heavily reliant on Gaelic mercenaries and allies right through to the closing years of the Nine Years' War.[16] Elizabethan strategy anticipated "maximum use of Irish aid," and accounts of the Nine Years' War are replete with Gaelic chiefs aiding the English even at the height of Tyrone's success. Even when Gaelic allies proved reluctant to provide expeditionary forces, they could be expected to keep order in their regions—essentially as "clients"— and to provide cattle to English forces.[17] Furthermore, accounts of Tudor armies continued to list mercenary kerne and galloglass. Although galloglass mercenaries declined in importance at the end of the century, English leaders continued to emphasize the critical skills kerne provided in rough country: Sir John Perrot in 1571 described them as indispensable, and Edward Barkley in 1582 advised that English footmen be reequipped as horsemen and kerne since "our English footmen are able by no means to annoy them for want of footmanship."[18] Despite modest immigration of English soldier-settlers, and despite English victories in open battle with Gaelic forces, Elizabethan armies in Ireland continued to depend heavily on Gaelic manpower.[19]

This dependence chafed against the growing fear of an Ireland united by Catholicism to resist English rule and even aid Spanish invasion. In consequence, Elizabeth grew more willing to dispatch expensive English troops in response to major uprisings. From there it proved only a short step to consider eliminating the Gaelic military class as a necessary prelude to lasting English control.[20]

Military developments in England and on the continent reinforced that thinking. Continental armies had been decisively shifting to combinations of pike and shot, albeit in varying ratios and combined formations.[21] Pike-and-shot formations had become core components of successful armies, but the men in them were not specialty troops chosen for skills associated with their lifestyle.[22] Furthermore, the discipline required for the linear tactics of pike and shot valued soldiers for passive discipline, rather than the aggressive ferocity associated with the Irish in their native formations.[23]

The English shift to pike and shot occurred in conjunction with a gradual move to relying on the royal army rather than locally raised units.[24] The change implied imagining recruits as individuals to be folded into a uniform military system rather than as skilled specialists. Units of kerne and galloglass in English service became fewer, but Gaelic Irishmen became a growing presence in nominally "English" companies.[25] When the royal army in Ireland expanded to suppress rebellions many companies originated in England but were fleshed out with local "mere Irish" recruits, especially after sustaining losses while on campaign.[26] As early as 1550 officials worried about the consequences of this pattern and sought to limit the Irish in any English company to between 3 and 10 percent of the total.[27] By the 1580s and 1590s the real (although technically illegal) percentage had gone up considerably. Nicholas Canny analyzed eight English bands in 1586, 1588, and 1589 that were heavily Irish; another three, led by Irish captains, likely were almost entirely Irish.[28] During the Nine Years' War the English regularly integrated Irishmen into existing English companies, despite repeated injunctions limiting the practice, to the point where one muster in 1601 revealed 657 Irishmen out of an entire force of 1,250, while other observers in 1597 claimed more generally that more than a half to three-quarters of the English army were in fact Irishmen.[29]

In the immediate aftermath of the Nine Years' War, the short-term solution appeared to be to diminish the Irish as "subjects" and restrict them from bearing "Armes in the pay of the state (which should euer be committed to the hands of the most faithfull Subiects)" and further, with rare parliamentary exceptions, to disarm them.[30] In the long term, the potential of the Irish as individual recruits won out, but for at least a half century their Catholicism made them suspect, and the English attempted to maintain a purely Protestant (if not strictly *English*) army in Ireland.

The Stuarts and Beyond

After 1603, the colonization of English and Scottish subjects in Ireland, deliberate policies of banishing or resettling Irish "swordsmen," and the increasing unification of Gaelic and Old English Catholic opposition to the Protestant Dublin administration make it difficult to refer to "Indigenous" military labor. Most records fail to distinguish between Gaelic Irish and Old English.[31] Nevertheless, Irish manpower continued to be a crucial English consideration. The English army in Ireland after 1603 (eventually known as the Irish Establishment or the Irish army) was nominally open only to Protestants.[32] Nevertheless, during the crisis preceding the Civil War the Earl of Strafford, as deputy, raised Irish troops—including "as many Oe's and Mc's as would startle a whole council board"—for use against Scottish Covenanters.[33] The Cromwellian settlement in Ireland then excluded Catholics from the army, but at the Restoration, the Stuarts reversed the policy.[34] Catholics quickly became the majority of the army, with predictable political results when James II tried to summon that army to England in response to William of Orange's 1688 invasion.[35] Late in 1688, William III again stripped the Catholics out of the ranks, even going so far as to imprison some 1,500 men from predominantly Catholic regiments.[36]

The eighteenth century saw a major shift in the use of Irish Catholic manpower. The Protestant ruling elite in Ireland saw the Irish Establishment forces as their bulwark against another Catholic uprising. In contrast, the ruling elite in the British parliament envisioned the Irish Establishment as a strategic reserve, safely located outside of England and financed by the Irish parliament. Over the long eighteenth century, repeated war and attendant demands for manpower not only brought more and more Irish Catholics into the British army, but may also have helped spur Catholic relief legislation.[37]

At the outset of the century Catholics were strictly weeded out of the ranks; Irish Protestants were forbidden from enlisting in the Irish Establishment to forestall "backdoor enlistments" of Catholics, and men were to be recruited solely in England and Scotland.[38] Irish Protestants were allowed to enlist in 1745, and the demands of the Seven Years' War further opened the door to Catholics. By 1757, Irishmen comprised 27.5 percent of the British army in North America.[39] Officially Catholics and dissenting Protestants were still excluded from service, but such men were clearly enlisting in considerable numbers as officials in Britain and Ireland tacitly agreed that Irish Catholics in regiments sent overseas posed no threat to the Protestant regime in Ireland. In 1771 the 15th Foot was "said to be almost entirely Catholic."[40]

During the Napoleonic Wars Ireland became a major source for British infantry. Besides filling the thirteen named Irish battalions, some 159,000 Irishmen joined English regiments between 1793 and 1814.[41] In 1809, 34 percent of the soldiers of the 57th Foot (West Middlesex) were Irish.[42] In one study of twenty-two British unit rosters from the Napoleonic wars only one (the Royal Dragoon Guards) contained no Irish surnames.[43] Peter Karsten argues that these volunteers did not "view themselves as joining the British army, but as joining 'the Army.' Seven centuries of British rule, of one sort or another, had led most Irish people to accept the fact that, like it or no, they were part of the United Kingdom." Karsten defines the social profile of such men as "Catholic, poor, sometimes of an adventurous, bellicose sort, apolitical, 'who saw themselves as soldiers' by occupation."[44] These Irish recruits stand in marked contrast to the collectively recruited, socially respected, and skilled men of the sixteenth century, and indeed to Native American peoples, who retained greater control over the conditions of their military service.

Patterns and Themes in Ireland

Several important patterns emerge in examining the English experience with Indigenous military labor in Ireland. Perhaps the clearest is the length and difficulty of the process of English conquest. Technology and tactical changes were less important than the continual co-option and dividing of the Indigenous Irish and the final reluctant commitment of massive resources from England. This strategy exemplified a key characteristic of any successful imperial power: the ability to act in a more uniform manner than the divided peoples it faced. But English centralization was far from perfect, as shown by the number of rebellions initiated by Anglo-Irish lords. Centralizing control over the British American colonies proved even more tenuous, but *in extremis* the colonies generally worked together to defend each other in ways that were not the case among the Gaelic Irish or Native Americans. Occasional moments of near pan-Indigenous cooperation—the Nine Years' War in Ireland (1689–97), King Philip's War in New England (1675–76), or later "Pontiac's War" (1763–66)—loom large, but Indigenous peoples were still found on both sides.

The retention of local, Indigenous control over the conditions of their military service reflected the imperial power's belief that Indigenes possessed unique and necessary military skills, a belief that lent those peoples power. This perspective allows us to see how Indigenous "peripheries" negotiated the terms of their relationship to the core.[45] In early modern Ireland only limited fractions of locally available military labor served the English directly as mercenaries. Most Irish soldiers served as retainers of a Gaelic lord, who calculated political advantages from cooperation with the English or not. In turn, the English envisaged feudal mechanisms of mobilization for their end of the negotiation. Although English and Gaelic versions of those mechanisms differed, there were strong similarities, particularly in contrast to forms of mobilization among Native Americans, and the English had to adjust to their expectations. Ironically, English reliance on Gaelic chiefs probably impeded efforts to peacefully incorporate Gaels as subjects under English law.[46]

Crucial to the tapping of Irish manpower, either as skilled mercenaries or through allied Gaelic chiefs, were personal relationships. In the fifteenth and sixteenth centuries, the Anglo-Irish lords acting for the English crown depended on personal and familial ties to bring allies into the field. Later, English administrators replaced Anglo-Irish ones, and English commanders had markedly different success in using Irish mercenaries and allies, depending on their sensitivity to personal relations among Gaels.[47] This ability proved even more essential in North America.

The English faced dramatic limitations when attempting to use Indigenous manpower outside of local contexts, especially when recruited as separate, special-skill troops. With the exceptions of Henry VIII's use of kerne in Scotland and France in the 1540s, Irish troops only fought outside of Ireland in circumstances of civil war, from Lambert Simnel's fifteenth-century claim to the throne to Strafford's army of 1639 and the ensuing English Civil War.[48] Indigenous manpower was used primarily against Indigenous enemies; when a subordinate people were considered "Indigenous" in military practice, imperial overlords generally only imagined them useful against Indigenes of a similar type. As the Irish shifted from being merely Indigenous to being *dangerous* and Indigenous, particularly as military technology shifted toward increasingly uniform troop types, the English desisted from employing the

Irish for military labor, in part because of the political dangers they posed. The exception proving the point was their use in civil wars when manpower needs were more desperate and political control contested. Later their transition from "Indigenous" to more acculturated, but still "subordinate" from the political and ideological viewpoint of the metropole, made them attractive candidates for recruitment into a uniform military system, where they literally disappeared into the uniform itself. Crucially, this recruitment of Irish labor into the military occurred despite the objections from local Protestant elites, who still found the Irish "dangerous" and feared the consequences of arming Catholics. Ironically, the Hanoverian British, like their Tudor predecessors, returned to treating the Irish as "subjects" to be incorporated into the army like any other subject; indeed the lord lieutenant of Ireland in 1777 believed that his recruitment of the Irish for the American war helped connect "parts of a great empire."[49]

Native Americans

The extent, complexity, and necessity of the English use of Native Americans in aid of colonial and then imperial expansion in North America are now a familiar theme in early American history. In 1984 Francis Jennings frankly argued that "Indian *cooperation* was the prime requisite for European penetration and colonization of the North American continent."[50] Subsequent scholarship marked out several basic characteristics, now considered axiomatic, regarding the military potential of Native Americans and its use by the English. First, the tremendous impact of disease and social disruption on Indian populations diminished their capacity for military resistance to colonization and may have encouraged them to ally with the new arrivals to enhance their power over traditional enemies. Second, initial English "policy" regarding alliances with Native Americans was inconsistent and decentralized: each colony developed its own approach. That said, virtually every Anglo-Indian war had Indians on both sides. English (and later British) reliance on Indian aid occurred within two different ideological contexts. Initially, the English imagined Indians as both "good" and "bad"; the former would not only make good allies, but eventually good Christians. Over time, Europeans increasingly perceived Indians as incorrigible, allies only out of necessity, and not susceptible to any larger project of civilization. Lastly, and crucially, scholars have established how the value of Native American military assistance escalated as French-English imperial competition heightened from 1689 to 1760, a period coinciding with a shift toward viewing Indians as uncivilizable. The defeat of the French made it easier for the British imperial center to diminish the value of Indians as subjects or as allies, even as white imperial subjects escalated their violent pressure on Indian land. Native American confederations in the mid-eighteenth century temporarily reversed declining estimations of Indian usefulness and suggested greater demographic power. Yet, despite regional and personal variations, a greater sense of linear progression occurred in North America than in Ireland, *if only* because of the demographic decline of Native Americans.[51]

Early Exploration and Contact

England, a late arrival to colonial competition in North America, brought two crucial perspectives on the possible roles of Indigenous peoples. The first derived from experience in Ireland, but this precedent had limited applicability.[52] The English viewed the stubbornly Catholic Irish population as more damned than a pagan people potentially open to Protestantism. Furthermore, Ireland's proximity to England made any loss of control far more dangerous than the loss of a North American colony might be. Lastly, Ireland had centuries of history as an English "colony," while early English explorers in North America (the Puritans excepted) anticipated establishing bases for preying on the Spanish or for finding gold—goals that differed markedly from sixteenth-century visions of Ireland. The second crucial perspective, engendered by England's latecomer status, was the Spanish presence and experience as refracted through English sensibilities. In essence, they feared the Spanish more than the Indians, who, they hoped, would share their anti-Spanish attitude.[53]

These twinned perspectives shaped the experience of the early colonists at Roanoke, at Jamestown, and in New England as they wrestled with how best to exploit Indian military potential. In practice English settlers attempted to project the kind of dominance they imagined the Spanish to have achieved. They staged ceremonies to crown Indian leaders as kings subject to Elizabeth or James (Manteo and Wahunsenacawh), and wrote treaties that nominally subordinated a people to English control (the Plymouth Colony's treaty with Massasoit, which they then repeated with his son Metacom).[54] The hard reality, however, was the initial demographic dominance of the Indians. Failing to persuade or dominate Indians in any significant numbers during those early years (roughly 1585–1630), the English resorted to a defensive policy reminiscent of mid-sixteenth-century Ireland—fortified garrisons and a coercive approach informed by an edge of paranoia.[55]

The Native American Military System

Irish mobilization techniques and tactical methods determined the potential and limits of their use by the English; similarly, Indian mobilization processes and tactics shaped their relations with the English. As we have seen earlier in this book, mobilization hinged on both community consensus and individual willingness to participate. Individual men agreed to mobilize for various reasons: personal hopes to achieve status; a family or clan's need for revenge; confidence in the abilities of a particular war leader to bring success; and assorted spiritual and material rewards of success. Europeans quickly learned to cultivate young men eager for the social status conveyed by successful combat. Conversely, tribal elders could use the well-known aggression of their young men as a diplomatic threat. The Onondagas and Cayugas once reminded the Virginia governor: "Our Young Warriors are like the Wolves of the Forrest as you Great Sachem of Virginia know."[56] Once embarked on a campaign, the cutting-off way of war in the heavily forested continent emphasized loose formations, individual initiative, marksmanship, and fluidity.[57]

Within this framework, as we saw in chapter 6, European technology had limited impacts. Firearms made open battle more lethal, and any Native tendency for close-order battle faded in favor of the already prominent raid and ambush. The flintlock musket or rifle relatively smoothly replaced the bow, but rendered Native Americans dependent on Europeans for gunpowder and for repairs. Perhaps most significant was the ability of Europeans, if provided with logistics and cannon, to overcome Native American fortifications. This new wrinkle had a twofold impact. Native villages were no longer defensible against that kind of threat, thus changing defensive tactics. Furthermore, Europeans could now persuade Native Americans to accompany expeditions as allies in hopes of plundering their enemy's villages—now vulnerable to cannon.

"Persuading," however, remains a key verb. The British could not mobilize Native Americans through force or conscription. In the European imagination "persuasion" often included threats of disaster, or more positively arguments of self-interest. For Native Americans a distinctive sense of "self-interest" was never absent, but persuasive mobilization implied warring in mutual partnership with someone else. One method to establish relationships was through trade. Exchanging goods both satisfied certain material and luxury needs and served as an act of reciprocity in which both parties acknowledged the worthiness and value of the other. Mobilization required multiple points of articulation between some central authority and the individual warrior; in

Anglo-Indian negotiations trade served as a crucial lubricant at the critical articulation point between a European emissary and a Native people. Indian Superintendent Edmund Atkins recommended that the British send gunsmiths to live among the Indians (as the French had done), noting that providing a gun was a beginning, but having a gunsmith in a village sustained an ongoing relationship.[58] The Natives were not shy about making this point. The Haudenosaunee Confederacy acknowledged in 1712 that "it is well known the original Foundation of their Alliance with the Christians were the Advantages they received by Trading with them. That antiently they made use of Earthen Pots, Stone Knives & Hatchets & Bows & Arrows, that after they had purchased from the Christ[ns] Good Arms they conquered their Enemies. . . . (say they) our first entering into a Coven[t] with you was Chiefly grounded upon Trade." Having acknowledged that truth, the Iroquois leaders then complained that the current low prices for their beaver furs "may be the occasion of breaking that Chain of Peace & Friendship wch hath subsisted between us."[59]

A trading relationship, however, was only the start. Most Native American mobilization occurred through kin relationships. Blood relationships defined one form of kin connection, and adoption a second. Even more important militarily were fictive kinships between individuals and between peoples.[60] References to the English (or French) king as "great father" were no mere affectations. Rather they laid a foundation for cooperation, although they did not guarantee aid.[61] The English often failed to understand the full meaning of both trade reciprocity and fictive kinship in setting conditions and boundaries on relationships, although their own cultural background provided them with analogous mobilization mechanisms that proved easily adaptable to the reciprocity/kinship dynamic. While early English efforts at designating "emperors" or "kings" usually flopped, the offering of specific tokens to signify such roles proved more successful. Paper commissions, medals, gorgets, scarlet uniform coats, and other tokens of rank in English society fitted neatly into Indian value systems as symbols of reciprocity and kinship.[62]

The First Settlements

Most of the major British American colonies went through an "early" phase in their military relationship with Indians that shared several features, regardless of absolute chronology of settlement. The chronologies of these relationships are thus "relative" to the maturity of a European settlement and to the limited or nonexistent commitment of resources from the central government.[63] The key variable in the early phase of all these settlements was the numerical inferiority of the English, who if engaged in offensive warfare relied heavily on numerically dominant contingents of allied Indians for crucial numbers and special skills.

Two regional examples are illustrative. Initial New England efforts against the Pequots in 1637 were frustrated by Pequot mobility and their unwillingness to engage in an open-field battle. Eventually the English persuaded the Narragansetts and Mohegans, the regional rivals to the Pequots, to join in the attack. The allied Indians provided the crucial guidance through the swamps of Connecticut to the Pequot village at Mystic and also provided the bulk of the allied army in the attack. The Narragansetts' supposed horrified reaction at the destruction of Mystic and its population did not stop them from fighting a battle against the Pequots immediately afterwards, and some remained with the English force for the duration of the campaign.[64] As I have suggested elsewhere, the Narragansetts' horror merely reflected the destruction of the prisoners they had hoped for, and not culture shock at a way of war that used fire and mass killing.[65]

Decades later, South Carolina showed a similar English dependency on Indians. English attacks on St. Augustine, the Tuscarora War, and the Yamasee War all depended on Indian allies to fill out the combined army. If those allies refused, as they did on numerous occasions, then English forces frequently had to abandon the campaign.[66] The 1702 attack on St. Augustine included 500–600 white men and 300–600 allied Indians from assorted Nations (Yamasees, Chiluques, Apalachicolas, and others). South Carolina's first expedition in the Tuscarora War of 1712 had 30 whites and 500 Yamasees; the second expedition in 1713 started with 33 whites and 800–900 Indians from different groups.[67]

South Carolina also provides examples of Indians acting independently of direct English military aid but in English interests, reflecting "client" activity. The term "client" denotes independent operations with simultaneous pursuit of Indigenous and English interests. Proprietors and colonists, however, differed over the best way to use the Indians as clients. The proprietors (generally resident in England) preferred a stable long-term relationship with one people who could serve as a defensive buffer against hostile powers further afield. South Carolinians, in contrast, were mainly interested in the Indian slave trade and the short-term profits it provided, generating war among nearby peoples to produce slaves, and then turning to another group. Successive Indian peoples served as slave raiders on peoples progressively further into the interior for sale into the slave market in Charlestown.[68] These client wars for slaves may have been the dominant pattern of warfare in the Southeast at least through 1715. Even the attack on St. Augustine in 1702, nominally a territorial attack on a Spanish fort, was at least partly if not wholly motivated by the slave trade, as was the later attack in 1739.

Virginia provides a telling exception to this pattern of early settlers relying on numerically dominant contingents of Indians. The Virginians' experience of the Powhatan attack in 1622 seems to have long soured them on Indians as allies, despite some official efforts to persuade some Indians to join their side, and despite the early contact-era efforts to incorporate the Powhatans as subject-allies.[69] Virginia's seventeenth-century wars after 1622 singularly lacked Indian allies. On the one occasion in 1656 when more than a hundred Pamunkeys mobilized to help Virginians deal with the "western Indians," the English fled at the outbreak of fighting and left the Pamunkeys to bear the brunt of the lost battle.[70] The lack of Virginian-Indian military cooperation reflected both English choice and Indian reaction to the clumsy if not violent interactions created by the Virginians. If there was an especially xenophobic colony, it was Virginia.[71]

The Maturing Settlements

As colonies matured (the mid- to late seventeenth century for New England, New York, and the Chesapeake, the early eighteenth for Pennsylvania and the southern colonies), white demographic expansion and continued noninterference from England shaped military relations with Native Americans. Colonial interest in trading with Indians withered as their interest in Indian land exploded. That shift paralleled the demographic decline of Indians under the greatest English influence, "Praying Indians" in New England, or "settlement Indians" more generally.[72] The weakness of centralized British control tended to engender competition among colonies, for Indian land and for what Indian trade remained, competition that also undermined British capabilities to raise large Indian allied contingents. When hostilities with Indians or with other Europeans broke out, British governors did reach out for Indian alliances, but increasingly found only small contingents of Indians whose limited numbers restricted their roles to those of guides and scouts. When traditional means of persuasion failed to stir adequate numbers of Indians, colonial governments created a more mercenary device: the scalp bounty. Bounties for enemy Indians' scalps could be paid to anyone who took them, though the flesh and hair of friendly and enemy Indians was virtually impossible to differentiate. Indians and white men both took Indian scalps indiscriminately; bits of flesh and hair could be taken from friends or enemies, and friends were usually easier to find. In filling this role Indians approached a more European notion of "mercenary" but utterly without oversight or direction.[73]

King Philip's War (1675–76) in New England exemplified all of these devices as well as a newly emerging approach to mobilizing Indian power. Officially New Englanders struggled desperately to raise Indian allies with only minimal initial success. Scalp bounties were quickly approved to encourage the militia and potential Indian help; some Praying Indians allied with the English, although English fears confined their participation.[74] Public opinion in Massachusetts strenuously opposed using Indians, while Connecticut did to a limited extent, dispatching "combined parties of white and Indian volunteers in search of the enemy with the promise of pay, provisions, and the profits of their plunder," and scalp bounties.[75] In the end, the most significant, even decisive, help came from an unexpected source and heralded a new beginning for English-Indian military cooperation. The Mohawks, instigated by the English though also moved by a long-standing enmity for New England Algonquians, attacked King Philip's encampment near the Hudson River. The Mohawks acted as clients: independent of English forces, serving their own interests but also English needs.[76] If doubts about their autonomy existed, the Mohawks summarily demonstrated it in October 1676: asked to aid New Englanders against Indians in Maine, they instead raided Mohegans friendly to New England, including the Praying Town of Natick in 1677.[77] Subsequent diplomatic negotiations between New York and the Haudenosaunee formalized relations at a crucial turning point in the British colonial project.

The Imperial Wars

At the end of the seventeenth century, a number of trends among both Indians and Europeans began converging, first observable in New England then farther south. Native American populations showed marked creative adjustments, particularly as Native Nations increasingly confederated to maintain their strength, often while geographically situated in a way that made them crucial players in the British and French imperial contests. In Europe, Britain and France lurched into a long century of warfare that would end only with the defeat of Napoleon. In response, the French, many operating out of Canada, became imperially proactive: their relations with New York and New England were more militant; they planted settlements on the Gulf of Mexico and the Mississippi River, destroyed English fishing stations in Newfoundland, and captured Hudson's Bay Company factories. Meanwhile, the British government began centralizing control over its disparate North

American colonies. This trend was not continuous, as witness the destruction of the Dominion of New England by colonists in the Revolution of 1688–89. The metropolitan government also shifted its attention to other imperial arenas and at times was simply neglectful. Nevertheless, imperial wars repeatedly drew the imperial eye back to North America until the conflagration beginning in 1754.

The first systematic English effort at Indian policy, as distinct from episodic engagements, occurred through successive governors of New York, Edmund Andros and Thomas Dongan, who helped forge the covenant chain with the Haudenosaunee.[78] The English interpreted the agreement as an Haudenosaunee yielding of sovereignty, or at least a recognition of English claims of sovereignty over any territory or people over which the Haudenosaunee could claim sovereignty.[79] This hope for exercising sovereignty through the Haudenosaunee reflected the long-standing objective of finding or creating a figurehead leader who could manipulate an entire Nation. The English envisaged the Haudenosaunee as conveyors of sovereignty for a host of peoples, as well as being allies and clients in wars, in the first instance providing much-needed manpower to English military expeditions, in the second providing a buffer between the English and the French.[80] Dongan went so far as to claim that he could "have three or four thousand of their men at call."[81]

Naturally the Haudenosaunee perceived the situation differently, and they rearranged the "terms" of their "client" status at will.[82] In 1701, after heavy costs from too-active participation during King William's War, the Haudenosaunee opted out of Queen Anne's War by concluding the Grand Peace between themselves and both the French and the English.[83] In subsequent imperial contests, New Yorkers profited from that peace as the French avoided crossing Haudenosaunee territory, while New Englanders in frontier towns paid the price for the lack of an active Haudenosaunee ally. Francis Jennings argues that over the next two decades the Haudenosaunee became increasingly dependent clients of the British.[84] Jon Parmenter challenges that view, arguing persuasively that the Haudenosaunee continued to manipulate and set terms to their own advantage, in part because the British continued to view Indian aid as indispensable.[85]

Indians were in fact indispensable during the imperial wars of the eighteenth century. The British continued to hope for full-scale client participation, encouraging whole Nations to act on their behalf, and occasionally with modest success. But even small contingents of Indians were invaluable for providing intelligence of the land and of enemy movements, thereby contributing to the security of columns marching deep in the wilderness. Without them English soldiers often proved unable to move: John Tracy complained to Governor Fitz-John Winthrop in 1700 that "our English souldiars wait and loosse their time for want of Indians not knowing the woods or manners of that work, and Indians we can git none." The New England expeditionary forces against Acadia and Canada may have been as much as 25 percent Native American during King William's War, and 13 and 14 percent in the expeditions of 1707 and 1710 during Queen Anne's War.[86]

Intercolonial friction and recognition that military success in imperial wars required Indian participation led the British government to consider further centralization of its control over Indian relations. In 1755 Edmund Atkins suggested that it was "generally known and understood . . . that the prosperity of our Colonies on the Continent, will stand or fall with our Interest and favour among [the Indians]. While they are our Friends, they are the Cheapest and strongest Barrier for the Protection of our Settlements; when Enemies, they are capable by ravaging in their method of War in spite of all we can do, to render those Possessions almost useless."[87]

In anticipation of another and larger imperial war, the British government appointed Indian superintendents in 1755, William Johnson and Edmund Atkins, for the northern and southern Nations, respectively. Johnson's ability to persuade Mohawks to fight on behalf of the British was based on his personal relationship with them. Born in Ireland and an adopted Mohawk, he was more adept than most Englishmen at understanding and using diplomatic forms.[88] Atkins, in contrast, modeled a more "imperial" approach to Indian diplomacy. Although clearly aware of the basic issues in mobilizing Indian help, he lacked Johnson's personal intimacy. Atkins's 1755 report revealed many of the basic hopes and problems with British visions of Indians as allies or clients. He planned, though in vain, to forge a new covenant with the Cherokees like that with the Haudenosaunee, which could become the core of a confederacy of the southern Indian Nations. Controlled by a centralized British administration, southern Indians would "make Peace or War with other Nations by joint Consent."[89]

The French and Indian War (1754–63) sent contradictory signals to British administrators. Serious British losses during the early years of the war reinforced the lesson that Indians were crucial in wilderness warfare. British military and diplomatic failures stripped away their Indian allies, and officers identified inadequate backcountry expertise as the source of their strategic problem. Lacking Indians, and finding colonial "backwoodsmen" both expensive and truculent, British officers tried to create their own version of a frontier soldier, with limited success. The lack of Indian allies and hostility among Indians in the Ohio valley, fanned by indiscriminate murders by white settlers, engendered punishing Indian raids on the Pennsylvania and Virginia frontiers.[90] The later years of the war seemed to send a different message. British successes came as the British committed more and more regular troops to the continent and they engaged in more conventional operations, to include sieges and even a traditional linear battle on the Plains of Abraham outside Quebec. What may have remained hidden from British vision, however, was the impact that their naval blockade had on the ability of the French both to supply their troops and to provide the necessary trade goods and gunpowder to their Indian allies. As French trade dried up, so did Native allies. Furthermore, as the British sent regular troops in ever-greater numbers, their diplomatic efforts with Indians finally began to bear fruit. Major diplomatic initiatives brought Mohawks and Cherokees into the war on the British side. Both groups formed allied contingents within British forces, although British officers remained suspicious of their value.[91] British regular forces and expeditionary militia armies that lacked major Indian allied contingents still employed small groups of "settlement Indians" as rangers or scouts within the expeditionary organization.[92]

After the war, with apparently mixed signals about the importance of the Indians and the French threat finally gone, General Jeffery Amherst curtailed the traditional diplomatic gifts the British had distributed to maintain relations with Indian allies. Meanwhile, colonists, in a manner similar to the English administrators of late sixteenth-century Ireland, saw their interests not in relations with the Indians, but in the acquisition of their land. The imperial failure both to maintain proper relationships and to control the rapacious behavior of white subjects quickly led to violent reaction, popularly known as "Pontiac's War," but in reality a multipolar uprising of Indians against their former allies.[93] A similar situation had erupted south of the Ohio River. The royal governor of South Carolina seriously violated Indian norms of relationships when he imprisoned numerous Cherokee headmen and set off a war that consumed the southern frontier from 1759 to 1761.[94]

The American Revolution

The dangers and costs of the Cherokee War and Pontiac's War convinced British imperial administrators to reestablish basic relationships with the western Indians, and they made at least nominal efforts to control land-hungry white colonists.[95] Their efforts left British administrators better positioned than the rebels to raise Indian assistance during the American Revolution. Convinced of Indians' military utility, the British had great hopes for using them against the Americans. Some British administrators recognized, however, that the political costs could be high; almost all were surprised at the financial cost, as well.

Native Americans contributed materially to the British war effort, but their help proved expensive.[96] Indian Agent John Stuart argued that despite high costs "we have not been able to do it without them," and indeed the numbers could be impressive: in the first ten months of 1781 some seventy-five war parties totaling almost 3,000 warriors set out from Fort Niagara.[97] But the situation at Niagara illustrates the difficulties of balancing costs and effectiveness. After the rebels' 1779 campaign into Iroquois country, Niagara became a refugee center with approximately 5,000 Indians camped in the area all demanding provisions. Costs for maintaining the women, children, and some warriors ballooned to £100,000 in 1781. Bruce Wilson calculates that the cost of "provisioning the Indians at the three major upper forts, Niagara, Detroit and Michilimackinac, reportedly exceeded the cost of the whole military establishment in Canada exclusive of provisions."[98] In contrast, during the French and Indian War Lord Loudoun's staff calculated that a regiment of 1,000 colonial rangers cost £42,400 in its first year of operations, slightly less thereafter, a cost considered exorbitant at the time.[99] British General John Burgoyne claimed, with some exaggeration, that 1,000 Indian warriors cost more than 20,000 regulars.[100] Thus, although the British had a potentially large pool of motivated Indian allies, they needed substantial resources to keep them, and frequently their dependents, on task. The Seminoles in Florida arrived in large numbers to assist the British, but lack of resources obliged British officials to turn them away. East Florida's governor, Patrick Tonyn, complained that he remained powerless without an ability to supply the Seminoles, leaving him "invested with the mere shadow of authority."[101]

Financial costs were compounded by profound political costs for involving Indians as allies. Their use pushed potentially neutral Americans into the rebel camp and disturbed the sensibilities of the political public in Britain, which in turn gave leverage to the opposition party. The rebels famously included the British use of Indian allies as a grievance in the Declaration of Independence, and evidence suggests that Cherokee attacks in 1776 converted many colonists to the rebel cause.[102] Troy Bickham suggests that in Britain public opinion quickly and overwhelmingly condemned the use of presumably savage Indian allies; such rejection, Bickham argues, did not extend to using slaves or Loyalists, nor entirely to the rebels (despite the opprobrium implicit in that term), thus supporting the idea of an eventual British rejection of Natives as potential subjects within the empire.[103]

Themes and Patterns

The skills that Indians provided to European forces in North America—intelligence, local knowledge, skill at irregular war, and security, all made necessary by the nature of the country—are well recognized by historians.[104] Yet they may be usefully reexamined through the framework suggested by John Landers's analysis of preindustrial economies in Europe and the relation between an organic economy and state expansion.[105] Landers argues that state expansion is fundamentally an areal extension of coercive authority, but not all "area" is equal. Natural barriers, such as mountains, swamps, and forests, complicate a state's capacity to impose its authority. Authority often followed trade, he argues, because trade constituted a separate and multipolar dynamic areal extension of influence, independent of state funding but partially subject to state control because of trade's ultimate links to the metropole. The creation and "smoothing" of trade routes eased the extension of truly coercive authority. In the huge expanse of North America, Native Americans proved susceptible to trade integration—the novelty of European goods provided an important initial entrée, and the cultural role of trade for establishing reciprocity lent the system durability. Trade pursued by independent European agents provided knowledge of routes and peoples behind which coercive authority could follow. Militarily, however, European forces, which customarily used roads to move troops and supplies, were not equipped or prepared to move through the roadless tracts of North America without aid.[106] Indians, therefore, provided the only available organic means of deploying coercive authority over long distances—either as clients acting on their own, or as guides and enablers for conventional European forces. Like Irish kerne, they provided special skills adapted to their environment. They provided that aid, however, on their own terms.

Two separate trends mitigated the indispensability of these Indians' skills. The demographic and areal expansion of white settlement pushed accessible organic fuel and labor sources deeper and deeper into the interior together with a capillary-like network of local roads. Eventually regular forces could march inland and find settler-provided food sources. Where such demographic expansion had not yet occurred, political will and capital was required to build otherwise uneconomic military roads, as Generals Edward Braddock and James Forbes did on the Virginia and Pennsylvania frontiers, respectively. On the northern front the "roads" were the St. Lawrence River and the Hudson River–Lake Champlain axis.[107] Military roads were built for political needs, not in response to the normal course of economic development. Yet military roads could not be built for all needs, and thus Indians retained their military value as "speciality skill troops" for much longer than did the Irish. In this sense Indians were famous as "pathfinders" and scouts; they were road substitutes and without them English forces sometimes could not move.[108] As clients, Indians became a second-order areal extension of coercive authority, but only in the context of competition with other imperial powers or other Indians. As "secondary" components they were not perceived as suitable for coercion within the European cultural and political sphere. Thus their use during the American Revolution generated intense cultural friction—similar to the reaction to the use of Irish troops in England.

Calling Indians "secondary agents," however, does a disservice to their persistent maintenance of autonomy. They retained their own vision of their interests, and always conditioned their aid upon agreement within their home societies. Dependence on certain European trade goods, especially gunpowder, constrained their flexibility in responding. Similarly, the French departure in 1763 deprived the Indians of diplomatic leverage, but Pontiac successfully, if temporarily, reasserted the need for reciprocity in the imperial-Indian relationship. Another factor favoring Indian autonomy, especially during the seventeenth century, was the variable, even competitive, policies of the different British colonies, though fortunately for the British, even greater variability existed among Indian peoples. Divide and conquer remained a viable strategy for both colonists and imperial administrators—even as it had in Ireland.[109]

Over the long term, the major difference between Ireland and North America turned on the acculturation of the Indigenous population. By 1600 the English were recruiting individual Irish soldiers into uniform military units. While fear of Catholicism slowed their full incorporation until the late eighteenth century, the long-term convergence of Irish subject with British soldier was clear. Native Americans, in contrast, remained "special-skill" warriors, used as allies, clients, or mercenaries through the end of the first British empire, a difference arising in part from their value as scouts and guides within a vast continental theater, and in part from the frequent English inability (or unwillingness) to differentiate between friendly and enemy Indians. From the 1587 Croatoan request for some token by which to identify them as friends to Edmund Atkins's issuing of special passports in 1760, Anglo-Americans repeatedly demonstrated that to be Indian *and* friendly required visible proof.[110] That persistent need for a badge masked a deeper and more visceral shift in attitudes toward Indians, whether as allies or in general. Early generations of colonists imagined the transformation of Indians into Christian and civilized Englishmen. The failure of assimilation efforts and the devastation of King Philip's War contributed to "policies of segregation and discriminatory legislation" and countenanced fears of Indians, even those who continued to serve colonists.[111] Matthew Kruer suggests that the same problem afflicted Virginians after 1675. The colonists there, he argues, "struggled to tell the difference between Native friends and Native enemies," and believing themselves in the midst of "terrible danger," a "mixture of embattled masculinity, cognitive fatigue, and growing hatred led some colonists to stop trying to tell them apart."[112] Like the Irish, Indians had gone from being different and useful, to being different and useful, but *dangerous*. Indian usefulness meant that they would continue to be employed, but positive Anglo-American attitudes remained contingent on the continued usefulness of Indians.[113] James Fitch wrote in 1696 that "if now our Indians are kindly used, you may hereafter have more, if other wise non will stir." In contrast, General John Campbell during the American Revolution reportedly thought of Indians as people to "be used like slaves or a people devoid of natural sense."[114] The Virginia colonists' aforementioned reluctance to use Indian allies may merely make them precocious rather than aberrant. Yet the greatest reason for a failure to incorporate Native Americans as subject-soldiers was the equally potent rejection of subjecthood by most Native Americans. Bribed, persuaded, bullied they might be, but conscripted or lured by pay and rations into a uniform military system they would not.

Conclusion

At the outset of this chapter, I suggested that there were five basic parallels in England's military relations with Ireland and with Native America. Perhaps the key issue that connects all five, however, is the relationship between subjecthood and military role. "Imagining" a nation is fundamental to the expansion and coherence of the modern state.[115] One way for an outsider to be included in that imagined community is through military service. Irishmen and Indians were valued for their military capabilities, but since their initial military role was to provide unique "Native" skills, such service actually worked *against* imagining them as subjects. In one example, after the Peace of Utrecht in 1713, Massachusetts settlers felt freer to violate the boundaries of the lands that had been set aside for their converted and allied Indians—who had served in some numbers in the preceding two wars. Military service in this sense had acted as a prop to legal protections, but because their service was "ethnic," based on specialty skills, their military labor provided a less durable claim on full subjecthood.[116] The homogenization of European armies around firearms progressively limited the usefulness of Indigenous skills, and persistent cultural fears of the "wild (Catholic) Irish" or the "savage Indian" delayed their full admission to a new uniform military. Furthermore, the Irish and Indians resisted becoming subjects, and the power of their resistance forced the English to adopt models of incorporation other than outright conquest. In the sixteenth century, both in Ireland and in North America, the English approached colonization via the "conquistador" model, assuming that conquest of the land would be followed by parceling it out into estates (plantations) protected by soldier-settlers.[117] The Indigenes proved resistant to these plans. In Ireland "conquest" and plantation only succeeded after an enormous climactic military effort *and* after the flight of the defeated Gaelic earls. In North America English settlement occurred more haphazardly, not as the result of any particular military success. Native resistance was prolonged and powerful, overcome in the end by disease, the slow violence of colonialism, and by the progressive expansion of a white settler infrastructure that could support the movements of a European-style military. Irish and Native resistance therefore forced the English to accommodate and *use* Native power rather than exterminate it. One form of accommodation was to hold out English subjecthood and English civility to the Irish and the Indians. Both groups in turn toyed with subjecthood, using it to their advantage where possible, but in the end rejecting it, and with that rejection the offer was progressively withdrawn only to be restored in a different (and attenuated) form much later.[118] A major reason for that mutual rejection was local English authorities seeking their own gain at the expense of the Indigenes, stoking conflict and actively undermining the metropole's nominal hopes for incorporation.[119]

CHAPTER EIGHT

War's Ends

War achieves ends. That does not mean that war "works," or achieves the ends that someone, or even anyone, wanted, but war changes things—even if only for the individuals caught up in it. The ends achieved may or may not reflect individual or communal motivations for participating, but when socially cohesive polities who create, distribute, and husband resources necessary for communal survival use collective violence against some other such polity, there will inevitably be some "political" consequences.[1] We have already explored how the material and cultural environment of Native societies shaped *how they fought*, but those things also shaped the nature of the consequences. To put it another way, the range of political outcomes was limited by the past experience of what outcomes seemed possible, were advantageous, were sustainable, and so on, given the nature of their material world. The Native American way of war was patterned by its material realities, and although it flexed and adapted to changes in those material realities, it did so within a cultural imaginary that defined what war *was*.

The same thing can be said about the expectations for war's *outcomes*. What was victory? What did you do with it? How did you ameliorate defeat? In modern strategic thought, planners devise "ways" of using violence according to the "means" at their disposal in order to achieve their political ends. Because of our European source base, historians of Native American Nations have often struggled to understand what political ends they were seeking (beyond basic survival when attacked). And because of European colonialism, very many of the wars that we see most clearly were in fact Native wars of self-defense, which need little explanation. As for wars among Indian Nations, European witnesses often imagined them as simply about revenge (communal and personal) or individual prestige. Some modern scholarship suggests that the desire to dominate new trade possibilities created by the arriving Europeans led to an expansion of wars among Indians competing for trade routes and hunting territories. Other scholars argue instead that cultural motives were more important—notably the desire to take prisoners for adoption and to both grieve losses and restore populations wracked by war and epidemics.[2] We also have clearly seen inter-Indian wars generated by European eagerness to trade goods for Indian slaves, at least through the early eighteenth century.[3] It therefore seems unavoidable that we ascribe at least some of the postcontact inter-Indian conflicts to a desire to access European goods in one way or another. Nevertheless, even when scholars have acknowledged that warfare was common and socially significant in relations among Native American Nations, there has been a tendency to avoid being clear about its political function. Timothy Pauketat, for example, a leading expert on Mississippian chiefdoms, after describing a carving of one Mississippian warrior killing or scalping another, somewhat inconclusively suggests that "this sort of warfare was probably intended to intimidate an enemy if not also to achieve a strategic military goal."[4]

More usefully, some ethnohistorians have begun to emphasize sovereignty, stressing that Native Nations made territorial claims and defended them. But even that emphasis on Native defense of sovereignty remains focused on the problem of survival in the face of European incursions and thus limits our understanding of how Native Nations imagined the political outcomes of offensive war. I would argue that their vision of possible political outcomes was rooted in their experience of wars with each other, not with Europeans, at least not during this period. Let us consider, for example, the broad concept of "conquest." Did Indian polities violently dispute territorial sovereignty, with victors claiming territory taken from the losers? This possibility has been harder to identify and define, in part because many anthropologists and historians long resisted the idea that Native American warfare was indeed lethal and that it often aimed to enhance one group's power at the expense of another.

Fortunately, many scholars now recognize the pre- and postcontact role of violent competition for resources in Native American societies, agreeing that Native Americans, in line with much of the rest of the world, fought with deadly intent and with both individual and group interests in mind. This recognition has greatly expanded how we think about the motivations for wars among Native Nations. David Silverman, for example, recently summarized Native American motivations for war as "the defense or expansion of territory; the seizure of captives for enslavement and adoption; the negotiation of tributary relationships between communities; the revenge of insults; the protection of kin from outside aggressors; and the plunder of enemy wealth."[5] Silverman's assessment is supported by that of Thomas Forsyth, Indian subagent for the Kickapoo, Sac, and Mesquaki Nations in the early nineteenth century, whose history of those peoples concluded that "the case[s] that leads to war are many, the want of Territory to hunt, depredations committed by one nation against another, and also the young Indians to raise their names, will make war against their neighbours without any cause whatever."[6] And to Silverman's list, based on evidence threaded thus far throughout this book, I would add individual desires for revenge that spiral into a broader conflict, communal desires to resist enslavement, long-standing group enmities that sustain a blood feud cycle, a desire to access trade goods, war for captives for internal labor (in addition to adoption, sale, or ransom), and finally, to maintain a reputation for being able to strike back.[7]

These motivations are not mutually exclusive, especially when one moves from individual to collective motivations. One French officer, for example, claimed that it "is also customary, when they have been victorious at war, for the chief of the war party to leave a tomahawk on the battlefield. The emblems of the tribe and the number of warriors he had with him are indicated on its handle. He does this as much to show valor, as to defy his enemies to come and attack him. Some tribes merely make the same signs on a tree, stripping off the outside bark."[8] Whatever other motivation had led that war party to that place at that time, they *also* sent a message that turned a military result into a political outcome. To mark the field in that way was an act of reputation management—an assertion of power, of the ability to strike back if threatened or attacked. But it does not tell us why they were there in the first place.

This particular anecdote is a prime example of why we must at least notionally separate motivations for war from expected possible outcomes. In arguing for a political function and accompanying strategy and planning within Native American warfare, I am not arguing that we throw out all the substantial evidence for the role of individual or familial motivations to assuage grief, satisfy a blood debt, or enhance personal status. In part because Native American societies lacked coercive control over their members, purely "personal" motives for violence had a relatively easy outlet. But when individuals, or clans, or towns acted violently, they did not do so as autonomous individuals divorced from the remainder of their Nation. Their actions had political import, affecting the enemy's sense of vulnerability or that enemy's desire for revenge, or enhancing the overall martial reputation (and thus security) of their own Nation. The tomahawk left on the battlefield may (or may not) have been carried there for personal reasons, but as a statement to others it had political power.

Wars among Indian Nations may have begun for all of the reasons Silverman or Forsyth listed, but when we examine the patterns of military activity and the limitations of Native "means" and "ways" we can also see how military behaviors correlated to desired or least *expected and possible* political ends. As an analogy, consider for a moment how our twenty-first-century cultural imaginary determines what we *think* are the possible political outcomes of modern war, represented by outcome-related words like cease-fires, no-fly zones, sanctions, United Nations resolutions, peacekeepers, refugee camps, and so on. Meanwhile, other somewhat older terms have mostly fallen *out* of the cultural imaginary, including reparations, unconditional surrender, colony, or conquest.[9]

In Native wars, the most dramatic outcomes were either some combination of submission and tribute or territorial displacement. The other political outcome—and probably the most common—was some form of status quo ante. In this sense the "coups" discussed in earlier chapters of this book were a form of war as punishment and reputation management, interpreted by some historians, I think rightly, as attacks intended to reset relationships (including spatial/territorial relationships) to some earlier status quo.[10] Although he did not fully understand the complexity of the cutting-off way of war and the possibility of repeated harassing raids, the same Frenchman who described the tomahawk left on the battlefield accurately observed that "it was rather general custom among the savage tribes, not to continue warfare when they have been victorious."[11] Most of the time.

A key reason for this relatively limited spectrum of political outcomes was the limitation of means within Native American systems of war. As a general rule, the rewards of military victory in the preindustrial world were shaped and limited by the nature of expeditionary logistics, which in turn was heavily shaped by the fundamentals of that society's subsistence system.[12] Anthropologists studying North American societies have been more sensitive to this issue than historians, in part because they have been interested in the centralized and hierarchical precontact Mississippian chiefdoms. Mark Rees, for example, noted that the "expansion and maintenance of coercive authority" in the chiefdoms of precontact Mississippian societies was "ultimately dependent on terrain, productivity, and transportation, involving travel time to and from a primary center. The scale and recurrence of coercive violence is closely related to the imposition of chiefly authority through consensual means of legitimation."[13] In other words, the capacity of a society to wield coercive violence at a distance from its center is a function of logistics, and in most preindustrial societies, logistics was a function of calories, geography, and distance/time. Native American logistical systems, as we see them in the early historic period (mostly the seventeenth and eighteenth centuries), were ill suited to take-and-hold territorial conquest, which tends to require the imposition of garrisons as a coercive force during a postvictory period of consolidation and regime installation. In this sense, one explanation for the emergence of more hierarchical chiefdoms in the Mississippi basin, on the Gulf Coast, and in the Chesapeake Bay area under Wahunsenacawh may reflect in part the relative ease of movement of bulk subsistence goods by water. In the absence of waterborne movement, Native logistical systems tended to support repeated raids, but neither continuous war—meaning war with forces in constant contact—nor the maintenance of forces away from their hometowns beyond a single season. Instead, as we will see, the political outcomes for Native American wars tended to be imposing tribute on enemy peoples or *emptying space*, that is, forcing an enemy people to displace further away. This latter outcome would still result in a claim of sovereignty: it became the victor's territory, and could even be literally marked out as such on the ground.[14]

In short, whatever reasons Native Americans may have had for going to war, the outcomes tended to be: (1) emptying and claiming space / displacing the defeated; (2) imposing tribute; (3) maintaining reputation and thus enhancing home security; (4) gaining captives (for various purposes); and of course, (5) self-defense / maintaining sovereignty. Self-defense needs little discussion. The quest for captives is relatively well understood, even if historians are only now realizing the full variety of the meanings for "captives." Those meanings could include, depending on time and nation, true kin-replacement adoptees, slaves for sale, ransomees, and semibound labor for local use. The issue of tribute, however, remains peripheral in the existing literature, and displacement is barely discussed at all, and therefore the rest of this chapter will focus on those two outcomes, both of which have a territorial and a subsistence dimension.

Territory and Sovereignty

We thus find ourselves coming back full circle to the description of Native American demographic space as laid out in chapter 1, to which we must now add a discussion of territorial sovereignty. Chapter 1 briefly summarized how native societies lived and ate within a territorial space, but we must revisit that process of living from a more political perspective, assessing how they claimed and contested sovereignty over those spaces. Acknowledging these claims then and now is important, as they have long been deliberately erased by colonial processes. As Juliana Barr notes, our awareness of Native territorial claims (especially beyond the immediate environs of a town cluster) has been undermined by colonial mapping practices: "Euro-American maps functioned as geopolitical 'statements of territorial appropriation' that erased Indian geography by replacing Indian domains with blank spaces of pristine

wilderness awaiting colonial development. Imperial maps published in Se-
ville, Paris, and London (but particularly those later in Washington D.C.)
sought to legitimize territorial claims (and delegitimize those of Indians) by
superimposing their own lines across the North American landscape."[15]

Native claims of sovereignty were extensive, but variably visible. No one at
the time, not even the most biased European witness, could fail to see the territorial claim embodied by the town itself and its surrounding fields. Less immediately obvious was a Nation's claim over the wider region immediately
around the existing cluster of towns. That wider region not only provided
seasonal resources (an oyster bank for example) and the close-in hunting
grounds, but also served as the space within which the towns themselves
would likely relocate every generation or so.[16] This relocation phenomenon
is widely understood as a consequence of timber needs, wood rot in the
buildings, field exhaustion, vermin growth, and so on.[17] Crucially, however,
the past history of such movement, and its hypothetical future, also established a claim, even as it allowed abandoned or not-yet-occupied spaces to be
lent out for use by other peoples in a friendly relationship. In the words of
historian Jeffers Lennox, in this case referencing the Northeast, "Indigenous
peoples recognized exclusive rights to land, but that exclusivity was never
permanent because villages would migrate every few years and abandon
what land they had been using." Ultimately, he argues, "Indigenous geographic
boundaries were more fluid and susceptible to established migratory patterns, but the boundaries existed, were enforced, and shaped how each group
related to their geography and to the region's other inhabitants."[18]

That need for future town sites combined with the even more extensive
need for distant hunting grounds to create conflict, as was made vividly clear
to William Bartram in the late eighteenth century as part of an explanation
for the frequent movement of Creek towns. The Creeks, he was told, regularly needed "fresh or new strong land for their plantations; and new, convenient and extensive range or hunting ground." It is important to note this
distinction between "convenient" and "extensive" hunting ground, which in
most cases was a seasonal issue—the latter grounds were used for extended
hunting trips in the winter. However, it is equally important to note that the
deerskin trade with Europeans greatly expanded both the length of the far
hunting season and the territorial requirements, and overharvesting may
have put even further pressure on the need for hunting grounds. This is another way in which European contact and trade possibilities exacerbated traditional rivalries, in this case over hunting grounds.[19] Close-in convenient
hunting supplemented the diet during the farming season, but winter hunts

typically ranged much further from the home village. Bartram's interlocutor then noted the consequences of this extensive need, as it "unavoidably forces them into contentions and wars with their confederates and neighbouring tribes; to avoid which they had rather move and seek a plentiful and peaceable retreat, even at a distance, than to contend with friends and relatives or embroil themselves in destructive wars with their neighbours." Avoiding conflict with friends and relatives, however, sometimes led them into conflicts with others. In a quest for more hunting land, the Creeks, it seemed, had sought the "destruction of the Yamases . . . which they at length fully accomplished; and by this conquest they gained a vast and invaluable territory, comprehending a delightful region and a most plentiful country for their favourite game, bear and deer."[20]

This example from the Creeks suggests the extent to which the spaces between town clusters might have been uninhabited, but they were neither unused nor unclaimed. As crucial parts of the seasonal pattern of subsistence, hunting and gathering grounds, which could be very extensive territories, were marked, claimed, and contested in various ways. As Anthony F. C. Wallace long ago demonstrated for northeastern Indians, "there were no 'common hunting grounds' where members of any tribe might enter and hunt at will." Joint use by separate peoples arrived at through "alliance, amalgamation or dependency" or even just temporary permission was common enough. But the evidence for sovereignty claims over hunting grounds is extensive, to include one Nation asking another for permission to hunt. Wallace provides the example of a 1690 peace agreement between the Haudenosaunee and the Wendat, Odawa, and others, as a part of which the Odawa received several wampum belts, "the third of which 'hung up a sun at the strait between Herier and Lake Huron, which should mark the boundaries between the two peoples,' and this sun should give them light when they were hunting.'"[21] Frenchman Pierre Pouchot, writing in the 1750s and referring generally to Indians of the Great Lakes and St. Lawrence region, described their seasonal trek to the interior for the winter hunt, noting that "they consider [the country] as belonging to their nation." He later emphasized that they were very attached to that land "and it is always a cause for war when one nation comes to hunt on territories of another. Indian travellers even take good care to leave the skins of the animals they have killed on the lands of another nation hanging from the trees so it [they] can get the benefit of them."[22] André Pénicaut, traveling up the Mississippi from the Gulf of Mexico at the outset of French colonization there, noted how the Bayagoulas delineated their boundary with the Houmas with a red stick, and furthermore that "these two nations were so jealous of the hunting in their territories that they would shoot at any of their neighbors whom they caught hunting beyond the limits marked by the red post."[23] In the 1750s the Abenakis threatened to go to war to protect their territorial integrity against English cutting timber or hunting beaver north of a specified boundary.[24] And Brett Rushforth has explored how the Indians of the seventeenth-century *pays d'en haut* staked and defended territorial claims to "hunting, fishing, and agricultural sites against their neighbors' pretensions." This defense was necessary in part because of the arrival of peoples displaced by Haudenosaunee attacks further to the east. Eventually the borders of each Nation settled down again, and a later European observer noted that

> the most uncultivated among them are well acquainted with the rights of their community to the domains they possess, and oppose with vigour every encroachment on them. Notwithstanding it is generally supposed that from their territories being so extensive, the boundaries of them cannot be ascertained, yet I am well assured that the limits of each nation in the interior parts are laid down in their rude plans with great precision.[25]

The precision of claims notwithstanding, political reality in the relationships between potentially hostile Nations meant that there was more than one kind of uninhabited land. Even if nominal claims to a hunting ground might literally abut, as in the case of the Houmas' and the Bayagoulas' red stick, safety in hunting meant that de facto buffer zones would grow up between hunting territories or within overlapping claims. Early Spanish wanderers in the Native Southeast frequently noted the wide expanse of seemingly vacant land between Nations—well before any European diseases would have affected the population. Aubrey Lauersdorf's research on the Apalachees explicitly calls these buffer zones, a concept also familiar to archaeologists who have identified uninhabited spaces between town clusters based on the archaeological record.[26] Such areas were extremely productive of game, precisely because they were *not* inhabited, and thus claiming them and even fighting for them became desirable.

Figure 8.1 (repeated here from chapter 1) portrays a generic version of all these territorial relationships. Where an archaeologist, or an ill-informed European traveler, might, based on the absence of habitation sites, conclude that the hunting areas were also unclaimed, only the *overlapping* claims constituted a true buffer zone, where both sides might find it dangerous to go, but which would also prove tempting, as a place where deer and other game would proliferate. Understanding these relationships between subsistence

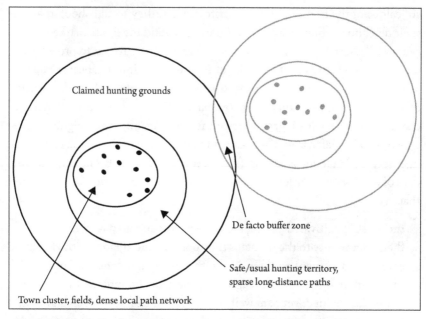

FIGURE 8.1 An idealized representation of Eastern Woodlands demographic space, showing the relationship between two town clusters and their territorial claims. Scaling does not allow for an appropriately large "claimed hunting grounds" circle; these circles could be very extensive. Drawn by the author.

and territorial space is essential to making sense of how submission and tribute worked, but especially in understanding how war to "empty space" functioned.

Submission and Tribute

Historians have long understood that some form of tribute from enforced submission existed among Native Nations, in part because it was highly visible in three crucial early contact zones: southern New England, the Chesapeake Bay, and the late Mississippian Southeast during the Spanish *entradas*. "Submission" in this context refers to the admission by one Nation that another's attacks had made their lives unsustainable, but that rather than move away, or continue to fight at a significant disadvantage, they offered to make peace, usually at the price of some form of tribute. In world-historical terms this was by far the most common outcome of military defeat (or sometimes the outcome of simply a military threat when the power differential was extremely lopsided). The nature of the tribute could vary from symbolic delivery of exotic goods to the bulk delivery of subsistence goods on a regular basis, or a commitment to serve as military allies in future wars, with nearly endless permutations and combinations of these three in varying levels of severity. Among Native American Nations tributary relations could be some form of bulk subsistence transfer (attested for each of the three regions just mentioned), but there were also more symbolic claims of "owning" a people, perhaps most famously the Haudenosaunee claim over the Lenapes. In that case, military defeat led the Lenapes to surrender control over their foreign policy and to allow a Haudenosaunee chief to live among them (although only briefly). But they retained autonomy in almost all other ways, including control over their own territory. In contrast, the Susquehannocks, also defeated by the Haudenosaunee, were treated more severely, being forced to depart their original home territory and to be absorbed as new kin into the Haudenosuanee Nations.[27]

More common, and certainly more visible, however, were tributary relationships that involved a transfer of goods, especially of maize, but also of wampum—a form of currency with real value in the complex operations of the northeastern fur trade. It is also important to note that tributary status, although hierarchical in the sense that it reflected a winner and a loser, also reflected an ongoing and reciprocal relationship—not unlike how we might think of patron-and-client systems. In general, subsistence would move to the patron, who in turn, at a minimum, extended his or her protection, but may also even have redistributed some of that tribute, since such redistribution was at the heart of much political authority within Native American Nations. Dylan Ruediger puts it neatly when he defines tribute "in its indigenous form" as a "circulatory and reciprocal exchange of goods from inferior to superior and back again."[28]

Various tributary relationships emerged, ended, evolved, and shifted throughout the greater New England area in the seventeenth and eighteenth centuries.[29] The Mahicans, for example, defeated by the Mohawks in the 1620s, paid a tribute in wampum, which Colin Calloway interprets as less about domination and more about cooperation and alliance, but it was definitely a consequence of defeat and it represented a rearrangement of their political relationship.[30] Similarly, Calloway narrates how the Sokokis in 1650 hoped to escape their annual tribute of wampum to the Haudenosaunee by joining an alliance against them, with the clear implication that tribute was burdensome.[31] Both Silverman and Allan Greer characterize the whole region as interwoven with tributary relationships. The former describes southern New England in the 1630s as an array of Wampanoags, Pequots, Mohegans, and

Narragansetts in dominant roles jostling among an assortment of more loosely organized Nipmucs, Woronocos, Pocumtucks, and so on, all of whom "competed with each other constantly for followers and to establish or escape hierarchical, tribute-paying relationships in which weaker parties paid wampum (shell beads), furs, and corn to stronger ones." Later in the century, Metacom of the Wampanoags began to lose his tributaries on Cape Cod and the nearby islands when they became "Praying Towns" under the sway of the Massachusetts Bay Colony and ceased paying tribute, as did those Nipmucs who had been paying tribute to Mohegans and Narragansetts.[32]

Submission followed by substantial tribute payments represented a significant acquisition of resources for the victor when they consisted of bulk subsistence or wampum. Although the "winners" may not have acquired either territory or absolute control over a population, they had acquired more resources and enhanced their reputation for power—which served to increase their security from attack. It is likely that the management of this kind of relationship was the sort of thing that led to the so-called coup-style attacks discussed in earlier chapters. A dominant Nation facing a truculent tributary could launch a brief flurry of raids as a political "reminder" of who was in charge. The attack or attacks would then be followed by a pause, to allow the tributary to make the appropriate submission in a newly reinforced subordinate relationship.[33]

One of the clearest pictures of how submission and tribute might have worked, and how it might ultimately lead to even greater centralization of power, comes from the workings of the Powhatan chiefdom. Here the process of subordinating a large number of smaller Nations had been well under way before the English arrival at Jamestown in 1607. During the last two decades of the sixteenth century and the first decade of the seventeenth, Wahunsenacawh, a chief among the Pamunkey people living on the James and York Rivers near present-day Richmond, gradually brought a wide array of the region's peoples into a tributary relationship. Although at times referred to as a confederacy, or an empire, at the time that it was encountered by the English colonists, it may be best to call it a paramount chiefdom. There seems little doubt about the extent of his power over much of that region's population. The conflicts that led to that arrangement are mostly obscure, having occurred prior to permanent English settlement. John Smith, our primary source, claims that Wahunsenacawh had inherited a chief's position over several groups near the falls, including the Powhatans, Arrohatecks, Appamattucks, Pamunkeys, Mattaponis, and Youghtanunds.[34] By the time John Smith and the other English arrived, however, he had extended his authority over many other peoples beyond this initial core. Fortunately for us, there are a few key glimpses into how Wahunsenacawh and other Indians in the region imagined the role of war in reconfiguring resources and relationships. The first glimpse comes from how he acquired rule over the Kecoughtans in the 1590s; the second was the submission of the Chickahominies in 1616; and finally there was the destruction of the Chesepians (or Chesapeakes) probably around 1607.

The Kecoughtans, living at the far eastern end of the peninsula between the York and James Rivers (a highly strategic position if one is worried about future visits from Europeans entering the bay), were a late addition to Wahunsenacawh's rule, having successfully resisted him for some time. With the death of their chief in the 1590s, however, and the accession of a weaker man, it became vulnerable and Wahunsenacawh attacked, "killing the Chief and most of them." The rest he forcibly resettled among his own people while turning the territory around Kecoughtan over to one of his sons. Some years later, Kecoughtan's survivors petitioned to live at Piankatank, which itself had been essentially wiped out and the land emptied by Wahunsenacawh in 1608, possibly in retaliation for the Piankatanks helping John Smith earlier that year. Wahunsenacawh attacked that village by surprise, killing twenty-four men and bringing the surviving women and children to his capital at Werowocomoco as "prisoners" who "doe him service."[35] In this case Wahunsenacawh's ends were both to increase his sense of security and to procure labor for use within his own personal circuit.

We have better documentation for the status of the Chickahominies, who, by the time the English arrived in Jamestown were apparently the only Nation still independent from Wahunsenacawh's tributary rule within the broad region lapped by the waters of Chesapeake Bay. According to William Strachey, however, they did "pay certayne dutyes" to Wahunsenacawh (symbolic tribute only?), and were willing to fight for him if paid in copper. So, in fact, they may have been "tributary" while other Indians were more "conquered." In other parts of the world, there are many shades of gray to the meaning of "tributary," but unfortunately our sources in this case are not precise. What is clear is that the Chickahominies remained substantially independent, to include their foreign policy. The latter became clear in 1614 when the Chickahominies sought to bolster their independence by entering into a treaty of alliance with the Jamestown colonists, who had been in persistent episodic conflict with Wahunsenacawh. Within a year, however, the colonists' many needs, arrogant insistence, and outright violence had alienated the Chickahominies, and they instead submitted as tributaries to Wahunsenacawh's rule (not later than 1616), although it is possible that they still retained a greater degree of autonomy than other peoples within the chiefdom.[36]

The third example, the Chesepians, is bleaker. Wahunsenacawh, apparently informed of a prophecy of an enemy to the east who would unseat him, utterly destroyed their village, leaving it initially vacant. It was soon reoccupied by the Nansemonds, another of Wahunsenacawh's submitted Nations.[37]

In these three examples we find that Wahunsenacawh warred to empty territory in fear of threats to his authority—threats possibly identified by their geographic situation as possible allies of future European visitors; he warred to establish tributary relationships over other towns; and he warred to establish control over people and redistribute them around his territory. This represents a wide range of political goals, a range that historian James Rice suggests closely resembles the actions of a state.[38] Wahunsenacawh's ambition had worked. His chiefdom had achieved a level of centralization that allowed for more radical incorporation of peoples, and even their forced movement *within* his territorial bounds. To rise to that level of power, however, seems to have begun with simple war for tribute: to force a group to submit to his authority at least to the point that they regularly sent him tribute in material form. On one occasion Wahunsenacawh showed John Smith a line of canoes on the riverbank, and indicated how they were used to collect tribute from assorted Nations along the bay—tribute of "Beads, Copper or Skins."[39] Interestingly, all of those items were objects conveying status, and Wahunsenacawh was seeking to control their distribution in a way that reinforced his dominance, although some scholars suggest that given the context (and Smith's limited fluency in the language) that it is difficult to tell whether this was really tribute or some form of exchange.[40] In addition to these status items, however, there is also evidence for Eastern Shore Indians providing substantial tribute in the form of corn.[41] And William Strachey made a broader claim that *each* subordinate chief held his land from Powhatan, "unto whom they pay 8 parts of 10 tribute of all the Commodities which their Country yieldeth, as of wheat, pease, beanes, 8 measures of 10, (and these measured out in little Caddies or Baskets which the great king appoints)."[42] Young Henry Spelman, who lived for over a year as a kind of adoptee among the Powhatans, and became an interpreter for the colony, affirmed the existence of such tribute, noting that each subordinate town gave up part of its harvest for storage by the Powhatan. Karen Kupperman argues that his possession of all that corn allowed Wahunsenacawh to redistribute it during the long winter, or as needed, and that this power of redistribution was the ultimate source of his broader political power.[43]

The forms of tributary submission narrated here for New England and the Chesapeake were not necessarily challenges to territorial sovereignty.

The Chickahominies and the many other tributary Nations in the Powhatan chiefdom still thought of and farmed their land as their own. They surrendered a part of their produce, but not their territorial claims. It was only as Wahunsenacawh's access to tribute increased, as did his claim on the military service of more and more towns, that he was able to enforce a more radical form of submission, including, as with the Kecoughtans, taking and holding territory and enslaving the inhabitants.

Emptying Space

There were other options, however, as hinted by the fate of the Chesepians. The Chesepians, a small Nation trapped against the ocean by a much bigger neighbor, had little option to move, and Wahunsenacawh did not give them the opportunity. Elsewhere in eastern North America, however, larger enemy Nations were unlikely to be completely destroyed in a single attack. Alternatively, concerted, successful, repeated raiding could make a region seem uninhabitable. Forcing an enemy Nation to move further away was a natural outgrowth of the nature of Native American demographic space. Making one's enemy move further away decreased their likely overlapping claim to hunting territory, increased one's own, and made it more logistically challenging for them to retaliate. This was a form of conquest, and many early European sources (some quoted already in this chapter) argued that Indians were as invested in territorial conquest as anyone. Thomas Forsyth, mentioned earlier as the early nineteenth-century agent among the Kickapoo, Sac, and Mesquaki Nations, noted that allies were often recruited for war by "promising them a portion of the enemy's country they may conquer."[44] Anthony F. C. Wallace, years ago, argued that land transfer among Indians could happen through "purchase (by Whites), conquest, and abandonment." "Conquest," he argued, "was clearly recognized in native theory during historic times, and it requires a Rousseauistic retrospective utopianism to suppose that it was not also recognized before contact."[45] Even so, there has been a tendency to miss the reality of Native conquest, in part, I argue, because we do not see territory being *occupied*. Instead, it was rendered empty.

Intriguingly, there are direct accounts of this precise relationship available from the long conflict and subsequent aftermath of the Creek-Cherokee War of 1715–54. Chapter 5 explored the impact of that war on the changing use of fortification in the Cherokee towns, and by coincidence it also happened to show the disappearance of quite a number of Cherokee towns—something that might seem initially to correspond simply to the known decline in total

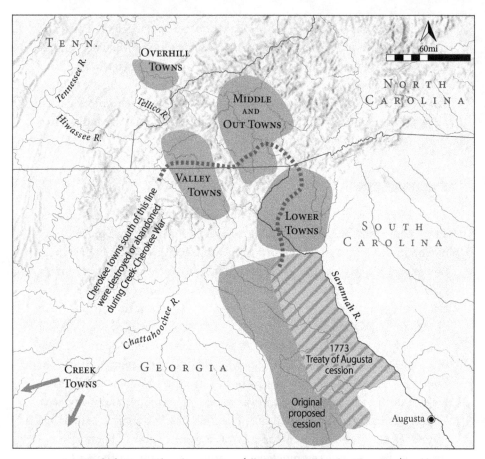

MAP 8.1 Creek claims to Cherokee territory (albeit contested by the Cherokees) and how they shaped the 1773 Treaty of Augusta. All the Cherokee towns south of the dotted line were destroyed or abandoned during the course of the war. Matilde Grimaldi.

population. It was only later that I realized that the spatial quality of their disappearance and the time span over which they did so corresponded to the Creek-Cherokee War. It seems likely that repeated Creek attacks on the most exposed Cherokee towns led those Cherokees to relocate (see the dividing line in map 8.1).

The narrative evidence supports that supposition. Desperate messages from leaders of the Cherokee Lower Towns in 1752 complained of losing population to Creek attacks, so badly that it "has occasioned all our Lower Towns to break up and wander all over the Nation, all but this Town and Ke-howe."[46] Nine chiefs from the Middle Towns also wrote to the South Carolina governor about the "great many which is driven amongst us by the enemy." This claim gained support from white trader James Beamer, who lamented the breakup of the Lower Towns, and the defenselessness of the remainder.[47] Historian Kathryn Braund interprets this last phase of the long war as intended to expand Creek hunting territory, and the 1754 peace treaty arbitrated by South Carolina included a Cherokee cession of land to the Creeks.[48]

In addition to this cession, the contraction of the Lower Towns cluster reduced the de facto Cherokee claim to the hunting lands further to the south. And two decades later that defeat was thrown in their face when the Cherokees sought to relieve their debts by ceding this land to the colonists in the early 1770s. The Creeks immediately objected, saying that they claimed "part of . . . [that] land in *right of conquest*, having obliged the Cherokees during the war between them to abandon it." Ultimately the original proposed cession was scaled back into the Treaty of Augusta of 1773, jointly signed by the Creeks and the Cherokees (see map 8.1). The whole dispute, however, highlights not only how the Creeks claimed to have gained ownership of new territories abutting the abandoned Cherokee towns, but also how the Cherokees persisted in asserting sovereignty over a huge hunting ground, thus creating overlapping claims that could become contested buffer zones.[49] Interestingly, in an earlier cession of Lower Towns land (engineered by Overhill Towns' leadership), the Overhill chief Oconostota claimed that ceding the land mattered little since it was "worn out" (hunted out?).[50]

It is rare to see Native Americans so clearly making this kind of legalistic claim on another Nation's territory through the "right of conquest." One notable other example was the Haudenosaunees' explicit assertion of control over Lenape territory in 1744, saying "since that Time we have conquered them, and their Country now belongs to us."[51] But even in the absence of sources spelling out these legalistic and explicit conquest claims, what we very often *do see* is the reaction of the defeated who chose to displace. The frequency with which defeated peoples chose to relocate suggests the extent to which it was a part of the normal cultural imaginary for responding to defeat. This is not to say that migration was easy or painless, but some Nations clearly chose it as preferable to submission. Such a choice reflected both their subsistence system and the logistical limits of their attackers. The attackers' campaign logistics could not sustain them remaining in country, since doing so would depend on both stored food found in the captured town and on the labor of the defeated, either held as captives, or forced to supply tribute as a now-subordinated population. Furthermore, we have seen how the operational pattern of the cutting-off way of war did not anticipate a single great victory; it instead often achieved its victory over time, through repeated raids that made life unbearable. As for the defeated, Native subsistence systems already depended on a certain level of mobility, whether seasonally for hunting or gathering, or decadal, in terms of moving the fields or even moving the town.

The loser, therefore, had the option of displacing and avoiding submission and a tributary status. The winner would return home and the newly vacant space between the enemies would expand, refilling with game, and with more of it claimed by the winner. This kind of displacement appears even in the earliest Spanish sources in the Southeast. In 1584, after a joint Spanish-Indian attack, the Potanos displaced west to avoid similar raids in the future. Intriguingly, the *holata* (chief) of the Potanos later negotiated a protective alliance with the Spanish in order to reoccupy the abandoned town site, suggesting that indeed, security was the prime consideration.[52] Examples of displacement proliferate rapidly when seen in this light: the migration of the Lenape, of half of the Tuscarora, and of the Shawnee, the coalescence of the Catawba combining multiple displaced peoples, and many more.[53]

In making this argument for displacement it is essential to again point out how words matter. As I argued in chapter 2, "skulking" unnecessarily and inaccurately minimizes the sophistication of Native American warfare. In this case, *displaced* is a far more accurate term for the defeated than *scattered*. Towns moved themselves entire, carrying their population, leadership, and culture with them. On some occasions a cluster of towns might not be able to relocate as a new intact cluster; the towns might combine, or be set up at some distance from each other, at least initially, but the people were not scattered. Brett Rushforth makes this point about the Wendats displaced into the *pays d'en haut*, and we can use their example over an even-longer time frame and across multiple displacements.[54] That story begins in part with Jacques Cartier's famous 1535 voyage up the St. Lawrence River and his encounter there with an Iroquoian-speaking people living in densely populated towns at both Stadacona (Quebec) and Hochelaga (Montreal). When Champlain returned to the same location in 1603 the people were gone, and archaeological and linguistic evidence suggests that they were at least related to the Wendat, and that some of the "missing" inhabitants had moved to the existing Wendat town sites on the north shore of Lake Ontario.[55] In the late 1640s the Wendat towns there were attacked and displaced by the Haudenosaunee (as discussed in chapter 2). It is this latter displacement, combined with other Nations also displaced by Haudenosaunee aggression at that time, that Rushforth is careful to characterize as not having been shattered or scattered, but undergoing a geographic dislocation— a normal response to defeat—rather than a "cultural reorientation."[56]

Although the Wendat displacement covered a very significant distance, sometimes the displacement, as with the Cherokee example just discussed, was *intraregional* rather than transregional. Wahunsenacawh suggested a similar form of intraregional displacement in his early dealings with Jamestown, telling Ralph Hamor that if the English became too aggressive, his "country was large enough" and he would just move further away and avoid violence with the English.[57] The Sugarees within the coalescing Catawba Nation moved their town at one point, albeit only slightly, because of all the towns in the Nation, it was the one most exposed to Haudenosaunee raids.[58]

Some of the displacements mentioned in this discussion were from colonial pressure (the Tuscaroras for example), but as suggested in chapter 1, the patterns for warfare and the cultural imaginary of political outcomes were set by wars among Indians, and those remained the most important types of conflicts for many decades after 1600. Wars of Indians against Indians set the patterns for both warfare and how to manage defeat. The defeated did not *always* displace; it was after all a dramatic option, fraught with all the labor necessary to plant new fields, build new homes, learn new paths, and so on. The Paspahegh chief Wowinchopunck admitted this truth to John Smith, but even so continued to threaten him with it. If the English kept attacking, he said, the Paspaheghs would just leave, and "you will have the worst by our absence, for we can plant any where, though with more labour, and we know you cannot live if you want our harvest. . . . If you proceed in reveng, we will abandon the Countrie."[59] Migration was never easy, and the sense of a home territory was real, thus the Potanos' *holata*'s desire to return to his original town site—it was his Nation's home. The difficulties of migration also explain the frequent resort of a displaced town to coalescing, at least temporarily, with a related or allied Nation, who could aid them through those hard initial transitional steps.[60]

As a political outcome, displacing an enemy increased the territory of the victor. It was not a take-and-hold form of conquest in the classic state style, in which a defeated population was subordinated to a new hierarchy now resident among them. But it did establish a claim to new hunting territory. And this form of conquest was a result that followed naturally (along with the other outcomes of taking captives and imposing tribute) from the cutting-off way of war and its logistical capabilities and limits. The flexible provisioning on the move could sustain a form of conquest by harassment.[61] Small parties, and sometimes large ones, could hit the enemy, return home, resupply, and return to the fight—sometimes, as related in chapter 3, they could use advanced hunting camps as their point of resupply. Because of the men's role in the annual subsistence system, they found it difficult to maintain a campaign year-round, but in the long term they could sustain low-intensity fighting for years at a time. It wasn't "continuous"; it was episodic, but also potentially long term, and repeated success would make a territory effectively uninhabitable. This is another way in which early European witnesses might misunderstand the larger intent of Indian warfare. Colin Calloway, for example, cites Garcilaso de la Vega's observations in the 1540s to conclude that Mississippian warfare did not include territorial conquest. De la Vega was looking for a city to be taken and held, or for garrisons to be distributed around the countryside. This was unsustainable in the cutting-off way of war. Its techniques, however—attacking, destroying, and retreating—*could* lead to conquest when sustained over the long term. Furthermore, as when the Powhatans were led by a successful leader like Wahunsenacawh over a long period of time, the cutting-off way could even lead to paramount chiefdom formation and more. For European witnesses, however, it was only natural that they looked for what they expected—open battle, siege, occupation, and conquest—while denigrating warfare that did not match those expectations.[62]

The Europeans soon encountered those very techniques and capabilities, as Native Americans turned them against the new arrivals, expecting that the harassment would ultimately displace them. John Smith described Jamestown as being under this kind of persistent harassment, claiming "wee had sometime peace and warre twice in a day, and very seldome a weeke, but we had some trecherous villany or other."[63] William Bradford in the Plymouth Colony reported on the Pequots' efforts to build an alliance against the English, arguing that the English were the real enemy, likely to take over the country if they were "suffered to grow and increase." To stop them, the Pequots proposed to avoid "open battle with them," but instead to "fire their houses, kill their cattle, and lie in ambush for them as they went abroad on their occasions; and all this they might easily do without any or little danger to themselves. The which course being held, they well saw the English could not long subsist but they would either be starved with hunger or be forced to forsake the country."[64] Bradford's focus on the avoidance of open battle is a reflection of his own prejudices, not a Pequot adaptation to European enemies. Otherwise, however, what he described was the normal cutting-off way of war waged to support a strategy of displacement. The same pattern continued into the eighteenth century. In Matthew Ward's account of the Lenapes' efforts in the 1750s to regain their land east of the Alleghenies, he concludes that their raids "principally focused on civilian targets, seeking to drive all settlers from the region." The Lenape had been forced to sell this land by the Haudenosaunee, and now they "sought to empty Berks and Northampton Counties . . . not only by destroying the settlers' farms and plantations but also by creating widespread panic and hysteria, causing the settlers to abandon their homes ahead of raids."[65]

NATIVE AMERICAN SYSTEMS of war were designed and carried out to coerce their enemies: to make them move and so gain territory; to make them submit and so increase resources and influence; and to gain captives for labor, for trade, and to sustain their societies. They fought to win, and although they faced increasingly steep demographic odds from the swelling European populations, they continued to do all those things effectively and with great geopolitical awareness. Their lives, their resistance, and their successes depended also on their skills at trade, diplomacy, and more, but their way of war, adaptive and flexible as it was, contributed mightily to the persistence and survival of Native people in North America. The stories of their individual Nations, their alliances, and their successes and failures bear recounting in that light.

Notes

Abbreviations in the Notes

Barnwell's Journal ▪ John Barnwell, "Journal of John Barnwell," *Virginia Magazine of History and Biography* 5, no. 4 (1897–98): 391–402; 6, no. 1 (1898–99): 42–55.

CCM ▪ J. S. Brewer and William Bullen, eds., *Calendar of the Carew Manuscripts Preserved in the Archiepiscopal Library at Lambeth, 1515–1624* (London: Longman & Co., 1867–73).

CSPI ▪ Great Britain Public Record Office, *Calendar of State Papers, Relating to Ireland, 1509–1670* (London: 1860–1912).

CSP-CS-AWI ▪ *Calendar of State Papers, Colonial Series, America and West Indies, 1574–1739*, CD-ROM, ed. Karen Ordahl Kupperman, John C. Appleby, and Mandy Banton, (London: Routledge in association with the Public Record Office).

Draper MSS ▪ The Draper Manuscript Collection, State Historical Society of Wisconsin, Madison, Wisc.

DRIA ▪ William L. McDowell, Jr., ed., *Documents Relating to Indian Affairs*, 2 vols. (Columbia, S.C.: Colonial Records of South Carolina, Series 2, 1958, 1970).

Four Masters ▪ Michael O'Clery, Cucogry O'Clery, Ferfeasa O'Mulconry, Cucogry O'Duigenan, Conary O'Clery, and John O'Donovan, *Annals of the Four Masters: Annala Rioghachta Eireann (Annals of the Kingdom of Ireland)* (Dublin: Hodges, Smith, and Co., 1854; repr. New York: AMS Press, 1966).

HNAI ▪ William C. Sturtevant, general editor. *The Handbook of North American Indians*, 20 vols. (Washington, DC: Smithsonian Institution Press, 1978–).

H.St.P. ▪ *State Papers Published Under the Authority of His Majesty's Commission, King Henry the Eighth*, 11 vols. (London: HMSO, 1830–52).

James Grant Papers ▪ Papers of James Grant of Ballindalloch, National Archives of Scotland, Edinburgh, Scotland—Microfilm ed., Library of Congress (Box numbers for the originals in Scotland originally corresponded to reel numbers in the microfilm edition, but were later changed by 1; cites herein are to the original box numbers as indicated on the film containers).

Johnson Papers ▪ Milton W. Hamilton, ed., *The Papers of Sir William Johnson*, 14 vols. (Albany: The University of the State of New York, 1921–65).

JR ▪ Reuben Gold Thwaites, ed., *The Jesuit Relations and Allied Documents: Travels and Explorations of the Jesuit Missionaries in New France, 1610–1791*, 73 vols. (Cleveland: Burrows Brothers, 1896–1901).

Lyttelton Papers ▪ William Lyttelton Papers, William L. Clements Library, University of Michigan, Ann Arbor.

NCCR ▪ William L. Saunders, ed., *The Colonial Records of North Carolina* (Raleigh, N.C.: various publishers, 1886–90).

NLI ▪ National Library of Ireland.

NYCD • E. B. O'Callaghan, et al., eds., *Documents Relative to the Colonial History of the State of New York* (Albany, N.Y.: 1853–87)
TNA • The National Archives (U.K.)

All spelling is left as found in the original sources except where previous editors have modernized it.

Chapter One

1. The precise timing of the arrival of maize in places like Ontario or New England is still debated, and it was preceded by other agricultural crops, so this is not about dating the arrival of "agriculture," only maize.

2. The best survey of changing war practices in precontact North America remains David H. Dye, *War Paths, Peace Paths: An Archaeology of Cooperation and Conflict in Native Eastern North America* (Lanham, Md.: AltaMira Press, 2009), esp. 144–45.

3. Although the first Spanish *entradas* in the Eastern Woodlands did not begin until the 1530s, it is likely that fishermen of various European nations were encountering Native Americans in the far northern reaches of the zone decades prior. And the fetishization of 1607 or 1584 as the date of the "first" English contacts ignores the powerful evidence for earlier Euro-Indian interactions and the speed with which knowledge and goods spread. John Smith found the Tockwoghs on the upper Chesapeake in 1608 already equipped with metal tools, presumably traded from more northerly nations' near-contemporaneous contacts with the French. In addition, there are the now well-documented travels of the Powhatan or Paspahegh named Paquiquineo/Don Luis from the Cheseapeake to Spain, Mexico, and Cuba and then back to the Chesapeake in the 1560s. Philip L. Barbour, ed., *The Complete Works of Captain John Smith* (Chapel Hill: University of North Carolina Press, 1986), 1:231; James Horn, *A Land As God Made It: Jamestown and the Birth of America* (New York: Basic Books, 2005), 1–9; and Helen C. Rountree, *Pocahontas, Powhatan, Opechancanough: Three Indian Lives Changed by Jamestown* (Charlottesville: University of Virginia Press, 2005), 26–28.

4. My very first book has a brief section on the patriot expeditions against the Cherokees during the American Revolution. It was my intense dissatisfaction with my own narrative that put me on the path to center Native American thinking about war.

5. I deliberately use the term "military forces" because they were the armed representatives of their society. Using the term puts Indians on the same semantic footing as the forces of the Old World. It is not, however, a claim of a separate military institution.

6. The sources and examples for this description are in chapter 2.

7. Patrick M. Malone, *The Skulking Way of War: Technology and Tactics among the New England Indians* (1991; repr., Baltimore: Johns Hopkins University Press, 1993).

8. Wayne E. Lee, "Conquer, Extract, and Perhaps Govern: Organic Economies, Logistics, and Violence in the Preindustrial World," in *A Global History of Early Modern Violence*, ed. Erica Charters, Marie Houllemare, and Peter H. Wilson (Manchester: Manchester University Press, 2020), 236–60.

9. David J. Silverman, *Thundersticks: Firearms and the Violent Transformation of Native America* (Cambridge, Mass.: Belknap Press of Harvard University Press, 2016).

10. John Landers, *The Field and the Forge: Population, Production, and Power in the Pre-Industrial West* (New York: Oxford University Press, 2003).

11. And to be clear, "group reputation" had key strategic consequences explored later in this book. For a look at the many ways Indians modified their environments, see William Cronon, *Changes in the Land: Indians, Colonists, and the Ecology of New England* (New York: Hill and Wang, 1983); and James Rice, *Nature and History in the Potomac Country: From Hunter-Gatherers to the Age of Jefferson* (Baltimore, Md.: Johns Hopkins University Press, 2009), esp. 5–6. These issues are also discussed further in chapter 3.

12. The following generic description is generally uncontroversial, sustained by detailed descriptions in a wide variety of sources. I have not felt compelled to cite more than is absolutely necessary for key specifics.

13. Gabriel Sagard, *The Long Journey to the Country of the Hurons*, ed. George M. Wrong and H. H. Langton (Toronto: The Champlain Society, 1939), 103–4.

14. R. Douglas Hurt, *Indian Agriculture in America: Prehistory to the Present* (Lawrence: University Press of Kansas, 1987), 27–31.

15. Hurt, *Indian Agriculture*, 29–33. Hurt suggests that the Wendats received 75 percent of their nutrition from agriculture, whereas interior Southeastern New England groups received only 25–50 percent from agriculture. In the Deep South, agriculturalists could in theory get enough food for the whole year just from corns, beans, and squash (although no doubt they greatly varied it when possible). More discussion of regional dietary variation is found in chapter 3.

16. This general pattern is well established in the literature, but as one example of the evolution of scholarly understanding of this pattern among the northern Iroquoians, note the dates of publication and see Bruce G. Trigger, "Settlement as an Aspect of Iroquoian Adaptation at the Time of Contact," *American Anthropologist*, New Series, 65, no. 1 (1963): 86–101; Susan Bamann, Robert Kuhn, James Molnar, and Dean Snow, "Iroquoian Archaeology," *Annual Review of Anthropology* 21 (1992): 435–60; and Eric E. Jones, "Population History of the Onondaga and Oneida Iroquois, A.D. 1500–1700," *American Antiquity* 75, no. 2 (2010): 387–407.

17. Peter A. Thomas, "Contrastive Subsistence Strategies and Land Use as Factors for Understanding Indian-White Relations in New England," *Ethnohistory* 23, no. 1 (1976): 1–12.

18. M. Boyd, T. Varney, C. Surette, and J. Surette, "Reassessing the Northern Limit of Maize Consumption in North America: Stable Isotope, Plant Microfossil, and Trace Element Content of Carbonized Food Residue," *Journal of Archaeological Science* 35 (2008) 2545–556; Hurt, *Indian Agriculture*, 33. See Bruce J. Bourque, *Twelve Thousand Years: American Indians in Maine* (Lincoln: University of Nebraska Press, 2001), 87, for Mi'kmaq raids on Indians living along the Kennebec River for corn, leading the latter ultimately to give up growing it.

19. Susan Sleeper-Smith, *Indigenous Prosperity and American Conquest: Indian Women of the Ohio River Valley, 1690–1792* (Chapel Hill: University of North Carolina Press, 2018), 51–53.

20. Timothy R. Pauketat, *Cahokia: Ancient America's Great City on the Mississippi* (New York: Viking Penguin, 2009), 2.

21. Mary Lucas Powell, "Ranked Status and Health in the Mississippian Chiefdom at Moundville," in *What Mean These Bones?: Studies in Southeastern Bioarchaeology*, ed. Mary Lucas Powell, Patricia S. Bridges, and Ann Marie Wagner Mires (Tuscaloosa: University of Alabama Press, 1991), 23.

206 Notes to Chapter Two

22. Kristin M. Hedman, "Late Cahokian Subsistence and Health: Stable Isotope and Dental Evidence," *Southeastern Archaeology* 25, no. 2 (2006): 258–74; Clark Spencer Larsen, *Bioarchaeology: Interpreting Behavior from the Human Skeleton,* 2nd ed. (Cambridge: Cambridge University Press, 2015), 305–7. Powell, "Ranked Status," however, suggests that this dietary difference was not as profound as often reported.

23. This discussion of Mississippian society derives from Timothy R. Pauketat, *Chiefdoms and Other Archaeological Delusions* (Lanham, Md.: AltaMira, 2007); and David G. Anderson, "Fluctuations between Simple and Complex Chiefdoms: Cycling in the Late Prehistoric Southeast," in *Political Structure and Change in the Prehistoric Southeastern United States,* ed. John F. Scarry (Gainesville: University Press of Florida, 1996), 245–46. The question of Mississippian cultural continuity into the historic period is contentious and complex. See Adam King, "The Historic Period Transformation of Mississippian Societies," in *Light on the Path: The Anthropology and History of the Southeastern Indians,* ed. Thomas J. Pluckhahn and Robbie Ethridge (Tuscaloosa: University of Alabama Press, 2006), 179–95; Robin Beck, *Chiefdoms, Collapse, and Coalescence in the Early American South* (New York: Cambridge University Press), 3–8; and Robbie Ethridge and Sheri M. Shuck-Hall, eds., *Mapping the Mississippian Shatter Zone: The Colonial Indian Slave Trade and Regional Instability in the American South* (Lincoln: University of Nebraska Press, 2009). There are many other site-specific studies, some collected in Charles Hudson and Carmen Chaves Tesser, eds., *The Forgotten Centuries: Indians and Europeans in the American South, 1521–1704* (Athens: University of Georgia Press, 1994). References for Mississippian warfare can be found in chapter 2.

24. Pierre Pouchot, *Memoirs on the Late War in North America, Between France and England* (Youngstown, N.Y.: Old Fort Niagara Association, 1994), 440.

25. This shift is discussed further in chapter 6. Also see David L. Preston, *The Texture of Contact: European and Indian Settler Communities on the Frontiers of Iroquoia, 1667–1783* (Lincoln: University of Nebraska Press, 2009) 35, 86–87, 125–28; and Kurt A. Jordan, *The Seneca Restoration, 1715–1754: An Iroquois Local Political Economy* (Gainesville: University Press of Florida, 2008), 163–68, 198–224.

26. James D. Rice, "War and Politics: Powhatan Expansionism and the Problem of Native American Warfare," *William and Mary Quarterly* 3d Ser., 77, no. 1 (2020): 31–32.

27. James Axtell, *Imagining the Other: First Encounters in North America* (Washington, D.C.: American Historical Association, 1991), 6–7.

28. I find Jill Lepore's discussion of King Philip versus Metacom to be persuasive on this subject. *The Name of War: King Philip's War and the Origins of American Identity* (New York: Alfred A. Knopf, 1998), xix–xx.

29. For good discussions of naming issues, see April Lee Hatfield, "Colonial Southeastern Indian History," *Journal of Southern History* 73 (2007): 575–76; Brooke Bauer and Elizabeth Ellis, "Indigenous, Native American, or American Indian? The Limitations of Broad Terms," *Journal of the Early Republic* (forthcoming). Thanks to Liz Ellis for sharing this article with me in draft.

Chapter Two

1. I explore the wider politics of this episode in Wayne E. Lee, *Barbarians and Brothers: Anglo-American Warfare, 1500–1865* (New York: Oxford University Press, 2011), 140–51.

2. Tobias Fitch, "Captain Fitch's Journal to the Creeks, 1725," in *Travels in the American Colonies,* ed. Newton D. Mereness (New York: Macmillan Co., 1916), 202–5.

3. This chapter is substantially new, but also reuses and expands on material from several of my earlier works, including Wayne E. Lee, "The Military Revolution of Native North America: Firearms, Forts, and Polities," in *Empires and Indigenes: Intercultural Alliance, Imperial Expansion, and Warfare in the Early Modern World,* ed. Wayne E. Lee (New York: New York University Press, 2011), 52–61; Wayne E. Lee, "Fortify, Fight, or Flee: Tuscarora and Cherokee Defensive Warfare and Military Culture Adaptation," *Journal of Military History* 68 (2004): 713–70; Wayne E. Lee, "Peace Chiefs and Blood Revenge: Patterns of Restraint in Native American Warfare in the Contact and Colonial Eras," *Journal of Military History* 71 (2007): 701–41; and Lee, *Barbarians and Brothers,* 151–56.

4. Daniel K. Richter, *The Ordeal of the Longhouse: The Peoples of the Iroquois League in the Era of European Colonization* (Chapel Hill: University of North Carolina Press, 1992), 35; Bruce G. Trigger, *The Huron: Farmers of the North,* 2nd ed. (Fort Worth: Holt, Rinehart and Winston, 1990), 54; Adam J. Hirsch, "The Collision of Military Cultures in Seventeenth-Century New England," *Journal of American History* 74, No. 4 (1988): 1191; J. Frederick Fausz, "Fighting 'Fire' with Firearms: The Anglo-Powhatan Arms Race in Early Virginia," *American Indian Culture and Research Journal* 3 (1979): 34; and Patrick M. Malone, *The Skulking Way of War: Technology and Tactics among the New England Indians* (1991; repr, Baltimore: Johns Hopkins University Press, 1993), 29–31. Timothy Shannon repeats this older interpretation with more nuance in his "The Native American Way of War in the Age of Revolutions, 1754–1814," in *War in an Age of Revolution,* ed. Roger Chickering and Stig Förster (Cambridge: Cambridge University Press, 2010), 139–43.

5. Nathaniel Knowles, "The Torture of Captives by the Indians of Eastern North America," *American Philosophical Society Proceedings* 82 (1940): 151–225; Daniel P. Barr, "'This Land Is Ours and Not Yours': The Western Delawares and the Seven Years' War in the Upper Ohio Valley, 1755–1758," in *The Boundaries between Us: Natives and Newcomers along the Frontiers of the Old Northwest Territory, 1750–1850,* ed. Daniel P. Barr (Kent, Ohio: Kent State University Press, 2006), 32; and Matthew C. Ward, *Breaking the Backcountry: The Seven Years' War in Virginia and Pennsylvania, 1754–1765* (Pittsburgh: University of Pittsburgh Press, 2003), 55.

6. Malone, *Skulking Way of War,* 65.

7. Colin G. Calloway, *The Western Abenakis of Vermont, 1600–1800: War, Migration, and the Survival of an Indian People* (Norman: University of Oklahoma Press, 1990), 56–58. Recent archaeological and linguistic research suggests that these St. Lawrence Iroquoians may have been ancestors to the Wendat; they were at least related. But the later Wendats may have been at least partly composed of the displaced St. Lawrence population. John Steckley, "Trade Goods and Nations in Sagard's Dictionary: A St. Lawrence Iroquoian Perspective," *Ontario History,* 104, no. 2 (2012): 139–54; James F. Pendergast, "The Ottawa River Algonquin Bands in a St. Lawrence Iroquoian Context," *Canadian Journal of Archaeology / Journal Canadien d'Archéologie* 23, no. 1/2 (1999): 63–136.

8. Ramsay Cook, *The Voyages of Jacques Cartier* (Toronto: University of Toronto Press, 1993), 67–68. There was a similar early contact story related to Englishmen in coastal North Carolina in 1584 of a massacre "some years earlier" of the Secotans by the Ponuike (led by a chief Piemacum) during a feast. David Beers Quinn, ed., *The Roanoke Voyages, 1584–1590:*

Documents to Illustrate the English Voyages to North America Under the Patent Granted to Walter Raleigh in 1584 (London: Hakluyt Society, 1955), 1: 113.

9. Malone, *Skulking Way of War*, 9.

10. Although I am focusing my critique here on Malone, to be fair, his analysis was only intended to describe events and behavior in seventeenth-century southern New England. Others have generalized his argument to the continent and to a wider chronology.

11. This truth will be argued throughout this book. For other works that have examined Native strategies in geopolitical terms, see James D. Rice, "War and Politics: Powhatan Expansionism and the Problem of Native American Warfare," *William and Mary Quarterly* 3d Ser., 77, no. 1 (2020): 3–32; William A. Starna and José António Brandão, "From the Mohawk-Mahican War to the Beaver Wars: Questioning the Pattern," *Ethnohistory* 51 (2004): 725–50; and Emerson W. Baker and John G. Reid, "Amerindian Power in the Early Modern Northeast: A Reappraisal," *William and Mary Quarterly* 3d Ser., 61, no. 1 (2004): 77–106.

12. George R. Milner, "Warfare in Prehistoric and Early Historic Eastern North America," *Journal of Archaeological Research* 7 (1999): 126–27; Patricia M. Lambert, "The Archaeology of War: A North American Perspective," *Journal of Archaeological Research* 10 (2002): 227–29; Maria Ostendorf Smith, "Osteological Indications of Warfare in the Archaic Period of the Western Tennessee Valley," in *Troubled Times: Violence and Warfare in the Past*, ed. Debra L. Martin and David W. Frayer (Amsterdam: Gordon and Breach, 1997), 241–66; Richard J. Chacon and Ruben G. Mendoza, eds., *North American Indigenous Warfare and Ritual Violence* (Tucson: University of Arizona Press, 2007); Kevin McBride, "War and Trade in Eastern New Netherland," in *A Beautiful and Fruitful Place: Selected Rensselaerswijk Seminar Papers, Volume 3*, ed. Margriet Lacy-Bruijn (Albany, N.Y.: New Netherland Institute, 2013), 279; Michael Strezewski, "Patterns of Interpersonal Violence at the Fisher Site," *Midcontinental Journal of Archaeology* 31 (2006): 249–80; and Maria Ostendorf Smith, "Beyond Palisades: The Nature and Frequency of Late Prehistoric Deliberate Violent Trauma in the Chickamauga Reservoir of East Tennessee," *American Journal of Physical Anthropology* 121 (2003): 303–18.

13. Charles Hudson, *Knights of Spain, Warriors of the Sun: Hernando De Soto and the South's Ancient Chiefdoms* (Athens: University of Georgia Press, 1997); David H. Dye, "The Transformation of Mississippian Warfare: Four Case Studies from the Mid-South," in *The Archaeology of Warfare: Prehistories of Raiding and Conquest*, ed. Elizabeth N. Arkush and Mark W. Allen (Gainesville: University Press of Florida, 2006), 101–47; David H. Dye, "Warfare in the Protohistoric Southeast, 1500–1700," in *Between Contacts and Colonies: Archaeological Perspectives on the Protohistoric Southeast*, ed. C. B. Wesson and M. A. Rees (Tuscaloosa: University of Alabama Press, 2002), 126–41; David H. Dye, "The Art of War in the Sixteenth-Century Central Mississippi Valley," in *Perspectives on the Southeast: Linguistics, Archaeology and Ethnohistory*, ed. Patricia B. Kwachka (Athens: University of Georgia Press, 1994), 44–60; David H. Dye, "Warfare in the Sixteenth-Century Southeast: The de Soto Expedition in the Interior," in *Columbian Consequences, Vol. 2, Archaeological and Historical Perspectives on the Spanish Borderlands East*, ed. David Hurst Thomas (Washington, D.C.: Smithsonian Institution Press, 1990), 211–22; David H. Dye, *War Paths, Peace Paths: An Archaeology of Cooperation and Conflict in Native Eastern North America* (Lanham, Md.: AltaMira Press, 2009), 152–55; David H. Dye, "The Transformation of Mississip-

pian Warfare: Four Case Studies from the Mid-South," in *The Archaeology of Warfare: Prehistories of Raiding and Conquest*, ed. Elizabeth N. Arkush and Mark W. Allen (Gainesville: University Press of Florida, 2006), 101–47; Karl T. Steinen, "Ambushes, Raids, and Palisades: Mississippian Warfare in the Interior Southeast," *Southeastern Archaeology* 11 (1992): 132–39; Matthew Jennings, *New Worlds of Violence: Cultures and Conquests in the Early American Southeast* (Knoxville: University of Tennessee Press, 2011); and George R. Milner, "Warfare, Population, and Food Production in Prehistoric Eastern North America," in *North American Indigenous Warfare and Ritual Violence*, ed. Richard J. Chacon and Rubén G. Mendoza (Tucson: University of Arizona Press, 2007), 182–201.

14. Roger Williams to Sir Henry Vane and John Winthrop, May 15, 1637, in Allyn Bailey Forbes, ed., *Winthrop Papers, Volume III: 1631–1637* (Boston: Massachusetts Historical Society, 1943), 413–14.

15. Keith F. Otterbein, "A History of Research on Warfare in Anthropology," *American Anthropologist* 101 (2000): 800; William Tulio Divale, *Warfare in Primitive Societies: A Bibliography* (Santa Barbara, Calif.: ABC-Clio, 1973), xxi–xxii; Thomas B. Abler, "European Technology and the Art of War in Iroquoia," in *Cultures in Conflict: Current Archaeological Perspectives*, ed. Diana Tkaczuk and Brian C. Vivian (Calgary: University of Calgary Archaeology Association, 1989), 278–79; Dye, *War Paths, Peace Paths*, 111–13; and Azar Gat, *War in Human Civilization* (Oxford: Oxford University Press, 2006), 116–32.

16. McBride, "War and Trade," 277–78.

17. The phrase is used in the sense of "to kill" in Shakespeare, while in the colonies it became one of the most common idioms in referring to warfare (especially with Indians). For examples of its use (in chronological order with dates of use in brackets where not otherwise indicated), see *Macbeth*, Act 4, Scene 3 [1606]; William Bradford, *Of Plymouth Plantation, 1620–1647* (New York: Random House, 1981), 129, 130 [1623], 327, 328 [1637]; Richter, "War and Culture," 548 [1689]; Powell Letter, Albemarle County Records, Microfilm CK002.10001, North Carolina Archives, Raleigh, N.C. [1704]; George Chicken, "Journal of Col. George Chicken's Mission from Charleston, S. C. to the Cherokees, 1725," in *Travels in the American Colonies*, ed. Newton D. Mereness (New York: Macmillan Co., 1916), 111–12; DRIA 1:101 [1751], 1:446 [1753]; *Pennsylvania Gazette*, September 15, 1763, March 8, 1764, June 28, 1764; and David Bjork, "Documents Regarding Indian Affairs in the Lower Mississippi Valley, 1771–1772," *Mississippi Valley Historical Review*, 13 (1926): 403 [1771]. Thanks to Peter Wood for the Powell letter.

18. Lieut. Edward Jenkins to Major Henry Gladwin, commandant of Detroit, dated from Ouiatinon, June 1, 1763, in Johnson Papers, 10:690–91.

19. George Chicken, "Journal of the March of the Carolinians into the Cherokee Mountains, in the Yemassee Indian War, 1715–16," *Yearbook of the City of Charleston* (1894), 342.

20. Using the term "war party" rather than "army" is a descriptive choice. As we will see in later chapters, groups of Indians on the offensive against their enemies were self-selected groups, who had usually gone through some form of ritual preparation prior to going to war. So the group was self-identified as one moving through the countryside for the purposes of war. Furthermore, characterizing it as an "army" would give the misimpression that it was large, hierarchical, and dependent on some network of logistics. A war party *might* be large, but a smaller group could follow the same basic patterns, and the English word "army" would not be appropriate.

21. Chapter 4 discusses the evidence for the loss of leader roles in the wake of casualties.

22. John Norton, *The Journal of Major John Norton, 1816*, ed. Carl F. Klinck and James J. Talman (Toronto: The Champlain Society, 1970), 262. Norton's supposed Cherokee father may be an invention. See Christina Snyder, *Slavery in Indian Country: The Changing Face of Captivity in Early America* (Cambridge, Mass.: Harvard University Press, 2010), 112.

23. JR 48: 75–77.

24. Accounts from white settlements suffering from such attacks tend to be a confused description of incidents happening all around them, with no sense of a pattern, but a persistent sense of being "under siege" with prisoners taken from homes, small parties ambushed and killed, and so on. This is why frontier communities in the late seventeenth and eighteenth centuries proliferated small private forts or blockhouses. As an example of the seemingly confused sense of events, see Edward Hand's description of the area around Ft. Pitt in the summer of 1777. Edward Hand to Kitty, Ft. Pitt, Aug. 25, 1777, Box 1, Edward Hand Papers, Historical Society of Pennsylvania, Philadelphia.

25. DRIA 2:413–17, 458–60.

26. Norton, *Journal*, 128–29.

27. DRIA 2:395.

28. James D. Rice, "War and Politics: Powhatan Expansionism and the Problem of Native American Warfare," *William and Mary Quarterly* 3d Ser., 77, no. 1 (2020): 18–19.

29. Quoted in Calloway, *Western Abenakis*, 122.

30. Spencer Records, 23CC, Draper MSS, 51.

31. Norton, *Journal*, 126–28.

32. Norton, *Journal*, 141–42.

33. Norton, *Journal*, 126–28.

34. There are differing interpretations of the probability of the Indians conducting "wars of conquest" prior to European contact. It has been argued, for example, that the presence of the European demand for furs led the Haudenosaunee to embark on a series of much more destructive wars, culminating in the near-complete destruction of the Wendats in 1648–1649. See: Richter, *Ordeal*, 54, 57, 60–62; and also the discussion in Bruce G. Trigger, "Early Native North American Responses to European Contact: Romantic versus Rationalistic Interpretations," *Journal of American History* 77 (1991): 1206–7. Craig Keener and Lawrence Keeley argue separately that precontact warfare actually was intensely destructive and regularly pursued for these kinds of extreme goals. Craig S. Keener, "An Ethnohistorical Analysis of Iroquois Assault Tactics Used against Fortified Settlements of the Northeast in the Seventeenth Century," *Ethnohistory* 46 (1999): 777–807, esp. 783, 788; Lawrence H. Keeley, *War before Civilization* (New York: Oxford University Press, 1996), esp. 113–26. For a compromise position see Abler, "European Technology," 279. It is certainly agreed, however, that Native societies could launch major offensives for the political purposes of communicating a set of messages to their enemies. Frederick W. Gleach, *Powhatan's World and Colonial Virginia: A Conflict of Cultures* (Lincoln: University of Nebraska Press, 1997), 43–54 (esp. 51); Ian K. Steele, *Warpaths: Invasions of North America* (New York: Oxford University Press, 1994); and Jill Lepore, *The Name of War: King Philip's War and the Origins of American Identity* (New York: Alfred A. Knopf, 1998), 118–19.

35. Lewis H. Larson, Jr., "Functional Considerations of Warfare in the Southeast during the Mississippi Period," *American Antiquity* 37 (1972): 390; Keener, "Iroquois Assault Tac-

tics; and Steele, *Warpaths*, 43, 231, 238 (for sieges). Compare Huron practices as described in Trigger, *Huron*, 53–55, and Iroquois practices in Keith F. Otterbein, "Huron vs. Iroquois: A Case Study in Inter-Tribal Warfare," *Ethnohistory* 26 (1979), 141–52.

36. George Edward Milne, *Natchez Country: Indians, Colonists, and the Landscapes of Race in French Louisiana* (Athens: University of Georgia Press, 2015), 194.

37. Wendell S. Hadlock, "War among the Northeastern Woodland Indians," *American Anthropologist*, New Ser. 49 (1947): 211.

38. Calloway, *Western Abenakis*, 73–74, provides a good summary. In 1669 Jeremias Van Rensselaer referred to the then six-year-long devastating war between the Mahicans and the Mohawks. *Correspondence of Jeremias van Rensselaer, 1651–1674*, ed. and trans. A. J. F. van Laer (Albany: The University of the State of New York, 1932), 413.

39. Richter, *Ordeal*, 103–4, is the most balanced assessment of the consequences. Also see Francis Jennings, *The Ambiguous Iroquois Empire* (New York: Norton, 1984), 132.

40. Dean R. Snow, *Mohawk Valley Archaeology: The Sites* (University Park, Pa.: Matson Museum of Anthropology, 1995), 411–13.

41. The two best modern descriptions are a single paragraph in Jon Parmenter, *The Edge of the Woods: Iroquoia, 1534–1701* (East Lansing: Michigan State University Press, 2010), 137, and an older article that has some geographic misunderstandings: Percy M. Van Epps, "The Battle of 1669 at Kinaquariones," *New York History* 13, no. 4 (1932): 420–30. Evan Haefeli usefully reconstructs the complex diplomacy surrounding the attack, as well as some of the aftermath (including a failed revenge attack by the Mohawks), in "Becoming a 'Nation of Statesmen': The Mohicans' Incorporation into the Iroquois League, 1671–1675," *New England Quarterly* 93 (2020): 433–35.

42. A recently arrived French missionary (Jean Pierron) provided one account in JR 53:137–45; the other is Daniel Gookin, *Historical Collections of the Indians of New England: Of Their Several Nations, Numbers, Customs, Manners, Religion and Government, Before the English Planted There* (Boston: 1792), 44–46.

43. Gookin, *Historical Collections*, 44.

44. JR 53:137.

45. Pierron hints at the end of his account that some Mohawk sentries had been killed during the Mahican initial approach, which Mahicans no doubt considered part of the overall engagement. So: one night's approach march, the next day's attack, battle, and retreat, plus another day's battle at Kinaquariones would have been a "three-day battle" in the telling. This is likely the source of Gookin's error.

46. Snow says the Mahicans were "armed with English guns but not much military sense," were "poorly equipped," and included children, falling back "exhausted after a few days," with most of them killed or captured when overtaken.

Dean R. Snow, *The Iroquois* (Oxford: Blackwell, 1994), 121. Calloway accepts that the Mahicans "laid siege" and then withdrew when they could not take the village. *Western Abenakis*, 74; Silverman skips completely over the role of the other Mohawk villages, and accepts the claim that the Mahicans retreated because they were running out of powder. *Thundersticks*, 46. Malone, *Skulking Way of War*, 65, also dismisses the Algonquians' attack as ineffective. Interestingly, Jennings, Richter, and Barr essentially skip over this episode, focusing instead on the nearly simultaneous war between the Haudenosaunee and the Susquehannocks.

47. Quote from JR 53:139. Such casualties were substantial for a society of only around 2,000 people; Richter suggests that these losses (combined with other recent events) led a council of Mohawk headmen to tell Pierron that their people would accept Christianity. *Ordeal*, 114.

48. For an example of the Chickasaws making almost exactly the same choices as the Mahicans, when attacking a party of Savannahs behind improvised fortifications in 1759, see Jerome Courtonee to Governor Lyttelton, Augusta, May 13, 1759, DRIA 2:489.

49. Craig S. Keener, "An Ethnohistorical Analysis of Iroquois Assault Tactics Used against Fortified Settlements of the Northeast in the Seventeenth Century," *Ethnohistory* 46 (1999): 777–807; Paul Hulton, ed., *The Work of Jacques le Moyne de Morgues: A Huguenot Artist in France, Florida and England* (London: Trustees of the British Museum, 1977), 1:149 and plate 123. Contra Malone, *Skulking Way of War*, 14; and Alden T. Vaughan, *New England Frontier: Puritans and Indians, 1620–1675*, 3rd ed. (Norman: University of Oklahoma Press, 1995), xxv.

50. Ian Kenneth Steele, *Warpaths: Invasions of North America* (New York: Oxford University Press, 1994), 138.

51. Steele, *Warpaths*, 64–65; Daniel P. Barr, *Unconquered: The Iroquois League at War in Colonial America* (Westport, Conn.: Praeger, 2006), 26–27; and Bruce G. Trigger, *Natives and Newcomers: Canada's "Heroic Age" Reconsidered* (Kingston and Montreal: McGill-Queen's University Press, 1985), 175–76.

52. Gleach, *Powhatan's World*, 43–44, reprints the colonists' descriptions of the battle, but Gleach does not believe it represented their normal way of fighting.

53. Hulton, *Work of Jacques le Moyne de Morgues*, 1:144 and plate 105.

54. Roger Williams, *A Key into the Language of America* (1643; repr., Bedford, Mass.: Applewood Books, 1997), 188–89.

55. Richter, *Ordeal*, 35. This result is how ethnohistorians have described battles by other tribal peoples witnessed in the twentieth century. See Keeley, *War before Civilization*, 59–61.

56. Contrast Daniel K. Richter's explanation of such large-scale occasions as "carefully planned, relatively bloodless, largely ceremonial confrontations between massed forces protected by wooden body armor and bedecked in elaborate headdresses." *Ordeal*, 35.

57. The most detailed account of the battle is from an eighteenth-century letter by Richard Hyde. Hyde claimed to have heard it from men close to Uncas during his life. There are good reasons to believe that Hyde would have had those connections through his grandfather William Hyde, who was an original founder of Norwich in the 1660s, and was therefore connected to John Mason, who was close to Uncas. In addition, William Hyde's daughter Hester married Stephen Post, who had been at Fort Saybrook during the Pequot War and was also a friend of Uncas (thanks to Kevin McBride for confirming these connections). The letter is quoted in full in Daniel Coit Gilman, *A Historical Discourse Delivered in Norwich, Connecticut, September 7, 1859* (Boston: Geo. C. Rand and Avery, 1859), 82–84. The battle is also discussed in Edward Johnson, *A History of New England . . . (Wonder Working Providence of Sions Saviour)* (London: Nathaniel Brooke, 1654), 182–85; John Winthrop, *The Journal of John Winthrop, 1630–1649*, abridged ed. (Cambridge, Mass.: Belknap Press, 1996), 236–37; William Bradford, *Of Plymouth Plantation, 1620–1647* (New York: Random House, 1981), 367; Michael Leroy Oberg, *Uncas: First of the Mohegans* (Ithaca, N.Y.: Cornell

University Press, 2003), 102–3; and Herbert Milton Sylvester, *Indian Wars of New England* (1910; repr., New York: Arno Press, 1979), 1:390–97.

58. For recent reviews of the development of this debate see José António Brandão, *"Your Fyre Shall Burn No More": Iroquois Policy Toward New France and Its Native Allies to 1701* (Lincoln: University of Nebraska Press, 1997), 5–18; Thomas S. Abler, "Iroquois Policy and Iroquois Culture: Two Histories and an Anthropological Ethnohistory," *Ethnohistory* 47 (2000): 483–91; and William A. Starna and José António Brandão, "From the Mohawk-Mahican War to the Beaver Wars: Questioning the Pattern," *Ethnohistory* 51 (2004): 725–50.

59. For the Iroqouis' success in obtaining guns and their impact, see most recently Silverman, *Thundersticks*, 21–55. Also see Keith F. Otterbein, "Why the Iroquois Won: An Analysis of Iroquois Military Tactics," *Ethnohistory* 11 (1964): 58; HNAI 15:352; and Bruce G. Trigger, *The Children of Aataentsic: A History of the Huron People to 1660* (Montreal: McGill-Queen's University Press, 1976), 2:627–33.

60. Silverman, *Thundersticks*, 37.

61. This account follows Otterbein, "Huron vs. Iroquois", who is basically summarizing the French Jesuit account found in JR 34:123–37.

62. JR 34:123.

63. Another example from the Cherokees almost exactly replicates the pattern at Gandaouagé: in this case an Iroquois war party attacked an outlying Cherokee town and successfully stormed it, taking most of the inhabitants prisoners, but the Cherokees of other nearby towns pursued, were able to cut the trail in front of the retreating Iroquois, and in the ensuing battle were able to rescue all of their people who had been taken captive. Norton, *Journal*, 263.

64. For the "half-moon" tactic, see Leroy V. Eid, "'A Kind of Running Fight': Indian Battlefield Tactics in the late Eighteenth Century," *Western Pennsylvania Historical Magazine* 71 (1988): 147–71Eid, "A Kind of Running Fight"; and Gleach, *Powhatan's World*, 43.

65. Norton, *Journal*, 129–30 (black bird description on 138).

66. Williams, *Key into the Language*, 184.

67. Philip L. Barbour, ed., *The Complete Works of Captain John Smith* (Chapel Hill: University of North Carolina Press, 1986), 1:255.

68. Depositions concerning Indian Disturbances in Virginia, June 1, 1758, DRIA 2:467; see also 2:468.

69. John Smith describes Jamestown as being under this kind of persistent harassment: "wee had sometime peace and warre twice in a day, and very seldome a weeke, but we had some trecherous villany or other" (before his efforts supposedly stopped it). John Smith, *Generall Historie*, II:159–60, reprinted in Karen Ordahl Kupperman, ed., *Captain John Smith: A Select Edition of His Writings* (Chapel Hill: University of North Carolina Press, 1998), 165. For other takes on this kind of harassment see: Keeley, *War before Civilization*, 116; Dye, "Warfare in the Sixteenth-Century Southeast"; Dye, "The Art of War in the Sixteenth-Century Central Mississippi Valley"; Hudson, *Knights of Spain*; Larson, "Functional Considerations"; Steinen, "Ambushes, Raids, and Palisades," 132–39; and Christina Snyder, "Conquered Enemies, Adopted Kin, and Owned People: The Creek Indians and Their Captives," *Journal of Southern History* 73 (2007): 268–69.

70. Keeley, *War Before Civilization*, 67–69, and George R. Milner, "Warfare in Prehistoric and Early Historic Eastern North America," *Journal of Archaeological Research* 7 (1999):

126–27 discuss the archaeological and ethnographic evidence for large-scale massacres. There are numerous examples of successful surprise attacks during the historic era resulting in high casualties. Keener, "Iroquois Assault Tactics," 785, describes several, but one only has to think of the successful initial Native American attacks in any number of seventeenth-century wars: the 1622 attack in Virginia (see chapter 4), the outbreak of King Philip's War in 1675, or the initial Tuscarora attacks described in chapter 5. Keener and Otterbein both argue that the technological imbalance between the Wendats and the Iroquois allowed even nonsurprise attacks to be highly lethal: Keener, "Iroquois Assault Tactics," 788–96; Otterbein, "Huron v. Iroquois," 148. The argument over the lethality of precontact Indian warfare is a bitter one; see Wayne E. Lee, "Early American Ways of War: A New Reconaissance, 1600–1815," *The Historical Journal* 44 (2001): 271–76.

71. Silverman, *Thundersticks*, makes this argument through several case studies around the continent. For the role of axes see Keener, "Iroquois Assault Tactics."

Chapter Three

1. Beverly W. Bond Jr., "The Captivity of Charles Stuart, 1755–57," *The Mississippi Valley Historical Review* 13, no. 1 (1926): 63.

2. Smith's capture is contextualized in David L. Preston, *Braddock's Defeat: The Battle of the Monongahela and the Road to Revolution* (New York: Oxford University Press, 2015), 197–99.

3. James Smith, *An Account of the Remarkable Occurrences in the Life and Travels of Col. James Smith, (Now a Citizen of Bourbon County, Kentucky,) During His Captivity With the Indians, in the Years 1755, '56, '57, '58, & '59 . . .* (Lexington, Ky.: Printed by John Bradford, 1799), 5–6, 45–46. A lightly annotated modern edition is available: James Smith, *Scoouwa: James Smith's Indian Captivity Narrative* (Columbus: Ohio Historical Society, 1978).

4. Journal of Captain John Montresor August 16, 1764, NYCD, 6:279.

5. Alert readers might immediately complain that European armies in Europe often lived off the countryside, and although this was partly true, doing so required a substantial farming population density, which did not exist on the edges of European settlement in the New World. This is not the venue to detail European logistics, but for population density requirements, see G. Perjés, "Army Provisioning, Logistics and Strategy in the Second Half of the 17th Century," *Acta Historica Academiae Scientiarum Hungaricae* 16 (1970): 1–51.

6. Ian K. Steele, in an otherwise excellent survey of Native American warfare, has almost no discussion of logistics, except in this comment about how Indians would teach Canadians to live off the land. *Warpaths: Invasions of North America* (New York: Oxford University Press, 1994), 135. He does show the Indians in King Philip's War were ultimately driven from their cornfields and had to "hunt in unfamiliar territory," Their accompanying families suffered as the war dragged on (see 106). As discussed below, Colin G. Calloway's attention to these details in *The Victory With No Name: The Native American Defeat of the First American Army* (New York: Oxford University Press, 2015) is exceptional.

7. See note 46 below.

8. There have been few real analyses of what strategic intentions Native American Nations had, especially in their wars against each other (other than obvious efforts at self-defense). For exceptions, see Emerson W. Baker and John G. Reid, "Amerindian Power in

the Early Modern Northeast: A Reappraisal," *William and Mary Quarterly* 3d Ser., 61, no. 1 (2004): 77–106; and James D. Rice, "War and Politics: Powhatan Expansionism and the Problem of Native American Warfare," *William and Mary Quarterly* 3d Ser., 77, no. 1 (2020): 3–32.

9. For variations, see the nation-by-nation analyses in HNAI vols. 14 and 15. For the over-all history and significance of agriculture (especially maize), see Susan Sleeper-Smith, *Indigenous Prosperity and American Conquest: Indian Women of the Ohio River Valley, 1690–1792* (Chapel Hill: University of North Carolina Press, 2018), esp. 27.

10. HNAI 15:298.

11. HNAI 15:258; James Rice, *Nature and History in the Potomac Country: From Hunter-Gatherers to the Age of Jefferson* (Baltimore, Md.: Johns Hopkins University Press, 2009), 42. These numbers do not necessarily conflict! Maize could have been the highest *single* supplier of calories and still only have been 25 percent of a highly varied diet.

12. HNAI 15:258. There is an excellent summary of seasonal subsistence and movement in the Potomac River basin in Rice, *Nature and History*, 35–42.

13. HNAI 15:217.

14. Bruce D. Smith, "Middle Mississippi Exploitation of Animal Populations: A Predictive Model," *American Antiquity* 39 no. 2 (1974): 274–91; and Charles L. Heath and E. Clay Swindell, "Coastal Plain Iroquoians Before and After European Contact: An Interpretive Study of Cashie Phase Archaeological Research in Northeastern North Carolina," in *The Archaeology of North Carolina: Three Archaeological Symposia*, ed. Charles R. Ewen, Thomas R. Whyte, and R. P. Stephen Davis, Jr. (Raleigh: North Carolina Archaeological Council Publication Number 30, 2011), www.rla.unc.edu/NCAC/Publications/NCAC30/index.html, esp. 10–37.

15. This pattern is repeated with endless minor variations in captivity narratives. For a very clear example, see James E. Seaver, *A Narrative of the Life of Mrs. Mary Jemison* (n.p.: Wm. P. Letchworth, 1877; facsimile reprint, Scituate, Mass.: Digital Scanning Inc., 2000), 63–64.

16. Josiah Priest, *A True Narrative of the Capture of David Ogden* (Lisle, N.Y.: Elmer E. Davis, 1840, 1882), 10–12 (quote); *Memoir of a French and Indian War Soldier by "Jolicoeur" Charles Bonin*, ed. Andrew Gallup (Bowie, Md.: Heritage Books, 1993), 154 (other examples below).

17. Jeanne Winson Adler, ed., *Chainbreaker's War: A Seneca Chief Remembers the American Revolution* (Hensonville, N.Y.: Black Dome Press, 2002), 78.

18. Mary Rowlandson, *The Sovereignty and Goodness of God*, ed. Neil Salisbury (Boston: Bedford Books, 1997), 111. Other examples from the captivity narratives of Isaac Jogues and Elizabeth Hanson, both in Richard VanDerBeets, ed., *Held Captive by Indians: Selected Narratives, 1642–1836* (Knoxville: University of Tennessee Press, 1994), 33–34, 142; and Joseph François Lafitau, *Customs of the American Indians Compared With the Customs of Primitive Times* (Toronto: The Champlain Society, 1974), 2:62.

19. Seaver, *Life of Jemison*, 77.

20. Cites for hunting on the move are found below.

21. For example, see Joe Ben Wheat, Harold E. Malde, and Estella B. Leopold, "The Olsen-Chubbuck Site: A Paleo-Indian Bison Kill," *Memoirs of the Society for American Archaeology* 26 (1972): i–ix, 1–180, esp. 108–9; and John D. Speth and Katherine A. Spielmann,

"Energy Source, Protein Metabolism, and Hunter-Gatherer Subsistence Strategies," *Journal of Anthropological Archaeology* 2, no. 1 (1983): 1–31.

22. "Estimated Daily Calorie Needs," www.fda.gov/media/112972/download (accessed November 30, 2020). Three U.S. Army "meals-ready-to-eat" are 3,750 calories: "Meals Read to Eat Nutrition Fact Sheet," www.qmo.amedd.army.mil/diabetes/MRE_Fact_Sheet.pdf (accessed August 21, 2022).

23. Based on Fred Anderson's calculations of a British Army ration in the Seven Years' War. There were a number of variations based on fresh or salt meat, beef or pork, beans or rice, and so on. But 2,500 calories is squarely in the middle of the estimate (not including alcohol, which could be a substantial addition if it was available as beer). Fred Anderson, *A People's Army: Massachusetts Soldiers and Society in the Seven Years' War* (Chapel Hill: University of North Carolina Press, 1984), 83–90; see also John Rees, "'The Foundation of an Army is the Belly': North American Soldiers' Food, 1756–1945," http://revwar75.com/library/rees/belly.htm#:~:text=North%20American%20Soldiers'%20Food%2C%20 1756%2D1945.

24. This varies based on the specific type of maize, and there is more variation when comparing a pound of flour to a pound of kernels, but the variation ranges between about 1,600 and 1,900 calories per pound. See www.fatsecret.com/calories-nutrition/generic/cornmeal-mush-made-with-water; www.fatsecret.com/calories-nutrition/generic/corn-dried-cooked?portionid=24014&portionamount=1.000; and www.fatsecret.com/calories-nutrition/usda/yellow-whole-grain-corn-meal.

25. For carcass/dressed weight of deer see Martin Marchello and Julie Garden-Robinson, "Wild Side of the Menu No. 2: Field to Freezer," www.ag.ndsu.edu/pubs/yf/foods/fn125.pdf. Venison is leaner than beef or pork and so is less caloric per pound. One scholar has calculated that a quart of dried corn mixed with fat as sagamite would yield 3,186 calories. This seems high. See George Colpitts, *Pemmican Empire: Food, Trae, and the Last Bison Hunts in the North American Plains, 1780–1882* (New York: Cambridge University Press, 2015), 53. Colpitts has an extensive caloric analysis here (including of calorie needs of men paddling loaded canoes all day), but his context mixes European and Indian practices.

26. David J. Silverman, *Thundersticks: Firearms and the Violent Transformation of Native America* (Cambridge, MA: Belknap Press of Harvard University Press, 2016), 43; Although it is possible that the Senecas used the Susquehanna River for part of the route, the Dutch sources do specify them having "marched." See NYCD 12:430, 431.

27. Jerome Courtonee to Governor Lyttelton, Augusta, May 13, 1759, DRIA 2:489.

28. Silverman, *Thundersticks*, 144.

29. Jean Lowry, *A Journal of the Captivity of Jean Lowry and Her Children* (Mercersburg, Pa.: Conococheague Institute, 2008).

30. John Norton, *The Journal of Major John Norton, 1816*, ed. Carl F. Klinck and James J. Talman (Toronto: The Champlain Society, 1970), 262.

31. Norton, *Journal*, 128–29.

32. One portage near Presque Isle was apparently only forty-five yards, although the primary one was much longer. "Journal of Captain John Montresor," in Sylvester K. Stevens and Donald H. Kent, eds, *Wilderness Chronicles of Northwestern Pennsylvania* (Harrisburg: Pennsylvania Historical Commission, 1941), 279; Preston, *Braddock's Defeat*, chapter 4. For a good overview of the complexity of the networks see John William Nelson, "The Ecology

of Travel on the Great Lakes Frontier: Native Knowledge, European Dependence, and the Environmental Specifics of Contact," *The Michigan Historical Review* 45.1 (2019): 1–26. There is a good summary of river portages as used by French fur traders (following Native routes) in Claiborne A. Skinner, *The Upper Country: French Enterprise in the Colonial Great Lakes* (Baltimore: Johns Hopkins University Press, 2008), 36–39.

33. M. J. Morgan, *Land of Big Rivers: French and Indian Illinois, 1699–1778* (Carbondale: Southern Illinois University Press, 2010), 34. Morgan also points to two other local boat-building traditions for more local river traffic, using skins or even just bundles of cane.

34. Pouchot, *Memoir,* 459–60; cf. Lafitau, *Customs,* 2:124–26.

35. Journal of William Preston, 1756, of the Sandy Creek Expedition, 21U Draper MSS.

36. Thomas Hariot, "Briefe and True Report," in *The Roanoke Voyages, 1584–1590: Documents to Illustrate the English Voyages to North America Under the Patent Granted to Walter Raleigh in 1584,* ed. David B. Quinn (London: Hakluyt Society, 1955), 1:364.

37. Peter H. Wood, "Missing the Boat: Ancient Dugout Canoes in the Mississippi-Missouri Watershed," *Early American Studies* 16, no. 2 (2018): 197–254, de Soto quote on 222. Wood provides numerous other examples of massive fleets of huge dugouts. It is not unreasonable to conclude, with respect to my ultimate aim of examining conquest methods, that the availability of this transport technology helped enable the consolidation of the large Mississippian chiefdoms.

38. "Ancient Dugout Canoe Found in Louisiana," www.archaeology.org/news/5678-170622-louisiana-dugout-canoe.

39. Johnson to Bouquet, June 18, 1764, Johnson Papers, 4:450–52.

40. Example described in Preston, *Braddock's Defeat,* 143–44.

41. Wood, "Missing the Boat," quotes at 239, 240–41.

42. Thomas S. Abler, ed., *Chainbreaker: The Revolutionary War Memoirs of Governor Blacksnake As Told to Benjamin Williams* (Lincoln: University of Nebraska Press, 1989), 34–40.

43. Smith, *Account,* 16–18.

44. Jogues in VanDerBeets, *Held Captive,* 12–13.

45. For a good example of intracluster paths, see the Wendat network in HNAI 15:369, and the discussion on p. 378 that points out how the paths usually followed high ground through wetlands and swamps; newcomers frequently got lost.

46. William E. Meyer, *Indian Trails of the Southeast (extract from the Forty-Second Annual Report of the Bureau of American Ethnology 1924–25* (Facsimile reprint, n.p.: Gustavs Library, 2009), foldout map; Frank N. Wilcox, *Ohio Indian Trails,* 3rd ed. (Cleveland, Ohio.: The Gates Press, 1934); Paul A. W. Wallace, *Indian Paths of Pennsylvania* (Harrisburg: Pennsylvania Historical and Museum Commission, 1998); Helen Hornbeck Tanner, "The Land and Water Communication Systems of the Southeastern Indians," in *Powhatan's Mantle: Indians in the Colonial Southeast,* ed. Peter H. Wood, Gregory A. Waselkov, and M. Thomas Hatley (Lincoln: University of Nebraska Press, 1989), 6–20.

47. Roger Williams, *A Key in to the Language of America [1643]* (Bedford, Mass.: Applewood Books, 1997), 11.

48. Lafitau, *Customs,* 2:114–15 (he does not specify which nation he is describing, but it is presumably the Wendat).

49. JR 68:145–49 (thanks to Elizabeth Ellis for pointing out this passage).

50. Pierre Pouchot, *Memoirs on the Late War in North America, Between France and England,* trans, Michael Cardy; ed. and annot. by Brian Leigh Dunnigan (Youngstown, N.Y.: Old Fort Niagara Publication, 1994), 446 (quote), 457, 478–49. Cf. Charles Bonin's account in *Memoir,* 69–70; JR 13:21–25.

51. Charles Johnston, *A Narrative of the Incidents Attending the Capture, Detention, and Ransom of Charles Johnston* (New York: J. & J. Harper, 1827; facsimile reprint in The Garland Library of Narratives of North American Indian Captivities, vol. 43, New York: Garland Publishing, 1975), 31.

52. Rowlandson, *Sovereignty,* 85–87.

53. Zadock Steele, *The Indian Captive: The Burning of Royalton Vermont* (North Stratford, N.H.: Ayer Company Publishers, 1971), 39–40 (originally published in 1818). For other captives carrying packs, both in hunting parties and upon capture, see John Gyles and Robert Eastburn, both in VanDerBeets, *Held Captive,* 108, 155; Smith, *Account,* 12, 16–18.

54. Seaver, *Life of Mary Jemison,* 42–43.

55. Abler, *Chainbreaker,* 143.

56. Virginia DeJohn Anderson, *Creatures of Empire: How Domestic Animals Transformed Early America* (New York: Oxford University Press, 2004), 201–2.

57. Brett Rushforth, "'A Little Flesh We Offer You': The Origins of Indian Slavery in New France," *William and Mary Quarterly,* 3d Ser., 60, no. 4 (2003): 794.

58. Pouchot, *Memoirs,* 457.

59. Kathryn E. Holland Braund, *Deerskins & Duffels: The Creek Indian Trade With Anglo America, 1685–1815* (Lincoln: University of Nebraska Press, 1993), 31; James Adair, writing in 1775, says almost every Cherokee household had horses, even after having had to eat them during the Anglo-Cherokee War, 1759–1761. *History of the American Indians,* ed. Samuel Cole Williams (New York: Promontory Press, 1930), 242.

60. Tyler Boulware, "'Skilful Jockies' and 'Good Sadlers': Native Americans and Horses in the Southeastern Borderlands," in Andrew K. Frank and A. Glenn Crothers, eds., *Borderland Narratives: Negotiation and Accommodation in North America's Contested Spaces, 1500–1850.* (Tallahassee: University Press of Florida, 2017), 70.

61. Jason W. Warren, *Connecticut Unscathed: Victory in the Great Narragansett War, 1675–1676* (Norman: University of Oklahoma Press, 2014), 52–53.

62. Ruth Ann Denaci, "The Penn's Creek Massacre and the Captivity of Marie Le Roy and Barbara Leininger," *Pennsylvania History: A Journal of Mid-Atlantic Studies* 74, no. 3 (2007): 312.

63. Seaver, *Life of Mary Jemison,* 78.

64. Smith, *Account,* 16–19.

65. Smith, *Account,* 27–29

66. Porters were demonstrably crucial to the logistics of Mesoamerican armies. Michel R. Oudijk and Matthew Restall, "Mesoamerican Conquistadors in the Sixteenth Century," in *Indian Conquistadors: Indigenous Allies in the Conquest of Mesoamerica,* ed. Laura Matthew and Michel R. Oudijk (Norman: University of Oklahoma Press, 2008), 38–42.

67. Pouchot, *Memoir,* 449 (cf. 457) (emphasis added). Norton tells a similar tale of the wife being directed to the kill: *Journal,* 126.

68. José António Brandão, ed., *Nation Iroquoise: A Seventeenth-Century Ethnography of the Iroquois* (Lincoln: University of Nebraska Press, 2003), 71–72.

69. The original source for the role of women in this incident is the Daniel Claus Memoranda Book, ff, 72–74 in the Daniel Claus and Family Papers, C-1485, 103767, MG 19 F1, Library and Archives Canada, microfilm, accessible at https://heritage.canadiana.ca/view/oocihm.lac_reel_c1485. At least one historian who has discussed this incident assumes that women were regularly present with Indian war parties. D. Peter MacLeod, *The Canadian Iroquois and the Seven Years' War* (Toronto: Dundurn Press, 1996), 74. Cf. Jon Parmenter, "After the Mourning Wars: The Iroquois as Allies in Colonial North American Campaigns, 1676–1760," *William and Mary Quarterly* 3d Ser., 64, no. 1 (2007): 65–67.

70. Lafitau, *Customs*, 2:138.

71. Christina Snyder summarizes the processes of torture/death and adoption for captives during the colonial era in *Slavery in Indian Country: The Changing Face of Captivity in Early America* (Cambridge, Mass.: Harvard University Press, 2010), chapters 3 and 4.

72. Lawrence A. Clayton, Vernon James Knight Jr., and Edward C. Moore, eds., *The DeSoto Chronicles: The Expedition of Hernando De Soto to North America in 1539–1543* (Tuscaloosa: University of Alabama Press, 1993), 1:77, 89, 94, 95, 121, 273 (the word used was *tameme*, clearly derived from the Mexica word *tlameme* (see 1:194); Snyder, *Slavery in Indian Country*, 13, 21, 24, 27–28.

73. Aubrey Lauersdorf, "Apalachee Diplomacy, Politics, and Power, 1528–1678" (Ph.D. Diss., University of North Carolina, 2020), 139–40.

74. Snyder, *Slavery in Indian Country*, 130ff.

75. Bonin, *Memoir*, 154.

76. JR 22: 265–67; Bruce G. Trigger, *The Children of Aataentsic: a History of the Huron People to 1660* (Montreal: McGill-Queen's University Press, 1976) 2:638; and William A. Starna and Ralph Watkins, "Northern Iroquoian Slavery," *Ethnohistory* 38 (1991): 51.

77. Starna and Watkins, "Northern Iroquoian Slavery," 34–57.

78. Brett Rushforth, *Bonds of Alliance: Indigenous and Atlantic Slaveries in New France* (Chapel Hill: University of North Carolina Press, 2013), 15–72, quote on 34–35.

79. Journal of William Preston, 1756, of the Sandy Creek Expedition, Draper Mss 21U (also in Preston's Journal of the Sandy Creek Expedition, February 9 to March 13, 1756, 1QQ Draper MSS, 123. A detailed documentary outline of the expedition is available at https://fiwf.org/sandy-creek-expedition-headwaters/.

80. Intelligence from Virginia, N.Y. August 14, 1763, Johnson Papers, 4:190–91.

81. Louise Phelps Kellogg, ed., *Frontier Advance on the Upper Ohio, 1778–1779* (Madison: State Historical Society of Wisconsin, 1916), 65, 70–71, 67–68, 86, 98.

82. Johnston, *Narrative of the Incidents*, 19–21, 25, 28–29, 46. For another example of "gorging" see Lafitau, *Customs*, 2:61.

83. Similar Native expectations are recorded for Haudenosaunee war parties from white settlers in the Susquehanna River valley. David L. Preston, *The Texture of Contact: European and Indian Settler Communities on the Frontiers of Iroquoia, 1667–1783* (Lincoln: University of Nebraska Press, 2009), 131.

84. Lauersdorf, "Apalachee Diplomacy," 102.

85. Garrett Wright, "Paawaariihusu^ɔ: Travel and the Central Great Plains" (Ph.D. Diss., University of North Carolina, 2019), 77.

86. Sleeper-Smith, *Indigenous Prosperity*, 35.

87. Morrill Marston, 1T Draper MSS, item 58.

88. Peter A. Thomas, "Contrastive Subsistence Strategies and Land Use as Factors for Understanding Indian-White Relations in New England," *Ethnohistory* 23 (1976): 12.

89. Quoted in Allan Greer, *Property and Dispossession: Natives, Empires and Land in Early Modern North America* (Cambridge: Cambridge University Press, 2018), 38.

90. Karen Ordahl Kupperman, *The Jamestown Project* (Cambridge, Mass.: Belknap Press of Harvard University Press, 2007), 170–74. A few examples from John Smith, *Proceedings* (1612) in *The Complete Works of Captain John Smith*, ed. Philip L. Barbour (Chapel Hill: University of North Carolina Press, 1986), 1: 212, 217, 239.

91. Henry Spelman noted that a good part of any individual house would be filled with baskets of dried corn, in addition to the storage house for the "king's" corn. Henry Spelman, *Relation of Virginia*, ed. Karen Ordahl Kupperman (New York: New York University Press, 2019), 72–73; Rice, *Nature and History*, 44; and Stephen R. Potter, *Commoners, Tribute, and Chiefs: The Development of Algonquian Culture in the Potomac Valley* (Charlottesville: University Press of Virginia, 1994), 172–73.

92. Sleeper-Smith, *Indigenous Prosperity*, 33. Sixteenth-century European armies often relied heavily on local populations for their logistics, and this seems to have been a pattern that they carried into their exploration of the Western Hemisphere. By the eighteenth century conventional European forces in North America had learned that they needed to carry their own provisions, partly because of low population densities in North America and partly because that practice came to dominate European military thinking on that continent. Lee, *Barbarians and Brothers*, 125–26, 186–87.

93. William Bartram, *Travels Through North & South Carolina, Georgia, East & West Florida, the Cherokee Country, the Extensive Territories of the Muscogulges, or Creek Confederacy, and the Country of the Chactaws; Containing An Account of the Soil and Natural Productions of Those Regions, Together with Observations on the Manners of the Indians* (Philadelphia: James & Johnson, 1791), 192, 209.

94. James H. Merrell, "Shamokin, 'the very seat of the Prince of darkness': Unsettling the Early American Frontier," in *Contact Points: American Frontiers From the Mohawk Valley to the Mississippi, 1750–1830*, ed. Andrew R. L. Cayton and Fredrika J. Teute (Chapel Hill: University of North Carolina Press, 1998), 22, 24–25.

95. Col. Daniel Brodhead to Pres. Reed, May 22, 1781, *Pennsylvania Archives, vol. 9* (Philadelphia: Joseph Severns & Co., 1854), 161–62.

96. Lauersdorf, "Apalachee Diplomacy," 203.

97. Seaver, *Life of Mary Jemison*, 78.

98. This may have been seed stored for the coming spring, rather than a traveling cache, but it nevertheless shows how food could be stored underground and without being under a roof. Mourt's Relation, as discussed in James Deetz and Patricia Scott Deetz, *The Times of Their Lives: Life, Love, and Death in Plymouth Colony* (New York: Random House, 2000), 46.

99. Adler, *Chainbreaker's War*, 102–3.

100. Hanson in VanDerBeets, *Held Captive*, 136, 137.

101. Steele, *Indian Captive*, 39–40.

102. Thomas Forsyth, "Manners and Customs of the Sauk and Fox Nation of Indians, 15th January 1827," 9T Draper MSS.

103. [William Smith], *An Historical Account of the Expedition against the Ohio Indians in the Year 1764, Under the Command of Henry Bouquet, Esq.* (Philadelphia: William Bradford, 1765), 39.

104. Washington to Robert Dinwiddie [Winchester, April 7, 1756], in George Washington, *The Papers of George Washington, Colonial Series*, ed. W. W. Abbott (Charlottesville, Va.: University Press of Virginia, 1983–), 2:333–34.

105. HNAI 15:298.

106. Calloway, *Victory*, 108, citing TNA CO 42/83: 170–81.

107. Calloway, *Victory*, 111.

108. Calloway, *Victory*, 113, citing "Indian Account" in *New Hampshire Gazette and General Advertiser*, March 7, 1792.

109. Norton, *Journal*, 181–82.

110. Mike Demick, "Warm Weather Means Hunters Should Take Extra Precautions with Game Meat," August 23, 2019, https://idfg.idaho.gov/press/warm-weather-means-hunters-should-take-precautions-game-meat#.

111. Pouchot, *Memoir*, 449.

112. Johnston, *Narrative of the Incidents*, 28–29.

113. Forsyth, "Manners and Customs," 9T, Draper MSS.

114. Calloway, *Victory*, discusses this passage on 111–12, but he misunderstands the division of labor. (Calloway is one of the few historians to deal with the impact of logistics on Native strategy and tactics, but he did make this small error.) Gerard T. Hopkins, *A Mission to the Indians, From the Indian Committee of Baltimore Yearly Meeting, to Fort Wayne, in 1804* (Philadelphia: T. E. Zell, 1862), 65. (The journalist in this source was being guided by William Wells, who had been present at the battle fighting alongside Little Turtle—he had been captured by the Miamis at the age of twelve. Wells later changed sides and joined the American army under General Anthony Wayne.)

115. This is discussed further in chapter 7.

116. Journal of William Preston, 1756, of the Sandy Creek Expedition, Draper Mss 21U.

117. NYCD 3:800–5.

118. NYCD 6:779–80.

119. Harmar's letter is printed in Ebenezer Denny, *Military Journal of Major Ebenezer Denny: An Officer in the Revolutionary and Indian Wars* (Philadelphia: J. B. Lippincott & Co., 1859), 422.

120. Stevens, *Wilderness Chronicles*, 145; Louise Phelps Kellogg, *Frontier Retreat on the Upper Ohio, 1779–1781* (Madison: Wisconsin Historical Society, 1917), 310–11.

121. Loudoun to Blair, February 13, 1758, Box 2, Folder 43; Byrd to Loudoun, March 1758, Box 2 Folder 68; Capt. Abraham Bosomworth, A Return of the Southern Indians, April 21, 1758, Box 2, Folder 133, all in the Headquarters Papers of Brigadier-General John Forbes Relating to the Expedition against Fort Duquesne in 1758, 1729–1759, Accession #10034, Special Collections, University of Virginia Library, Charlottesville, Va. Copies kindly provided to me by David Preston.

122. Pouchot, *Memoir*, 475–78. Pouchot may be echoing earlier French authors here; Lafitau says something very similar about when the attackers approach their target and "they stop shooting guns in huting and begin to live on provisions of flour which they have brought. They dampen it with a little cold water or eat it dry and down it with a great cup [of water]." Lafitau, *Customs*, 2:141.

123. James Smith discussed this dynamic in the anecdote that opened this chapter.

124. Gabriel Sagard, *The Long Journey to the Country of the Hurons* (Toronto: The Champlain Society, 1939), 152–53.

125. These attacks were discussed in chapter 2.

Chapter Four

1. Much of this chapter duplicates with permission the text of Wayne E. Lee, "Peace Chiefs and Blood Revenge: Patterns of Restraint in Native American Warfare in the Contact and Colonial Eras," *Journal of Military History* 71 (2007): 701–41. In addition to updating some of the citations, some sections have been shortened while others have been expanded, particularly with regard to prisoners as slaves. A version of this essay that focuses more specifically on the problems of escalation and intercultural contact forms the core of chapters 5 and 6 in Wayne E. Lee, *Barbarians and Brothers: Anglo-American Warfare, 1500–1865* (New York: Oxford University Press, 2011).

2. There is a good summary of this status issue in Christina Snyder, "Conquered Enemies, Adopted Kin, and Owned People: The Creek Indians and Their Captives," *Journal of Southern History* 73 (2007): 267; and David H. Dye, *War Paths, Peace Paths: An Archaeology of Cooperation and Conflict in Native Eastern North America* (Lanham, Md.: AltaMira Press, 2009), 176.

3. Sources for these generalizations are discussed throughout the chapter.

4. The argument for rapid and largely unseen change as a result of European contact is now well rehearsed, but its implications for military behavior are still not clearly understood nor agreed upon. See Keith F. Otterbein, "A History of Research on Warfare in Anthropology," *American Anthropologist* 101 (2000): 794–805 and the follow-up commentaries in the same journal by Neil Whitehead, 102 (2000): 834–37; Leslie E. Sponsel, 102 (2000): 837–41; Otterbein, 102 (2000): 841–44; and R. K. Dentan, 104 (2002): 278–80; R. Brian Ferguson and Neil L. Whitehead, eds., *War in the Tribal Zone: Expanding States and Indigenous Societies* (Santa Fe, N.M.: School of American Research Press, 1992); and R. Brian Ferguson, "Violence and War in Prehistory," in *Troubled Times: Violence and Warfare in the Past*, ed. Debra L. Martin and David W. Frayer (Amsterdam: Gordon and Breach, 1997), 339–42.

5. Barbara Ehrenreich, *Blood Rites: Origins and History of the Passions of War* (New York: Henry Holt and Co., 1997), 132–43.

6. Essentially this is another caveat. During much of the competitive imperial colonization period, many Native American peoples limited the impact of war by manipulating their position at the crux of competing European empires, playing one side against the other to limit their own exposure. Although in part such a diplomatic role was made possible because of Native political structures discussed herein, the specific nature of the imperial standoff is not considered. Daniel K. Richter, "Native Peoples of North America and the Eighteenth-Century British Empire," in *The Oxford History of the British Empire, Vol. II: The Eighteenth Century*, ed. P. J. Marshall (Oxford: Oxford University Press, 1998), 357–60.

7. Frederic W. Gleach, *Powhatan's World and Colonial Virginia: A Conflict of Cultures* (Lincoln: University of Nebraska Press, 1997), 88–105; J. Frederick Fausz, "Patterns of Anglo-Indian Aggression and Accommodation along the Mid-Atlantic Coast, 1584–1634," in *Cultures in Contact: The Impact of European Contacts on Native American Cultural Institu-*

tions, A.D. 1000–1800, ed. William W. Fitzhugh (Washington, D.C.: Smithsonian Institution Press, 1985), 235–36; Karen Ordahl Kupperman, *The Jamestown Project* (Cambridge, Mass.: Belknap Press of Harvard University Press, 2007), 103–7; James Horn, *A Land As God Made It: Jamestown and the Birth of America* (New York: Basic Books, 2005), 12–16; and Helen C. Rountree, *Pocahontas's People: The Powhatan Indians of Virginia Through Four Centuries* (Norman: University of Oklahoma Press, 1996), 24–25.

8. *The Complete Works of Captain John Smith*, ed. Philip L. Barbour (Chapel Hill: University of North Carolina Press, 1986), 1:237.

9. Gleach, *Powhatan's World*, 130.

10. Horn, *Land as God Made It*, 249–50 discusses the succession (quote at 251). Helen C. Rountree sees the succession as more straightforward from Wahunsenacawh to Opitchapam to Opechancough. *Pocahontas, Powhatan, Opechancanough: Three Indian Lives Changed by Jamestown* (Charlottesville: University of Virginia Press, 2005), 23, 29–31.

11. Gleach, *Powhatan's World*, 142; Karen Ordahl Kupperman, *Indians and English: Facing Off in Early America* (Ithaca, N.Y.: Cornell University Press, 2000), 102.

12. Horn, *Land as God Made It*, 253.

13. Gleach calls the attack a "coup" in an effort to emphasize the limited goals of this style of warfare. Gleach, *Powhatan's World*, 148–58. This is not a reference to the "counting coup" practices of Plains Indians. For other narratives of the 1622 attack and the subsequent war see Edmund S. Morgan, *American Slavery, American Freedom* (New York: W.W. Norton & Co., 1975), 98–101; and William L. Shea, *The Virginia Militia in the Seventeenth Century* (Baton Rouge: Louisiana State University Press, 1983), 25–50.

14. See the map of the attacks in Horn, *Land as God Made It*, 256.

15. Gleach, *Powhatan's World*, 49–53; Kupperman, *Indians and English*, 196.

16. Chapter 5 discusses the outbreak of this war in more detail. The main source is George Chicken, "Journal of the March of the Carolinians into the Cherokee Mountains, in the Yemassee Indian War, 1715–16," *Yearbook of the City of Charleston* (1894): 315–54. See also Tom Hatley, *The Dividing Paths: Cherokees and South Carolinians Through the Revolutionary Era* (Oxford: Oxford University Press, 1995), 24–25; John Phillip Reid, *A Better Kind of Hatchet: Law, Trade, and Diplomacy in the Cherokee Nation During the Early Years of European Contact* (University Park: Pennsylvania State University Press, 1976), 61–73; John Philip Reid, *A Law of Blood: The Primitive Law of the Cherokee Nation* (New York: New York University Press, 1970), 175; and Verner Crane, *The Southern Frontier, 1670–1732* (Durham, N.C.: Duke University Press, 1929), 162–86.

17. For more on the Yamasee War, see William L. Ramsey, "'Something Cloudy in Their Looks': The Origins of the Yamasee War Reconsidered," *The Journal of American History* 90 (2003): 44–75; Alan Gallay, *The Indian Slave Trade: The Rise of the English Empire in the American South, 1670–1717* (New Haven, Conn.: Yale University Press, 2002), 338–41; Steven J. Oatis, *A Colonial Complex: South Carolina's Frontiers in the Era of the Yamasee War, 1680–1730* (Lincoln: University of Nebraska Press, 2008); and William L. Ramsey, *The Yamasee War: A Study of Culture, Economy, and Conflict in the Colonial South* (Lincoln: University of Nebraska Press, 2008).

18. Chicken, "Journal of the March (1715–16)," 345.

19. This process of fortification and abandonment is explored in more detail in chapters 5 and 8.

20. For Taliwa, see Hatley, *Dividing Paths*, 93; for the Creek attacks of 1752 and the subsequent peace, see David Corkran, *The Cherokee Frontier, 1740–1762* (Norman: University of Oklahoma Press, 1962), 35–37.

21. These claims are discussed in chapter 8.

22. Chicken, "Journal of the March (1715–16)," 342.

23. In many peoples, a fourth motive functioned in parallel with the political, blood feud, and status motives, and that was the acquisition of prisoners for adoption. This is discussed more fully below.

24. Anthony F. C. Wallace, *The Death and Rebirth of the Seneca* (New York: Vintage Books, 1969), 44.

25. A sophisticated and detailed discussion of the blood feud is Reid, *Law of Blood*. Among many others, see Charles Hudson, *The Southeastern Indians* (Knoxville: University of Tennessee Press, 1976), 230–32, 239–40; Richard White, *The Middle Ground: Indians, Empires, and Republics in the Great Lakes Region, 1650–1815* (Cambridge: Cambridge University Press, 1991), 80; and Gordon M. Sayre, *Les Sauvages Américains: Representations of Native Americans in French and English Colonial Literature* (Chapel Hill: University of North Carolina Press, 1997), 279–80.

26. Hudson, *Southeastern Indians*, 242, based on James Adair, *History of the American Indians*, ed. Samuel Cole Williams (New York: Promontory Press, 1930; repr. New York: Argonaut Press, 1966), 407. See also Cadwallader Colden's description of the possibility of such inter-Nation resolution of blood feud between the Adirondacks and the Iroquois. *The History of the Five Indian Nations of Canada* (London, 1747), 22. For other examples of intergroup attempts to assuage a blood feud before it got started see Kupperman, *Indians and English*, 106; Tobias Fitch, "Captain Fitch's Journal to the Creeks, 1725," in *Travels in the American Colonies*, ed. Newton D. Mereness (New York: Macmillan Co., 1916), 203; Reid, *Law of Blood*, 171–72; James Merrell, *Into the American Woods: Negotiators on the Pennsylvania Frontier* (New York: Knopf, 1999), 116–21; Colin G. Calloway, *The Western Abenakis of Vermont, 1600–1800: War, Migration, and the Survival of an Indian People* (Norman: University of Oklahoma Press, 1990), 165, 189–90; Wendell S. Hadlock, "War among the Northeastern Woodland Indians," *American Anthropologist* New Ser. 49 (1947): 213–14; and Kathleen Du-Val, "Cross-Cultural Crime and Osage Justice in the Western Mississippi Valley, 1700–1826," *Ethnohistory* 54 (2007): 699–702.

27. Talk of Tistoe and The Wolf of Keowee to Governor Lyttelton, March 5, 1759, Lyttelton Papers.

28. Matthew Kruer, "Bloody Minds and Peoples Undone: Emotion, Family, and Political Order in the Susquehannock-Virginia War," *William and Mary Quarterly* 3d Ser., 74, no. 3 (2017): 402; Matthew Kruer, *Time of Anarchy: Indigenous Power and the Crisis of Colonialism in Early America* (Cambridge, Mass.: Harvard University Press, 2021), esp. 16.

29. Reid, *Better Kind of Hatchet*, 9.

30. Ferguson argues that this lack of coercive structures was the most fundamental limitation on prestate warfare. Ferguson, "Violence and War in Prehistory," 336.

31. For one example of this ideology at work see John Winthrop, *The Journal of John Winthrop, 1630–1649*, unabridged edition, ed. Richard S. Dunn, James Savage, and Laetitia Yeandel (Cambridge, Mass.: Harvard University Press, 1996), 252.

32. Edward Waterhouse, *A Declaration of the State of the Colony in Virginia* (London, 1622; repr., New York: Da Capo Press, 1970), 22–23.

33. Lawrence H. Keeley, *War Before Civilization* (New York: Oxford University Press, 1996), 116; David H. Dye, "Warfare in the Sixteenth-Century Southeast: The de Soto Expedition in the Interior," in *Columbian Consequences, Vol. 2: Archaeological and Historical Perspectives on the Spanish Borderlands East,* ed. David Hurst Thomas (Washington, D.C.: Smithsonian Institution Press, 1990), 211–22; David H. Dye, "Warfare in the Protohistoric Southeast, 1500–1700," in *Between Contacts and Colonies: Archaeological Perspectives on the Protohistoric Southeast,* ed. Cameron B. Wesson and Mark A. Rees (Tuscaloosa: University of Alabama Press, 2002), 131–32; Karl T. Steinen, "Ambushes, Raids, and Palisades: Mississippian Warfare in the Interior Southeast," *Southeastern Archaeology* 11 (1992): 132–39; David G. Anderson, "Fluctuations between Simple and Complex Chiefdoms: Cycling in the Late Prehistoric Southeast," in *Political Structure and Change in the Prehistoric Southeastern United States,* ed. John F. Scarry (Gainesville: University Press of Florida, 1996), 245–46; Mark A. Rees, "Coercion, Tribute, and Chiefly Authority: The Regional Development of Mississippian Political Culture," *Southeastern Archaeology* 16, no. 2 (1997): 113–33; and Timothy R. Pauketat, *Chiefdoms and Other Archaeological Delusions* (Lanham, Md.: AltaMira Press, 2007).

34. Thomas E. Davidson, "Relations between the Powhatans and the Eastern Shore," in *Powhatan Foreign Relations,* 146–47, 150; William Strachey, *The Historie of Travell into Virginia Britania (1612),* 2nd Ser., vol. 103, ed. Louis B. Wright and Virginia Freund (London: Hakluyt Society, 1953), 87; Russell Dylan Ruediger, "Tributary Subjects: Affective Colonialism, Power, and the Process of Subjugation in Colonial Virginia, c. 1600–c. 1740," (Ph.D. Diss., Georgia State University, 2017); and Stephen R. Potter, *Commoners, Tribute and Chiefs: The Development of Algonquian Culture in the Potomac Valley* (Charlottesville: University of Virginia Press, 1993). There are other examples of the absorption of people as a blend of tributary and adoption, including the hopes of the Narragansett allies of the English in 1637, who lamented the killing of so many Pequots at Mystic whom they had hoped to control after their defeat. Lee, *Barbarians and Brothers,* 154–55.

35. HNAI 15:315; Leroy V. Eid, "'National War' among Indians of Northeastern North America," *Canadian Review of American Studies* 16 (1985): 125–54. For Mississippian conquest warfare see note 61.

36. Quote is from Joseph François Lafitau, *Customs of the American Indians Compared With the Customs of Primitive Times,* ed. William N. Fenton and Elizabeth L. Moore (Toronto: The Champlain Society, 1974), 2:101.

37. Neal Salisbury, *Manitou and Providence: Indians, Europeans, and the Making of New England, 1500–1643* (Oxford: Oxford University Press, 1982), 229. For other discussions of "political" goals for Native American warfare see Gleach, *Powhatan's World,* 51–54; and Thomas C. Parramore, "The Tuscarora Ascendancy," *North Carolina Historical Review* 59 (1982): 322–23.

38. Thus the Keowee Cherokees' threat to draw in other towns as quoted above.

39. See note 33. This concept is discussed further in chapter 8.

40. Roger Williams to Sir Henry Vane and John Winthrop, May 15, 1637, in Allyn Bailey Forbes, ed., *Winthrop Papers, Volume III: 1631–1637* (Boston: Massachusetts Historical Society, 1943), 413.

41. For example, the Montagnais and the Haudenosaunee once agreed to "spare the blood of our followers" and submit to the judgment of a wrestling contest. JR 1:269–70.

42. Hudson, *Southeastern Indians*, 257; Daniel K. Richter, *The Ordeal of the Longhouse: The Peoples of the Iroquois League in the Era of European Colonization* (Chapel Hill: University of North Carolina Press, 1992), 40. See also below in the section on making peace.

43. For examples of the red stick or red flag see Hudson, *Southeastern Indians*, 243; and Adair, *History*, 408. Similarly, there is the famous story of the Narragansett chief, Canonicus, sending a clear warning of impending war to the Plymouth colonists in the form of a rattlesnake's skin wrapped around a bundle of arrows. Governor Bradford's response of returning the skin stuffed with powder and shot sufficiently impressed Canonicus that he backed off from his challenge. William Bradford, *Of Plymouth Plantation, 1620–1647* (New York: Random House, 1981), 106; Alden T. Vaughan, *New England Frontier: Puritans and Indians, 1620–1675*, 3rd ed. (Norman: University of Oklahoma Press, 1995), 79–80.

44. Karen Ordahl Kupperman, ed., *Captain John Smith: A Select Edition of His Writings* (Chapel Hill: University of North Carolina Press, 1998), 165. For a modern parallel consider the United States' bombing of Libya in 1986, or the cruise missile strikes in Sudan and Afghanistan in 1998. Drone strikes in general in countries outside declared zones of hostility also fit into this paradigm.

45. Richter, "Native Peoples," 357.

46. Hatley, *Dividing Paths*, 44–45. The original document is available as: John Sharp to Governor Nicholson, November 12, 1724, in *Calendar of State Papers, Colonial Series, American and West Indies, 1574–1739*, CD-ROM, ed. Karen Ordahl Kupperman, John C. Appleby, and Mandy Banton (London: Routledge, 2000), Item 429v, 34:280.

47. See chapter 5. The blaming of young men was a common diplomatic ploy throughout the Eastern Woodlands; see DuVal, "Cross-Cultural Crime," 698, for one example from further west.

48. Hudson, *Southeastern Indians*, 243–44; Adair, *History*, 167–78.

49. John Gyles, "Memoirs of Odd Adventures, Strange Deliverances, etc.," in *Puritans among the Indians: Accounts of Captivity and Redemption, 1676–1724*, ed. Alden T. Vaughan and Edward W. Clark (Cambridge, Mass.: Harvard University Press, 1981), 120.

50. Mary Rowlandson, *The Sovereignty and Goodness of God*, ed. Neil Salisbury (Boston: Bedford Books, 1997), 100.

51. HNAI 15:685–86. Examples can expand almost infinitely. For the Haudenosaunee, see HNAI 15:315–16.

52. Alfred A. Cave, *The Pequot War* (Amherst: University of Massachusetts Press, 1996), 22; J. Frederick Fausz, "Fighting 'Fire' with Firearms: The Anglo-Powhatan Arms Race in Early Virginia," *American Indian Culture and Research Journal* 3 (1979): 41–42; and Corkran, *Cherokee Frontier*, 155.

53. Gregory Evans Dowd, *A Spirited Resistance: The North American Indian Struggle for Unity, 1745–1815* (Baltimore: The Johns Hopkins University Press, 1992), 1–22 contains an extensive discussion of the relationship of the spiritual, the material, and war.

54. George Turner to Governor Lyttelton, July 2, 1758, in DRIA 2:471. Colin Calloway documents a similar instance of the Creeks delaying a war party until the completion of the Green Corn ceremony. *The American Revolution in Indian Country: Crisis and Diversity in Native American Communities* (Cambridge: Cambridge University Press, 1995), 62.

55. JR 47:227. War parties also carried medicine bundles or other sacred objects whose loss could send the warriors home. Hudson, *Southeastern Indians*, 244, 247; Adair, *History*, 409; Gleach, *Powhatan's World*, 53; and HNAI 15:685, 695–96.

56. James Axtell, "The White Indians of Colonial America," *William and Mary Quarterly* 3d Ser., 32, no. 1 (1975): 67; Rowlandson, *Sovereignty and Goodness*, 107, note 82; Thomas S. Abler, "Scalping, Torture, Cannibalism and Rape: An Ethnohistorical Analysis of Conflicting Values in War," *Anthropologica* 34 (1992): 13; Dowd, *Spirited Resistance*, 9–10; Armstrong Starkey, *European and Native American Warfare, 1675–1815* (Norman: University of Oklahoma Press, 1998), 28, 81; Cave, *Pequot War*, 20; Elizabeth Hanson, "God's Mercy Surmounting Man's Cruelty," in *Puritans among the Indians*, 242 (see also the editors' comments at 14); Adair, *History*, 171–72; and James Drake, "Restraining Atrocity: The Conduct of King Philip's War," *New England Quarterly* 70, no. 1 (1997): 50.

57. Hatley, *Dividing Paths*, 107; Adair, *History*, 260–61; and Fintan O'Toole, *White Savage: William Johnson and the Invention of America* (New York: Farrar, Straus and Giroux, 2005), 264. Richard White reports another instance of Indians taking revenge for the rape of women in the 1760s. *Middle Ground*, 345.

58. Hudson, *Southeastern Indians*, 252. See also Starkey, *Warfare*, 28.

59. HNAI 15:628. See also the Miamis' postraid ritual, which although not as directly confining, deprived the warriors of their personal sacred bundles for several days, presumably preventing them from returning to war immediately. HNAI 15:685.

60. As an example, Claudio Saunt describes the limited coercive power within Creek communities prior to the late eighteenth century in *A New Order of Things: Property, Power, and the Transformation of the Creek Indians* (New York: Cambridge University Press, 1999), 1, 21–22.

61. Native American societies that had combined, or partially combined, this tripartite power structure into one person were typically more militant and aggressive. Frederic Gleach has made this argument for Powhatan's power in Virginia: for reasons unknown, Powhatan had successfully combined civil, military, and religious authority in his person, and thus was able to embark on building a paramount chiefdom. Gleach, *Powhatan's World*, 31. Similarly, the more centralized and urbanized Mississippian societies of the late prehistoric Southeast were ruled by "priest-kings" who combined civil, military, and sacred functions, and waged aggressive conquest warfare in competition with each other and with surrounding less centralized peoples. Charles Hudson, *Knights of Spain, Warriors of the Sun: Hernando De Soto and the South's Ancient Chiefdoms* (Athens: University of Georgia Press, 1997), 17; David H. Dye, "The Art of War in the Sixteenth-Century Central Mississippi Valley," in *Perspectives on the Southeast: Linguistics, Archaeology and Ethnohistory*, ed. Patricia B. Kwachka (Athens: University of Georgia Press, 1994), 54–56; Dye, "Warfare in the Sixteenth-Century Southeast," 213–14; Dye, *War Paths, Peace Paths*, 151–55; and Matthew Jennings, *New Worlds of Violence: Cultures and Conquests in the Early American Southeast* (Knoxville: University of Tennessee Press, 2011), 1–80.

62. Adair, *History*, 167–68.

63. Colden, *History*, 6–7; Gyles, "Memoirs," 120; JR 47:221–31; and Sayre, *Sauvages Américains*, 275–76.

64. See, for example, Richter, *Ordeal*, 34–35; Cave, *Pequot War*, 3; Bruce G. Trigger, *The Children of Aataentsic: A History of the Huron People to 1660* (Montreal: McGill-Queen's University Press, 1976), 1:69; Saunt, *New Order of Things*, 21; and Hadlock, "War," 211.

65. Pierre Francois Xavier de Charlevoix, *Journal of a Voyage to North America* (London, 1761), 1:360, cited in Stephen Brumwell, *Redcoats: The British Soldier and War in the Americas, 1755–1763* (New York: Cambridge University Press, 2002), 204. See also the Iroquois mobilization process described in José António Brandão, ed., *Nation Iroquoise: A Seventeenth-Century Ethnography of the Iroquois* (Lincoln: University of Nebraska Press, 2003), 67, 73, 75.

66. Adair, *History*, 416.

67. HNAI 15:676. See also Stephen Aron, *How the West Was Lost: The Transformation of Kentucky from Daniel Boone to Henry Clay* (Baltimore: Johns Hopkins University Press, 1996), 34; and Sayre, *Sauvages Américains*, 270.

68. Cave, *Pequot War*, 157.

69. Some anthropologists and ethnohistorians would disagree with this statement, arguing that the casualty counts documented in the historic era (such as the 1649 Haudenosaunee attack discussed in chapter 2) resulted from European influence.

70. Craig S. Keener, "An Ethnohistorical Analysis of Iroquois Assault Tactics Used against Fortified Settlements of the Northeast in the Seventeenth Century," *Ethnohistory* 46 (1999): 777–807; and Paul Hulton, ed., *The Work of Jacques le Moyne de Morgues: A Huguenot Artist in France, Florida and England* (London: Trustees of the British Museum, 1977), 1:149 and plate 123. Compare Patrick M. Malone, *The Skulking Way of War: Technology and Tactics among the New England Indians* (1991; repr., Baltimore: Johns Hopkins University Press, 1993),, 14; and Vaughan, *New England Frontier*, xxv. Dye argues that Mississippian chiefdoms *did* rely on mass assaults in the precontact era, reflecting greater coercive authority over a larger regional population. *War Path, Peace Paths*, 145.

71. George R. Milner, "Warfare in Prehistoric and Early Historic Eastern North America," *Journal of Archaeological Research* 7 (1999): 126–27; Patricia M. Lambert, "The Archaeology of War: A North American Perspective," *Journal of Archaeological Research* 10 (2002): 227–29; and Maria Ostendorf Smith, "Osteological Indications of Warfare in the Archaic Period of the Western Tennessee Valley," in *Troubled Times*, 241–66.

72. This does not mean that "ritualism" disappeared, just the ritual battle. Fausz, "Fighting Fire"; Starkey, *Warfare*, 24–25; Richter, *Ordeal*, 54; and Otterbein, "Why the Iroquois Won," 59–60. Note that these sources argue for the shift in tactics due to firearms. My argument, with significant influence from Otterbein and Divale, is for a broader shift from a duality of war styles (ritual battle and deadly ambush) to a stricter reliance on the ambush based on the shifting balance of offense versus defense. Otterbein, "History," 800; William Tulio Divale, *Warfare in Primitive Societies: A Bibliography* (Santa Barbara, Calif.: ABC-Clio, 1973), xxi–xxii; and Thomas B. Abler, "European Technology and the Art of War in Iroquoia," in *Cultures in Conflict: Current Archaeological Perspectives*, ed. Diana Tkaczuk and Brian C. Vivian (Calgary: University of Calgary Archaeology Association, 1989), 278–79. Lawrence Keeley's emphasis in *War Before Civilization* on the per capita lethality of primitive warfare in general is an important stimulus to this argument. See also chapter 6 in this book.

73. Leroy V. Eid, "'A Kind of Running Fight': Indian Battlefield Tactics in the late Eighteenth Century," *Western Pennsylvania Historical Magazine* 71 (1988): 147–71; DRIA 2:467, 468; and Gleach, *Powhatan's World*, 43.

74. Francis Jennings, *The Invasion of America: Indians, Colonialism, and the Cant of Conquest* (New York: W. W. Norton & Co., 1975), 152–53; Malone, *Skulking Way of War*, 103–4.

75. Lion Gardiner, "Relation," 131–32, cited in Cave, *Pequot War*, 133.

76. Paul A. Robinson, "Lost Opportunities: Miantonomi and the English in Seventeenth-Century Narragansett Country," in *Northeastern Indian Lives, 1632–1816*, ed. Robert S. Grumet (Amherst: University of Massachusetts Press, 1996), 22–23.

77. John Underhill, *Newes From America* (London, 1638; repr., New York: Da Capo Press, 1971), 42–43.

78. See note 70, esp. Keener, "Ethnohistorical Analysis," 783, 785.

79. D. Owsley and H. Berryman, "Ethnographic and Archaeological Evidence of Scalping in the Southeastern United States," *Tennessee Archaeologist* 31 (1975): 41–60; Gardiner, "Relation," 131–32, cited in Cave, *Pequot War*, 134. There is also strong archaeological evidence for prehistoric killing of women. Richard G. Wilkinson, "Violence against Women: Raiding and Abduction in Prehistoric Michigan," in *Troubled Times*, 21–44. The extent of such killing is debated, but it certainly occurred. See Brian Ferguson's summary essay, "Violence and War in Prehistory," in the same volume, 321–55.

80. Karen Anderson, *Chain Her by One Foot: The Subjugation of Native Women in Seventeenth-Century New France* (New York: Routledge, 1991), 169–78; Richter, *Ordeal*, 35–36; and Hudson, *Southeastern Indians*, 254–55. Hudson also indicates that intertwined with torture as an expression of grief was a spiritual component. That is, torture also served a ritual purpose. Cf. Trigger, *Children*, 1:73–74. For a survey of the different torture rituals see Nathaniel Knowles, "The Torture of Captives by the Indians of Eastern North America," *American Philosophical Society Proceedings* 82 (1940): 151–225.

81. José António Brandão, *"Your Fyre Shall Burn No More": Iroquois Policy Toward New France and Its Native Allies to 1701* (Lincoln: University of Nebraska Press, 1997), 130–31; Richter, "War and Culture"; Richter, *Ordeal*, 30–74; and Jon Parmenter, *The Edge of the Woods: Iroquoia, 1534–1701* (East Lansing: Michigan State University Press, 2010), 103.

82. See, for example, Helen C. Rountree, "The Powhatans and Other Woodland Indians as Travelers," in *Powhatan Foreign Relations, 1500–1722*, ed. Helen C. Rountree (Charlottesville: University Press of Virginia, 1993), 50; Starkey, *Warfare*, 29–30; James Merrell, *The Indians' New World* (Chapel Hill: University of North Carolina Press, 1989), 30–31; and Colin G. Calloway, *New Worlds for All: Indians, Europeans, and the Remaking of Early America* (Baltimore: Johns Hopkins University Press, 1997), 142–51.

83. Brett Rushforth, *Bonds of Alliance: Indigenous and Atlantic Slaveries in New France* (Chapel Hill: University of North Carolina Press, 2013), 35–72. Also see Christina Snyder, *Slavery in Indian Country: The Changing Face of Captivity in Early America* (Cambridge, Mass.: Harvard University Press, 2010); and Robin Beck, *Chiefdoms, Collapse, and Coalescence in the Early American South* (New York: Cambridge University Press, 2013).

84. For a good discussion of the various uses of prisoners see Ian K. Steele, "Surrendering Rites: Prisoners on Colonial North American Frontiers," in *Hanoverian Britain and Empire: Essays in Memory of Philip Lawson*, ed. Stephen Taylor, Richard Connors, Clyve Jones, and Philip Lawson (Woodbridge, UK: Boydell Press, 1998), 138–42. Richter argues that the whole nature of Iroquois warfare (reliance on surprise, avoidance of assaulting forts, ritualized battles) was determined by this desire to take prisoners. *Ordeal*, 37–38.

85. Increase Mather, "Quentin Stockwell's Relation of his Captivity and Redemption," in *Puritans among the Indians*, 81; Ian K. Steele, *Betrayals: Fort William Henry & the "Massacre"* (New York: Oxford University Press, 1990), 121.

86. Richter, *Ordeal*, 40.

87. James Axtell, "The Scholastic Philosophy of the Wilderness," in *The European and the Indian: Essays in the Ethnohistory of Colonial North America* (Oxford: Oxford University Press, 1981), 138–50; Wayne E. Lee, *Crowds and Soldiers in Revolutionary North Carolina: The Culture of Violence in Riot and War* (Gainesville: University Press of Florida, 2001), 119–29. I cannot stress strongly enough that obviously Europeans did not adhere to their own norms, but even so, they frequently used this prisoner issue as a rhetorical tool to point to Indian "barbarity."

88. John Lawson, *A New Voyage to Carolina* (London, 1709; repr., Chapel Hill: University of North Carolina Press, 1967), 207.

89. John Demos, *The Unredeemed Captive* (New York: Vintage Books, 1994), 24, 29, 33, 38–39.

90. JR 34:135–37.

91. Adair, *History*, 427.

92. Steele, *Betrayals*, 113, 131, 184.

93. Chicken, "Journal of the March (1715–16)," 345–46. Roger Williams's dictionary is again helpful in imagining this process, including such phrases as "let us parley" or "let us cease Armes." Roger Williams, *A Key into the Language of America* (1643; repr., Bedford, Mass.: Applewood Books, 1997), 189. See also JR 70:195.

94. A third party would not be implicated in the ongoing cycle of blood revenge, and therefore could approach the warring sides in greater safety. The English often saw themselves as filling this third-party role, but usually for their own economic reasons, since they preferred to trade with all comers. See for example the Pequots' appeal to the English in 1634. Cave, *Pequot War*, 69–70. Similarly, the Indians sought to use Rhode Island as an intermediary between themselves and the other New England colonies at the outset of King Philip's War. John Easton, "A Relacion of the Indyan Warre," in *Narratives of the Indians Wars, 1675–1699*, ed. Charles H. Lincoln (New York: Charles Scribner, 1913), 8–9.

95. JR 27:246–73. See Richter, *Ordeal*, 41 and Hudson, *Southeastern Indians*, 257 for more details on the peacemaking process.

96. Quotes from Gardiner, "Relation," 131–32 cited in Cave, *Pequot War*, 133. For another example of the protection of embassies, see Rowlandson, *Sovereignty and Goodness*, 102–3, especially where the Wampanoag leadership expressed regret that some "Matchit" [bad] Indian had stolen provisions from the English embassy.

97. HNAI 15:314–15; Gleach, *Powhatan's World*, 34–35; and Aron, *How the West*, 34.

98. Hudson, *Southeastern Indians*, 223–24. For Chickasaw peace chiefs, see Robbie Ethridge, *From Chicaza to Chickasaw: The European Invasion and the Transformation of the Mississippian World, 1540–1715* (Chapel Hill: University of North Carolina Press, 2010), 228.

99. "The Examination and Relation of James Quannapaquait," in Rowlandson, *Sovereignty and Goodness*, 124–25; Lafitau, *Customs*, 2:101–3; Calloway, *Western Abenakis*, 172; and Saunt, *A New Order*, 23–25.

100. HNAI 15:192, 314–15. One European observer, for example, exactly reversed the real power relationship among the Cherokees: "Every Town has a Head Warrior, who is in great

Esteem among them, and whose Authority seems to be greater than their Kings, because their King is looked upon as little else than a Civil Magistrate, except it so happens that he is at the same Time a Head Warrior." Sir Alexander Cuming, "Journal of Sir Alexander Cuming (1730)," in *Early Travels in the Tennessee Country, 1540–1800*, ed. Samuel Cole Williams (Johnson City, Tenn.: The Watauga Press, 1928), 122.

101. Rennard Strickland, *Fire and the Spirits: Cherokee Law From Clan to Court* (Norman: University of Oklahoma Press, 1975), 47–48; Hudson, *Southeastern Indians*, 222; HNAI 15:192, 315; Wallace, *Death and Rebirth*, 40; James Axtell, *Natives and Newcomers: The Cultural Origins of North America* (New York: Oxford University Press, 2001), 139; Fred Gearing, *Priests and Warriors: Social Structures for Cherokee Politics in the 18th Century* (Menasha, Wisc.: American Anthropological Association, Memoir 93, 1962); Calloway, *New Worlds for All*, 111; and Lisa Brooks, *Our Beloved Kin: A New History of King Philip's War* (New Haven, Conn.: Yale University Press, 2018), 30. See also the theoretical discussion of this issue in Ferguson, "Violence and War," 336.

102. This issue of peace chiefs, as well as the role of women in decision-making, is explored further in chapter 6.

103. For pushing men to war, see Wallace, *Death and Rebirth*, 101; and Richter, *Ordeal of the Longhouse*, 60, 224. For pushing an end to war, see Saunt, *New Order of Things*, 25; and Hudson, *Southeastern Indians*, 187.

104. The role of Europeans in diminishing women's influence within Native societies forms a substantial literature: see Anderson, *Chain Her*; and Calloway, *New Worlds for All*, 191.

105. Saunt, *New Order of Things*, 25.

106. Evan Haefeli's work on the treaty making between the Lenape and the Mohicans with the Haudenosaunee is particularly illuminating in the complex role that fictive kin identification (and specifically gender-based identifiers for whole Nations) played in creating a mechanism to sustain peace. Presumably, identifying a formerly enemy Nation as now kin helped undermine the imperatives of the blood feud. "Becoming a 'Nation of Statesmen': The Mohicans' Incorporation into the Iroquois League, 1671–1675," *New England Quarterly* 93 (2020): 414–61; and "The Great Haudenosaunee-Lenape Peace of 1669: Oral Traditions, Colonial Records, and the Origin of the Delaware's Status as 'Women,'" *New York History* (Forthcoming).

107. Reid, *Better Kind of Hatchet*, 10; Richter, *Ordeal*, 40, 44–45.

108. Kupperman, *Indians and English*, 197–99. Kupperman provides a more extensive analysis of the exchange of children in Karen Ordahl Kupperman, *Pocahontas and the English Boys: Caught Between Cultures in Early Virginia* (New York: NYU Press, 2021).

109. The Cherokees discussed in chapter 5 refused the English request for help in 1715 against the Yamasees, as they had too many kin connections, but agreed to fight other groups. Contemporaries and historians have long observed the role that kinship played in affecting Haudenosaunee military choices. Karim M. Tiro has shown the warnings passed back and forth between the divided members of the Haudenosaunee during the American Revolution: "A 'Civil' War? Rethinking Iroquois Participation in the American Revolution," *Explorations in Early American Culture* 4 (2000): 148–65, and personal communication. Also see Stephen Brumwell, *White Devil: A True Story of War, Savagery, and Vengeance in Colonial America* (Cambridge, Mass.: Da Capo Press, 2005), 193–94. This role of kinship in channeling and restraining war is also a central argument of Brooks, *Our Beloved Kin*.

110. Ralph Hamor, *A True Discourse of the Present State of Virginia (1615)* (London, 1615; repr., New York: Da Capo Press, 1971), 38.

111. Gleach, *Powhatan's World*, 152–54; Rountree, "Powhatans," 50.

112. Kupperman, *Indians and English*, 198–99; Kupperman, *Pocahontas*, 6, 33. For a discussion of diplomatic marriages in another context see Hudson, *Southeastern Indians*, 234.

113. Reid, *Better Kind of Hatchet*, 9–10; Cave, *Pequot War*, 157 (for the Pequots' killing of English-allied Mohegans living among them after the disaster at Mystic).

114. Ian K. Steele, "Surrendering Rites," 138; Hatley, *Dividing Paths*, 94; Richter, *Ordeal*, 111; Reid, *Better Kind of Hatchet*, 111; Trigger, *Huron*, 53; Cave, *Pequot War*, 66–67; Wayne E. Clark and Helen C. Rountree, "The Powhatans and the Maryland Mainland," in *Powhatan Foreign Relations*, 132; and R. Demere to Gov. Lyttelton, July 23, 1757; R. Demere to Gov. Lyttelton, June 26, 1757; and White Outerbridge to Gov. Lyttelton, March 8, 1757, all in Lyttelton Papers. Reid points out, however, that such resident aliens could also be loose cannons, acting on their own needs and thus creating trouble for the community in which they lived. *Law of Blood*, 163–72.

115. The Jesuit Jean de Brébeuf saw this warning function as the main intent of sending and receiving visitors to and from the village. JR 10:229. See also the warnings passed along by one of Robert Rogers's Indian scouts to the target of Rogers's impending attack. Calloway, *Western Abenakis*, 178. There is a similar example in *Western Abenakis*, 212.

116. Gleach, *Powhatan's World*, 49–53; Kupperman, *Indians and English*, 196.

117. "Examination and Relation," in Rowlandson, *Sovereignty and Goodness*, 120.

118. The Europeans viewed such "go-betweens" much differently. For an extended treatment of the initial successes and ultimate failures of intermediaries between Europeans and Indians see Merrell, *Into the American Woods*. Note, however, that I am treating "resident alien" as a much more specific category than Merrell's "go-betweens."

119. Ethridge, *From Chicaza*, 228; Greg O'Brien, *Choctaws in a Revolutionary Age, 1750–1830* (Lincoln: University of Nebraska Press, 2002), 63.

120. There are two other significant peacekeeping structures worth mentioning, but space forbids detailed treatment. The first was the Haudenosaunee Confederacy, an elaborate governmental device designed to keep the peace between its five (later six) members (Mohawk, Cayuga, Oneida, Onondaga, Seneca, and later Tuscarora). It seems to have originated to quell blood feuds among those groups that at the time were deemed out of control. It was not necessarily designed to conduct diplomacy with outside groups, but to preserve peace internal to the confederacy. Richter, *Ordeal*, 30–49; Wallace, *Death and Rebirth*, 44–47. The other was the ball game, known to posterity as lacrosse. There is some suggestion that intertribal lacrosse matches, known as the "little brother of war," may have served as an outlet for young men's aggression, although it did not seem to deal with revenge issues or serve as a substitute for "grand" or national war. Thomas Vennum, *American Indian Lacrosse: Little Brother of War* (Washington, D.C.: Smithsonian Institution Press, 1994).

121. Chapters 5, 6, and 8 of my *Barbarians and Brothers* explore the problem of intercultural escalation in much greater detail. Also see Peter Way, "The Cutting Edge of Culture: British Soldiers Encounter Native Americans in the French and Indian War," in *Empire and Others: British Encounters With Indigenous Peoples, 1600–1850*, ed. Martin Daunton and Rick Halpern (Philadelphia: University of Pennsylvania Press, 1999), 123–48; Adam J. Hirsch,

"The Collision of Military Cultures in Seventeenth-Century New England," *Journal of American History* 74, no. 4 (1988): 1187–212; Gregory T. Knouff, "Soldiers and Violence on the Pennsylvania Frontier," in *Beyond Philadelphia: The Pennsylvania Hinterland in the American Revolution*, ed. John B. Frantz and William Pencak (University Park: Pennsylvania State University Press, 1998), 171–93; and Lee, *Crowds and Soldiers*, 117–29. A variant of this argument postulates that Europeans arrived in North America during the horribly violent era of the Religious Wars, and that they brought that form of unrestrained warfare with them. In the face of an "uncivilized" enemy, the colonists preserved that way of war despite changes in Europe itself. John Ferling, *A Wilderness of Miseries: War and Warriors in Early America* (Westport, Conn.: Greenwood Press, 1980), 29–54; John Morgan Dederer, *War in America to 1775: Before Yankee Doodle* (New York: New York University Press, 1990), 127, 129–36; Malone, *Skulking Way of War*, 102; and Ronald Dale Karr, "'Why Should You Be So Furious?': The Violence of the Pequot War," *Journal of American History* 85 (1998): 876–909.

122. The idea that European technology increased lethality is a commonplace in histories of Native American warfare (for example: Malone, *Skulking Way of War*, 65; Donald E. Worcester and Thomas E. Schilz, "The Spread of Firearms among the Indians on the Anglo-French Frontiers," *American Indian Quarterly* 8 (1984): 103; and Calloway, *Western Abenakis*, 56, 61, 88). The role of a desire for European trade goods in leading to an increased frequency of war for control of trade routes or trade items (notably fur) is more complex. For reviews of the development of this debate see Brandão, *"Your Fyre,"* 5–18; Thomas S. Abler, "Iroquois Policy and Iroquois Culture: Two Histories and an Anthropological Ethnohistory," *Ethnohistory*, 47 (2000): 483–91; William A. Starna and José António Brandão, "From the Mohawk-Mahican War to the Beaver Wars: Questioning the Pattern," *Ethnohistory* 51 (2004): 725–50; George T. Hunt, *The Wars of the Iroquois: A Study in Intertribal Trade Relations* (Madison: University of Wisconsin Press, 1940); and Richter, *Ordeal*, 55–74. For a general theory of European-induced escalation, see Ferguson and Whitehead, *War in the Tribal Zone*; and Ferguson, "Violence and War," 339–42. Alan Gallay, however, in *Indian Slave Trade*, has convincingly demonstrated the increased frequency of Indian warfare as a result of their participation in the European slave trade, a participation that also dramatically altered the function and scale of prisoner taking. Since Gallay, a number of scholars have explored and expanded on the consequences of enslaving Indians on the extent and destructiveness of inter-Indian warfare. Matthew Jennings, *New Worlds of Violence: Cultures and Conquests in the Early American Southeast* (Knoxville: University of Tennessee Press, 2011); Robbie Ethridge and Sheri M. Shuck-Hall, eds., *Mapping the Mississippian Shatter Zone: The Colonial Indian Slave Trade and Regional Instability in the American South* (Lincoln: University of Nebraska Press, 2009); David J. Silverman, *Thundersticks: Firearms and the Violent Transformation of Native America* (Cambridge, Mass.: Belknap Press of Harvard University Press, 2016); Denise I. Bossy, "The South's Other Slavery: Recent Research on Indian Slavery," *Native South* 9 (2016): 27–53; and Matthew Kruer, *Time of Anarchy: Indigenous Power and the Crisis of Colonialism in Early America* (Cambridge, Mass.: Harvard University Press, 2021).

123. Richter, *Ordeal*, 58, 60.

124. James Drake argues that there was even a basic misunderstanding of the meaning of "hostage" during King Philip's War. James David Drake, *King Philip's War: Civil War in New England, 1675–1676* (Amherst: University of Massachusetts Press, 1999), 115–16.

125. Hamor, *True Discourse*, 44.

126. Jill Lepore, *The Name of War: King Philip's War and the Origins of American Identity* (New York: Alfred A. Knopf, 1998), 21.

127. Bradford, *Plymouth Plantation*, 108–9. Kathleen J. Bragdon suggests that Hobomock lived in Plymouth for about twenty years. *Native People of Southern New England, 1500–1650* (Norman: University of Oklahoma Press, 1996), 290.

128. Drake, *King Philip's War*, 87; Lepore, *Name of War*, 156–58. For a moving story of how two Praying Indians struggled to prove their loyalty in the face of persistent doubt see "The Examination and Relation of James Quannapaquait," in Rowlandson, *Sovereignty and Goodness*, 118–28.

129. Two famous examples in Pennsylvania were the Paxton Boys massacre in 1763 and Gnadenhutten in 1782: see Benjamin Franklin, "Narrative of the Late Massacres," in *The Papers of Benjamin Franklin*, ed. Leonard W. Labaree (New Haven, Conn.: Yale University Press, 1967), 11:42–69; and White, *Middle Ground*, 389–91. For other similar incidents see Jenny Hale Pulsipher, "Massacre at Hurtleberry Hill: Christian Indians and English Authority in Metacom's War," *William & Mary Quarterly* 3d Ser., 53, no. 3 (1996): 459–86; Dowd, *Spirited Resistance*, 65–87; and Aron, *How the West*, 49.

130. See Steele, "Surrendering Rites," 152–54 for a rare example of all sides' expectations of prisoner treatment being met, although the details of that success clearly delineate the fragility of the process.

131. Steele, "Surrendering Rites," 155–56.

132. See note 127 and White, *Middle Ground*, 345.

133. Karr argues in a similar vein about the failure to establish "reciprocity" in "Why Should You Be So Furious," esp. 888.

Chapter Five

1. The bulk of this chapter is reprinted here with permission from Wayne E. Lee, "Fortify, Fight, or Flee: Tuscarora and Cherokee Defensive Warfare and Military Culture Adaptation," *Journal of Military History* 68 (2004): 713–70. Some material has been cut out as it would be repetitive of chapter 2. Some additional sources have been added, and I have altered the discussion of bastions somewhat to reflect a more accurate set of definitions. Some of my criticisms of the existing literature are no longer quite accurate, but much of it remains true, so I have left that text substantially unchanged, while adding references to newer work in the notes.

2. Although many more had been killed by smallpox brought in by the 1759 expedition and through strains on subsistence created by three consecutive expeditions.

3. To be sure, similar stories could be told of Indians and fortifications in the Northeast, but there is greater clarity in the Southeast with its more uniform experience of contact moving inland from the coast toward the mountains. The complicating French presence to the west was more distant and less threatening than it was in the Northeast.

4. I refer here to the widespread contacts between fishermen and Indians in the North Atlantic and also to the arrival of the occasional Spaniard in the Southeast long before more literate sources arrived. Brian Ferguson and Neil Whitehead argue that the contact between states and more simple societies rapidly alters the nature of war even beyond the

immediate contact zone. R. Brian Ferguson and Neil L. Whitehead, eds., *War in the Tribal Zone: Expanding States and Indigenous Societies* (Santa Fe, N.M.: School of American Research Press, 1992).

5. Patrick M. Malone, *The Skulking Way of War: Technology and Tactics among the New England Indians* (1991; repr., Baltimore: Johns Hopkins University Press, 1993); Daniel K. Richter, "War and Culture: The Iroquois Experience," *William and Mary Quarterly* 3d Ser., 40, no. 4 (1983): 528–59; Daniel K. Richter, *The Ordeal of the Longhouse: The Peoples of the Iroquois League in the Era of European Colonization* (Chapel Hill: University of North Carolina Press, 1992); Frederick J. Fausz, "Patterns of Anglo-Indian Aggression and Accommodation along the Mid-Atlantic Coast, 1584–1634," in *Cultures in Contact: The Impact of European Contacts on Native American Cultural Institutions, A.D. 1000–1800*, ed. William W. Fitzhugh (Washington, D.C.: Smithsonian Institution Press, 1985), 225–68; Frederick J. Fausz, "Fighting 'Fire' with Firearms: The Anglo-Powhatan Arms Race in Early Virginia," *American Indian Culture and Research Journal* 3 (1979): 33–50; Craig S. Keener, "An Ethnohistorical Analysis of Iroquois Assault Tactics Used against Fortified Settlements of the Northeast in the Seventeenth Century," *Ethnohistory* 46 (1999): 777–807; Gordon M. Sayre, *Les Sauvages Americains: Representations of Native Americans in French and English Colonial Literature* (Chapel Hill: University of North Carolina Press, 1997); George T. Hunt, *The Wars of the Iroquois: A Study in Intertribal Trade Relations* (Madison: University of Wisconsin Press, 1940); Jose Antonio Brandao, *"Your Fyre Shall Burn No More": Iroquois Policy toward New France and Its Native Allies to 1701* (Lincoln: University of Nebraska Press, 1997); Craig S. Keener, "An Ethnohistoric Perspective on Iroquois Warfare During the Second Half of the Seventeenth Century (A.D. 1649–1701)" (Ph.D. Diss., Ohio State University, 1998); Thomas B. Abler, "European Technology and the Art of War in Iroquoia," in *Cultures in Conflict: Current Archaeological Perspectives*, ed. Diana Tkaczuk and Brian C. Vivian (Calgary: University of Calgary Archaeology Association, 1989), 273–82; Brian J. Given, *A Most Pernicious Thing: Gun Trading and Native Warfare in the Early Contact Period* (Ottawa: Carleton University Press, 1994); and Bruce G. Trigger, *The Children of Aataentsic: a History of the Huron People to 1660* (Montreal: McGill-Queen's University Press, 1976).

6. David J. Silverman, *Thundersticks: Firearms and the Violent Transformation of Native America* (Cambridge, Mass.: Belknap Press of Harvard University Press, 2016).

7. Thomas Parramore has documented the extensive trade networks of the Tuscarora, and in fact their regional dominance over both Indians and English up through the end of the seventeenth century. Thomas C. Parramore, "The Tuscarora Ascendancy," *North Carolina Historical Review* 59 (1982): 307–26.

8. Compare James H. Merrell, *The Indians' New World: Catawbas and Their Neighbors From European Contact Through the Era of Removal* (Chapel Hill: University of North Carolina Press, 1989), ix. Ian K. Steele, *Warpaths: Invasions of North America* (New York: Oxford University Press, 1994) is a fairly sensitive survey of Indian warfare and their adaptation to change, but is conducted on such a sweeping scale that the details of the process are elided.

9. Figure 5.2 is based on John E. Byrd and Charles L. Heath, "The Rediscovery of the Tuscarora Homeland: A Final Report of the Archaeological Survey of the Contentnea Creek Drainage, 1995–1997," report submitted to the National Park Service and the North Carolina Division of Archives and History, Raleigh, 1997 (available in the Office of State Archaeology, Greene County Surveys, #4153); Parramore, "Tuscarora Ascendancy," 318; and

David Sutton Phelps, "Archaeology of the North Carolina Coast and Coastal Plain: Problems and Hypotheses," in *The Prehistory of North Carolina: An Archaeological Symposium*, ed. Mark A. Mathis and Jeffrey J. Crow, (Raleigh: Division of Archives and History, North Carolina Department of Cultural Resources, 1983), 37.

10. Archaeologists refer to the precontact Native culture associated with the Tuscarora homeland in North Carolina as the "Cashie" phase, and they have come to believe that the Cashie phase began around 800 C.E., arising from an Iroquoian migration in 600 C.E.., and later becoming the historic Tuscarora. Byrd and Heath, "Rediscovery," 8–9; H. Trawick Ward and R. P. Stephen Jr. Davis, *Time Before History: The Archaeology of North Carolina* (Chapel Hill: University of North Carolina Press, 1999), 223–25; and Phelps, "Archaeology of the North Carolina Coast," 43. For the Tuscaroras' regional power see Parramore, "Tuscarora Ascendancy," 307–12.

11. Douglas W. Boyce, "Did a Tuscarora Confederacy Exist?," in *Four Centuries of Southern Indians*, ed. Charles M. Hudson (Athens: University of Georgia Press, 1975), 38.

12. HNAI 15:283; Parramore, "Tuscarora Ascendancy," 315, fn. 38.

13. Boyce, "Tuscarora Confederacy?," 34; Parramore, "Tuscarora Ascendancy," 323.

14. Parramore, "Tuscarora Ascendancy," 313; Douglas W. Boyce, "'As the Wind Scatters the Smoke': The Tuscaroras in the Eighteenth Century," in *Beyond the Covenant Chain: The Iroquois and Their Neighbors in Indian North America, 1600–1800*, ed. Daniel K. Richter and James H. Merrell (Syracuse, N.Y.: Syracuse University Press, 1987), 152.

15. Barnwell's Journal, 394.

16. Baron Christoph von Graffenried, *Christoph Von Graffenried's Account of the Founding of New Bern* (Raleigh, N.C.: Edwards & Broughton, Co., 1920), 266.

17. Ward and Davis, *Time Before History*, 275; Byrd and Heath, "Rediscovery," 10.

18. Phelps, "North Carolina Coast," 46; Ward and Davis, *Time Before History*, 224.

19. Graffenried, *Account of the Founding*, 272. The presumption here is that his transfer took place early enough in the conflict that whatever palisading he witnessed had already been in place before the war.

20. Byrd and Heath, "Rediscovery," 10; personal conversation with John Byrd and Charles Heath, April 20, 2001. Tuscarora conflict with groups to the north continued into the eighteenth century: Minutes of Council of Virginia, October 23, 1702, CSP-CS-AWI, item 1093, v20:690. David La Vere, *The Tuscarora War: Indians, Settlers, and the Fight for the Carolina Colonies* (Chapel Hill: University of North Carolina Press, 2013), 44 reviews the evidence on this more thoroughly.

21. Parramore, "Tuscarora Ascendancy," 311.

22. This fits in with the broader regional portrait of both fortified and unfortified villages as common features in the precontact landscape. John White's drawings of coastal Algonkian settlements include both types of villages. P. H. Hulton and David Beers Quinn, eds., *The American Drawings of John White, 1577–1590* (London & Chapel Hill, N.C.: University of North Carolina Press, 1964), 2: plates 31 and 35; Lewis H. Larson, Jr., "Functional Considerations of Warfare in the Southeast during the Mississippi Period," *American Antiquity* 37 (1972), 384. Further discussion of prehistoric palisading follows.

23. Paul Hulton, ed., *The Work of Jacques le Moyne de Morgues: A Huguenot Artist in France, Florida and England* (London: The Trustees of the British Museum, 1977), plate 122, text 1:149. See also Ward and Davis, *Time Before History*, 213–16.

24. Evidence for the northern Iroquois palisades is surveyed in Keener, "Iroquois Assault Tactics," 780–86. See also the illustrations in Bruce G. Trigger, *Natives and Newcomers: Canada's Heroic Age Reconsidered* (Toronto: University of Toronto Press, 1985), 180; Trigger, *Children*, 1:43–44; and the Pequot fortifications at Mystic, reproduced in Hirsch, "Collision of Military Cultures," 1189.

25. Le Moyne's drawing does not show a ditch, but his extensive caption describes one. Hulton, *Work*, 1:149. As for the Tuscarora, the Jordan's Landing site apparently had such a ditch, although the excavator has referred to it simply as a borrow pit for earth thrown up against the palisade wall. Phelps, "North Carolina Coast," 44–46; Abler, "European Technology," 276. Compare Larson, "Functional Considerations," 384.

26. Palisade walls two or three posts thick are attested for the northern Iroquoian peoples, and for sites in precontact western North Carolina (Pisgah culture) as well. Keener, "Iroquois Assault Tactics," 781–82; Ward and Davis, *Time Before History*, 161–63. For a complete survey, see David E. Jones, *Native North American Armor, Shields, and Fortifications* (Austin: University of Texas Press, 2004).

27. Larson, "Functional Considerations"; David J. Hally, "The Chiefdom of Coosa," in *The Forgotten Centuries: Indians and Europeans in the American South, 1521–1704*, ed. Charles Hudson and Carmen Chaves Tesser (Athens: The University of Georgia Press, 1994), 233. Both of these sources provide archaeological evidence for the extensive use of straight-line palisade walls supplemented by numerous projecting bastions in the Mississippian Southeast. Excavations at Town Creek in North Carolina reveal a similar pattern, but with a more circular palisade and with fewer bastions (and therefore less functional). See Ward and Davis, *Time Before History*, 125, and Charles Hudson, *Elements of Southeastern Indian Religion* (Leiden: E. J. Brill, 1984), plate XVIIIb. For more on southeastern palisading in general, see below and Hudson, *Elements*, 211–13. For a broader summary of Mississippian fortifications and bastion use see George R. Milner, "Warfare in Prehistoric and Early Historic Eastern North America," *Journal of Archaeological Research* 7 (1999), 119–20; Dye, *War Paths*, 145–46, 148, 155; and George R. Milner, "Warfare, Population, and Food Production in Prehistoric Eastern North America," in *North American Indigenous Warfare and Ritual Violence*, ed. Richard J. Chacon and Rubén G. Mendoza (Tucson: University of Arizona Press, 2007), 187–90. Some useful information is also in David E. Jones, *Native North American Armor, Shields, and Fortifications* (Austin: University of Texas Press, 2004).

28. James Rice, *Nature and History in the Potomac Country: From Hunter-Gatherers to the Age of Jefferson* (Baltimore, Md.: Johns Hopkins University Press, 2009), 33; "Potomac Creek Site: Stage 1: Uncomfortable Immigrants (ca. AD 1300–1400)," at www.wm.edu/sites/wmcar/research/potomac/stage-one/index.php (accessed February 14, 2022).

29. The Tuscarora and Coastal Algonkians of North Carolina are considered to be roughly the southern "edge" of the cultural region associated with the Northeast Woodlands. Southeastern Mississippian culture's northernmost extent was the southern part of North Carolina, highlighted by the platform mound village style (such as at Town Creek). Byrd and Heath, "Rediscovery," 5; Ward and Davis, *Time Before History*, 125; and Bruce G. Trigger, "Cultural Unity and Diversity," in *Handbook of North American Indians—Northeast*, 798–804. The Tuscaroras may also have seen European-style bastioned fortifications by 1711. Jamestown had had such bastions, as had the Roanoke fort. The Tuscaroras' relations with the Spanish may have included a viewing of the fortifications at St. Augustine,

and the fortifications at Charlestown also followed the European *trace italienne* design. Parramore, "Tuscarora Ascendancy," 310–11; Larry Ivers, *Colonial Forts of South Carolina, 1670–1775* (Columbia: University of South Carolina Press, 1970), 40–42; and Harry S. Mustard, "On the Building of Fort Johnson," *South Carolina Historical Magazine* 64 (1963): 129–35.

30. Milner, "Warfare," 123–25; Patricia M. Lambert, "The Archaeology of War: A North American Perspective," *Journal of Archaeological Research* 10 (2002): 227.

31. Parramore, "Tuscarora Ascendancy," esp. 307.

32. Boyce, "As the Wind," 152.

33. Parramore, "Tuscarora Ascendancy," 318–21.

34. David La Vere provides the most recent and thorough discussion of the motives for the war and the course of events. *Tuscarora War*, 3–4, 12, 16–17, 64 (on causes).

35. La Vere, *Tuscarora War*, 53–54; Ward, *Time Before History*, 274; Lawrence Lee, *Indian Wars in North Carolina, 1663–1763* (Raleigh, N.C.: Carolina Charter Tercentenary Commission, 1963; repr., Raleigh: North Carolina Division of Archives and History, 1997), 20; and Alonzo Thomas Dill, Jr., "Eighteenth Century New Bern: Part III, Rebellion and Indian Warfare," *North Carolina Historical Review* 22 (1945): 300–305.

36. Parramore, "Tuscarora Ascendancy," 319–20.

37. For the various groupings of Indians either hostile or neutral see Boyce, "Tuscarora Confederacy," 36; and La Vere, *Tuscarora War*, 30, 43, 58–59.

38. Gleach, *Powhatan's World*, 51–53, 158; Parramore, "Tuscarora Ascendancy," 322–23; and Karl T. Steinen, "Ambushes, Raids, and Palisades: Mississippian Warfare in the Interior Southeast," *Southeastern Archaeology* 11 (1992): 132–39, esp. 134. Compare Jill Lepore, *The Name of War: King Philip's War and the Origins of American Identity* (New York: Alfred A. Knopf, 1998), 118–19.

39. Parramore, "Tuscarora Jack," 122; Parramore, "Tuscarora Ascendancy," 322–23. The northern Tuscaroras were confused on this point, having been told by their Virginia contacts that the southern villages had attacked the Germans, not the English, and that the English would therefore quickly make peace. Barnwell's Journal, 398.

40. Lt. Gov. Spotswood to Lord Dartmouth, February 8, 1711, CSP-CS-AWI, item 638, 25:355–57. Graffenried commented on the general lack of fortifications in the area. *Account of the Founding*, 239. For North Carolina's inability to respond and for the hasty construction of garrison houses see Christine Anne Styrna, "The Winds of War and Change: the Impact of the Tuscarora War on Proprietary North Carolina, 1690–1729" (Ph.D. Diss., College of William & Mary, 1990), 144–45. Detailed accounts of the Indian attacks are few and generally secondhand: NCCR 1:808–13, 815, 819–20, 825–29.

41. Wayne E. Lee, *Crowds and Soldiers in Revolutionary North Carolina: The Culture of Violence in Riot and War* (Gainesville: University Press of Florida, 2001), 125–27; Dill, "Rebellion and Indian Warfare," 299–300.

42. Styrna identifies South Carolina's motives as a desire for Indian slaves, a motive that North Carolina explicitly acknowledged. "Winds of War," 156–57; NCCR 1:900.

43. La Vere's *Tuscarora War* is now the best complete narrative. Older versions are Hugh T. Lefler, *Colonial North Carolina: A History* (New York: Scribner, 1973), 67–76; Lee, *Indian Wars*, 20–38; and Dill, "Rebellion and Indian Warfare."

44. This account is provided by Christoph von Graffenried, who had been taken prisoner immediately prior to the initial attack, and who was moved back and forth between

villages as part of negotiations. He was thus in a position to witness the Tuscaroras' response to this first attack. *Account of the Founding,* 273–74. The reliance on swamps to conceal one's population from attack is of course an old technique, not one turned to simply because of Europeans. David H. Dye, "Warfare in the Sixteenth-Century Southeast: The de Soto Expedition in the Interior," in *Columbian Consequences, Vol. 2: Archaeological and Historical Perspectives on the Spanish Borderlands East,* ed. David Hurst Thomas (Washington, D.C.: Smithsonian Institution Press, 1990), 219.

45. For "refuge" fortifications see John Keegan, *A History of Warfare* (New York: Alfred A. Knopf, 1993), 139–40. This is of course the function of fortifications as discussed in chapter 2.

46. Barnwell described a number of the forts he encountered as unfinished, and there were clearly some more complex than others. Graffenried recorded the Tuscarora decision to fortify in advance of Barnwell's arrival. *Account of the Founding,* 243. For the placement of the forts at some distance from the towns see Byrd and Heath, "Rediscovery," 31.

47. The following account is based on Barnwell's Journal; Graffenried, *Account of the Founding*; Parramore, "Tuscarora Jack"; and Byrd and Heath, "Rediscovery." Note that there is some disagreement between Parramore and Byrd and Heath over Barnwell's route, but the archaeological evidence would seem to support Byrd and Heath's interpretation.

48. Barnwell's Journal, 394–95.

49. Barnwell's Journal, 395. Other sources indicate that in fact there may have been mostly noncombatants within the fort, contradicting Barnwell's assumptions about men in the forts and women and children hiding in the swamps. Parramore, "Tuscarora Jack," 123–24.

50. Barnwell's Journal, 396, 398, 400.

51. Barnwell's Journal, 400.

52. Barnwell's Journal, 44–45. The following is drawn entirely from Barnwell's Journal, 43–47.

53. Phelps, "North Carolina Coast," 46; Ward and Davis, *Time Before History,* 224.

54. Barnwell's Journal, 45.

55. For a short discussion and a diagram, see Wayne E. Lee, *Waging War: Conflict, Culture, and Innovation in World History* (New York: Oxford University Press, 2016), 228–31. For early European forts in the New World using this system, see Eric C. Klingelhofer, *First Forts: Essays on the Archaeology of Proto-Colonial Fortifications* (Leiden and Boston: Brill, 2010).

56. Barnwell claimed that during the truce negotiations he saw evidence that the Indians had dug "reintrenchments" within the fort as a precaution against the walls being taken.

57. The following is in Barnwell's Journal, 50–52.

58. Barnwell's Journal, 51. Graffenried relates how he suggested that they bring in the artillery then rusting at the governor's residence on the Albemarle. *Account of the Founding,* 244. Graffenried's version of events conflates the two sieges of Hancock's Fort, but it is clear that the artillery only became available at the second siege. In February, Lieutenant Governor Spotswood of Virginia had suggested that artillery would be necessary to attack the Indians in their forts, and had requested some from England. Lt. Gov. Spotswood to Lord Dartmouth, February 8, 1711, CSP-CS-AWI, Item 638, 25:355–57.

59. Graffenried, *Account of the Founding,* 244.

60. Barnwell cited the lack of supplies as the main reason for having to cease operations. He was roundly criticized within North Carolina for his decision. Governor Spotswood to the Council of Trade, May 8, 1712, CSP-CS-AWI, item 408, 26:279; Graffenried, *Account of the Founding*, 245.

61. The truce terms, his march into the fort, and the quote are from Barnwell's Journal, 50–54.

62. Lt. Gov. Spotswood to the Council of Trade, May 8, 1712, CSP-CS-AWI, item 408, 26:277–81.

63. For the Indian population hiding in the swamps during the siege, see Barnwell's Journal, 43.

64. Lt. Gov. Spotswood to the Council of Trade, May 8, 1712, CSP-CS-AWI, item 408, 26:277–81.

65. Barnwell claimed that the men slept in the small forts, with the women and children in the swamps, but he admits to killing ten women in the assault on Narhantes (Torhunta), while other evidence examined by Thomas Parramore hints that virtually the whole "garrison" of that fort might have been the old, women, and children. Barnwell's Journal, 395–96; Parramore, "Tuscarora Jack," 123–24.

66. Keegan, *History of Warfare*, 139.

67. Graffenried, *Account of the Founding*, 245; Joseph W. Barnwell, "The Second Tuscarora Expedition," *South Carolina Historical and Genealogical Magazine* 10 (1909): 33.

68. Quote from Graffenried, *Account of the Founding*, 245.

69. There is much less information available about Moore's expedition, although the siege of Neoheroka itself is well documented. Barnwell, "Second Tuscarora Expedition," is still the best modern account. In addition to the sources cited in Barnwell, see Graffenried, *Account of the Founding*, 245 (where he mistakenly refers to Neoheroka as Catechna); and Lt. Gov. Spotswood to the Council of Trade, June 2, 1713, CSP-CS-AWI, item 355, 27:184–87.

70. Barnwell, "Second Tuscarora Expedition," 35–36.

71. A tracing of the diagram is printed in Barnwell, "Second Tuscarora Expedition," as a foldout map; the original is in the collections of the South Carolina Historical Society. The excavation results have not yet been published, but preliminary papers have been presented: John E. Byrd, "The Search for Forts of the Tuscarora War Era," paper presented at the Society for American Archaeology Conference, New Orleans, La., 2001; Charles L. Heath and David S. Phelps, "Architecture of a Tuscarora Fortress: Neoheroka Fort and the Tuscarora War," paper presented at the Society for American Archaeology Conference, Seattle, Wash., 1998. A summary of the excavations is at "Neoheroka Fort (Greene County)," https://ancientnc.web.unc.edu/indian-heritage/by-region/northern-coastal-plain/neoheroka-fort/ (accessed February 8, 2022). The tercentenary of the siege generated a website that collates a variety of documents and images, as well as a detailed analysis of Moore's diagram of the siege: John A. Tucker, "Nooherooka 300," https://collectio.ecu.edu/chronicles/About/Nooherooka-300 (accessed February 8, 2022).

72. The following description is based on the narrative and the legend printed on Moore's diagram, as well as excavation details discussed in the preliminary papers cited above, and in personal communications with John Byrd and Charles Heath.

73. The excavators of Neoheroka have suggested (I think rightly) that the bunkers represented neither a European nor a Native American traditional style of fortification. Heath and Phelps, "Architecture," 2.

74. Heath and Phelps, "Architecture," 4.

75. Graffenried, *Account of the Founding*, 245.

76. The number of whites killed and wounded actually exceeds the number Moore brought with him from South Carolina. The presumption is that he had been reinforced with some North Carolinians. Barnwell's research indicates that Captain Maul's company (the one badly shot up between bastions E and D) was from North Carolina. "Second Tuscarora Expedition," 37, fn. 9. Captain Maul started the battle with forty-seven men, of whom only twenty were alive and uninjured at the end.

77. The casualty counts are from the diagram, and from Moore's letter to Pollock, dated March 27, 1713, reprinted in Barnwell, "Second Tuscarora Expedition," 39. There is something vaguely suspicious about the prisoner total of 392 equaling the total of the dead (scalped plus burned also equaling 392). The map text suggests 270 Tuscarora men killed and over 500 prisoners for a total loss of at least 800.

78. Lt. Gov. Spotswood to the Council of Trade, June 2, 1713, CSP-CS-AWI, item 355, 27:184–87. For further discussion of the Tuscaroras' hope for Iroquois help, see Styrna, "Winds of War," 140–41. For the abandonment of the other fort, "Cohunche," see Barnwell, "Second Tuscarora Expedition," 40.

79. Lee, *Indian Wars*, 37–38; La Vere, *Tuscarora War*, 170–200.

80. David La Vere argues that the pine logs used at Neoheroka rendered the fort particularly vulnerable to fire: "Of Fortifications and Fire: The Tuscarora Response to the Barnwell and Moore Expeditions during North Carolina's Tuscarora War, 1712 and 1713," *North Carolina Historical Review* 94 (2017): 363–90.

81. DRIA 1:101 (quote), 258; George Chicken, "Journal of Col. George Chicken's Mission from Charleston, S. C. to the Cherokees, 1725," in *Travels in the American Colonies*, ed. Newton D. Mereness (New York: Macmillan Co., 1916), 128.

82. This is a subject worth further exploration, but for a few of the many examples of the importance attached to volley or cannonfire honorary salutes, the meaning of white, red, British, or French flags, or other syncretic military symbolism, see George Chicken, "Journal of the March of the Carolinians into the Cherokee Mountains, in the Yemassee Indian War, 1715–16," *Yearbook of the City of Charleston* (1894), 330, 332; DRIA 1:119, 2:68, 111–12, 124, 125, 136, 199–200, 321, 322, 349; Timberlake, *Memoirs*, 118; and Christopher French, "Journal of an Expedition to South Carolina," *Journal of Cherokee Studies* 2 (1977): 280. As for the use of firearms, the speed and completeness of this shift for the Cherokees also need further exploration, but for most of the period covered here seem to have been fairly complete. Hatley, *Dividing Paths*, 14, 46.

83. The following description of Cherokee society is derived from Gerald F. Schroedl, "Cherokee Ethnohistory and Archaeology from 1540 to 1838," in *Indians of the Greater Southeast: Historical Archaeology and Ethnohistory*, ed. Bonnie G. McEwan (Gainesville: University Press of Florida, 2000), 204–41; Rennard Strickland, *Fire and the Spirits: Cherokee Law From Clan to Court* (Norman: University of Oklahoma Press, 1975); Reid, *A Better Kind of Hatchet*; Phillip K. Reid, *A Law of Blood: The Primitive Law of the Cherokee Nation*

(New York: New York University Press, 1970); Tom Hatley, *The Dividing Paths: Cherokees and South Carolinians Through the Revolutionary Era* (Oxford: Oxford University Press, 1995); and Fred Gearing, *Priests and Warriors: Social Structures for Cherokee Politics in the 18th Century* (Menasha, Wisc.: American Anthropological Association, Memoir 93, 1962). Population changes are discussed in Russell Thornton, *The Cherokees: A Population History* (Lincoln: University of Nebraska Press, 1990); Peter H. Wood, "The Changing Population of the Colonial South: An Overview by Race and Region, 1685–1790," in *Powhatan's Mantle: Indians in the Colonial Southeast*, ed. Peter H. Wood, Gregory A. Waselkov, and M. Thomas Hatley (Lincoln: University of Nebraska Press, 1989), 61–66; and Ward and Davis, *Time Before History*, 231–33.

84. Alexander Longe, "A Small Postscript on the ways and manners of the Indians called Cherokees [1725]," *Southern Indian Studies* 21 (1969): 44 (quote); Reid, *Better Kind of Hatchet*, 6, 9.

85. Theda Perdue, "Cherokee Relations with the Iroquois in the Eighteenth Century," in *Beyond the Covenant Chain: The Iroquois and Their Neighbors in Indian North America, 1600–1800*, ed. Daniel K. Richter and James H. Merrell (Syracuse, N.Y.: Syracuse University Press, 1987), 136.

86. Strickland, *Fire and the Spirits*, 47–48.

87. Schroedl, "Cherokee Ethnohistory"; Roy S. Dickens, Jr., *Cherokee Prehistory: The Pisgah Phase in the Appalachian Summit Region* (Knoxville: University of Tennessee Press, 1976), 14–15; Bennie C. Keel, *Cherokee Archaeology: A Study of the Appalachian Summit* (Knoxville: University of Tennessee Press, 1976), 215–16; and Ward and Davis, *Time Before History*, 187. Captain Christopher French noted in 1761 that the houses were "straggling," to the point of not being "commanded by muskett shot." Christopher French, "Journal of an Expedition," 297–98.

88. The following summary is based on Keel, *Cherokee Archaeology*, 214; Dickens, *Cherokee Prehistory*, 16; Roy S. Dickens, Jr., "Mississippian Settlement Patterns in the Appalachian Summit Area: The Pisgah and Quallah Phases," in *Mississippian Settlement Patterns*, ed. Bruce D. Smith (New York: Academic Press, 1978), 119; Ward and Davis, *Time Before History*, 179–81; David G. Moore, ed., *The Conference on Cherokee Prehistory* (Swannanoa, N.C.: Warren Wilson College, 1986); Schroedl, "Cherokee Ethnohistory," 209–12; R. P. Stephen Davis, Jr., "The Cultural Landscape of the North Carolina Piedmont at Contact," in *The Transformation of the Southeastern Indians, 1540–1760*, ed. Robbie Ethridge and Charles Hudson (Jackson: University Press of Mississippi, 2002), 135–54; Christopher B. Rodning, "Reconstructing the Coalescence of Cherokee Communities in Southern Appalachia," in *Transformation of the Southeastern Indians*, 155–76; and Hudson, *Knights of Spain*, 185–98.

89. The best combination of a critical reading of the De Soto and Juan Pardo narratives with current archaeological evidence (especially with regard to fortifications) is Hudson, *Knights of Spain*.

90. For the location of Mississippian fortified towns in the Overhill Towns area see Hally, "Chiefdom of Coosa."

91. Dickens, *Cherokee Prehistory*, 46, 50, 96, 97; Keel, *Cherokee Archaeology*, 218; Dickens, "Mississippian Settlement Patterns," 131; and Ward and Davis, *Time Before History*, 160–78, 186–87.

92. "Henry Woodward's Westoe Voyage," in *Narratives of Early Carolina, 1650–1708*, ed. Alexander S. Salley (New York: Charles Scribner's Sons, 1911), 133.

93. Abraham Wood, "Letter of Abraham Wood Describing Needham's Journey (1673)," in *Early Travels in the Tennessee Country, 1540–1800*, ed. Samuel Cole William (Johnson City, Tenn.: Watauga Press, 1928), 28. There is some dispute over whether this "Tomahittan" village was actually "ethnically" Cherokee. See Davis, "Cultural Landscape," 141.

94. Wood, "Letter of Abraham Wood," 28–29; Crane, *Southern Frontier*, 40–41; Hatley, *Dividing Paths*, 22; DRIA 2:xii; and Styrna, "Winds of War," 122.

95. Crane, *Southern Frontier*, 24, 75–77, 79–80; *Boston News-Letter*, Monday, April 24–May 1, 1704.

96. For more on the Yamasee War see Steven J. Oatis, *A Colonial Complex: South Carolina's Frontiers in the Era of the Yamasee War, 1680–1730* (Lincoln: University of Nebraska Press, 2008); William L. Ramsey, *The Yamasee War: A Study of Culture, Economy, and Conflict in the Colonial South* (Lincoln: University of Nebraska Press, 2008); and Hatley, *Dividing Paths*, 23–26; and Verner Crane, *The Southern Frontier, 1670–1732* (Durham, N.C.: Duke University Press, 1929), 162–86.

97. Hatley, *Dividing Paths*, 24; Reid, *Better Kind of Hatchet*, 61–73.

98. Chicken, "Journal of the March (1715)," 315–54.

99. Town locations for maps 5.3 and 5.4 are derived from Betty Anderson Smith, "Distribution of Eighteenth-Century Cherokee Settlements," in *The Cherokee Indian Nation: A Troubled History*, ed. Duane H. King (Knoxville: University Of Tennessee Press, 1979), 46–60 (town name spellings generally follow Smith); John Oliphant, *Peace and War on the Anglo-Cherokee Frontier, 1756–63* (Baton Rouge: Louisiana State University Press, 2001), 124, 160; Schroedl, "Cherokee Ethnohistory," 205; and contemporary maps reprinted in Lawrence Henry Gipson, *The British Empire Before the American Revolution* (New York: Alfred A. Knopf, 1956) 9:50, 55; "A New Map of the Cherokee Nation," in *Journal of Cherokee Studies* 2 (1977): 334; and Henry Timberlake, *The Memoirs of Lieut. Henry Timberlake* (Johnson City, Tenn.: Watauga Press, 1927; repr. New York: Arno Press, 1971), foldout map. Schroedl has misidentified the Keowee River and therefore has misplaced the Lower Towns. Also useful is an undated, unsigned letter sent to James Grant prior to his 1761 expedition that describes the relative positions of many of the interior towns. Box 32, James Grant Papers. Cuming's journal and Hunter's map from 1730 indicate a number of other Middle Towns near Etchoe, but their subsequent history is less clear, and so they are not shown here. Their absence in later records may be further proof of the town abandonment discussed below. Sir Alexander Cuming, "Journal of Sir Alexander Cuming (1730)," in *Early Travels in the Tennessee Country*, 115–43.

100. Chicken, "Mission (1725)," 345. Reid discusses the nature of this incident as an initiation of war in *Law of Blood*, 175.

101. Crane, *Southern Frontier*, 200–201; Chicken, "Journal of Mission (1725)," 95–96.

102. Chicken, "Mission (1725)," 111–12, 149, 150, 153, 157. An incident with a trader in 1724 also revealed that Nayowee (Noyowe) was fortified. John Sharp to Governor Nicholson, November 12, 1724, CSP-CS-AWI, item 429v, 34:280.

103. Chicken, "Mission (1725)," 146 (quote), 148, 149–50, 152.

104. Chicken, "Mission (1725), 156.

105. Tobias Fitch, "Captain Fitch's Journal to the Creeks, 1725," in *Travels in the American Colonies*, ed. Newton D. Mereness (New York: Macmillan Co., 1916), 198. For other examples of early eighteenth-century southeastern war parties skulking around a fort see Fitch, "Captain Fitch's Journal," 202; Chicken, "Mission (1725)," 160–61; and DRIA 2:395.

106. Jennings, *New Worlds of Violence*, 167; Smith, "Distribution of Cherokee Settlements," 48–49; Hatley, *Dividing Paths*, 82–83; David Corkran, *The Cherokee Frontier, 1740–1762* (Norman: University of Oklahoma Press, 1962), 36; DRIA 1:246ff, 255; and Samuel C. Williams, "An Account of the Presbyterian Mission to the Cherokees, 1757–1759," *Tennessee Historical Magazine* 2d Ser., 1 (1931): 130. Some of the destroyed towns were rebuilt in the same vicinity after the peace, notably Keowee, Oconne, and Quanessee.

107. Thornton, *Cherokees*, 29, 35.

108. Thomas Walker, "Dr. Thomas Walker's Journal (1750)," in *Early Travels in the Tennessee Country*, 171. The fort described by Walker is presumed to be one occupied by a Cherokee refugee community as described by Hatley, *Dividing Paths*, 82–83.

109. DRIA 1:56 (a request for swivel guns, presumably for a fort?), 255 (Iwassee), 261 (Great Tellico).

110. DRIA 2:413–17, 459–60 (quotes).

111. *South Carolina Gazette*, May 21–26, 1759; DRIA 2:489; and Milo Milton Quaife, ed., *The Siege of Detroit in 1763: The Journal of Pontiac's Conspiracy and John Rutherfurd's Narrative of a Captivity* (Chicago: Lakeside Press, 1958), 150–51.

112. For a good sense of the Cherokees' awareness of English potential military capability, see DRIA 1:446.

113. T. F. Brewer and J. Baillie, "The Journal of George Pawley's 1746 Agency to the Cherokee," *Journal of Cherokee Studies* 16 (1991), 15–16, 19; DRIA 1:186, 191.

114. Hatley, *Dividing Paths*, 94.

115. See the discussion in chapter 4.

116. For trade purposes, see Hatley, *Dividing Paths*, 95–98; DRIA 1:447, 2:223–24, 2:153–54; and Brewer and Baillie, "Journal of George Pawley," 15. Quote from DRIA 1:186.

117. DRIA 2:xiii. For a detailed recounting of the diplomatic maneuvering that preceded the building of Ft. Prince George, and the divisions of Cherokee opinion on the subject, see Corkran, *Cherokee Frontier*, 35–36, 38–49. For a description of Ft. Prince George, see *South Carolina Gazette*, December 29, 1759; and Alexander Hewatt, *An Historical Account of the Rise and Progress of the Colonies of South Carolina and Georgia* (London, 1779; repr., Spartanburg, S.C.: The Reprint Company, 1971), 2:204–5.

118. DRIA 1:221. For other examples of Cherokee awareness of the essentialness of cannon to rendering a fort formidable see DRIA 2:125, 127, 259; and Brewer and Baillie, "The Journal of George Pawley," 16, 19.

119. The fort is described in William Lyttelton to Jeffrey Amherst, August 25, 1756, Sir Jeffery Amherst Papers, WO 34/35, TNA. Governor Dinwiddie of Virginia later claimed that they never planned to garrison the fort. Robert Dinwiddie to Gov. Lyttelton, Sept. 18, 1756, Lyttelton Papers.

120. The best and most convenient description of the construction of Ft. Loudoun is the pamphlet produced at the Fort Loudoun park: Paul Kelley, *Historic Fort Loudoun* (Vonore, Tenn.: Fort Loudoun Association, 1958).

121. Corkran, *Cherokee Frontier*, 46; Daniel Ingram, *Indians and British Outposts in Eighteenth-Century America* (Gainesville: University Press of Florida, 2012), 27–58. For the Cherokee manipulating the Virginia expedition into building its fort at a separate location from the one intended for the South Carolina fort see Ingram, *Indians and British Outposts*,

37–39; DRIA 2:163; Andrew Lewis to Raymond Demere, July 7, 1756, Lyttelton Papers; and William Lyttelton to Jeffrey Amherst, August 25, 1756, Amherst Papers, WO 34/35, TNA.

122. Hatley suggests that the Cherokees were taken aback by the size and scale of the eventual fort, arguing that they intended to have a permanent British "presence" in their midst, for the diplomatic and economic motives discussed above, not a British "army." *Dividing Paths*, 95–96. This is disingenuous: by 1756 there were a number of continuously garrisoned forts in South Carolina, most especially Fort Prince George in the Lower Towns. There could have been little doubt among the Cherokees about what "fort" meant.

123. DRIA 1:186; Ingram, *Indians and British Outposts*, 45–46. Compare the Catawbas' request for a similar fort in 1757: Arthur Dobbs to Gov. Lyttelton, May 27, 1757, Lyttelton Papers.

124. DRIA 2:217; John William Gerard De Brahm, "De Brahm's Account (1756)," in *Early Travels in the Tennessee Country*, 190–91.

125. The military commander, Captain Raymond Demere, sided with the Indians in the dispute over siting. His letters and De Brahm's account differ as to who eventually won the argument, and so, therefore, do the historians' accounts. The park rangers at Ft. Loudoun today offer the interpretation that De Brahm preferred a high knoll that could not be commanded by artillery from the surrounding hills, but the Indians' objections led to a compromise site. The fort was built partly on a smaller eminence close to the river, and partly on the flat river plain (as it is reconstructed today). DRIA 2:217–18; De Brahm, "De Brahm's Account (1756)," 190–91; Corkan, *Cherokee Frontier*, 90–91; and Kelley, *Fort Loudoun*, 11–12. For earlier correspondence over the purpose of the fort and therefore its best siting see DRIA 2:75, 99.

126. DRIA 2:260. For the type and number of cannon see DRIA 2:198, 219, 251, 259, 264.

127. Capt. Demere reported that some of the Cherokees had built houses inside the Virginia fort in 1756, but Henry Timberlake's sketch of 1762 notes that the fort had been destroyed by the Cherokees. DRIA 2:217; Timberlake, *Memoirs*, foldout map.

128. DRIA 2:217.

129. Timberlake, *Memoirs*, foldout map, and particularly his descriptions of Chota and Settico, 59 and 62.

130. Montgomery to Amherst, June 4, 1760, in *Amherst Papers, 1756–1763: The Southern Sector*, ed. Edith Mays (Bowie, Md.: Heritage Books, 1999), 122–23; *South Carolina Gazette*, June 7–16, 1760 (Extraordinary); and Philopatrios [Christopher Gadsen], *Some Observations on the Two Campaigns Against the Cherokee Indians, in 1760 and 1761. In a Second Letter From Philopatrios* (Charlestown, S.C.: Peter Timothy, 1762), 79.

131. The "wealth of sources" includes all of the Montgomery's and Grant's correspondence directed to General Jeffery Amherst (including Grant's journal of the 1761 campaign) [*Amherst Papers, 1756–1763* and Amherst Papers, WO 34/35, 34/40, TNA]; Grant's papers with correspondence covering all three campaigns [James Grant Papers]; the detailed coverage printed in the *South Carolina Gazette* and *Maryland Gazette* for each campaign; the journals of several officers [French, "Journal of an Expedition," esp. 297–98; Major Alexander Monypenny, "Diary of March 20–May 31, 1761," *Journal of Cherokee Studies* 2 (1977): 320–31; Timberlake, *Memoirs*]; Governor Lyttelton's papers describing the 1759 expedition [Lyttelton Papers]; the competing versions of Grant's campaign in Philopatrios, *Some Observations*, and Henry Laurens, "A Letter signed Philolethes," in Philip M. Hamer and

George C. Rogers, eds., *The Papers of Henry Laurens* (Columbia: University of South Carolina Press, 1972), 3:275–55, esp. 312; a history written by a participant shortly after the war [Thomas Mante, *The History of the Late War in North America, and the Islands of the West-Indies . . .* (London: W. Strahan and T. Cadell, 1772)]; and other early histories of the war [Alexander Hewatt, *An Historical Account of the Rise and Progress of the Colonies of South Carolina and Georgia* (London, 1779; repr., Spartanburg, S.C.: The Reprint Company, 1971); and George Milligen, *A Short Description of the Province of South-Carolina (1763),* in *Colonial South Carolina: Two Contemporary Descriptions,* ed. Chapman J. Milling (Columbia: University of South Carolina Press, 1951)]. Colonel William Byrd directly stated that there were no "strong Holds" in any of the Middle Towns. Col. Byrd to General Amherst, March 21, 1761, 4 ZZ, Draper MSS. Finally, De Brahm, who had seen many Cherokee villages in the 1750s, but who had no notion of developments over the last several decades, wrote that "the Indians have *as yet* no Notion of shutting themselves in Forts." John William Gerard De Brahm, *De Brahm's Report of the General Survey in the Southern District of North America* (Columbia: University of South Carolina Press, 1971), 110 (emphasis added).

132. *South Carolina Gazette,* May 21–26, 1759; DRIA 2:459–60, 489.

133. There are numerous narratives of the Cherokee War, but the most recent and authoritative are Daniel J. Tortora, *Carolina in Crisis: Cherokees, Colonists, and Slaves in the American Southeast, 1756–1763* (Chapel Hill: University of North Carolina Press, 2015); Oliphant, *Peace and War;* Hatley, *Dividing Paths;* and Corkran, *Cherokee Frontier.* The brief summary of the war's causes and course is based on those sources and the documents in DRIA, the Lyttleton Papers, the Amherst Papers, and the James Grant Papers.

134. White Outerbridge to Lyttelton, Sept. 11, 1759, Lyttelton Papers; Adair, *History,* 260.

135. A survey of reports from Governor Lyttelton's correspondents in the Cherokee country in the summer and fall of 1759 gives this impression of "not quite war" very strongly. There are many reports of backcountry attacks; meanwhile the Fort Prince George garrison and the traders around it continued more or less normal interactions with the local Cherokees—if under heightened tension, and with the occasional threat of attack. In one sense Fort Prince George was fulfilling its exact function in Cherokee diplomacy; the Cherokees continued to negotiate with these representatives living among them, downplaying the ongoing violence, and thus delaying the outbreak of an all-out war. See in particular Richard Coytmore to Lyttelton, September 8, 1759; and James Beamer to Lyttelton, September 10, 1759, both in Lyttelton Papers.

136. This notion of continued limits to Cherokee intentions ("not quite war") during this period is supported by the successful resupply of Fort Loudoun by eighty hogs driven over the mountains without interference after Lyttelton's departure. John Stuart to Allan Stuart, May 15, 1760, Box 32, James Grant Papers.

137. The siege and eventual fate of Fort Loudoun are beyond the scope of this article. See P. M. Hamer, "Fort Loudoun in the Cherokee War, 1758–1761," *North Carolina Historical Review* 2 (1925): 442–58, and the sources cited above.

138. Again, this narrative is drawn from Oliphant, Hatley, and Corkran, tempered with Montgomery's official correspondence to Amherst (in *Amherst Papers, 1756–1763*) and the narratives published in the *South Carolina Gazette* in the late summer and fall of 1760.

139. Montgomery to Amherst, July 2, 1760, in *Amherst Papers, 1756–1763,* 127–28.

140. Montgomery to Amherst, July 2, 1760, in *Amherst Papers, 1756–1763,* 127.

141. See the discussion on attacking European pack trains in chapter 6.

142. Grant explained Montgomery's decision in Grant to Lt. Gov. Bull, July 3, 1760, reprinted in Philopatrios, *Some Observations*, 87. Amherst believed that logistics was the most difficult problem in fighting the Indians. "On War in North America," MS in Amherst Papers, WO 34/102, pp. 2, 15, TNA.

143. Logistics was also a key reason for Montgomery's departure from Fort Prince George prior to the conclusion of a peace. He blamed the lack of pay and clothing for the provincials and rangers, as well as the disrepair of their wagons and the worn-out condition of their horses. Montgomery to Amherst, September 11[?] 1760, Box 48, James Grant Papers. Grant explained Montgomery's decision in Grant to Lt. Gov. Bull, July 3, 1760, reprinted in Philopatrios, *Some Observations*, 87.

144. *South Carolina Gazette*, August 13–16, 1760 (quote), October 18–26, 1760; Lt. Gov. Bull to Genl. Amherst, April 15, 1761, Amherst Papers, WO 34/35, TNA. Bull also hints that the younger Cherokees had been boasting to the Creeks in the months after Montgomery's retreat. Bull to Attakullakulla, March 30, 1761, Box 33, James Grant Papers. See also Steele, *Warpaths*, 231.

145. *South Carolina Gazette*, August 16–23, 1760. This source and those in the previous note are the best we have for insight into the Cherokee perspective. Admittedly the issue of the Cherokees' diplomatic "attitude" is highly complex, varying from town to town. Little Carpenter in particular continued to press for peace. Even he, however, noted during this period that "we have given the blow," but hoped it would be forgotten. Talk of Little Carpenter, March 12, 1761, Box 33, James Grant Papers. See also Lach. Mackintosh to Grant, March 15, 1761, Box 33, James Grant Papers. Many Carolinians saw Montgomery's retreat as an ominous portent as well. See for example, Lt. Gov. William Bull to Montgomery, July 12, 1760, Box 32, James Grant Papers; and Oliphant, *Peace and War*, 132–33. For the surrender of Loudoun, see Hamer, "Fort Loudoun."

146. It is worth noting that the Cherokees apparently hoped to use the cannon captured at Fort Loudoun against Fort Prince George. They were relying on the knowledge of soldiers captured at Fort Loudoun, but their escape scuttled the plan. *South Carolina Gazette*, September 6–13, 1760, October 11–18, 1760.

147. There are numerous accounts of this second battle of Etchoe: see Hewatt, *Historical Account*, 2:248–49; Grant's Journal, Amherst Papers, WO 34/40, TNA; Grant to William Byrd, July 11, 1761, Box 29, James Grant Papers; Laurens, "A Letter Signed Philolethes," in *Papers of Henry Laurens*, 3:308–11; French, "Journal of an Expedition," 283; and Oliphant, *Peace and War*, 159–62, especially note 145. For the attack on the packhorses, see Court-Martial record of Captain John Dargan, August 4, 1761, Army Series, Box 33, James Grant Papers; and Grant's Journal (letterbook draft) in Army Series, Box 29, James Grant Papers.

148. Grant to Amherst, July 10, 1761, in *Amherst Papers, 1756–1763*, 280.

149. The best reconstruction of his march is in Oliphant, *Peace and War*, 160.

150. Hatley correctly points out that the separate, concurrent Virginia expedition under William Byrd (and later Adam Stephen), although it never penetrated to the Overhill Towns, was in a position threatening to do so, and probably further pressured the Cherokees to negotiate. *Dividing Paths*, 139. Although Byrd did not think his force capable of reaching the Overhill Towns alone, he met with several Overhill headmen and threatened (emptily) to destroy their towns unless they sued for peace. Byrd to Grant, July 19, 1761, Box 33,

James Grant Papers. The original intention was for the Grant and Byrd forces to converge, Grant from the east, the Virginians from the north. Amherst to Lt. Gov. Fauquier, February 13, 1761, and Col. William Byrd to Amherst, March 21, 1761, in 4ZZ, Draper MSS; Col. William Byrd to Amherst, March 11, 1761, in Mays, *Amherst Papers,* 207–28; and Col. Adam Stephen to Gov. Fauquier, September 7, 1761, Amherst Papers, WO 34/37, TNA.

151. John Grenier, *The First Way of War: American War Making on the Frontier, 1607–1814* (Cambridge: Cambridge University Press, 2005). See also William L. Shea, *The Virginia Militia in the Seventeenth Century* (Baton Rouge: Louisiana State University Press, 1983), 20, 33; Fausz, "Patterns of Anglo-Indian Aggression," in *Cultures in Contact,* 246; Lee, *Crowds and Soldiers,* 121; and Colin G. Calloway, *New Worlds for All: Indians, Europeans, and the Remaking of Early America* (Baltimore: Johns Hopkins University Press, 1997), 109. Amherst's manuscript manual on war in North America advocates an even more radical plan, suggesting that the villages be destroyed and the women and children be captured to draw out the men. "On War in North America," MS in Amherst Papers, WO 34/102, p. 13, TNA.

152. Amherst to Montgomery, March 6, 1760, and Amherst to Grant, December 15, 1760, in Mays, *Amherst Papers,* 82–83, 153–54. Amherst presumed that diplomatic submission would follow such punishment. Amherst to Montgomery, June 18, 1760, Box 48, James Grant Papers. Grant foresaw the probable withdrawal strategy of the Cherokees, and asked Amherst for advice on what to do if burning the towns did not bring them to the peace table. Amherst could not offer any helpful suggestions. Amherst to Grant, December 21, 1760, Box 32, James Grant Papers.

153. This is the main thrust of Philopatrios, *Some Observations.* See also John Rattray to Grant, July 18, 1761, Box 33, James Grant Papers. Discussion in Tortora, *Carolina in Crisis,* 155–62.

154. Hewatt, *Historical Account,* 251; Laurens, "A Letter Signed Philolethes," in *Papers of Henry Laurens,* 3:287.

155. Grant to Amherst, January 17, 1761, and Grant to Amherst, December 24, 1761, in *Amherst Papers, 1756–1763,* 176, 337.

156. Keeley, *War Before Civilization,* 44, 75, 175. This is also the explanation usually given for the defeat of the intertribal alliance in King Philip's War; see Steele, *Warpaths,* 106. I am making a distinction here between the Europeans' need for constant logistical supply (they had no ability to live off the country in the frontier zones of North America) and the Indians' structural inability to demographically and materially support continuous war (due to their greater population-to-participation ratio and their new dependence on European military materiel). Keeley argues that logistics was the Europeans' greatest strength, and in the long term that was true; in the short term it was their point of greatest vulnerability. See also Armstrong Starkey, "European-Native American Warfare in North America, 1513–1815," in *War in the Early Modern World, 1450–1815,* ed. Jeremy Black (Boulder, Colo.: Westview Press, 1999), 252; Robert M. Utley, "Cultural Clash on the Western North American Frontier," in *The Military and Conflict Between Cultures,* ed. James C. Bradford (College Station: Texas A&M University Press, 1997), 103; Calloway, *New Worlds,* 103; and Matthew C. Ward, "Fighting the 'Old Women,'" *Virginia Magazine of History and Biography* 103 (1995): 297–320.

157. Oliphant, *Peace and War,* 131, 161; Laurens, "A Letter Signed Philolethes," in *Papers of Henry Laurens,* 3:287 (quote), 288; Grant's Journal, Amherst Papers, PRO WO 34/40. Little Carpenter claimed only twenty-two men and some women were killed at the 1761 battle,

with about double that in the 1760 battle. John Stuart to Grant, September 26, 1761, and October 17, 1761, Box 33, James Grant Papers.

158. M. Thomas Hatley, "The Three Lives of Keowee: Loss and Recovery in Eighteenth-Century Cherokee Villages," in *Powhatan's Mantle*, 155–56.

159. There is a strong possibility that the Pequots at Mystic were primarily women, children, and the elderly, but the point remains. Native American refuge forts were highly vulnerable to prepared European attack. Ronald Dale Karr, "'Why Should You Be So Furious?': The Violence of the Pequot War," *Journal of American History* 85 (1998): 876–909, esp. 876, 905.

160. Grant to Amherst, November 18, 1761, in *Amherst Papers, 1756–1763*, 330.

161. Philopatrios, *Some Observations*, 73; Grant to Amherst, November 18, 1761, in *Amherst Papers, 1756–1763*, 330; Hatley, *Dividing Paths*, 161; and Robin F. A. Fabel, *Colonial Challenges: Britons, Native Americans, and Caribs, 1759–1775* (Gainesville: University Press of Florida, 2000), 87.

162. First two quotes from Calloway, *Western Abenakis*, 88–89, 59; and Utley, "Cultural Clash." For other brief discussion of palisade abandonment, see Steele, *Warpaths*, 135; Armstrong Starkey, *European and Native American Warfare, 1675–1815* (Norman: University of Oklahoma Press, 1998), 23–24; Larson, "Functional Considerations," 384; and Keener, "Iroquois Assault Tactics," 801.

163. General Return of Troops commanded by Col. Adam Stephen, November 28, 1761, Amherst Papers, WO 34/37, PRO. These were the Tuscaroras from the northern villages who had remained in North Carolina after 1715. For the Virginia expedition, see note 171 below. Grant's Indian allies included Mohawks, Catawbas, Chickasaws, Stockbridges, and others. Their activities are a frequent subject of his journal.

164. It is interesting to note the different sequence of choices made by the Catawbas, as recounted in Merrell, *Indians' New World*, 124–25, 127.

165. Malone points out the European-style modifications made to Narragansett forts in the 1670s. *Skulking Way*, 98–101. The Susquehannocks in the 1660s and 1670s improved a European-built fort, and used it in conjunction with cannon to fight off both Native and European besiegers. They eventually abandoned the fort at the close of the Virginia siege in 1675. Steele, *Warpaths*, 52–54; Matthew Kruer, *Time of Anarchy: Indigenous Power and the Crisis of Colonialism in Early America* (Cambridge, Mass.: Harvard University Press, 2021), 56–59.

166. Douglas B. Bamforth, "Indigenous People, Indigenous Violence: Precontact Warfare on the North American Great Plains," *Man*, n.s., 29 (1994): 111.

167. See note 117.

168. Leroy V. Eid, "'A Kind of Running Fight': Indian Battlefield Tactics in the late Eighteenth Century," *Western Pennsylvania Historical Magazine* 71 (1988): 147–71, esp. 155–68.

169. In 1760 the Cherokees used an ambush to attack the baggage after the main body passed by a previously hidden body of Indians. In 1761 the Cherokees seem to have used the half-moon technique to slide along the edges of the march column and then attack the rear (the rear had also been briefly attacked earlier that day). For details of the 1760 battle, see Montgomery to Amherst, July 2, 1760, in *Amherst Papers, 1756–1763*, 127–29; Hewatt, *Historical Account*, 2:231–32; Mante, *History*, 290–93; *South Carolina Gazette*, July 5–12, July 12–19, July 19–26; letters of James Grant in Philopatrios, *Some Observations*, 81–87; and Oliphant, *Peace and War*, 130–31. For 1761, see note 147.

170. Montgomery also had to destroy flour to provide packhorses for his wounded. Montgomery to Amherst, July 2, 1760, in *Amherst Papers, 1756–1763*, 128.

171. Grant to William Byrd, July 11, 1761, Box 29, James Grant Papers. The draft version of Grant's journal with the crossed-out passage is in Box 29, James Grant Papers.

172. John Stuart to Grant, September 18, 1761, Box 33, James Grant Papers.

173. Bruce G. Trigger, "Early Native North American Responses to European Contact: Romantic versus Rationalistic Interpretations," *Journal of American History* 77 (1991): 1214.

174. A similar story of flexibility could be told in regard to Indian adaptation of aspects of European military materiel and ritual, as well as shifts in their offensive strategies, particularly siege techniques against European forts.

Chapter Six

1. The bulk of this chapter originally appeared as Wayne E. Lee, "The Military Revolution of Native North America: Firearms, Forts, and Polities," in *Empires and Indigenes: Intercultural Alliance, Imperial Expansion, and Warfare in the Early Modern World*, ed. Wayne E. Lee (New York: New York University Press, 2011), 49–80. It is reprinted here with permission. Some material has been added, and some from that original version has been moved to other chapters in this book.

2. Key interventions are Geoffrey Parker, *The Military Revolution: Military Innovation and the Rise of the West, 1500–1800*, 2nd ed. (Cambridge: Cambridge University Press, 1996); Clifford Rogers, ed., *The Military Revolution Debate: Readings on the Transformation of Early Modern Europe* (Boulder, Colo.: Westview Press, 1995); and Jeremy Black, *A Military Revolution? Military Change and European Society 1550–1800* (London: Macmillan, 1991). A recent reevaluation is Azar Gat, "What Constituted the Military Revolution of the Early Modern Period?" in *War in an Age of Revolution, 1775–1815*, ed. Roger Chickering and Stig Förster (Cambridge: Cambridge University Press, 2010), 21–48. Tonio Andrade usefully compares these processes in Europe to similar issues in China in *The Gunpowder Age: China, Military Innovation, and the Rise of the West in World History* (Princeton, N.J.: Princeton University Press, 2016).

3. Brian M. Downing, *The Military Revolution and Political Change* (Princeton, N.J.: Princeton University Press, 1992).

4. Wayne E. Lee, *Barbarians and Brothers: Anglo-American Warfare, 1500–1865* (New York: Oxford University Press, 2011), chap. 3; Geoffrey Parker, ed., *The Cambridge History of Warfare* (New York: Cambridge University Press, 2005), 1–11.

5. Harold Peterson, *Arms and Armor in Colonial America, 1526–1783* (New York: Bramhall House, 1956), 19, 43–46; Nathaniel B. Shurtleff, *Records of the Governor and Company of the Massachusetts Bay in New England* (Boston: W. White, 1853), 1:26; and William H. Browne, ed., *Archives of Maryland* (Baltimore: Maryland Historical Society, 1885), 3:100–101. The Jamestown colonists had a mix of matchlocks, wheel locks, and snaphaunces in 1609, but they rapidly moved away from matchlocks, as attested by a 1625 arms inventory. See J. Frederick Fausz, "Fighting 'Fire' with Firearms: The Anglo-Powhatan Arms Race in Early Virginia," *American Indian Culture and Research Journal* 3 (1979): 39, 44. Dixie Ray Haggard correctly cautions, however, that we should not consider the early "primitive flintlocks" as comparably reliable as their more familiar eighteenth-century versions. "The First

Invasion of Georgia and the Myth of Westo Power, 1656–1684," *Journal of Military History* 86 (2022), 544–51.

6. The evidence for all of these specifics has been brought out in earlier chapters.

7. Roger Williams, *A Key into the Language of America* (1643; repr., Bedford, Mass.: Applewood Books, 1997), 184–86.

8. Ian K. Steele, *Warpaths: Invasions of North America* (New York: Oxford University Press, 1994), 13–14; Brian J. Given, *A Most Pernicious Thing: Gun Trading and Native Warfare in the Early Contact Period* (Ottawa: Carleton University Press, 1994); and Armstrong Starkey, *European and Native American Warfare, 1675–1815* (Norman: University of Oklahoma Press, 1998), 20–21. David Silverman provides a brief counter to this conclusion in *Thundersticks: Firearms and the Violent Transformation of Native America* (Cambridge, Mass.: Belknap Press of Harvard University Press, 2016), 8–14. More recently, Haggard has restated the superiority of the bow, especially compared to seventeenth-century muskets with "primitive flintlocks," as part of an argument that the Westos were not rendered superior by access to seventeenth-century guns of any type. "First Invasion," 544–51.

9. Silverman, *Thundersticks*, 14–18; Abler, "European Technology," 275; James Hart Merrell, *The Indians' New World: Catawbas and Their Neighbors from European Contact through the Era of Removal* (Chapel Hill: University of North Carolina Press, 1989), 60, 153, 162–64; and José António Brandão, *'Your Fyre Shall Burn No More': Iroquois Policy toward New France and Its Native Allies to 1701* (Lincoln: University of Nebraska Press, 1997), 99–101. More evidence for this desire follows later.

10. Silverman, *Thundersticks*, esp. 18–20.

11. Kenneth Warren Chase, *Firearms: A Global History to 1700* (Cambridge: Cambridge University Press, 2003), 199–202.

12. Clifford J. Rogers, "Tactics and the Face of Battle," in *European Warfare, 1350–1750*, ed. David Trim and Frank Tallett (Cambridge: Cambridge University Press, 2010), 203–35.

13. Given, *Most Pernicious Thing*, 119 (for musket energy). The modern bow-hunting community has had an active and vigorous debate over the nature and type of kinetic energy expended by arrows. See www.huntingcircle.com/kinetic_energy.php (accessed June 9, 2009, site discontinued); Ed Ashby, "Momentum, Kinetic Energy, and Arrow Penetration (And What They Mean for the Bowhunter)," available at www.tradgang.com/ashby/Momentum Kinetic Energy and Arrow Penetration.htm (accessed June 10, 2009). English longbows of the period delivered somewhat more kinetic energy, but there is no evidence that Indian bows were comparable to English ones. See Rogers, "Tactics and the Face of Battle"; Patrick M. Malone, *The Skulking Way of War: Technology and Tactics among the New England Indians* (1991; repr., Baltimore: Johns Hopkins University Press, 1993), 17–18. Haggard, "First Invasion," errs in comparing Native bows to English longbows. Modern hunting bows are reasonable comparanda to Native American bows in terms of kinetic energy and effects on unarmored flesh. Indians did not need heavy-draw-weight bows designed to defeat metal armor. The best evidence from the few surviving Indian bows suggests relatively low draw weights compared to Eurasian warbows. Although this is hardly systematic evidence, I also write informed by years of experience as a traditional archer and black-powder weapons experimenter.

14. Quoted in Fausz, "Fighting 'Fire' with Firearms," 37.

15. For the common use of armor and shields in nongun contexts, see David H. Dye, *War Paths, Peace Paths: An Archaeology of Cooperation and Conflict in Native Eastern North America*

(Lanham, Md.: AltaMira Press, 2009), 14–15; and David E. Jones, *Native North American Armor, Shields, and Fortifications* (Austin: University of Texas Press, 2004), 57–62, 135–39. For the disappearance of armor as guns came into common use, see the summary in Daniel P. Barr, *Unconquered: The Iroquois League at War in Colonial America* (Westport, Conn.: Praeger, 2006), 27–29. Florida bowmen deeply impressed the Spanish in the early sixteenth century, penetrating their armor and as much as six inches of wood. See Steele, *Warpaths*, 12–13. At Jamestown, an Indian bowman pierced an English wooden shield but broke his arrow on a steel version. See George Percy, "Observations Gathered out of a Discourse . . . ," in *Jamestown Narratives*, ed. Edward Wright Haile (Champlain, Va.: Roundhouse, 1998), 95–96.

16. Williams, *Key into the Language*, 189; *Dead Birds* (1963, directed by Robert Gardner). Abler discusses this at greater length in "European Technology," 274–75.

17. Peterson, *Arms and Armor*, 227.

18. Alfred A. Cave, *The Pequot War* (Amherst: University of Massachusetts Press, 1996), 137.

19. Personal communication with Kevin McBride, June 2009.

20. More research is needed on who had access to rifled guns and when. Although rifling was a relatively old technology used in elite hunting weapons, it was uncommon even in Europe into the seventeenth century, and the famous American version, the "Pennsylvania Rifle," was not invented until the early eighteenth century. See Peterson, *Arms and Armor*, 192–93. Some sources from the Southeast (at least), indicate that they were only just becoming common among the Creeks in the 1750s. See Daniel Pepper to Governor Lyttelton, November 30, 1756, in DRIA 2:296.

21. Peter A. Thomas, "In the Maelstrom of Change: The Indian Trade and Cultural Process in the Middle Connecticut River Valley, 1635–1665" (reprint of 1979 Ph.D. diss., University of Massachusetts; New York: Garland, 1990), 248–50; JR 49:139–41; NYCD 13:355–56; David Wilton to John Winthrop Jr., December 25, 1663, Winthrop Papers, Boston: Massachusetts Historical Society. A similar feint outside a fort is recorded for the Narragansetts in 1645 in Thomas Peters to John Winthrop, ca. May 1645, in Allyn Bailey Forbes, ed., *Winthrop Papers, Volume V, 1645–1649* (Boston: Massachusetts Historical Society, 1947), 5:19.

22. Leroy V. Eid, "'A Kind of Running Fight': Indian Battlefield Tactics in the late Eighteenth Century," *Western Pennsylvania Historical Magazine* 71 (1988): 147–71; DRIA 2:467, 468; Frederick W. Gleach, *Powhatan's World and Colonial Virginia: A Conflict of Cultures* (Lincoln: University of Nebraska Press, 1997), 43; and Williams, *Key into the Language*, 184.

23. Quoted in Wayne E. Lee, Anthony E. Carlson, David L. Preston, and David Silbey, *The Other Face of Battle: America's Forgotten Wars and the Experience of Combat* (New York: Oxford University Press, 2021), 49 (quote), 53, 55.

24. John Landers, *The Field and the Forge: Population, Production, and Power in the Pre-Industrial West* (New York: Oxford University Press, 2003), esp. 98–100, 273–74.

25. John Craig deposition, March 30, 1756, p. 78, vol. 2, Penn Manuscripts, Indian Affairs, Penn Family Papers, Collection no. 485A, HSP, as quoted in Amy C. Schutt, *Peoples of the River Valleys: The Odyssey of the Delaware Indians* (Philadelphia: University of Pennsylvania Press, 2007), 109.

26. In addition to the note about Monongahela above, see Eid, "Kind of Running Fight," 163; and David Preston, *Braddock's Defeat: The Battle of the Monongahela and the Road to Revolution* (New York: Oxford University Press, 2015), 235.

27. Henry Bouquet to Jeffrey Amherst, August 5, 1763, *The Papers of Col. Henry Bouquet,* ed. Sylvester K. Stevens and Donald H. Kent (Harrisburg: Pennsylvania Historical Commission, 1942), series 21649, Pt. 1, 227; William Smith, *Historical Account of Bouquet's Expedition against the Ohio Indians in 1764* (1765; repr., Cincinnati: Robert Clarke, 1907), 20, 36, 82, 89–90.

28. Allan R. Millett, "Caesar and the Conquest of the Northwest Territory," *Timeline* (Ohio Historical Society) 14 (1997): 17–21 (thanks to Allan Millett for pointing this piece out to me); John Sugden, *Blue Jacket: Warrior of the Shawnees* (Lincoln: University of Nebraska Press, 2000), 159, 164–66.

29. Silverman, *Thundersticks,* 135–36.

30. Several letters, Johnson Papers, 10:815–17.

31. Merrell, *Indians' New World,* 79; John Oliphant, *Peace and War on the Anglo-Cherokee Frontier, 1756–63* (Baton Rouge: Louisiana State University Press, 2001), 161; and Silverman, *Thundersticks,* 133–34.

32. See note 48.

33. Oliphant, *Peace and War,* 137–38. Henry Timberlake recorded the Cherokees firing "two pieces of cannon" as a salute when he departed Chote in 1762. These may have been swivel guns that the Cherokees had earlier received from the South Carolinians. *The Memoirs of Lieut. Henry Timberlake* (1927; repr., New York: Arno Press, 1971), 118. The British were sure to include a clause requiring the Cherokees to surrender those cannon in the 1761 treaty. Treaty with Cherokees (December 18, 1761) enclosed in letter from Gov. Boone to Amherst, January 18, 1762, Amherst Papers, WO 34/35, TNA.

34. JR 63:245.

35. George Edward Milne, *Natchez Country: Indians, Colonists, and the Landscapes of Race in French Louisiana* (Athens: University of Georgia Press, 2015), 193.

36. DRIA 2:125, 127, 328. What appears to be a swivel gun ball emerged from excavations of a 1780s Catawba house site in summer 2009 (personal communication from Stephen R. P. Davis Jr.). Haggard claims the Westos were accompanied by some white Virginians who aided them with two swivel guns during their forays into coastal Georgia, but his claim that such a gun would have broken open palisades does not hold up. Such guns did not have that capability. "First Invasion," 553–54.

37. Matthew C. Ward, "'The European Method of Warring Is Not Practiced Here': The Failure of British Military Policy in the Ohio Valley, 1755–1759," *War in History* 4, no. 3 (1997): 258, notes that Indians in the summer of 1756 attacked nine small frontier stockades on the Virginia-Pennsylvania frontier and destroyed five, but these were not cannon-equipped *trace italienne* forts. From the late seventeenth century onward, combined French and Indian raids on the northeastern frontier regularly overwhelmed isolated forts and stockades. And most famously, several British forts were surprised and taken at the outset of Pontiac's War. See Steele, *Warpaths,* 141, 198–99, 237.

38. For the debate on the intensity and lethality of warfare, see chapter 4.

39. George R. Milner, "Warfare in Prehistoric and Early Historic Eastern North America," *Journal of Archaeological Research* 7 (1999): 123–25.

40. Much of the following paragraph is based on the essays in Gaynell Stone, ed., *Native Forts of the Long Island Sound Area* (Stony Brook, N.Y.: Suffolk County Archaeological Association, 2006), especially those by Kevin McBride, Ralph S. Solecki, and Charlotte C. Taylor.

Lorraine Williams, however, argues that Fort Shantok had a precontact phase, although her argument is fragile, as it based on the use of trench-set posts, thereby implying a lack of European tools. Elizabeth Chilton states categorically that as of 2005, there is no evidence for "formal villages, palisaded settlements, intensive horticulture, or warfare . . . in New England prior to European contact." See her "Farming and Social Complexity in the Northeast," in *North American Archaeology*, ed. Timothy R. Pauketat and Diana DiPaolo Loren (Malden, Mass.: Blackwell, 2005), 50. I have discussed this issue extensively with Kevin McBride, research director for the Mashantucket Pequot, who also sees no evidence for fortification in southern New England in the precontact era. See as well Kathleen Bragdon, *Native Peoples of Southern New England, 1500–1650* (Norman: University of Oklahoma Press, 1996), 149.

41. See the reports in *Native Forts* for Forts Corchaug, Shantok, Massapeag, Fort Hill/ Weinshauks, Monhantic, Ninigret, Block Island, and Montauk. For the Narragansetts' Great Swamp Fort and other similarly improved forts from the King Philip's War era, see Malone, *Skulking Way of War*, 98–101.

42. For a brief summary of wall and bastion design in the precontact Mississippian chiefdoms, see George R. Milner, "Warfare, Population, and Food Production in Prehistoric Eastern North America," in *North American Indigenous Warfare and Ritual Violence*, ed. Richard J. Chacon and Rubén G. Mendoza (Tucson: University of Arizona Press, 2007), 187–90.

43. In addition to Craig S. Keener's broad survey in "An Ethnohistorical Analysis of Iroquois Assault Tactics Used against Fortified Settlements of the Northeast in the Seventeenth Century," *Ethnohistory* 46 (1999): 777–807, see, for example, the three palisaded sites reported in Robert E. Funk and Robert D. Kuhn, *Three Sixteenth-Century Mohawk Iroquois Village Sites* (Albany: New York State Museum, 2003).

44. Keener, "Ethnohistorical Analysis," 789–91.

45. JR 10:53, quoted in Keener, "Ethnohistorical Analysis," 786.

46. Keener, "Ethnohistorical Analysis," 780–86, 800; Thomas B. Abler, "European Technology and the Art of War in Iroquoia," in *Cultures in Conflict: Current Archaeological Perspectives*, ed. Diana Tkaczuk and Brian C. Vivian (Calgary: University of Calgary Archaeology Association, 1989), 276–77.

47. See note 21.

48. JR 48:141. The French also built a fort in the 1650s for the Onondaga women and children to use as a refuge, and additionally supplied a blacksmith for firearm repair. Jon Parmenter, *The Edge of the Woods: Iroquoia, 1534–1701* (East Lansing: Michigan State University Press, 2010), 105. An additional case study could be made of the Susquehannocks' successful use of European fortification technology, including cannon. The basic sources are Steele, *Warpaths*, 52–54; Michael Leroy Oberg, *Dominion and Civility: English Imperialism and Native America, 1585–1685* (Ithaca, N.Y.: Cornell University Press, 1999), 195–99; Matthew Kruer, *Time of Anarchy: Indigenous Power and the Crisis of Colonialism in Early America* (Cambridge, Mass.: Harvard University Press, 2021); Francis Jennings, *The Ambiguous Iroquois Empire* (New York: Norton, 1984), 127–28; William L. Shea, *The Virginia Militia in the Seventeenth Century* (Baton Rouge: Louisiana State University Press, 1983), 98–99; JR 68:77; *Archives of Maryland* 2:481–501; 3:417, 420–21; 15:48–49; Barry C. Kent, *Susuquehanna's Indians* (Harrisburg: Pennsylvania Historical and Museum Commission, 1984), 39–53; Charles M. Andrews, *Narratives of the Insurrections, 1675–1690* (New York: Scribner, 1915),

18–19, 47–48; and CO 5/1371, f. 188, in Virginia Colonial Records Project microfilm collection. Apparently in preparation for a war with the French, the Natchez built two squared- or pentagonal-bastioned forts in the late 1720s. Milne, *Natchez Country*, 178, 192. Additional examples of modified forts in the Southeast are described in Jones, *Native North American Armor*, 130–35.

49. R. David Edmunds and Joseph L. Peyser, *The Fox Wars: The Mesquakie Challenge to New France* (Norman: University of Oklahoma Press, 1993), 66–74, 79–86.

50. Max Mintz, *Seeds of Empire: The American Revolutionary Conquest of the Iroquois* (New York: New York University Press, 1999); Joseph R. Fischer, *A Well-Executed Failure: The Sullivan Campaign against the Iroquois, July–September 1779* (Columbia: University of South Carolina Press, 1997); Barbara Graymont, *The Iroquois in the American Revolution* (Syracuse, N.Y.: Syracuse University Press, 1972); and Lee, *Barbarians and Brothers,* chap. 8.

51. For another perspective on this problem, see George Raudzens, "Outfighting or Outpopulating? Main Reasons for Early Colonial Conquests, 1493–1788," in *Technology, Disease, and Colonial Conquests, Sixteenth to Eighteenth Centuries: Essays Reappraising the Guns and Germs Theories,* ed. George Raudzens (Leiden: Brill, 2001), 31–58.

52. Silverman, *Thundersticks*, 12–16.

53. Malone, *Skulking Way of War*, 93–95, cites the evidence for a Wampanoag blacksmith burial, as well as documentary evidence for a Narragansett blacksmith during King Philip's War. See Kevin McBride, "Monhantic Fort: The Pequot in King Philip's War," in *Native Forts,* 331–32. The tools have not yet been published, but Kevin McBride kindly allowed me to examine the metal finds and tools from Monhantic (now stored at the Mashantucket Pequot Research Center and Library). In addition, a mid- to late seventeenth-century Narragansett cemetery in Rhode Island contains a man buried with a blacksmith hammer, a horseshoe, and other blacksmithing tools. See Paul Alden Robinson, "The Struggle Within: The Indian Debate in Seventeenth-Century Narragansett Country" (Ph.D. diss., SUNY Binghamton, 1990), 285 (burial 38); and Paul A. Robinson, Marc A. Kelley, and Patricia E. Rubertone, "Preliminary Biocultural Interpretations from a Seventeenth-Century Narragansett Indian Cemetery in Rhode Island," in *Cultures in Contact: The Impact of European Contacts on Native American Cultural Institutions, A.D. 1000–1800,* ed. William W. Fitzhugh (Washington, D.C.: Smithsonian Institution Press, 1985), 120.

54. I make this judgment partly based on personal experience as an amateur blacksmith (forge-welding a barrel, for example, is a complicated task requiring specialized tools and precise temperature control), but the records of requests for gunsmiths are equally clear. See Wilbur R. Jacobs, ed., *The Appalachian Indian Frontier: The Edmond Atkin Report and Plan of 1755* (Lincoln: University of Nebraska Press, 1967), 8–10; Merrell, *Indians' New World,* 60; DRIA 1:104, 2:372; JR 57:29; *Propositions Made by the Five Nations of Indians* (New York: William Bradford, 1698), 5; Daniel K. Richter, *The Ordeal of the Longhouse: The Peoples of the Iroquois League in the Era of European Colonization* (Chapel Hill: University of North Carolina Press, 1992), 220–21; and Johnson Papers, 1:307.

55. Steele, *Warpaths*, 106.

56. Bert S. Hall, *Weapons and Warfare in Renaissance Europe: Gunpowder, Technology, and Tactics* (Baltimore: Johns Hopkins University Press, 1997), 41–104.

57. Examples can multiply endlessly. Consulting the indexes under "gunpowder" or even casual consultation focusing on recorded Indian speeches in such sources as DRIA, NYCD,

and Peter Wraxall, *An Abridgment of the Indian Affairs... Transacted in the Colony of New York, From the Year 1678 to the Year 1751* (Cambridge, Mass.: Harvard University Press, 1915), conveys the extent of the problem.

58. Gleach, *Powhatan's World*, 142; Karen Ordahl Kupperman, *Indians and English: Facing Off in Early America* (Ithaca, N.Y.: Cornell University Press, 2000), 102; Charles Hudson, *The Southeastern Indians* (Knoxville: University of Tennessee Press, 1976), 222–24; Rennard Strickland, *Fire and the Spirits: Cherokee Law from Clan to Court* (Norman: University of Oklahoma Press, 1975), 47–48; HNAI 15:192, 315; Anthony F. C. Wallace, *The Death and Rebirth of the Seneca* (New York: Vintage Books, 1969), 40; James Axtell, *Natives and Newcomers: The Cultural Origins of North America* (New York: Oxford University Press, 2001), 139; Fred Gearing, *Priests and Warriors: Social Structures for Cherokee Politics in the 18th Century* (Menasha, Wisc.: American Anthropological Association, Memoir 93, 1962); Colin G. Calloway, *New Worlds for All: Indians, Europeans, and the Remaking of Early America* (Baltimore: Johns Hopkins University Press, 1997), 111; Kathleen DuVal, *The Native Ground: Indians and Colonists in the Heart of the Continent* (Philadelphia: University of Pennsylvania Press, 2006), 71–73, 90–91, 105; and Bruce G. Trigger, *Natives and Newcomers: Canada's Heroic Age Reconsidered* (Toronto: University of Toronto Press, 1985), 93, 171; Lisa Brooks demonstrates how other factors, such as European legal systems, could also undermine traditional forms of authority in *Our Beloved Kin: A New History of King Philip's War* (New Yaven, Conn.: Yale University Press, 2018), 49.

59. Although northeastern Algonquians did not divide war and peace powers as strictly, they still ruled through a consensus-building process, something that European trade also disrupted. See Neal Salisbury, *Manitou and Providence: Indians, Europeans, and the Making of New England, 1500–1643* (New York: Oxford University Press, 1982), 42–43, 118–19; Bragdon, *Native Peoples*, 140–43, 146–48; and Howard S. Russell, *Indian New England before the Mayflower* (Hanover, N.H.: University Press of New England, 1980), 19–20.

60. Nathaniel Sheidley presents a generational version of this argument in "Hunting and the Politics of Masculinity in Cherokee Treaty-Making, 1763–75," in *Empire and Others: British Encounters with Indigenous Peoples, 1600–1850*, ed. Martin Daunton and Rick Halpern (Philadelphia: University of Pennsylvania Press, 1999), 167–85.

61. Daniel Ingram, *Indians and British Outposts in Eighteenth-Century America* (Gainesville: University Press of Florida, 2012), 11–12. Ingram makes clear that the forts were seen by the Indians to provide a variety of functions, but refuge defense was clearly one of them.

62. Bruce Wilson, "The Struggle for Wealth and Power at Fort Niagara, 1775–1783," *Ontario History* 68 (1976): 137–54.

63. Trigger, *Natives and Newcomers*, 269–70.

64. Merrell, *Indians' New World*, 57–58.

65. Merrell, *Indians' New World*, 124–25, 127, 162.

66. Roy S. Dickens Jr., *Cherokee Prehistory: The Pisgah Phase in the Appalachian Summit Region* (Knoxville: University of Tennessee Press, 1976), 15; H. Trawick Ward and R. P. Stephen Davis Jr., *Time before History: The Archaeology of North Carolina* (Chapel Hill: University of North Carolina Press, 1999), 187.

67. James E. Seaver, *A Narrative of the Life of Mrs. Mary Jemison* (n.p.: Wm. P. Letchworth, 1877; facsimile reprint, Scituate, Mass.: Digital Scanning Inc., 2000), 124–27. There is a long analysis of the eighteenth-century Senecas' shift to disaggregated settlements in Kurt A.

Jordan, *The Seneca Restoration, 1715–1754: An Iroquois Local Political Economy* (Gainesville: University Press of Florida, 2008), 163–95, 198–224.

68. The process varied widely from locale to locale and people to people. Some lands never transitioned to private parcels (for example, those of the Pequot). Daniel R. Mandell studied this process for the Massachusetts Indians in the eighteenth century to include shifting settlement patterns. The details are complex and involved more than mere defensive needs, but those, too, played a role. See *Behind the Frontier: Indians in Eighteenth-Century Eastern Massachusetts* (Lincoln: University of Nebraska Press, 1996).

69. This is the main argument of Silverman, *Thundersticks*.

70. Most of the debate on this war focuses on the motives for the Iroquois attacks, not on the reasons for their success. See Richter, *Ordeal*, 63–64; Keith F. Otterbein, "Why the Iroquois Won: An Analysis of Iroquois Military Tactics," *Ethnohistory* 11 (1964): 56–63; Keith F. Otterbein, "Huron vs. Iroquois: A Case Study in Inter-Tribal Warfare," *Ethnohistory* 26 (1979): 141–52; Elizabeth Tooker, "The Iroquois Defeat of the Huron: A Review of Causes," *Pennsylvania Archaeologist* 33 (1963): 115–23; Trigger, *Natives and Newcomers*, 266–69; and George T. Hunt, *The Wars of the Iroquois: A Study in Intertribal Trade Relations* (Madison: University of Wisconsin Press, 1940). Brian Given, however, argues that European guns were irrelevant to the outcome (*Most Pernicious Thing*, 8–10). Keener's conclusion, discussed earlier, that a combination of guns and iron axes made the difference, is probably correct. See Keener, "Ethnohistorical Analysis," 789–91. Keener's conclusion is supported by Silverman, *Thundersticks*, 21–55.

71. Salisbury, *Manitou and Providence*, 69–70.

72. Merrell, *Indians' New World*, 40; Marvin T. Smith, *Archaeology of Aboriginal Culture Change in the Interior Southeast: Depopulation during the Early Historic Period* (Gainesville: University Press of Florida, 1987), 132–33. Alan Gallay is less certain that the gun provided the crucial advantage, but he follows Malone on the inefficacy of the gun versus the bow, and his own survey of the evidence suggests at least that Europeans believed the gun trade enabled the succession of slave-raiding peoples. See *The Indian Slave Trade: The Rise of the English Empire in the American South, 1670–1717* (New Haven, Conn.: Yale University Press, 2002), 41, 60–61, 147, 211. Silverman, *Thundersticks*, 56–91, is more certain about the significance of guns to this dynamic, *vice* Haggard, "First Invasion," who revisits and supports the idea that guns played little role in the success of the Westos in their rise to primacy in the late seventeenth-century Indian slave trade.

73. Silverman, *Thundersticks*, 35–39 gives the guns more credit, but also emphasizes the rapid rebalancing as guns proliferated.

74. Haggard, "First Invasion," 554–55.

75. Silverman, *Thundersticks*, 57; The key scholarship on this remains Gallay, *Indian Slave Trade*. See also Christina Snyder, *Slavery in Indian Country: The Changing Face of Captivity in Early America* (Cambridge, Mass.: Harvard University Press, 2010); and Denise I. Bossy, "The South's Other Slavery: Recent Research on Indian Slavery," *Native South* 9 (2016): 27–53.

76. See the discussion of scalp bounties in chapter 7.

77. James Axtell, "The White Indians of Colonial America," *William and Mary Quarterly* 3d Ser., 32, no. 1 (1975): 59–61; Ian K. Steele, "Surrendering Rites: Prisoners on Colonial North American Frontiers," in *Hanoverian Britain and Empire: Essays in Memory of Philip*

Lawson, ed. Stephen Taylor, Richard Connors, Clyve Jones, and Philip Lawson (Woodbridge, U.K.: Boydell Press, 1998), 137–57.

78. James D. Rice surveys much of this new literature in "Early American Environmental Histories," *William and Mary Quarterly* 3d Ser., 75, no. 3 (2018): 401–32, and I owe Rob Nixon's "Slow Violence" phrase to him (424). Alfred W. Crosby's book remains the foundational study of the demographic impact of disease: *Ecological Imperialism: The Biological Expansion of Europe, 900–1900* (Cambridge: Cambridge University Press, 1986), but he also introduced the notion of how other forms of settler-induced environmental change could undermine traditional subsistence and social systems. For other studies, see William Cronon, *Changes in the Land: Indians, Colonists, and the Ecology of New England* (New York: Hill and Wang, 1983); and Virginia DeJohn Anderson, *Creatures of Empire: How Domestic Animals Transformed Early America* (Oxford: Oxford University Press, 2004). For the synergism of war and disease, and especially slave raiding, see Elizabeth A. Fenn, *Pox Americana: The Great Smallpox Epidemic of 1775–82* (New York: Hill & Wang, 2001); Paul Kelton, *Epidemics and Enslavement: Biological Catastrophe in the Native Southeast, 1492–1715* (Lincoln: University of Nebraska Press, 2007); and David S. Jones, "Virgin Soils Revisited," *William and Mary Quarterly* 3d Ser., 60, no. 4 (2003): 703–42. The concept of the Shatter Zone is from Robbie Ethridge, "Creating the Shatter Zone: Indian Slave Traders and the Collapse of the Southeastern Chiefdoms," in *Light on the Path: The Anthropology and History of the Southeastern Indians*, ed. Charles M. Hudson, Thomas J. Pluckhahn, and Robbie Franklyn Ethridge (Tuscaloosa: University of Alabama Press, 2006), 207–18. Ethridge expands this argument in Robbie Ethridge, *From Chicaza to Chickasaw: The European Invasion and the Transformation of the Mississippian World, 1540–1715* (Chapel Hill: University of North Carolina Press, 2010).

79. The process of eighteenth-century confederation, reconfiguration, and even ethnogenesis has generated a large literature. For a summary, see Daniel K. Richter, "Native Peoples of North America and the Eighteenth-Century British Empire," in *The Oxford History of the British Empire*, vol. 2: *The Eighteenth Century*, ed. P. J. Marshall (New York: Oxford University Press, 1998), 356–61.

Chapter Seven

1. This chapter was originally published as "Subjects, Clients, Allies, or Mercenaries? The British use of Irish and Amerindian military power, 1500–1815," in *Britain's Oceanic Empire: Atlantic and Indian Ocean Worlds, c. 1550–1850*, ed. H. V. Bowen, Elizabeth Mancke, and John G. Reid (Cambridge: Cambridge University Press, 2012), 179–217. It is reprinted here with permission, with the material on Ireland greatly reduced. Readers interested in Irish issues should see that earlier version. I have preferred "Anglo-Irish" to describe the Englishmen living in Ireland at the beginning of the sixteenth century, although I am aware of debate on this subject. For the seventeenth century they are more appropriately referred to as the Old English. For English failure to commit resources, see Bruce P. Lenman, *England's Colonial Wars 1550–1688: Conflicts, Empire and National Identity* (Harlow, U.K.: Pearson Education, 2001), 16.

2. Matthew R. Bahar, *Storm of the Sea: Indians and Empires in the Atlantic's Age of Sail* (New York: Oxford University Press, 2019).

3. This division of functions extends the analysis in Cynthia H. Enloe, *Ethnic Soldiers: State Security in Divided Societies* (Athens: University of Georgia Press, 1980).

4. Colm Lennon, *Sixteenth-Century Ireland*, rev. ed. (Dublin: Gill & Macmillan, 2005), 75. Compare Kildare's actions at the battle of Knockdoe in 1504: "The Book of Howth," in CCM, 6:183, 185. It is also noteworthy that English accounts of the battle barely mention the Gaelic allies, but the Irish accounts of the era regularly list the large presence of Gaelic lords in Kildare's army. See one example: *Four Masters*, 5:1305.

5. H.St.P., 2:12–13.

6. There are many examples of the complex composition of Tudor armies operating in Ireland; see H.St.P., 2:32–33, 35–38, 57–58, 147, 75–76, 233, 234, 262–63, 524; 3:193. For general discussions, see John Dymmok, *A Treatice of Ireland* (Dublin: Irish Archaeological Society, 1842), 8; Steven G. Ellis, "The Tudors and the Origins of the Modern Irish State: A Standing Army," in *A Military History of Ireland*, ed. Thomas Bartlett and Keith Jeffery (Cambridge: Cambridge University Press, 1996), 117, 120; and G. A. Hayes-McCoy, "The Army of Ulster, 1593–1601," *Irish Sword* 1 (1949–1953): 105–10.

7. H.St.P., 3:169–73; an example from 1566 is in SP 63/19/85, TNA.

8. Dymmok, *Treatice*, 7–8. Much of Dymmok's *Treatice* is copied from older versions of a standard text describing Ireland that exists in multiple copies. He added certain details appropriate to 1600. See "A Treatise of Ireland," MS 669, National Library of Ireland, Dublin; *Historical Manuscript Commission Report 3 for 1872* (London: Henry Hansard and Son, 1890), appendix, p. 115; and David B. Quinn, "Edward Walshe's 'Conjectures' Concerning the State of Ireland [1552]," *Irish Historical Studies* 5 (1946): 303.

9. Cyril Falls, *Elizabeth's Irish Wars* (London: Methuen, 1950), 67; K. W. Nicholls, *Gaelic and Gaelicized Ireland in the Middle Ages*, 2nd ed. (Dublin: Lilliput Press, 1972, 2003), 95–98; and Ellis, *Ireland*, 42, 44.

10. James O'Neill, *The Nine Years War, 1593–1603* (Dublin: Four Courts Press, 2017), 53.

11. A cursory examination of the *Four Masters* (for this period, vol. 5) will confirm this impression of endemic warfare. See also R. R. Davies, *The First English Empire: Power and Identities in the British Isles, 1093-1343* (Oxford: Oxford University Press, 2000),124–25; Katharine Simms, "Warfare in the Medieval Gaelic Lordships," *Irish Sword* 12 (1975/76): 98–109; and David Edwards, "The Escalation of Violence in Sixteenth-Century Ireland," in *Age of Atrocity: Violence and Political Conflict in Early Modern Ireland*, ed. David Edwards, Pádraig Lenihan, and Clodagh Tait (Dublin: Four Courts Press, 2007), 39–46.

12. T. W. Moody and F. X. Martin, eds., *The Course of Irish History* (Boulder, Colo.: Roberts Rinehart Publishers, 1994), 179 (quote); H.St.P. 3:347–48; "Book of Howth," in CCM, 6:195.

13. H.St.P. 3:443–48; Dean Gunter White, "Henry VIII's Irish Kerne in France and Scotland, 1544–1545," *Irish Sword* 3 (1958): 213–25.

14. The literature is vast; the seminal text is Nicholas P. Canny, *The Elizabethan Conquest of Ireland: A Pattern Established, 1565-76* (Hassocks, UK: Harvester Press, 1976). Helpful summaries are David Armitage, *The Ideological Origins of the British Empire* (Cambridge: Cambridge University Press, 2000), 24–25; and David Edwards, "Ideology and Experience: Spenser's View and Martial Law in Ireland," in *Political Ideology in Ireland, 1541–1641*, ed. Hiram Morgan (Dublin: Four Courts Press, 1999), 127–57. I provide a somewhat more

detailed treatment in Wayne E. Lee, *Barbarians and Brothers: Anglo-American Warfare, 1500–1865* (New York: Oxford University Press, 2011), 23–27.

15. James O'Neill's recent book *The Nine Years War* is the best summary of the war, and also provides a good overview of the complex debate among Irish historians about Elizabethan policies of "reform." See 15–18.

16. Edwards, "Collaboration without Anglicisation," 92–93, explores the contradiction between wanting to eliminate the Gaelic military class and simultaneously relying on Gaelic leaders to provide military assistance.

17. Falls, *Elizabeth's Irish Wars*, 341 (quote); Standish O'Grady, ed., *Pacata Hibernia: Ireland Appeased and Reduced*, 2 vols. (London: Downey & Co., 1896), 1:xxii–lxiii.

18. Falls, *Elizabeth's Irish Wars*, 70; CSPI 2:400 (quote). Interestingly, Barkley is repeating advice word for word offered by Humphrey Gilbert in 1579 (CCM 2:176).

19. Other examples of the significant presence of Gaelic troops in English armies (including via feudal-style obligations): Ciaran Brady, ed., *A Viceroy's Vindication? Sir Henry Sidney's Memoir of Service in Ireland, 1556–78* (Cork, Ireland: Cork University Press, 2002), 46–47, 51, 100–101; CCM, 1:375–56, 378, 406–8; Falls, *Elizabeth's Irish Wars*, 157–58; Ellis, *Ireland*, 288; and Perrot, *Chronicle*, 29–33, 93. There are countless examples in the State Papers.

20. Canny, *Elizabethan Conquest*, 130; Nicholas P. Canny, *Making Ireland British, 1580-1650* (Oxford: Oxford University Press, 2001), 130–31.

21. Geoffrey Parker, *The Military Revolution: Military Innovation and the Rise of the West, 1500–1800*, 2nd ed. (Cambridge: Cambridge University Press, 1996), 18; Kevin Forkan, "Strafford's Irish Army, 1640–41" (M.A. Thesis, National University of Ireland, Galway, 1999), 38; and Donal O'Carroll, "Change and Continuity in Weapons and Tactics, 1594–1601," in *Conquest and Resistance: War in Seventeenth-Century Ireland*, ed. Padraig Lenihan (Leiden: Brill, 2001), 231–34.

22. O'Carroll, "Change and Continuity in Weapons and Tactics," 211–56; Bert S. Hall, *Weapons and Warfare in Renaissance Europe: Gunpowder, Technology, and Tactics* (Baltimore, Md.: Johns Hopkins University Press, 1997), 170, 234.

23. For the shift in preferring men who could "stand fast" versus those with "ferocious aggressiveness" see Robert L. O'Connell, *Of Arms and Men* (New York: Oxford University Press, 1989), 118–19.

24. Canny, *Making Ireland British*, 60.

25. The decline in both total numbers and/or relative percentage of kerne in royal pay can be traced in assorted musters or paybooks from 1558 to 1595: SP 63/1/5; SP 63/7/61; SP 63/14/26 (i); SP 63/13/60 (i); Mary O'Dowd, ed., *Calendar of State Papers Ireland: Tudor Period 1571–1575*, rev. ed. (Kew: Public Record Office, 2000), 1–3; CCM 2:462–64, 3:127; and Carew MS 597, f. 87a–88a, Lambeth Palace Library, London.

26. Canny, *Making Ireland British*, 68.

27. Such orders were regularly repeated with slight modifications of the percentages. Roger B. Manning, *An Apprenticeship in Arms: The Origins of the British Army 1585–1702* (Oxford: Oxford University Press, 2006), 20; CCM, 1:355, 3:72; Canny, *Making Ireland British*, 68, 72; CSPI 1:239; 5:267–69; and SP 61/2/57.

28. CSPI 1:269; Canny, *Making Ireland British*, 97.

29. Falls, *Elizabeth's Irish Wars*, 200, 201, 215, 217, 225, 244, 326; Ellis, *Ireland*, 339, 343; CSPI 6:231, 249, 450; and Hiram Morgan, ed., "A Booke of Questions and Answars Concerning the Warrs or Rebellions of the Kingdome of Irelande [Nicholas Dawtrey, ca. 1597],"

Analecta Hibernia 36 (1995): 93. For one ordinance forbidding Irishmen in English companies, "excepte those of the pale," see "Certain Ordynaunces to be observed dureinge the warrs of Ireland," British Library Add. MSS 19,831. The 1601 muster is in Fynes Moryson, *An Itinerary: Containing His Ten Years Travell* (Glasgow: J. MacLehose, 1907), 2:403.

30. Hughes, *Shakespeare's Europe*, 251.

31. Canny, *Making Ireland British*, 200–205, 240, 412–14.

32. One exception was the Irish regiment composed heavily of Gaels sent on the disastrous 1627 Isle of Rhé expedition, and later allowed to remain on the Irish Establishment. Aidan Clarke, "Sir Piers Crosby, 1590–1646: Wentworth's 'Tawney Ribbon,'" *Irish Historical Studies* 26: 142–60.

33. Forkan, "Strafford's Irish Army"; Jane H. Ohlmeyer, *Civil War and Restoration in the Three Stuart Kingdoms*, 2nd ed. (Dublin: Four Courts Press, 2001), 84 (quote); Canny, *Making Ireland British*, 291, 296, 458; James Scott Wheeler, *The Irish and British Wars, 1637–1654: Triumph, Tragedy, and Failure* (London: Routledge, 2002), 75.

34. John Childs, *The Army of Charles II* (London: Routledge & Kegan Paul, 1976), 208.

35. Alan J. Guy, "The Irish Military Establishment, 1660–1776," in *Military History of Ireland*, 213–14.

36. John Childs, *The British Army of William III, 1689–1702* (Manchester: Manchester University Press, 1987), 10–13.

37. Thomas Bartlett, "'A Weapon of War Yet Untried': Irish Catholics and the Armed Forces of the Crown, 1760–1830," in *Men, Women and War*, ed. T. G. Fraser and Keith Jeffery (Dublin: Lilliput Press, 1993), 66–85.

38. R. E. Scouller, *The Armies of Queen Anne* (Oxford: Clarendon Press, 1966), 125, 293; Guy, "Irish Military Establishment," 217; Thomas Bartlett, "'Weapon of War,'" 68–69. The recruitment of Irish Catholics into the navy seems to have been both common and without political backlash. Stephen Conway, *War, State, and Society in Mid-Eighteenth-Century Britain and Ireland* (Oxford: Oxford University Press, 2006), 182–83.

39. Stephen Brumwell, *Redcoats: The British Soldier and War in the Americas, 1755–1763* (New York: Cambridge University Press, 2002), 318. The religious affiliations of these Irishmen in British regiments are uncertain.

40. Terence Denman, "'*Hibernia officina militum*': Irish Recruitment to the British Regular Army, 1660–1815," *Irish Sword* 20 (1996): 150–63; and S. H. F. Johnston, "The Irish Establishment," *The Irish Sword* 1 (1949–53): 35 (quote).

41. Peter Karsten, "Irish Soldiers in the British Army, 1792–1922: Suborned or Subordinate?," in *Motivating Soldiers: Morale or Mutiny*, ed. Peter Karsten (New York: Garland Publishing, 1998), 36.

42. Michael Glover, *Wellington's Army in the Peninsula 1808–1814* (New York: Hippocrene Books, 1977), 25.

43. Mark Bois, "Men, Cohesion and Battle: The Inniskilling Regiment at Waterloo" (M.A. Thesis, University of Louisville, 2006), 84.

44. Karsten, "Irish Soldiers," 57.

45. Thomas D. Hall, "Incorporation in the World-System: Toward a Critique," *American Sociological Review* 51 (1986): 398; Thomas D. Hall, "Frontiers, Ethnogenesis, and World-Systems: Rethinking the Theories," in *A World Systems Reader*, ed. Thomas D. Hall (Lanham, Md.: Rowman & Littlefield, 2000), 237–70.

46. Ellis, *Ireland*, 285.

47. Falls, *Elizabeth's Irish Wars*, 34.

48. For Simnel's abortive invasion, see Ellis, *Ireland*, 85.

49. Quoted in P. J. Marshall, *The Making and Unmaking of Empires: Britain, Indian, and America C. 1750-1783* (Oxford: Oxford University Press, 2005), 341. Note that Marshall sees a persistent English refusal to imagine the Irish as "British," but the trajectory of recruiting Irishmen is markedly different than the recruitment of Native Americans, suggesting gradations of "not-British." P. J. Marshall, "A Nation Defined by Empire, 1755–1776," in *Uniting the Kingdom? The Making of British History*, eds., Alexander Grant and Keith J. Stringer (London: Routledge, 1995), 208–22.

50. Francis Jennings, *The Ambiguous Iroquois Empire* (New York: W. W. Norton & Co., ·1984), 367, emphasis in original. See also Daniel K. Richter, "Native Peoples of North America and the Eighteenth-Century British Empire," in *The Oxford History of the British Empire, Vol. II: The Eighteenth Century*, ed. P. J. Marshall (Oxford: Oxford University Press, 1998), 347–71.

51. Recent treatments have emphasized the continuing importance of Native military power even after the seventeenth-century epidemics, something that few British administrators would have contested, but it remains fair in hindsight to acknowledge the long-term diminution of power associated with demographic decline. Emerson W. Baker and John G. Reid, "Amerindian Power in the Early Modern Northeast: A Reappraisal," *William and Mary Quarterly* 3d Ser., 61 (2004): 77–106; Jon Parmenter, "After the Mourning Wars: The Iroquois as Allies in Colonial North American Campaigns, 1676–1760," *William and Mary Quarterly* 3d Ser., 64, no. 1 (2007): 39–82.

52. The Irish precedent is now a commonplace in early American history, but continues to need development. See Canny, *Elizabethan Conquest*; Howard Mumford Jones, *O Strange New World—American Culture: the Formative Years* (New York: Viking Press, 1952); Stephen Saunders Webb, "Army and Empire: English Garrison Government in Britain and America, 1569 to 1763," *William and Mary Quarterly* 3d Ser., 34, no. 1 (1977): 1–31; and Nicholas Canny, "England's New World and the Old, 1480s–1630s," in *The Oxford History of the British Empire, Vol. I: The Origins of Empire*, ed. Nicholas Canny (Oxford: Oxford University Press, 1998), 148–69.

53. Edmund S. Morgan, *American Slavery, American Freedom* (New York: W. W. Norton & Co., 1975), 6–24.

54. As Lisa Brooks points out, the Plymouth-Metacom treaty subordinated Metacom to the English king, but not to Plymouth. *Our Beloved Kin: A New History of King Philip's War* (New Haven, Conn.: Yale University Press, 2018), 53.

55. Webb, "Army and Empire," 7–8; Neal Salisbury, *Manitou and Providence: Indians, Europeans, and the Making of New England, 1500–1643* (Oxford: Oxford University Press, 1982), 99–100, 123.

56. Quote from Peter Wraxall, *An Abridgment of the Indian Affairs . . . Transacted in the Colony of New York, From the Year 1678 to the Year 1751* (Cambridge, Mass.: Harvard University Press, 1915), 11, 100; Colin G. Calloway, *The American Revolution in Indian Country: Crisis and Diversity in Native American Communities* (Cambridge, Mass.: Cambridge University Press, 1995), 143.

57. As discussed in chapter 2.

58. Wilbur R. Jacobs, ed., *The Appalachian Indian Frontier: The Edmond Atkin Report and Plan of 1755* (Lincoln: University of Nebraska Press, 1967), 8–10.

59. Wraxall, *Abridgment*, 95 (quote), 111, 153; Jacobs, *Appalachian Indian Frontier*, 13.

60. British officials eventually came to recognize and cultivate men who more clearly understood this role of relationships in dealing with Indians. Richard R. Johnson, "The Search for a Usable Indian: An Aspect of the Defense of Colonial New England," *Journal of American History* 64 (1977): 629–30; Bruce Wilson, "The Struggle for Wealth and Power at Fort Niagara, 1775–1783," *Ontario History* 68 (1976): 142; and Jacobs, *Appalachian Indian Frontier*, 80.

61. Nancy Shoemaker, *A Strange Likeness: Becoming Red and White in Eighteenth-Century North America* (New York: Oxford University Press, 2004), 117–21.

62. Shoemaker, *Strange Likeness*, 35–60; Calloway, *American Revolution*, 60, 135, 250–51, 257; Jacobs, *Appalachian Indian Frontier*, 85; Milton W. Hamilton, "Guy Johnson's Opinions on the American Indian," *Pennsylvania Magazine of History and Biography* 77, no. 3 (1953): 321; Kathleen DuVal, *The Native Ground: Indians and Colonists in the Heart of the Continent* (Philadelphia: University of Pennsylvania Press, 2006), 135; and Alan Gallay, *The Indian Slave Trade: The Rise of the English Empire in the American South, 1670–1717* (New Haven, Conn.: Yale University Press, 2002), 138–40.

63. Webb calculates that for the entire seventeenth century the usual British regular presence on the North American continent was only 300 troops, and rarely more than 1,000. "Army and Empire," 23.

64. Alfred A. Cave, *The Pequot War* (Amherst: University of Massachusetts Press, 1996), 153–54.

65. See chapter 4.

66. Gallay, *Indian Slave Trade*, 84–86.

67. Charles W. Arnade, *The Siege of St. Augustine in 1702* (Gainesville: University of Florida Press, 1959), 5, 32; See also chapter 5 of this book.

68. Gallay, *Indian Slave Trade*, 53–54, 59–61, 134.

69. Early contact produced some major alliances, most notably the Chickahominies who agreed to become Englishmen, committing their 500 bowmen to aid the English. Ralphe Hamor, *A True Discourse of the Present Estate of Virginia* (London, 1615; repr., Amsterdam: Da Capo Press, 1971), 11–15; Karen Ordahl Kupperman, *Indians and English: Facing Off in Early America* (Ithaca, N.Y.: Cornell University Press, 2000), 72.

70. William L. Shea, *The Virginia Militia in the Seventeenth Century* (Baton Rouge: Louisiana State University Press, 1983), 79; see also 38, 46, 68.

71. There were later momentary exceptions, whose fragility proves the point: James H. Merrell, *The Indians' New World: Catawbas and Their Neighbors From European Contact Through the Era of Removal* (Chapel Hill: University of North Carolina Press, 1989), 57–58, 91 (Saponis served as border guards at Fort Christanna from 1714, but they rejected European acculturation in 1717); Michael Leroy Oberg, *Dominion and Civility: English Imperialism and Native America, 1585–1685* (Ithaca, N.Y.: Cornell University Press, 1999), 202 (Occaneechees agree to ally with Nathaniel Bacon, but then were killed by him and his men).

72. The role of settlement Indians as subjects or as soldiers in English (or American revolutionary) armies needs further work. Jenny Hale Pulsipher, *Subjects Unto the Same King: Indians, English, and the Contest for Authority in Colonial New England* (Philadelphia:

University of Pennsylvania Press, 2005); Gallay, *Indian Slave Trade*, 54, 94–95; Johnson, "Search for the Usable Indian," 644–45; Richter, "Native Peoples of North America," 360–61; Jason W. Warren, *Connecticut Unscathed: Victory in the Great Narragansett War, 1675–1676* (Norman: University of Oklahoma Press, 2014); Michelle Schohn, "The Pee Dee Indian People of South Carolina," in *People of One Fire* 3 (May 2008): 9–12; and Brian D. Carroll, "'Savages' in the Service of Empire: Native American Soldiers in Gorham's Rangers, 1744–1762," *New England Quarterly* 85, no. 3 (2012): 383–429. Jason Mancini at the Mashantucket Pequot Research Center has also done substantial work on the military and maritime service of Connecticut settlement Indians in American service, and he has shared much of that data with me. A published version is available as Jason R. Mancini and David J. Naumec, *Connecticut's African & Native American Revolutionary War Enlistments: 1775–1783* (Mashantucket, Conn.: Mashantucket Pequot Museum and Research Center, 2005).

73. John Grenier, *The First Way of War: American War Making on the Frontier, 1607–1814* (Cambridge: Cambridge University Press, 2005), 39–43, 65. Edmund Atkins in 1755 complained of the indiscriminateness of the bounty system and of its usurpation of a more centralized management of Indians. Jacobs, *Appalachian Indian Frontier*, xxiv. In one unusual circumstance a group of ninety-five Mohegans, Pequots, and Niantics served fifteen weeks in a garrison on the Maine frontier in 1704, receiving pay and scalp bounties. Johnson, "Search for a Usable Indian," 630–31.

74. James David Drake, *King Philip's War: Civil War in New England, 1675–1676* (Amherst: University of Massachusetts Press, 1999), 101–4.

75. Johnson, "Search for a Usable Indian," 627; Patrick M. Malone, *The Skulking Way of War: Technology and Tactics among the New England Indians* (1991; repr., Baltimore: Johns Hopkins University Press, 1993), 107–15; Warren, *Connecticut Unscathed.*

76. Johnson, "Search for a Usable Indian," 633–34; Parmenter, "After the Mourning Wars," 42–43; and Allen W. Trelease, *Indian Affairs in Colonial New York: The Seventeenth Century* (Ithaca, N.Y.: Cornell University Press, 1960; Lincoln: University of Nebraska Press, 1997), 231, 233–34.

77. Trelease, *Indian Affairs*, 236–37.

78. Richter, "Native Peoples of North America," 353 provides a short summary. For an overview of the historiography see Parmenter, "After the Mourning Wars," 77–82.

79. Trelease, *Indian Affairs*, 245, 253–94; Jennings, *Ambiguous Iroquois Empire*, 191–92. Royal instructions to the governors of New York in later years assumed the submission and subjecthood of the Haudenosaunee. NYCD 3:690.

80. Calloway, *American Revolution*, 37; Gallay, *Indian Slave Trade*, 138–40; Eric Hinderaker, "The "Four Indian Kings" and the Imaginative Construction of the First British Empire," *William and Mary Quarterly* 3d Ser., 53 (1996): 487–526; and Colin G. Calloway, *New Worlds for All: Indians, Europeans, and the Remaking of Early America* (Baltimore: Johns Hopkins University Press, 1997), 111. New York's active hope to use the Covenant Chain in this expandable way can be seen in their reaction to the arrival of a delegation of Miamis in 1711. Wraxall, *Abridgment of the Indian Affairs*, 87. Edmund Atkins hoped for a similarly expansive covenant with the Cherokees: see below.

81. NYCD 3:393.

82. Johnson, "Search for a Usable Indian," 642–43; Trelease, *Indian Affairs*, 265–67; Richard L. Haan, "Covenant and Consensus: Iroquois and English, 1676–1760," in *Beyond the*

Covenant Chain: The Iroquois and Their Neighbors in Indian North America, 1600–1800, ed. Daniel K. Richter and James H. Merrell (Syracuse, N.Y.: Syracuse University Press, 1987), 51, 53–54.

83. Gilles Havard, *The Great Peace of Montreal of 1701: French-Native Diplomacy in the Seventeenth Century* (Montreal and Kingston: McGill-Queen's University Press, 2001).

84. Jennings, *Ambiguous Iroquois Empire*, 211, 289–90.

85. Parmenter, "After the Mourning Wars," esp. 74.

86. Johnson, "Search for a Usable Indian," 628, 631, quote from 640.

87. Jacobs, *Appalachian Indian Frontier*, 3–4.

88. Fintan O'Toole, *White Savage: William Johnson and the Invention of America* (New York: Farrar, Straus and Giroux, 2005).

89. Jacobs, *Appalachian Indian Frontier*, 92.

90. Matthew C. Ward, *Breaking the Backcountry: The Seven Years' War in Virginia and Pennsylvania, 1754–1765* (Pittsburgh, Pa.: University of Pittsburgh Press, 2003).

91. Parmenter, "After the Mourning Wars," 70–75, briefly reviews Haudenosaunee participation after 1757, emphasizing, however, its conditionality and their continued manipulation of the alliance. David H. Corkran suggests that the "presents" provided to Cherokee contingents during this era were the functional equivalent of mercenary pay, traditionally redistributed by headmen, but designed to keep them in the field longer than otherwise possible. *The Cherokee Frontier* (Norman: University of Oklahoma Press, 1962), 129.

92. The Stockbridges regularly served as a "ranger" company in British forces. Brumwell, *Redcoats*, 210–11. The fifty-two Tuscaroras of North Carolina played a similar role on behalf of the Virginia militia that marched against the Cherokees in 1761. General Return of Troops commanded by Col. Adam Stephen, November 28, 1761, Amherst Papers, WO 34/37, TNA.

93. Calloway, *American Revolution*, 21. For Pontiac's War in general, see Gregory Evans Dowd, *War Under Heaven: Pontiac, the Indian Nations, and the British Empire* (Baltimore, Md.: The Johns Hopkins University Press, 2002).

94. Discussed in chapter 5. Another roughly contemporaneous indigenous effort to force an adjustment in the imperial relationship occurred in Nova Scotia. John G. Reid, "*Pax Britannica* or *Pax Indigena?*: Planter Nova Scotia (1760–1782) and Competing Strategies of Pacification," *Canadian Historical Review* 85 (2004): 683–84.

95. Marshall, *Making and Unmaking*, 190–93.

96. In addition to the other works cited here, key works on British Indian policy during the war include Paul Lawrence Stevens, "His Majesty's 'Savage' Allies: British Policy and the Northern Indians During the Revolutionary War—The Carleton Years, 1774–1778" (Ph.D. Diss., State University of New York at Buffalo, 1984); Robert Allen, *His Majesty's Indian Allies: British Indian Policy in the Defence of Canada, 1774–1815* (Toronto: Dundurn Press, 1992); and Jim Piecuch, *Three Peoples, One King: Loyalists, Indians, and Slaves in the Revolutionary South, 1775–1782* (Columbia: University of South Carolina Press, 2008). The costs to Native Americans were of course even more extraordinary, as shown in Calloway, *American Revolution*.

97. Calloway, *American Revolution*, 225, 144.

98. Wilson, "Struggle for Wealth and Power," 139.

99. Grenier, *First Way of War*, 133.

100. John Ferling, *Almost a Miracle: The American Victory in the War of Independence* (Oxford: Oxford University Press, 2007), 213.

101. Quoted in Calloway, *American Revolution*, 262

102. Ferling, *Almost a Miracle*, 226–27, 264; Wayne E. Lee, *Crowds and Soldiers in Revolutionary North Carolina: The Culture of Violence in Riot and War* (Gainesville: University Press of Florida, 2001), 142–43.

103. Troy O. Bickham, *Savages Within the Empire: Representations of American Indians in Eighteenth-Century Britain* (Oxford: Oxford University Press, 2005), 243–71; Marshall, *Making and Unmaking*, 190–93. The political and financial costs did not prevent Britain from again relying heavily on Native aid during the War of 1812, but they did so again without a serious commitment to the Indians as subjects.

104. A typical summary is Colin G. Calloway, *Crown and Calumet: British-Indian Relations, 1783–1815* (Norman: University of Oklahoma Press, 1987), 196–202.

105. John Landers, *The Field and the Forge: Population, Production, and Power in the Pre-Industrial West* (New York: Oxford University Press, 2003), esp. 98.

106. Compare Ferling's analysis of the British army's problem during the American Revolution, *Almost a Miracle*, 565.

107. Ian K. Steele, *Warpaths: Invasions of North America* (New York: Oxford University Press, 1994), 214. A manuscript guide to war in North America spends most of its length discussing how to build and secure roads into the wilderness. "On War in North America," Amherst Papers, WO 34/102, TNA.

108. Johnson, "Search for a Usable Indian," 640. Peter Schuyler's journal of his 1691 expedition to Canada provides a vivid daily account of the logistical, intelligence, and "mobility" services provided by his contingent of Indians. NYCD 3:800–805.

109. Jeremy Black suggests that dividing and conquering was at the root of much European preindustrial colonial success. "Introduction," in *War in the Early Modern World, 1450–1815*, ed. Jeremy Black (Boulder, Colo.: Westview Press, 1999), 13.

110. Kupperman, *Indians and English*, 188; Jacobs, *Appalachian Indian Frontier*, xxv.

111. Johnson, "Search for a Usable Indian," 648–49 (quote). Recent discussions of these changes in attitude include Pulsipher, *Subjects unto the Same King*; Patrick Griffin, *American Leviathan: Empire, Nation, and Revolutionary Frontier* (New York: Hill & Wang, 2007); Peter Silver, *Our Savage Neighbors: How Indian War Transformed Early America* (New York: W. W. Norton, 2008); and Lee, *Barbarians and Brothers*, chaps. 6 and 8.

112. Matthew Kruer, *Time of Anarchy: Indigenous Power and the Crisis of Colonialism in Early America* (Cambridge, Mass.: Harvard University Press, 2021), 241.

113. Marshall, *Making and Unmaking*, 190–93; Calloway, *Crown and Calumet*, 123. Calloway also suggests that the preservation of Canada in 1812–1814 was in many respects due to Indian aid. *Crown and Calumet*, 220–22.

114. Johnson, "Search for a Usable Indian," 647; Calloway, *American Revolution*, 228.

115. Benedict R. Anderson, *Imagined Communities: Reflections on the Origin and Spread of Nationalism* (London: Verso, 1983).

116. Daniel R. Mandell, *Behind the Frontier: Indians in Eighteenth-Century Eastern Massachusetts* (Lincoln: University of Nebraska Press, 1996), 40, 42–43, 51, 66.

117. David B. Quinn, *The Elizabethans and the Irish* (Ithaca, N.Y.: Published for the Folger Shakespeare Library by Cornell University Press, 1966), 106–7; Canny, *Elizabethan Conquest.*

118. I do not refer here to the strictly legal definition of "subject," but rather to a more generalized sense of acceptance and incorporation into the imagined polity. Compare Jacob Selwood, "'English-Born Reputed Strangers': Birth and Descent in Seventeenth-Century London," *Journal of British Studies* 44 (October 2005): 728–53; and Gavin Loughton, "Calvin's Case and the Origins of the Rule Governing 'Conquest' in English Law," *Australian Journal of Legal History* 8 (2004), www.austlii.edu.au/au/journals/AJLH/2004/8.html. There is also a large and growing literature on the shifting English legal vision of their sovereignty over the Indians as subjects. In addition to Griffin, Pulsipher, Oberg, and Silver, already cited herein, see especially Ken MacMillan, *Sovereignty and Possession in the English New World: The Legal Foundations of Empire, 1576–1640* (Cambridge: Cambridge University Press, 2006); Jack P. Greene, ed., *Exclusionary Empire: English Liberty Overseas, 1600–1900* (Cambridge: Cambridge University Press, 2009); Anthony Pagden, *Lords of All the World: Ideologies of Empire in Spain, Britain and France C. 1500–c. 1800* (New Haven, Conn.: Yale University Press, 1995); and Patricia Seed, *Ceremonies of Possession in Europe's Conquest of the New World, 1492–1640* (Cambridge: Cambridge University Press, 1995).

119. See Quinn, *Elizabethans and Irish*, 125; Pulsipher, *Subjects unto the Same King*; Oberg, *Dominion and Civility*, esp. 136, 150.

Chapter Eight

1. I write this conclusion in the midst of the 2022 Russian invasion of Ukraine, and I cannot help but reflect on how Vladimir Putin's motivations for invading (the "cause" of the war) may have very little to do with the ultimate political outcome. Historical examination of motivations is very different from examining the outcome. As historians, we must do both, but we should not confuse the two.

2. The paradigmatic work for the latter interpretation remains Daniel K. Richter, "War and Culture: The Iroquois Experience," *William and Mary Quarterly* 3d Ser., 40 (1983): 528–59 and his *The Ordeal of the Longhouse: The Peoples of the Iroquois League in the Era of European Colonization* (Chapel Hill: University of North Carolina Press, 1992), 30–74. These varying interpretations are discussed in more detail in chapter 4.

3. See chapters 4 and 5.

4. Timothy R. Pauketat, *Cahokia: Ancient America's Great City on the Mississippi* (New York: Viking Penguin, 2009), 167.

5. David J. Silverman, *Thundersticks: Firearms and the Violent Transformation of Native America* (Cambridge, Mass.: Belknap Press of Harvard University Press, 2016), 9.

6. Thomas Forsyth, "Manners and Customs of the Sauk and Fox Nations of Indians, 15th January 1827," manuscript copy in 9T, Draper MSS.

7. Colin G. Calloway, *The Western Abenakis of Vermont, 1600–1800: War, Migration, and the Survival of an Indian People* (Norman: University of Oklahoma Press, 1990), 68 for his assessment of motivations for war that include (1) ending tribute; (2) Revenge; and (3) accessing trade. Note that he rightly constructs this in such a way that these goals are not mutually exclusive.

8. Andrew Gallup, ed., *Memoir of a French and Indian War Soldier by "Jolicoeur" Charles Bonin* (Bowie, Md.: Heritage Books, 1993), 154.

9. The Russian invasion of Ukraine has returned the notion of "conquest" to the cultural imaginary, but the very shock of it is equally obvious in global political discourse.

10. I believe Neil Salisbury mistook usual outcomes for intentions, when he said that "to the Narragansett warfare was a contest in which one sought to intimidate and scatter one's enemies through a combination of physical and supernatural weapons. The result might be a favorable shift in the balance of power but certainly not the elimination of any existing communal entities." *Manitou and Providence: Indians, Europeans, and the Making of New England, 1500–1643* (Oxford: Oxford University Press, 1982), 229.

11. Gallup, *Memoir*, 154.

12. I introduce this theoretical problem in Wayne E. Lee, "Conquer, Extract, and Perhaps Govern: Organic Economies, Logistics, and Violence in the Preindustrial World," in Erica Charters, Marie Houllemare, and Peter H. Wilson, eds., *A Global History of Early Modern Violence* (Manchester: Manchester University Press, 2020), 236–60.

13. Mark A. Rees, "Coercion, Tribute, and Chiefly Authority: The Regional Development of Mississippian Political Culture," *Southeastern Archaeology* 16, no. 2 (1997): 113–33 (quote at 116).

14. Evidence for this is discussed more fully below. For the reality of territorial ambition even among nonstate peoples, see the cross-cultural discussion in Lawrence H. Keeley, *War Before Civilization* (New York: Oxford University Press, 1996), 99–112, 116.

15. Juliana Barr, "Geographies of Power: Mapping Indian Borders in the "Borderlands" of the Early Southwest," *William and Mary Quarterly* 3d series, 68, no. 1 (2011): 5–46 (quote at 7). Also see Kathleen DuVal, *The Native Ground: Indians and Colonists in the Heart of the Continent* (Philadelphia: University of Pennsylvania Press, 2006), 28. Barr's article provides a deeper dive into various theoretical issues of territory versus territoriality that need not detain us here.

16. See below for "convenient" hunting grounds.

17. James H. Merrell, *The Indians' New World: Catawbas and Their Neighbors From European Contact Through the Era of Removal* (Chapel Hill: University of North Carolina Press, 1989), 124–25; Allan Greer, *Property and Dispossession: Natives, Empires and Land in Early Modern North America* (Cambridge: Cambridge University Press, 2018), 39.

18. Jeffers Lennox, *Homelands and Empires: Indigenous Spaces, Imperial Fictions, and Competition for Territory in Northeastern North America, 1690–1763* (Toronto: University of Toronto Press, 2017), 10.

19. Dean R. Snow, "Wabanaki 'Family Hunting Territories,'" *American Anthropologist* New Series, 70, no. 6 (1968): 1143–51. On the expansion of the deerskin trade in the Southeast, see Daniel J. Tortora, *Carolina in Crisis: Cherokees, Colonists, and Slaves in the American Southeast, 1756–1763* (Chapel Hill: University of North Carolina Press, 2015), 15–17; Kathryn E. Holland Braund, *Deerskins & Duffels: The Creek Indian Trade With Anglo America, 1685–1815* (Lincoln: University of Nebraska Press, 1993), 69–72; and Tom Hatley, *The Dividing Paths: Cherokees and South Carolinians Through the Revolutionary Era* (Oxford: Oxford University Press, 1995), 164–66.

20. Gregory A. Waselkov and Kathryn E. Holland Braund, eds., *William Bartram on the Southeastern Indians* (Lincoln: University of Nebraska Press, 1995), 92.

21. Anthony F. C. Wallace, "Political Organization and Land Tenure among the Northeastern Indians, 1600–1830," *Southwestern Journal of Anthropology* 13, no. 4 (1957): 301–21, quotes at 311–12, 318.

22. Pierre Pouchot, *Memoirs on the Late War in North America, Between France and England* (Youngstown, N.Y.: Old Fort Niagara Association, 1994), 451, 461.

23. Richebourg Gaillard McWilliams, ed. and trans., *Fleur De Lys and Calumet: Being the Pénicaut Narrative of French Adventure in Louisiana* (Baton Rouge: Louisiana State University Press, 1953), 25–26. Charles Bonin may have misunderstood what was happening when he described how victorious Indians would make signs on a tree "stripping off the outside bark." Gallup, *Memoir*, 154.

24. Calloway, *Western Abenakis*, 162–63.

25. Brett Rushforth, *Bonds of Alliance: Indigenous and Atlantic Slaveries in New France* (Chapel Hill: University of North Carolina Press, 2013), 24. For other examples of boundary claiming see George Loskiel, *History of the Mission of the United Brethren among the Indians in North America* (London, 1794), 129. A legend about Catawba encroachment on the Cherokees is related in Henry Rowe Schoolcraft, *The Indian Tribes of the United States* (Philadelphia: J. B. Lippincott & Co., 1884), 1:407; and Lisa Brooks, *Our Beloved Kin: A New History of King Philip's War* (New Haven, Conn.: Yale University Press, 2018), 29.

26. Aubrey Lauersdorf, "Apalachee Diplomacy, Politics, and Power, 1528–1678" (Ph.D. Diss., University of North Carolina, 2020), 45–46. A brief discussion of buffer zones is in Steven A. LeBlanc and Katherine E. Register, *Constant Battles: The Myth of the Peaceful, Noble Savage* (New York: St. Martin's Press, 2003), 140, 155. David H. Dye, *War Paths, Peace Paths: An Archaeology of Cooperation and Conflict in Native Eastern North America* (Lanham, Md.: AltaMira Press, 2009) discusses buffer zones extensively.

27. Francis Jennings, *The Ambiguous Iroquois Empire* (New York: W. W. Norton & Co., 1984), 154–55, 159–61. Evan Haefeli discusses the nature of the Lenape submission to the Haudenosaunee in the last third of the seventeenth century, including the supposed issue of their being gendered "female" as meaning "defeated," in two articles (and I'm grateful to him for sending me one still forthcoming). "Becoming a 'Nation of Statesmen': The Mohicans' Incorporation into the Iroquois League, 1671–1675," *New England Quarterly* 93 (2020): 425–33; and "The Great Haudenosaunee-Lenape Peace of 1669: Oral Traditions, Colonial Records, and the Origin of the Delaware's Status as 'Women,'" *New York History* (Forthcoming). There are other examples of the absorption of people as a blend of tributary and adoption, including the hopes of the Narragansett allies of the English in 1637, who lamented the killing of so many Pequots at Mystic whom they had hoped to control after their defeat. Wayne E. Lee, *Barbarians and Brothers: Anglo-American Warfare, 1500–1865* (New York: Oxford University Press, 2011), 154–55.

28. Russell Dylan Ruediger, "Tributary Subjects: Affective Colonialism, Power, and the Process of Subjugation in Colonial Virginia, c. 1600–c. 1740" (Ph.D. Diss., Georgia State University, 2017), 118.

29. Neal Salisbury argues that these tributary relationships were solely as the result of contact, as disadvantaged bands were forced to resort to Indian middlemen to access European trade, paying tribute to do so. Other scholars are not so sure, and suggest that tributary relationships may have been more normal even precontact. Neal Salisbury, *Manitou and Providence: Indians, Europeans, and the Making of New England, 1500–1643* (Oxford: Oxford University Press, 1982), 48, 147; Kathleen J. Bragdon, *Native People of Southern New England, 1500–1650,* (Norman: University of Oklahoma Press, 1996), 147–50; and Kathleen J. Bragdon,

Native People of Southern New England, 1650–1775 (Norman: Univerity of Oklahoma Press, 2009), 96–99.

30. Calloway, *Western Abenakis*, 63.

31. Calloway, *Western Abenakis*, 68, citing Gabriel Druillettes, "Journal of an Embassy from Canada to the United Colonies of New England in 1650, by Father Gabriel Druillettes," ed. John Gilmeary Shea, *Collections of the New York Historical Society* 2d ser., 3, pt. 1, 317–23.

32. Silverman, *Thundersticks*, 96 (quote), 104. Cf. Greer, *Property and Dispossession*, 41–42; and Kevin McBride, "War and Trade in Eastern New Netherland," in *A Beautiful and Fruitful Place: Selected Rensselaerswijk Seminar Papers, Volume 3*, ed. Margriet Lacy-Bruijn (Albany, N.Y.: New Netherland Institute, 2013), 281.

33. See the discussion of so-called "coups" in chapter 5.

34. Helen C. Rountree, *Pocahontas's People: The Powhatan Indians of Virginia Through Four Centuries* (Norman: University of Oklahoma Press, 1996), 25; John Smith, *A Map of Virginia* in Philip L. Barbour, ed., *The Complete Works of Captain John Smith* (Chapel Hill: University of North Carolina Press, 1986), 1:173. For evidence of regional conflict prior to English arrival, see E. Randolph Turner III, "Native American Protohistoric Interactions in the Powhatan Core Area," in *Powhatan Foreign Relations, 1500–1722*, ed. Helen C. Rountree (Charlottesville: University Press of Virginia, 1993), 89–90. Strachey also reports these inheritances, but is likely using Smith as his source.

35. William Strachey, *The Historie of Travell into Virginia Britania (1612)*, 2nd Ser., vol. 103, ed. Louis B. Wright and Virginia Freund (London: Hakluyt Society, 1953), 68; Strachey in Edward Wright Haile, ed., *Jamestown Narratives: Eyewitness Accounts of the Virginia Colony* (Champlain, Va.: Roundhouse, 1998), 604, 626–27; Smith, *A Map of Virginia*, 175; and Helen C. Rountree, *Pocahontas, Powhatan, Opechancanough: Three Indian Lives Changed by Jamestown* (Charlottesville: University of Virginia Press, 2005), 44–45.

36. Strachey, *Historie*, 68–69; Rountree, *Pocahontas's People*, 60–61; Rountree, "Introduction," in *Powhatan Foreign Relations*, 6–7; J. Frederick Fausz, *The Day Kikotan Became Hampton: England's First Indian War, 1609–1614* (Hampton, Va.: Port Hampton Press, 2010), 7–9; and Ruediger, "Tributary Subjects," 116–21.

37. Strachey, *Historie*, 104–5; Rountree, *Pocahontas's People*, 27–28.

38. James D. Rice, "War and Politics: Powhatan Expansionism and the Problem of Native American Warfare," *William and Mary Quarterly* 3d Ser., 77, no. 1 (2020): 31–32.

39. John Smith, *A True Relation [1608]*, in Barbour, *Complete Works*, 1:69.

40. Thomas E. Davidson, "Relations between the Powhatans and the Eastern Shore," in *Powhatan Foreign Relations*, 146–47.

41. Davidson, "Powhatans and the Eastern Shore," 150.

42. Strachey, *Historie*, 87 (spelling modernized, also in Haile edition at 644). See Stephen R. Potter, *Commoners, Tribute, and Chiefs: The Development of Algonquian Culture in the Potomac Valley* (Charlottesville: University Press of Virginia, 1993), 17–19, 172–73.

43. Karen Ordahl Kupperman, *Pocahontas and the English Boys: Caught Between Cultures in Early Virginia* (New York: NYU Press, 2021), 52. Contararily, James Horn seems to downplay the scope and significance of subsistence tribute in bulk. *A Land As God Made It: Jamestown and the Birth of America* (New York: Basic Books, 2005), 14.

44. Thomas Forsyth, "Manners and Customs of the Sauk and Fox Nation of Indians, 15th January 1827" MS, in 9T, Draper MSS.

45. Anthony F. C. Wallace, "Political Organization and Land Tenure among the Northeastern Indians, 1600–1830," *Southwestern Journal of Anthropology* 13, no. 4 (1957): 318.

46. Talk from Skiogusto Kehowe and the Good Warrior to Governor Glen, Estuttowe, April 15, 1752, DRIA 1:247.

47. Talk of the Head Men of Ioree, April 17, 1752, DRIA 1:254; James Beamer to Governor Glen, April 26, 1752, DRIA 1:256–57.

48. Kathryn E. Holland Braund, *Deerskins & Duffels: The Creek Indian Trade With Anglo America, 1685–1815* (Lincoln: University of Nebraska Press, 1993), 132–33. A fuller narrative is in David Corkran, *The Cherokee Frontier, 1740–1762* (Norman: University of Oklahoma Press, 1962), 22–25, 33–36; and David H. Corkran, *The Creek Frontier, 1540–1783* (Norman: University of Oklahoma Press, 1967), 113–14, 128–30, 146–48, 150–53.

49. As discussed in chapter 5; see Lee, "Conquer, Extract, and Perhaps Govern," 248–51. The documents on the Creek-Cherokee land dispute were kindly provided by Bryan Rindfleisch: Habersham to George Galphin, Esqr. of Silver Bluff, "sent to Mr. Pooler to forward," from Savannah, October 1, 1772 (Folder 4); *South Carolina Gazette; and Country Journal, 1765–1775*, July 16, 1771, MS CscG. South Caroliniana Library, University of South Carolina, Columbia, S.C.; "John Stuart to Earl of Hillsborough," Charleston, June 12, 1772 in *Documents of the American Revolution, 1770–1783, Vol. V*, ed. K. G. Davies (Shannon, Ireland: Irish University Press, 1972–), 114–17; "Memorial of Governor James Wright to Earl of Hillsborough," [?] December 12, 1771, in Davis, *Documents of the American Revolution, Vol. III*: 269–72. To be clear, the fuller depopulation of the Lower Towns only occurred during the Anglo-Cherokee War of 1759–62, but what matters here is the Creek claim from the earlier war. As Lisa Brooks points out, Indians quickly became familiar with English legal forms and would turn that language to their own use, and such is possible here as well. *Our Beloved Kin*, 41.

50. John T. Juricek, *Endgame for Empire: British-Creek Relations in Georgia and Vicinity, 1763–1776* (Gainesville: University Press of Florida, 2015), 155. Juricek also narrates the processes leading to the Treaty of Augusta, 156–85; see esp. 178, in which a Creek speaker humiliates the Cherokees present at the negotiations by referring to their defeat in a feminizing manner, having "long ago obliged them to wear the petticoat."

51. Europeans often described the seventeenth-century Haudenosaunee wars as wars of conquest, and they certainly do seem to have established at least a tributary empire of sorts. I think it likely that they were making explicit territorial claims on hunting grounds in Pennsylvania, Huronia, and the upper Ohio valley. Thanks to David Preston and Michael Oberg for discussions on this issue. Quote: Carl Van Doren and J. P. Boyd, eds., *Indian Treaties Printed by Benjamin Franklin, 1736–1762* (Philadelphia, Pa.: The Historical Society of Pennsylvania, 1938), 53, also available at http://treatiesportal.unl.edu/earlytreaties/treaty.00003.html. There is also an intriguing comment by the Weckquasgeck leadership about Mohawk claims to their land. A possible European buyer of their land wondered how they could sell it, having just been pushed off it by the Mohawks. They replied that the Mohawks could kill them and take their goods, but "will not say they have any pretence to [our] Land." Discussed in Haefeli, "Becoming a 'Nation of Statesmen,'" 443.

52. Lauersdorf, "Apalachee Diplomacy," 74. Of note, the *holata* also promised to bring his allies into the relationship, suggesting tributary connective tissue here as well.

53. For one look at the many movements of nations around the Southeast across the precontact/contact divide, see Marvin T. Smith, "Aboriginal Population Movements in

the Early Historic Period Interior Southeast," in *Powhatan's Mantle: Indians in the Colonial Southeast,* ed. Peter H. Wood, Gregory A. Waselkov, and M. Thomas Hatley (Lincoln: University of Nebraska Press, 1989), 21–34.

54. A similar set of stories could be told with respect to the repeated displacement of the Lenapes and Shawnees (among others) into the western Ohio valley.

55. Calloway, *Western Abenakis,* 57; John Steckley, "Trade Goods and Nations in Sagard's Dictionary: A St. Lawrence Iroquoian Perspective," *Ontario History* 104, no. 2 (2012): 139–54.

56. Brett Rushforth, *Bonds of Alliance: Indigenous and Atlantic Slaveries in New France* (Chapel Hill: University of North Carolina Press, 2013), 24.

57. Ralph Hamor, "A True Discourse of the Present Estate of Virginia [1615]," in Haile, *Jamestown Narratives,* 835, 837; Kupperman, *Pocahontas and the English Boys,* 37.

58. Merrell, *Indians' New World,* 124–25.

59. Quoted in Horn, *Land as God Made It,* 128.

60. Elizabeth N. Ellis documents a great deal of this kind of movement among the *petites nations* of the lower Mississippi valley, including the accompanying friction. Elizabeth N. Ellis, *The Great Power of Small Nations: Indigenous Diplomacy in the Gulf South* (Philadelphia: University of Pennsylvania Press, 2023). See also Kurt A. Jordan, *The Seneca Restoration, 1715–1754: An Iroquois Local Political Economy* (Gainesville: University Press of Florida, 2008), 168 for their intraregional move in response to a 1687 French expedition.

61. For other takes on this kind of harassment see Keeley, *War Before Civilization,* 116; David H. Dye, "Warfare in the Sixteenth-Century Southeast: The de Soto Expedition in the Interior," in *Columbian Consequences, Vol. 2: Archaeological and Historical Perspectives on the Spanish Borderlands East,* ed. David Hurst Thomas (Washington, D.C.: Smithsonian Institution Press, 1990), 211–22; David H. Dye, "The Art of War in the Sixteenth-Century Central Mississippi Valley," in *Perspectives on the Southeast: Linguistics, Archaeology and Ethnohistory,* ed. Patricia B. Kwachka (Athens: University of Georgia Press, 1994); Charles Hudson, *Knights of Spain, Warriors of the Sun: Hernando De Soto and the South's Ancient Chiefdoms* (Athens: University of Georgia Press, 1997); Lewis H. Larson, Jr., "Functional Considerations of Warfare in the Southeast during the Mississippi Period," *American Antiquity* 37 (1972): 383–92; Karl T. Steinen, "Ambushes, Raids, and Palisades: Mississippian Warfare in the Interior Southeast," *Southeastern Archaeology* 11 (1992): 132–39; and Christina Snyder, "Conquered Enemies, Adopted Kin, and Owned People: The Creek Indians and Their Captives," *Journal of Southern History* 73 (2007): 268–69.

62. Colin G. Calloway, *New Worlds for All: Indians, Europeans, and the Remaking of Early America* (Baltimore: Johns Hopkins University Press, 1997), 94.

63. John Smith, *Generall Historie,* II: 159–60, reprinted in Karen Ordahl Kupperman, ed., *Captain John Smith: A Select Edition of His Writings* (Chapel Hill: University of North Carolina Press, 1998), 165.

64. William Bradford, *Of Plymouth Plantation, 1620–1647* (New York: Random House, 1981), 329–30.

65. Matthew C. Ward, *Breaking the Backcountry: The Seven Years' War in Virginia and Pennsylvania, 1754–1765* (Pittsburgh: University of Pittsburgh Press, 2003), 50–51. Compare Stephen Aron, *How the West Was Lost: The Transformation of Kentucky From Daniel Boone to Henry Clay* (Baltimore: Johns Hopkins University Press, 1996), 40.

Index

Page numbers in *italics* refer to figures and maps.

weapons. *See specific types*

Wells, William, 64, 221n114

Wendats: agriculture of, 5, 59; diet of, 38; displacement of, 198, 207n7; firearms of, 154; fire prevention by, 88; fortifications of, 152–53; Haudenosaunee war with, 30–32, 68–69, 81, 148, 154, 198; horses of, 52; palisades of, 31, 148; towns of, 5, 69; trading partners of, 30–31; traveling food of, 68–69

Werowocomoco, 193

Westos, 120, 155

White, John, 103, *104*, 110, 119

wilderness: European views on, 5, 37, 187; mapping of, 187; warfare in, 141, 144, 174–75

William III (king of England), 164

William of Orange, 164

Williams, Roger, 48, 88

Wilson, Bruce, 177

Winchester, 66

windage, 136

Winthrop, Fitz-John, 175

withdrawal, strategy of, 131, 132. *See also* retreat

women: food carried by, 53–55; in hunting, 53, 64; killing of, in total war practices, 88, 90; political power of, 92–93, 151; as prisoners, adoption of, 90; in purification rituals, 85; as restraints on war, 92–93; sexual violence against, 83, 84; status of, 53–55; in war parties, 26, 27, 53, 67. *See also* feminized roles

Wood, Abraham, 120

Wood, Peter, 44, 45

Woodward, Henry, 120

Woronocos, 192

Wowinchopunck, 199

xenophobia, 172

Yamasees: in Creek–Cherokee War, 75; Creeks in conflict with, 15–16, 188; pursuit of attackers by, 15–16; in Tuscarora War, 109; in Yamasee War, 120–22, 145, 171

Youghtanunds, 192

Printed in the USA
CPSIA information can be obtained
at www.ICGtesting.com
LVHW041405220923
758939LV00033B/449

9 781469 673783